T0185426

Mastering the Raspberry Pi

Warren W. Gay

Mastering the Raspberry Pi

Copyright © 2014 by Warren W. Gay

This work is subject to copyright. All rights are reserved by the Publisher, whether the whole or part of the material is concerned, specifically the rights of translation, reprinting, reuse of illustrations, recitation, broadcasting, reproduction on microfilms or in any other physical way, and transmission or information storage and retrieval, electronic adaptation, computer software, or by similar or dissimilar methodology now known or hereafter developed. Exempted from this legal reservation are brief excerpts in connection with reviews or scholarly analysis or material supplied specifically for the purpose of being entered and executed on a computer system, for exclusive use by the purchaser of the work. Duplication of this publication or parts thereof is permitted only under the provisions of the Copyright Law of the Publisher's location, in its current version, and permission for use must always be obtained from Springer. Permissions for use may be obtained through RightsLink at the Copyright Clearance Center. Violations are liable to prosecution under the respective Copyright Law.

ISBN-13 (pbk): 978-1-4842-0182-4

ISBN-13 (electronic): 978-1-4842-0181-7

Trademarked names, logos, and images may appear in this book. Rather than use a trademark symbol with every occurrence of a trademarked name, logo, or image we use the names, logos, and images only in an editorial fashion and to the benefit of the trademark owner, with no intention of infringement of the trademark.

The use in this publication of trade names, trademarks, service marks, and similar terms, even if they are not identified as such, is not to be taken as an expression of opinion as to whether or not they are subject to proprietary rights.

While the advice and information in this book are believed to be true and accurate at the date of publication, neither the authors nor the editors nor the publisher can accept any legal responsibility for any errors or omissions that may be made. The publisher makes no warranty, express or implied, with respect to the material contained herein.

Publisher: Heinz Weinheimer
Lead Editor: Michelle Lowman
Development Editor: Douglas Pundick
Technical Reviewer: Stewart Watkiss
Editorial Board: Steve Anglin, Mark Beckner, Ewan Buckingham, Gary Cornell, Louise Corrigan, Jim DeWolf, Jonathan Gennick, Jonathan Hassell, Robert Hutchinson, Michelle Lowman, James Markham, Matthew Moodie, Jeff Olson, Jeffrey Pepper, Douglas Pundick, Ben Renow-Clarke, Dominic Shakeshaft, Gwenan Spearing, Matt Wade, Steve Weiss
Coordinating Editor: Kevin Walter
Copy Editor: Sharon Wilkey
Compositor: SPi Global
Indexer: SPi Global
Artist: SPi Global
Cover Designer: Anna Ishchenko

Distributed to the book trade worldwide by Springer Science+Business Media New York, 233 Spring Street, 6th Floor, New York, NY 10013. Phone 1-800-SPRINGER, fax (201) 348-4505, e-mail orders-ny@springer-sbm.com, or visit www.springeronline.com. Apress Media, LLC is a California LLC and the sole member (owner) is Springer Science + Business Media Finance Inc (SSBM Finance Inc). SSBM Finance Inc is a Delaware corporation.

For information on translations, please e-mail rights@apress.com, or visit www.apress.com.

Apress and friends of ED books may be purchased in bulk for academic, corporate, or promotional use. eBook versions and licenses are also available for most titles. For more information, reference our Special Bulk Sales–eBook Licensing web page at www.apress.com/bulk-sales.

Any source code or other supplementary material referenced by the author in this text is available to readers at www.apress.com. For detailed information about how to locate your book's source code, go to www.apress.com/source-code/.

Raspberry Pi Foundation schematics used with permission.

I dedicate this book to the memory of my father, Charles Wallace Gay, who passed away this year. He didn't remember it when we discussed it last, but he was responsible for sparking my interest in electronics at an early age. He had brought home from his used-car business two D cells, a piece of blue automotive wire, and a flashlight bulb. After showing me how to hold them together to complete the circuit and light the bulb, I was hooked for life.

I am also indebted to my family for their patience. Particularly my wife, Jacqueline, who tries to understand why I need to do the things I do with wires, solder, and parts arriving in the mail. I am glad for even grudging acceptance, because I'm not sure that I could give up the thrill of moving electrons in some new way. Sometimes hobby electronics projects have no real justification beyond "because we can!"

Contents at a Glance

Contents

About the Author

Warren W. Gay started out in electronics at an early age, dragging discarded TVs and radios home from public school. In high school he developed a fascination for programming the IBM 1130 computer, which resulted in a career plan change to software development. After attending Ryerson Polytechnical Institute, he has enjoyed a software developer career for over 30 years, programming mainly in C/C++. Warren has been programming Linux since 1994 as an open source contributor and professionally on various Unix platforms since 1987.

Before attending Ryerson, Warren built an Intel 8008 system from scratch before there were CP/M systems and before computers got personal. In later years, Warren earned an advanced amateur radio license (call sign VE3WWG) and worked the amateur radio satellites. A high point of his ham radio hobby was making digital contact with the Mir space station (U2MIR) in 1991.

Warren works at Datablocks.net, an enterprise-class ad serving software services company. There he programs C++ server solutions on Linux back-end systems.

About the Technical Reviewer

Stewart Watkiss graduated from the University of Hull, United Kingdom, with a masters degree in electronic engineering. He has been a fan of Linux since first installing it on a home computer during the late 1990s. While working as a Linux system administrator, he was awarded Advanced Linux Certification (LPIC 2) in 2006, and created the Penguin Tutor website to help others learning Linux and working toward Linux certification (`www.penguintutor.com`).

Stewart is a big fan of the Raspberry Pi. He owns several Raspberry Pi computers that he uses to help to protect his home (Internet filter), provide entertainment (XBMC), and teach programming to his two children. He also volunteers as a STEM ambassador, going into local schools to help support teachers and teach programming to teachers and children.

Acknowledgments

In the making of a book, there are so many people involved. I first want to thank Michelle Lowman, acquisitions editor, for her enthusiasm for the initial manuscript and pulling this project together. Enthusiasm goes a long way in an undertaking like this.

I'd also like to thank Kevin Walter, coordinating editor, for handling all my email questions and correspondence, and coordinating things. I greatly appreciated the technical review performed by Stewart Watkiss, checking the facts presented, the formulas, the circuits, and the software. Independent review produces a much better end product.

Thanks also to Sharon Wilkey for patiently wading through the copy edit for me. Judging from the amount of editing, I left her plenty to do. Thanks to Douglas Pundick, development editor, for his oversight and believing in this book. Finally, my thanks to all the other unseen people at Apress who worked behind the scenes to bring this text to print.

I would be remiss if I didn't thank my friends for helping me with the initial manuscript. My guitar teacher, Mark Steiger, and my brother-in-law's brother, Erwin Bendicks, both volunteered their time to help me with the first manuscript. Mark has no programming or electronics background and probably deserves an award for reading through "all that *stuff*." I am indebted also to my daughter Laura and her fiancé Michael Burton, for taking the time to take my photograph and the Raspberry Pi cover image, while they plan their wedding.

There are so many others I could list who helped me personally to reach a point in my life where I could write a book like this. To all of you, please accept my humble thanks, and may God bless.

■ ■ ■

## CHAPTER 1

Why This Book?

This book developed out of a need for an in-depth work about the Raspberry Pi that just didn't seem to exist. If I had found one, I would have gladly purchased it. A quick survey revealed a large number of "how to get started" books. But I pined for something with the kind of meat that appeals to engineering types. Give me numbers, formulas, and design procedures.

Almost all of that information is available out there on the Internet *somewhere*. But I discovered that some questions take considerable time to research. If you know exactly where to look, the answer is right there. But if you're just starting out with the Raspberry Pi, you have several online Easter-egg hunts ahead of you. How much is your time worth?

Here's a short sample of some of the questions answered in this book:

- How much current can a general purpose input/output (GPIO) port source or sink?

- What is the resistance of the GPIO internal pull-up/pull-down resistor?

- Which GPIO does the 1-Wire interface use?

- What is the GPIO voltage range for a 0 bit or 1 bit?

- How do you budget the GPIO power?

Some of these questions have simple answers, while others require an "it depends" explanation. You might be wondering why you need to know the internal GPIO pull-up resistance. Chapter 27 discusses this in connection with motor driver interfaces and what happens at boot time. A number of questions arise when you start designing interfaces to the outside world. While you may not aspire to be an electronics engineer, it helps to think like one.

Who Needs This Book?

This is an important question and the answer, of course, depends on what you are looking for. So let's cut to the chase. This book is

- Not an easy "how to get started" book (These are plentiful.)

- Not a book about Scratch, Python, or Ruby programming

- Not a "download package X, configure it, and install it thusly" book

- Not a media server or retro games console handbook

- Not a book on how to use or administer Linux

This book is targeted to those who have the following:

- A college/university level or hobbyist interest

- Some exposure to Linux (Raspbian Linux)

- Some exposure to the C programming language

- Some exposure to digital electronics

This Book Is Primarily About

In very broad terms, this book can be described primarily as follows:

- A Raspberry Pi hardware reference, with software exploration

- An electronics interfacing projects book, exploring the hardware and software to drive it

In a nutshell, it is a *reference* and *projects* book for the Raspberry Pi. The reference coverage is *extensive* compared to other offerings. A considerable section of the book is also dedicated to projects. I believe that this combination makes it one of the best choices for a book investment.

An ever-increasing number of interface boards can be purchased for the Pi, and the choices increase with each passing month. However, this book takes a "bare metal" approach and does not use any additional extender/adapter board solutions. You can, of course, use them, but they are not required.

This text also uses a "poor student" approach, using cheap solutions that can be purchased as Buy It Now sales on eBay. These then are directly interfaced to the GPIO pins, and I discuss the challenges and safety precautions as required. This approach should also meet the needs of the hobbyist on a limited budget.

You should have a beginning understanding of the C programming language to get the most out of the software presented. Since the projects involve electronic interfacing, a beginning understanding of digital electronics is also assumed. The book isn't designed to teach electronics, but some formulas and design procedures are presented.

Even those with no interest in programming or electronics will find the wealth of reference material in this book worth owning. The back of the book contains a bibliography for those who want to research topics further.

Learning Approach

Many times a construction article in a magazine or a book will focus on providing the reader with a *virtual kit*. By this, I mean that every tool, nut and bolt, component, and raw material is laid out, which if properly assembled, will achieve the project's end purpose. This is fine for those who have no subject area knowledge but want to achieve that end result.

However, this book does *not* use that approach. The goal of this book is to help you learn *how to design* solutions for your Rasberry Pi. You cannot learn design if you're not allowed to think for yourself! For this reason, I encourage the substitution of parts and design changes. Considerable effort is expended in design procedure. This book avoids a "here is exactly how you do it" approach that many online projects use.

I explain the challenges that must be reviewed, and how they are evaluated and overcome. One simple example is the 2N2222A transistor driver (see Chapter 12), where the design procedure is provided. If you choose to use a different junk box transistor, you can calculate the base resistor needed, knowing its H_{FE} (or measured on a digital multimeter). I provide a recipe of sorts, but you are not required to use the exact same ingredients.

In some cases, a project is presented using a purchased assembled PCB driver. One example (in Chapter 27) is the ULN2003A stepper motor driver PCB that can be purchased from eBay for less than $5 (free shipping). The use of the PCB is entirely optional, since this single-chip solution can be breadboarded. The PCB, however, offers a cheap, ready-made solution with LED indicators that can be helpful in developing the solution. In many cases, the assembled PCB can be purchased for about the same price as the components themselves. Yet these PCB solutions don't rob you of the interface design challenge that remains. They simply save you time.

It is intended that you, the reader, *not* use the presented projects as exact recipes to be followed. Use them as *guidelines*. Explore them as presented first if you like, but do not be afraid to substitute or alter them in some way. By the time you read this book, some PCBs used here may no longer be available. Clever eBay searches for chip numbers may turn up other manufactured PCB solutions. The text identifies the kind of things to watch out for, like unwanted pull-up resistors and how to locate them.

By all means, change the presented software! It costs nothing to customize software. Experiment with it. The programs are purposely provided in a "raw" form. They are *not* meant to be deployed as finished solutions. They are boiled down as much as possible to be easily read and understood. In some cases, error checking was removed to make the code more readable. All software provided in this book is placed in the public domain with no restrictions. Mold it to your needs.

If you follow the projects presented—or better, try them all—you'll be in a good position to develop new interface projects of your own design. You'll know what questions to ask and how to research solutions. You'll know how to interface 3-volt logic to 5-volt logic systems. You'll know how to plan for the state of the GPIO outputs as the Raspberry Pi boots up, when driving external circuits. Experience is the best teacher.

Organization of This Book

This book is organized into four major parts. The first part is an introduction, which does *not* present "how to get started" material but does cover topics like static IP addressing, SSH, and VNC access. I'll otherwise assume that you already have all the "getting started" material that you need.

Part 2 is a large reference section dedicated to the Raspberry Pi hardware. It begins with power supply topics, header strips (GPIO pins), LEDs, and how to wire a reset button. Additional chapters cover SDRAM, CPU, USB, Ethernet (wired and wireless), SD cards, and UART (including RS-232 adapters). A large focus chapter on GPIO is presented. Additional chapters cover Linux driver access to 1-Wire devices, the I2C bus, and the SPI bus. Each chapter examines the hardware and then the software API for it.

In Part 3, important software aspects of the Raspberry Pi are examined. This part starts with a full exploration of the boot process, initialization (from boot to command prompt), and vcgencmd and its options. The Linux console and the serial console are documented. Finally, software development chapters on cross- compiling the kernel are covered in detail.

Part 4 is the fun part of the book, where you apply what you learned to various projects. All of the projects are inexpensive and easy to build. They include interfacing 1-Wire sensors, an I2C GPIO extender, a nunchuk as a mouse, an infrared reader, unipolar and bipolar stepper motor drivers, switch debouncing, PWM, and a remote sensor/console. There is also a real-time clock project for the Model A owner (which can be tried on the Model B). These cover the majority of the interfacing use cases that you will encounter.

The meanings of acronyms used in this advanced level book will be taken for granted. As the reader, you are likely familiar with the terms used. If however, you find yourself in need of clarification, Appendix A contains an extensive glossary of terms.

Software in This Book

I generally dislike the "download this guy's package X from here and install it thusly" approach. The problem is that the magic remains buried inside package X, which may not always deliver in the ways that you need. Unless you study their source code, you become what ham radio people call an *appliance operator*. You learn how to install and configure things but you don't learn how they work.

For this reason, a bare metal approach is used. The code presented is unobstructed by hidden software layers. It is also independent of the changes that might occur to magic package X over time. Consequently, it is hoped that the programs that compile today will continue to compile successfully in the years to come.

Python programmers need not despair. Knowing how things are done at the bare metal level can help your understanding. Learning exactly what happens at the system level is an improvement over a vague idea of what a Python package is doing for you. Those who write packages for Python can be inspired by this book.

The software listings have been kept as short as possible. Books filled with pages of code listings tend to be "fluffy." To keep the listing content reduced, the unusual technique of #include-ing shared code is often used. Normally, program units are compiled separately and linked together at the end. But that approach requires header files, which would just fill more pages with listings.

The source code used in this book is available for download from this website:

```
git://github.com/ve3wwg/raspberry_pi.git
```

There you can also obtain the associated make files. The git clone command can be used on your Raspberry Pi as follows:

```
$ git clone git://github.com/ve3wwg/raspberry_pi.git
```

To build a given project, simply change to the project subdirectory and type the following:

```
$ cd ./raspberry_pi
$ make
```

If you are making program changes and want to force a rebuild from scratch, simply use this:

```
$ make clobber all
```

Final Words

If you are still reading, you are considering purchasing or have purchased this book. That makes me truly excited for you, because chapters of great Raspberry Pi fun are in your hands! Think of this book as a Raspberry Pi owners manual with fun reference projects included. Some may view it as a cookbook, containing basic idea recipes that can be tailored to personal needs. If you own a Raspberry Pi, you need this book!

A lot of effort went into including photos, figures, and tables. These make the book instantly more useful as a reference and enjoyable to read. Additional effort went into making the cross-references to other areas of the book instantly available.

Finally, this is the type of book that you can lie down on the couch with, read through once, while absorbing things along the way. Afterward, you can review the chapters and projects that interest you most. Hopefully, you will be inspired to try all of the projects presented!

## CHAPTER 2

The Raspberry Pi

Before considering the details about each resource within the Raspberry Pi, it is useful to take a high-level inventory. In this chapter, let's just list what you get when you purchase a Pi.

In later chapters, you'll be looking at each resource from two perspectives:

- The hardware itself—what it is and how it works

- The driving software and API behind it

In some cases, the hardware will have one or more kernel modules behind it, forming the device driver layer. They expose a software API that interfaces between the application and the hardware device. For example, applications communicate with the driver by using ioctl(2) calls, while the driver communicates with the I2C devices on the bus. The /sys/class file system is another way that device drivers expose themselves to applications. You'll see this when you examine GPIO in Chapter 12.

There are some cases where drivers don't currently exist in Raspbian Linux. An example is the Pi's PWM peripheral that you'll look at in Chapter 30. Here we must map the device's registers into the application memory space and drive the peripheral directly from the application. Both direct access and driver access have their advantages and disadvantages.

So while our summary inventory here simply lists the hardware devices, you'll be examining each from a hardware and software point of view in the chapters ahead.

Models

A hardware inventory is directly affected by the model of the unit being examined. The Raspberry Pi comes in two models:

- Model A (introduced later as a hardware-reduced model)

- Model B (introduced first and is the full hardware model)

Figure 2-1 shows the Model B and its interfaces. Table 2-1 indicates the differences between the two models.

Figure 2-1. *Model B interfaces*

Table 2-1. *Model Differences*

Resource	Model A	Model B
RAM	256 MB	512 MB
USB ports	1	2
Ethernet port	None	10/100 Ethernet (RJ45)
Power consumption[10]	300 mA (1.5 W)	700 mA (3.5 W)
Target price[9]	$25.00	$35.00

As you can see, one of the first differences to note is the amount of RAM available. The revision 2.0 (Rev 2.0) Model B has 512 MB of RAM instead of 256 MB. The GPU also shares use of the RAM. So keep that in mind when budgeting RAM.

In addition, the Model A does not include an Ethernet port but can support networking through a USB network adapter. Keep in mind that only one USB port exists on the Model A, requiring a hub if other USB devices are needed.

Finally, the power consumption differs considerably between the two models. The Model A is listed as requiring 300 mA vs. 700 mA for the Model B. Both of these figures should be considered low because consumption rises considerably when the GPU is active (when using the desktop through the HDMI display port).

The maximum current flow that is permitted through the 5 V micro-USB connection is about 1.1 A because of the fuse. However, when purchasing a power supply/adapter, it is recommended that you seek supplies that are rated higher than 1.2 A because they often don't live up to their specifications. Chapter 4 provides more details about power supplies.

Hardware in Common

The two Raspberry Pi models share some common features, which are summarized in Table 2-2.[9] The Hardware column lists the broad categories; the Features column provides additional specifics.

Table 2-2. *Common Hardware Features*

Hardware	Features	Comments
System on a chip	Broadcom BCM2835	CPU, GPU, DSP, SDRAM, and USB port
CPU model	ARM1176JZF-S core	With floating point
Clock rate	700 MHz	Overclockable to 800 MHz
GPU	Broadcom VideoCore IV	
	OpenGL ES 2.0	3D
	OpenVG	3D
	MPEG-2	
	VC-1	Microsoft, licensed
	1080p30 H.264	Blu-ray Disc capable, 40 Mbit/s
	MPEG-4	AVC high-profile decoder and encoder
	1 Gpixel/s, 1.5 Gtexels/s	24 GFLOPS with DMA
Video output	Composite RCA	PAL and NTSC
	HDMI	Rev 1.3 and 1.4
	Raw LCD panels	Via DSI
Audio output	3.5 mm jack	
	HDMI	
Storage	SD/MMC/SDIO	Card slot
Peripherals	8 × GPIO	
	UART	
	I2C bus	100 kHz
	SPI bus	Two chip selects, +3.3 V, +5 V, ground
Power source	5 V via micro-USB	

Which Model?

One of the questions that naturally follows a model feature comparison is why the Model A? Why wouldn't everyone just buy Model B?

Power consumption is one deciding factor. If your application is battery powered, perhaps a data-gathering node in a remote location, then power consumption becomes a critical factor. If the unit is supplemented by solar power, the Model A's power requirements are more easily satisfied.

Cost is another advantage. When an Arduino/AVR class of application is being considered, the added capability of the Pi running Linux, complete with a file system on SD, makes it irresistible. Especially at the model A price of $25.

Unit cost may be critical to students in developing countries. Networking can be sacrificed, if it still permits the student to learn on the cheaper Model A. If network capability is needed later, even temporarily, a USB network adapter can be attached or borrowed.

The main advantage of the Model B is its networking capability. Networking today is so often taken for granted. Yet it remains a powerful way to integrate a larger system of components. The project outlined in Chapter 29 demonstrates how powerful ØMQ (ZeroMQ) can be in bringing separate nodes together.

CHAPTER 3

Preparation

While it is assumed that you've already started with the Raspberry Pi, there may be a few things that you want to do before working through the rest of this book. For example, if you normally use a laptop or desktop computer, you may prefer to access your Pi from there. Consequently, some of the preparation in this chapter pertains to network access.

If you plan to do most or all of the projects in this book, I highly recommend using something like the Adafruit Pi Cobbler (covered later in this chapter). This hardware breaks out the GPIO lines in a way that you can access them on a breadboard. If you're industrious, you could build a prototyping station out of a block of wood. I took this approach but would buy the Adafruit Pi Cobbler if I were to do it again (this was tedious work).

Static IP Address

The standard Raspbian SD card image provides a capable Linux system, which when plugged into a network, uses DHCP to automatically assign an IP address to it. If you'd like to connect to it remotely from a desktop or laptop, then the dynamic IP address that DHCP assigns is problematic.

There are downloadable Windows programs for scanning the network. If you are using a Linux or Mac host, you can use Nmap to scan for it. The following is an example session from a MacBook Pro, using the MacPorts collection nmap command. Here a range of IP addresses are scanned from 1–254:

```
$ sudo nmap -sP 192.168.0.1-254
Starting Nmap 6.25 (http://nmap.org) at 2013-04-14 19:12 EDT
. . .
Nmap scan report for mac (192.168.0.129)
Host is up.
Nmap scan report for rasp (192.168.0.132)
Host is up (0.00071s latency).
MAC Address : B8:27:EB:2B:69:E8 (Raspberry Pi Foundation)
Nmap done : 254 IP addresses (6 hosts up) scanned in 6.01 seconds
$
```

In this example, the Raspberry Pi is clearly identified on 192.168.0.132, complete with its MAC address. While this discovery approach works, it takes time and is inconvenient.

If you'd prefer to change your Raspberry Pi to use a static IP address, see the "Wired Ethernet" section in Chapter 9 for instructions.

Using SSH

If you know the IP address of your Raspberry Pi or have the name registered in your hosts file, you can log into it by using SSH. In this example, we log in as user pi on a host named rasp (in this example, from a Mac):

```
$ ssh pi@rasp
pi@rasp's password:
Linux raspberrypi 3.2.27+ #250 PREEMPT ... armv6l
...
Last login : Fri Jan 18 22:19:50 2013 from 192.168.0.179
$
```

Files can also be copied to and from the Raspberry Pi, using the scp command. Do a man scp on the Raspberry Pi to find out more.

It is possible to display X Window System (X-Window) graphics on your laptop/desktop, if there is an X-Window server running on it. (Windows users can use Cygwin for this, available from www.cygwin.com.) Using Apple's OS X as an example, first configure the security of your X-Window server to allow requests. Here I'll take the lazy approach of allowing all hosts (performed on the Mac) by using the xhost command:

```
$ xhost +
access control disabled, clients can connect from any host
$
```

From the Raspberry Pi, connected through the SSH session, we can launch Xpdf, so that it opens a window on the Mac:

```
$ export DISPLAY=192.168.0.179:0
$ xpdf &
```

Here, I've specified the Mac's IP address (alternatively, an /etc/hosts name could be used) and pointed the Raspberry Pi to use the Mac's display number :0. Then we run the xpdf command in the background, so that we can continue to issue commands in the current SSH session. In the meantime, the Xpdf window will open on the Mac, while the Xpdf program runs on the Raspberry Pi.

This doesn't give you graphical access to the Pi's desktop, but for developers, SSH is often adequate. If you want remote graphical access to the Raspberry's desktop, see the next section, where VNC is introduced.

VNC

If you're already using a laptop or your favorite desktop computer, you can conveniently access your Raspberry Pi's graphical desktop over the network. Once the Raspberry Pi's VNC server is installed, all you need is a VNC client on your accessing computer. Once this is available, you no longer need a keyboard, mouse, or HDMI display device connected to the Raspberry Pi. Simply power up the Pi on your workbench, with a network cable plugged into it.

You can easily install the VNC server software on the Pi at the cost of about 10.4 MB in the root file system. The command to initiate the download and installation is as follows:

```
$ sudo apt-get install tightvncserver
```

After the software is installed, the only remaining step is to configure your access to the desktop. The vncserver command starts up a server, after which you can connect remotely to it.

Using SSH to log in on the Raspberry Pi, type the following command:

```
$ vncserver :1 -geometry 1024x740 -depth 16 -pixelformat rgb565
```

You will require a password to access your desktop.

```
Password:
Verify:
Would you like to enter a view-only password (y/n ) ? n
New 'X' desktop is rasp:1

Creating default startup script/home/pi/.vnc/xstartup Starting applications specified ↪
in/home/pi/.vnc/xstartup
Log file is/home/pi/.vnc/rasp:1.log
$
```

The password prompts are presented only the first time that you start the VNC server.

Display Number

In the vncserver command just shown, the first argument identifies the display number. Your normal Raspberry Pi X-Window desktop is on display :0. So when you start up a VNC server, choose a new unique display number like :1. It doesn't have to be the number 1. To a limited degree, you can run multiple VNC servers if you find that useful. For example, you might choose to start another VNC server on :2 with a different display resolution.

Geometry

The -geometry 1024x740 argument configures the VNC server's resolution in pixels. This example's resolution is unusual in that normally 1024×768 would be used for a display resolution, a common geometry choice for monitors. But this need not be tied to a *physical* monitor resolution. I chose the unusual height of ×740 to prevent the VNC client program from using scrollbars (on a Mac). Some experimentation may be required to find the best geometry to use.

Depth

The -depth 16 argument is the pixel-depth specification. Higher depths are possible, but the resulting additional network trafficc might curb your enthusiasm.

Pixel Format

The last command-line argument given is -pixelformat rgb565. This particular example specifies that each pixel is 5 bits, 6 bits, 5 bits—for red, green and blue, respectively.

Password Setup

To keep unauthorized people from accessing your VNC server, a password is accepted from you when you start the server for the first time. The password chosen can be changed later with the vncpasswd command.

Server Startup

If you often use VNC, you may want to define a personal script or alias to start it on demand. Alternatively, have it started automatically by the Raspberry Pi as part of the Linux initialization. See Chapter 17 for more information about initialization scripts.

VNC Viewers

To access your VNC server on the Raspberry Pi, you need a corresponding VNC viewer on the client side. On the Mac, you can use the MacPorts collection to install a viewer:

```
$ sudo port install vnc
```

Once the viewer is installed, you can access your VNC server on the Raspberry Pi at 192.168.0.170, display :1, with this:

```
$ vncviewer 192.168.0.170:1
```

If you have your Raspberry Pi in the hosts file under rasp, you can use the name instead:

```
$ vncviewer rasp:1
```

When the VNC viewer connects to the server, you will be prompted for a password. This obviously keeps others out of your VNC server.

For Ubuntu Linux, you can install the xvnc4viewer package. For Windows, several choices are available, such as RealVNC and TightVNC.

If you find that the screen resolution doesn't work well with your client computer, experiment with different VNC server resolutions (-geometry). I prefer to use a resolution that doesn't result in scrollbars in the viewer. Scrolling around your Raspberry Pi desktop is a nuisance. You can eliminate the need for scrolling by reducing the geometry dimensions.

Stopping VNC Server

Normally, you don't need to stop the VNC server if you are just going to reboot or shut down your Raspberry Pi. But if you want to stop the VNC server without rebooting, this can be accomplished. Supply the display number that you used in the VNC server startup (:1 in this example) using the -kill option:

```
$ vncserver -kill :1
```

This can be useful as a security measure, or to save CPU resources when the server isn't being used. This can also be useful if you suspect a VNC software problem and need to restart it.

Prototype Station

The danger of working with the tiny Raspberry Pi's PCB is that it moves all over the surface as wires tug at it. Given its low mass, it moves easily and can fall on the floor and short wires out in the process (especially around curious cats).

For this reason, I mounted my Raspberry Pi on a nice block of wood. A small plank can be purchased from the lumberyard for a modest amount. I chose to use teak since it looks nice and doesn't crack or warp. Even if you choose to use something like the Adafruit Pi Cobbler, you may find it useful to anchor the Raspberry Pi PCB. Mount the PCB on the wood with spacers. Figure 3-1 shows my prototype station.

Figure 3-1. *A simple prototype station*

Retro Fahnestock clips were installed and carefully wired to a connector on header strip P1 (the wiring was the most labor-intensive part of this project).

■ **Tip**   Fahnestock clips can be economically purchased at places like www.tubesandmore.com (part # S-H11-4043-6).

A small PCB for the RS-232 interface was acquired from eBay ($2.32 total) and mounted at the end of the station. Wires from the RS-232 PCB were routed back to RX/TX and +3.3 V clips and simply clipped into place (this allows you to disconnect them, if you wish to use those GPIO pins for some other purpose). The RS-232 PCB is permanently grounded for convenience.

The RS-232 PCB is necessary only for those who wish to use a serial console or to interface with some other serial device. The PCB acquired was advertised on eBay as "MAX232CSE Transfer Chip RS-232 To TTL Converter Module COM Serial Board." The converter (based on the MAX232CSE chip) will work with TTL or 3.3 V interfaces. Connecting the RS-232 converter's VCC connection to the Raspberry Pi +3.3 V supply makes it compatible with the Pi.

■ **Caution**   Do not connect the RS-232 converter to +5 V, or you will damage the Pi. For additional information about this, see Chapter 11.

In Figure 3-1 you can see a simple bracket holding a small push button (top right). This has been wired up to P6 for a reset button. This is not strictly required if your power supply is working correctly (power-on reset works rather well). Unlike an AVR setup, *you are not likely to use reset very often.* Chapter 5 has more details about this.

The LED was added to the station last. It was soldered to a pair of half-inch finishing nails, nailed into the wood. The LED's cathode has a 220 Ω resister soldered in series with it to limit the current and wired to ground. The anode is connected to the Fahnestock clip labeled LED. The LED can be tested by connecting an alligator lead from the LED clip to the +3.3 V supply clip (this LED also tolerates +5 V). Be sure to choose a low- to medium-current LED that requires about 10 mA or less (16 mA is the maximum source current from a GPIO pin).

To test your prototyping station, you may want to use the script listed in the "GPIO Tester" section in Chapter 12. That script can be used to blink a given GPIO pin on and off in 1-second intervals.

Adafruit Pi Cobbler

A much easier approach to prototype connections for GPIO is to simply purchase the Adafruit Pi Cobbler kit, which is available from the following site:

```
learn.adafruit.com/adafruit-pi-cobbler-kit/overview
```

This kit provides you with these features:

- Header connector for the Pi's P1
- Ribbon cable
- Small breakout PCB
- Breakout header pins

After assembly, you plug the ribbon cable onto the header P1. At the other end of the ribbon cable is a small PCB that provides 26 pins that plug into your prototype breadboard. A small amount of assembly is required.

Gertboard

Students might consider using a Gertboard, which is available from this site:

```
uk.farnell.com
```

The main reason behind this recommendation is that the Raspberry Pi's connections to the outside world are sensitive, 3.3 V, and vulnerable to static electricity. Students will want to connect all manner of buttons, switches, motors, and relays. Many of these interfaces require additional buffers and drivers, which is what the Gertboard is there for.

In addition to providing the usual access to the Pi's GPIO pins, the Gertboard also provides these features:

- Twelve *buffered* I/O pins
- Three push buttons
- Six open collector drivers (up to 50 V, 500 mA)
- A motor controller (18 V, 2 A)
- A two-channel 8/10/12 bit digital-to-analog converter
- A two-channel 10-bit analog-to-digital converter
- A 28-pin DIP ATmega microcontroller

This provides a ready-made learning environment for the student, who is anxious to wire up something and just "make it work." Many of the 3-volt logic and buffering concerns are eliminated, allowing the student to focus on projects.

Bare Metal

Despite the availability of nice adapters like the Gertboard, the focus of this text is on interfacing directly to the Pi's 3 V GPIO pins. Here are some of the reasons:

- No specific adapter has to be purchased for the projects in this book.

- Any specified adapter can go out of production.

- You'll not likely use an expensive adapter on each *deployed* Pi.

- Bare metal interfacing will exercise your design skills.

If we were to do projects with only wiring involved, there wouldn't be much learning involved. Facing the design issues that arise from working with weak 3 V GPIOs driving the outside world will be much more educational.

The third bullet speaks to finished projects. If you're building a robot, for example, you're not going to buy Gertboards everywhere you need to control a motor or read sensor data. You're going to want to economize and build that yourself. This book is designed to help you *face* those kinds of challenges.

CHAPTER 4

■ ■ ■

Power

One of the most frequently neglected parts of a system tends to be the power supply—at least when everything is working. Only when things get weird does the power supply begin to get some scrutiny.

The Raspberry Pi owner needs to give the power supply extra respect. Unlike many AVR class boards, where the raw input voltage is followed by an onboard 5 V regulator, the Pi expects its power to be regulated at the input. The Pi does include onboard regulators, but these regulate to lower voltages (3.3 V and lower).

Figure 4-1 illustrates the rather fragile Micro-USB power input connector. There is a large round capacitor directly behind the connector that people often grab for leverage. It is a mistake to grab it, however, as many have reported "popping it off" by accident.

Figure 4-1. *Micro-USB power input*

Calculating Power

Sometimes power supplies are specified in terms of voltage, and power handling capability in watts. The Pi's input voltage of 5 V must support a *minimum* of 700 mA (Model B). Let's compute a power supply figure in watts (this does not include any added peripherals):

$$P = V \times I$$
$$= 5 \times 0.7$$
$$= 3.5\,W$$

The 3.5 W represents a minimum requirement, so we should overprovision this by an additional 50%:

$$P = 3.5 \times 1.50$$
$$= 5.25\,W$$

The additional 50% yields a power requirement of 5.25 W.

■ **Tip**   Allow 50% extra capacity for your power supply. A power supply gone bad may cause damage or many other problems. One common power-related problem for the Pi is loss of data on the SD card.

Current Requirement

Since the power supply being sought produces one output voltage (5 V), you'll likely see adapters with advertised *current* ratings instead of power. In this case, you can simply factor a 50% additional current instead:

$$I_{supply} = I_{Pi} \times 1.50$$
$$= 0.700 \times 1.50$$
$$= 1.05\,A$$

To double-check our work, let's see whether this agrees with the power rating we computed earlier:

$$P = V \times I$$
$$= 5 \times 1.05$$
$$= 5.25\,W$$

The result does agree. You can conclude this section knowing that you *minimally* need a 5 V supply that produces one of the following:

- 5.25 W or more
- 1.05 A or more (ignoring peripherals)

Supplies that can meet either requirement, should be sufficient. However, you should be aware that not all advertised ratings are what they seem. Cheap supplies often fail to meet their own claims, so an additional margin must always be factored in.

Peripheral Power

Each additional circuit that draws power, especially USB peripherals, must be considered in a power budget. Depending on its type, a given USB peripheral plugged into a USB 2 port can expect up to 500 mA of current, assuming it can obtain it. (Pre Rev 2.0 USB ports were limited to 140 mA by polyfuses.)

Wireless adapters are known to be power hungry. Don't forget about the keyboard and mouse when used, since they also add to the power consumption. If you've attached an RS-232 level shifter circuit (perhaps using MAX232CPE), you should budget for that small amount also in the 3 V supply budget. This will indirectly add to your +5 V budget, since the 3 V regulator is powered from it. (The USB ports use the +5 V supply.) Anything that draws power from your Raspberry Pi should be tallied.

Model B Input Power

The Raspberry Pi's input voltage is fixed at exactly 5 V (±0.25 V). Looking at the schematic in Figure 4-2, you can see how the power enters the micro-USB port on the pin marked VBUS. Notice that the power flows through fuse F3, which is rated at 6 V, 1.1 A. If after an accidental short, you find that you can't get the unit to power up, check that fuse with an ohmmeter.

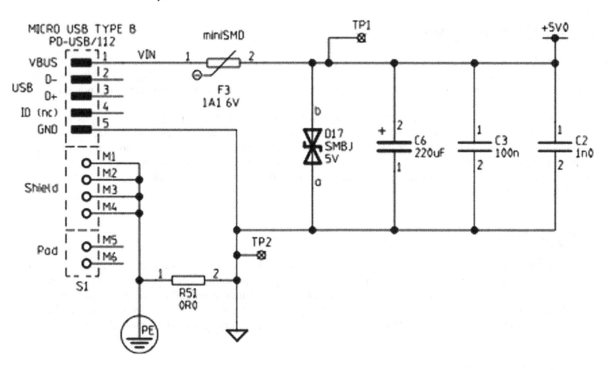

Figure 4-2. *Model B Rev 2.0 input power*

If you bring the input +5 V power into the Pi through header P1, P5, or TP1, for example, you will lose the safety of the fuse F3. So if you bypass the micro-USB port to bring in power, you may want to include a safety fuse in the supplying circuit.

Figure 4-3 shows the 3.3 V regulator for the Pi. Everything at the 3.3 V level is supplied by this regulator, and the current is limited by it.

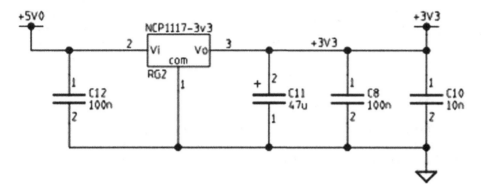

Figure 4-3. *3.3 V power*

Model A Input Power

Like the Model B, the Model A receives its power from the micro-USB port. The Model A power requirement is 300 mA, which is easily supported by a powered USB hub or desktop USB 2 port. A USB 2 port is typically able to supply a maximum of 500 mA unless the power is divided among neighboring ports. You may find in practice, however, that not all USB ports will deliver 500 mA.

As with the Model B, factor the power required by your USB peripherals. If your total nears or exceeds 500 mA, you may need to power your Model A from a separate power source. Don't try to run a wireless USB adapter from the Model A's USB port if the Pi is powered by a USB port itself. The total current needed by the Pi and wireless adapter will likely exceed 500 mA. Supply the wireless adapter power from a USB hub, or power the Pi from a 1.2 A or better power source. Also be aware that not all USB hubs function correctly under Linux, so check compatibility if you're buying one for that purpose.

3.3 Volt Power

Since the 3.3 V supply appears at P1-01, P1-17, and P5-02, it is useful to examine Figure 4-3 (shown previously) to note its source. This supply is indirectly derived from the input 5 V supply, passing through regulator RG2. The maximum excess current that can be drawn from it is 50 mA; the Raspberry Pi uses up the remaining capacity of this regulator.

When planning a design, you need to budget this 3 V supply carefully. Each GPIO output pin draws from this power source an additional 3 to 16 mA, depending on how it is used. For more information about this, see Chapter 12.

Powered USB Hubs

If your power budget is stretched by USB peripherals, you may want to consider the use of a *powered* USB hub. In this way, the *hub* rather than your Raspberry Pi provides the necessary power to the downstream peripherals. The hub is especially attractive for the Model A because it provides additional ports.

Again, take into account that not all USB hubs work with (Raspbian) Linux. The kernel needs to cooperate with connected USB hubs, so software support is critical. The following web page lists known working USB hubs:

`http://elinux.org/RPi_Powered_USB_Hubs`

Power Adapters

This section pertains mostly to the Model B because the Model A is easily supported by a USB 2 port. We'll first look at an unsuitable source of power and consider the factors for finding suitable units.

An Unsuitable Supply

The example shown in Figure 4-4 was purchased on eBay for $1.18 with free shipping (see the upcoming warning about fakes). For this reason, it was tempting to use it.

Figure 4-4. *Model A1265 Apple adapter*

This is an adapter/charger with the following ratings:

- *Model*: A1265

- *Input*: 100–240 VAC

- *Output*: 5 V, 1 A

When plugged in, the Raspberry Pi's power LED immediately lights up, which is a good sign for an adapter (vs. a charger). A fast rise time on the power leads to successful power-on resets. When the voltage was measured, the reading was +4.88 V on the +5 V supply. While not ideal, it is within the range of acceptable voltages. (The voltage must be between 4.75 and 5.25 V.)

The Apple unit seemed to work fairly well when HDMI graphics were *not* being utilized (using serial console, SSH, or VNC). However, I found that when HDMI was used and the GPU had work to do (move a window across the desktop, for example), the system would tend to seize up. This clearly indicates that the adapter does not fully deliver or regulate well enough.

■ **Caution**   Be very careful of counterfeit Apple chargers/adapters. The Raspberry Pi Foundation has seen returned units damaged by these. For a video and further information, see `www.raspberrypi.org/archives/2151`.

E-book Adapters

Some people have reported good success using e-book power adapters. I have also successfully used a 2 A Kobo charger.

Best Power Source

While it is possible to buy USB power adapters at low prices, it is wiser to spend more on a high-quality unit. It is not worth trashing your Raspberry Pi or experiencing random failures for the sake of saving a few dollars.

If you lack an oscilloscope, you won't be able to check how clean or dirty your supply current is. A better power adapter is cheaper than an oscilloscope. A shaky/noisy power supply can lead to all kinds of obscure and intermittent problems.

A good place to start is to simply Google "recommended power supply Raspberry Pi." Do your research and include your USB peripherals in the power budget. Remember that wireless USB adapters consume a lot of current—up to 500 mA.

■ **Note**   A random Internet survey reveals a range of 330 mA to 480 mA for wireless USB adapter current consumption.

Voltage Test

If you have a DMM or other suitable voltmeter, it is worthwhile to perform a test after powering up the Pi. This is probably the very first thing you should do, if you are experiencing problems.

Follow these steps to perform a voltage test:

1.   Plug the Raspberry Pi's micro-USB port into the power adapter's USB port.

2.   Plug in the power adapter.

3.   Measure the voltage between P1-02 (+5 V) and P1-25 (Ground): expect +4.75 to +5.25 V.

4.   Measure the voltage between P1-01 (+3.3 V) and P1-25 (Ground): expect +3.135 to +3.465 V.

■ **Caution**   Be very careful with your multimeter probes around the pins of P1. *Be especially careful not to short the +5 V to the +3.3 V pin*, even for a fraction of a second. Doing so will zap your Pi! If you feel nervous or shaky about this, leave it alone. You may end up doing more harm than good. As a precaution, put a piece of wire insulation (or spaghetti) over the +3.3 V pin.

The left side of Figure 4-5 shows the DMM probes testing for +5 V on header strip P1. Again, be very careful not to touch more than one pin at a time when performing these measurements. *Be particularly careful not to short between 5 V and 3.3 V*. To avoid a short-circuit, use a piece of wire insulation, heat shrink tubing, or even a spaghetti noodle over the other pin.

Figure 4-5. *Measuring voltages*

The right side of Figure 4-5 shows the positive DMM probe moved to P1-01 to measure the +3.3 V pin. Appendix B lists the ATX power supply standard voltage levels, which include +5 ± 0.25 V and +3.3 ± 0.165 V.

Battery Power

Because of the small size of the Raspberry Pi, it may be desirable to run it from battery power. Doing so requires a regulator and some careful planning. To meet the Raspberry Pi requirements, you must form a power budget. Once you know your maximum current, you can flesh out the rest. The following example assumes that 1 A is required.

Requirements

For clarity, let's list our battery power requirements:

- Voltage 5 V, within ± 0.25 V
- Current 1 A

Headroom

The simplest approach is to use the linear LM7805 as the 5 V regulator. But there are some disadvantages:

- There must be some headroom above the input voltage (about 2 V).

- Allowing too much headroom increases the power dissipation in the regulator, resulting in wasted battery power.

- A lower maximum output current can also result.

Your batteries should provide a minimum input of 5+2 V (7 V). Any lower input voltage to the regulator will result in the regulator "dropping out" and dipping below 5 V. Clearly, a 6 V battery input will not do.

LM7805 Regulation

Figure 4-6 shows a very simple battery circuit using the LM7805 linear regulator. Resistor R_L represents the load (the Raspberry Pi).

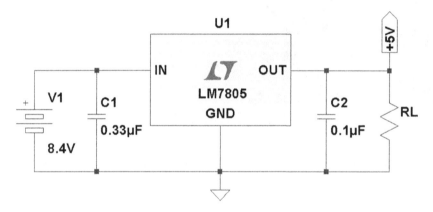

Figure 4-6. *Regulated battery supply*

The 8.4 V battery is formed from seven NiCad cells in series, each producing 1.2 V. The 8.4 V input allows the battery to drop to a low of 7 V before the minimum headroom of 2 V is violated.

Depending on the exact 7805 regulator part chosen, a typical heat-sinked parameter set might be as follows:

- *Input voltage*: 7–25 V

- *Output voltage*: 1.5 A (heat-sinked)

- *Operating temperature*: 125°C

Be sure to use a heat sink on the regulator so that it can dissipate heat energy to the surrounding air. Without one, the regulator can enter a thermal shutdown state, reducing current flow to prevent its own destruction. When this happens, the output voltage will drop below +5 V.

Keep in mind that the amount of power dissipated by the battery is more than that received by the load. If we assume that the Raspberry Pi is consuming 700 mA, a minimum of 700 mA is also drawn from the battery through the regulator (and it could be slightly higher). Realize that the regulator is dissipating additional energy because of its higher input voltage. The total power dissipated by the regulator and the load is as follows:

$$P_d = P_L \times P_R$$
$$= 5\,V \times 0.7\,A + (8.4\,V - 5\,V) \times 0.7\,A$$
$$= 3.5\,W + 2.38\,W$$
$$= 5.88\,W$$

The regulator must dissipate the difference between the input and the output voltages (2.38 W). This additional energy heats up the regulator with the energy being given away at the heat sink. Because of this, designers avoid using a high input voltage on linear regulator circuits.

If the regulator is rated at a maximum of 1.5 A at 7 V (input), the power maximum for the regulator is about 10.5 W. If we apply an input voltage of 8.4 V instead of 7, we can derive what our 5 V maximum current will be:

$$I_{max} = \frac{P_{max}}{V_{in}}$$
$$= \frac{10.5\,W}{8.4\,V}$$
$$= 1.25\,A$$

From this, we find that the 8.4 V battery regulator circuit can provide a maximum of 1.25 A at the output, without exceeding the regulator's power rating. Multiply 8.4 V by 1.25 A to convince yourself that this equals 10.5 W.

DC-DC Buck Converter

If the application is designed for data acquisition, for example, it is desirable to have it run as long as possible on a given set of batteries or charge cycle. A switching regulator may be more suitable than the linear regulator.

Figure 4-7 shows a very small PCB that is about 1.5 SD cards in length. This unit was purchased from eBay for $1.40, with free shipping. At these prices, why would you build one?

Figure 4-7. *DC-DC buck converter*

They are also simple to use. You have + and – input connections and + and – output connections. Feed power in at one voltage and get power out at another voltage. This is so simple that you'll forgive me if I omit the diagram for it.

But don't immediately wire it up to your Raspberry Pi, until you have calibrated the output voltage. While it *might* come precalibrated for 5 V, it is best not to count on it. If the unit produces a higher voltage, you might fry the Pi.

The regulated output voltage is easily adjusted by a multiturn trim pot on the PCB. Adjust the pot while you read your DMM.

The specifications for the unit I purchased are provided in Table 4-1 for your general amusement. Notice the wide range of input voltages and the fact that it operates at a temperature as low as –40°C. The wide range of input voltages and current up to 3 A clearly makes this a great device to attach to solar panels that might vary widely in voltage.

Table 4-1. *DC-DC buck converter specifications*

Parameter	Min	Max	Units	Parameter	Min	Max	Units
Input voltage	4.00	35.0	Volts	Output ripple		30.9	mA
Input current		3.0	Amps	Load regulation	±0.5	%	
Output voltage	1.23	30.0	Volts	Voltage regulation	±2.5	%	
Conversion efficiency		92	%	Working temperature	–40	+85	°C
Switching frequency		150	kHz	PCB size		45×20×12	mm
				Net weight		10	g

The specification claims up to a 92% conversion efficiency. Using 15 V on the input, I performed my own little experiment with measurements. With the unit adjusted to produce 5.1 V at the output, the readings shown in Table 4-2 were taken.

Table 4-2. *Readings taken from experiment*

Parameter	Input	Output	Units
Voltage	15.13	5.10	Volts
Current	0.190	0.410	Amps
Power	2.87	2.09	Watts

From the table we expected to see more power used on the input side (2.87 W). The power used on the output side was 2.09 W. The efficiency then becomes a matter of division:

$$\frac{2.09}{2.87} = 0.728$$

From this we can conclude that the measured conversion efficiency was about 72.8%.

How well could we have done if we used the LM7805 regulator? The following is a best case estimate, since I don't have an actual current reading for that scenario. But we do know that at least as much current that flows out of the regulator must flow into it (likely more). So what is the absolute best that the LM7805 regulator could theoretically do? Let's apply the same current draw of 410 mA for the Raspberry Pi at 5.10 V, as shown in Table 4-3. (This was operating without HDMI output in use.)

Table 4-3. *Hypothetical LM7805 power use*

Parameter	Input	Output	Units
Voltage	7.1	5.10	Volts
Current	0.410	0.410	Amps
Power	2.91	2.09	Watts

The power efficiency for this best case scenario amounts to this:

$$\frac{2.09}{2.91} = 0.718$$

The absolute best case efficiency for the LM7805 regulator is 71.8%. But this is achieved at its *optimal* input voltage. Increasing the input voltage to 12 V causes the power dissipation to rise considerably, resulting in a 42.5% efficiency (this calculation is left to the reader as an exercise). Attempting to operate the LM7805 regulator at 15.13 V, as we did with the buck converter, would cause the efficiency to drop to less than 33.7%. Clearly, the buck converter is much more efficient at converting power from a higher voltage source.

Signs of Insufficient Power

In the forums, it has been reported that ping sometimes doesn't work from the desktop (with HDMI), yet works OK in console mode.[42] Additionally, I have seen that desktop windows can freeze if you move them (HDMI). As you start to move the terminal window, for example, the motion would freeze part way through, as if the mouse stopped working.

These are signs of the Raspberry Pi being power starved. The GPU consumes more power when it is active, performing accelerated graphics. Either the desktop freezes (GPU starvation) or the network interface fails (ping). There may be other symptoms related to HDMI activity.

Another problem that has been reported is resetting of the Raspberry Pi shortly after starting to boot. The board starts to consume more power as the kernel boots up, which can result in the Pi being starved.[43]

If you lose your Ethernet connection when you plug in a USB device, this too may be a sign of insufficient power.[44]

While it may seem that a 1 A power supply should be enough to supply a 700 mA Raspberry Pi, you will be better off using a 2 A supply instead. Many power supplies simply don't deliver their full advertised ratings.

The micro-USB cable is something else to suspect. Some are manufactured with thin conductors that can result in a significant voltage drop. Measuring the voltage as shown previously in the "Voltage Test" section may help diagnose that. Try a higher-quality cable to see whether there is an improvement.

No Power

If your Pi appears dead, even though power is present at the input, the input polyfuse could have blown. If this was a recent event, allow the unit to cool down. The polymer in the fuse recrystallizes, but this can take several hours. If you think the F3 poly fuse is permanently destroyed, see the Linux wiki page[45] for how to test it.

CHAPTER 5

■ ■ ■

Header Strips, LEDs, and Reset

In this chapter, an inventory of the Raspberry Pi header strips, LEDs, and reset button connections is covered. These are important interfaces from the Pi to the outside world. You may want to use a bookmark for Table 5-3, which outlines the general purpose input/output (GPIO) pins on header strip P1.

Status LEDs

The Model A Raspberry Pi has a subset of the Model B LED indicators because it lacks the Ethernet port. The Model B has three additional LEDs, each showing the network status. Table 5-1 provides a list of LED statuses.

Table 5-1. *Status LEDs*

LED	Color	Model A	Model B	Comment
ACT	Green	OK	ACT	SD card access activity
PWR	Red	Yes	Yes	Power supply
FDX	Green	N/A	Yes	LAN: Full duplex
LNK	Green	N/A	Yes	LAN: Link
100	Yellow	N/A	100	Labeled incorrectly on Rev 1.0 as 10M: 10/100 Mbit link

OK or ACT LED

This green LED indicates SD card I/O activity. This active low LED is internally driven by the kernel on GPIO 16 (see the kernel source file bcm2708.c in arm/mach-bcm2708).

PWR LED

This red LED simply indicates that the Raspberry Pi has power. Figure 5-1 shows that the power LED is supplied from the 3.3 V regulator.[14] Consequently, the LED indicates only that power is arriving through the 3.3 V regulator.

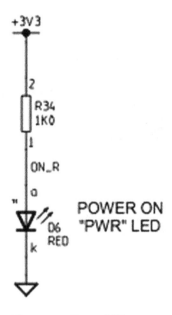

Figure 5-1. *Power LED*

The power LED indicator is not necessarily an indication that the power is *good*. It simply indicates that power is present. The LED can be lit and still not have sufficient voltage present for the CPU to operate correctly.

If there is any doubt about how good the power supply is, refer to the "Voltage Test" section in Chapter 4, which has information about how to perform a voltage test.

FDX LED

This green LED indicates that the Ethernet port is operating in *full-duplex* mode.

LNK LED

This green LED indicates that the Ethernet port has an active link-level status.

10M or 10/100 LED

Model B Rev 1.0 had this LED incorrectly labelled as *10M*. The correct label is 100, which is found on Rev 2.0 boards. This yellow LED indicates that the 100 Mbit link is active (otherwise, it is a 10 Mbit link).

Header P1

The Raspberry Pi includes a 13x2 pin strip identified as P1, which exposes GPIO pins. This includes the I2C, SPI, and UART peripherals as well as the +3.3 V, +5.0 V, and ground connections. Table 5-2 shows the pin assignments for the Model B, Rev 1.0 PCB.

Table 5-2. *Rev 1.0 GPIO Header Connector P1 (Top View)*

Lower Left				Upper Left
3.3 V power	P1-01	P1-02	5 V power	
GPIO 0 (I2C0_SDA)+*R1=1.8k*	P1-03	P1-04	5 V power	
GPIO 1 (I2C0_SCL)+*R2=1.8k*	P1-05	P1-06	Ground	
GPIO 4 (GPCLK 0/1-Wire)	P1-07	P1-08	GPIO 14 (TXD)	
Ground	P1-09	P1-10	GPIO 15 (RXD)	
GPIO 17	P1-11	P1-12	GPIO 18 (PCM_CLK)	
GPIO 21 (PCM_DOUT)	P1-13	P1-14	Ground	
GPIO 22	P1-15	P1-16	GPIO 23	
3.3 V power	P1-17	P1-18	GPIO 24	
GPIO 10 (MOSI)	P1-19	P1-20	Ground	
GPIO 9 (MISO)	P1-21	P1-22	GPIO 25	
GPIO 11 (SCKL)	P1-23	P1-24	GPIO 8 (CE0)	
Ground	P1-25	P1-26	GPIO 7 (CE1)	
Lower Right				**Upper Right**

■ **Caution**   The Model A can supply a maximum of 500 mA from the +5 V pins of P1. The model B has a lower maximum limit of 300 mA. These limits are due to the fusible link F3 on the PCB (shown previously in Figure 4-2 in Chapter 4). Note also for both models, the +3.3 V pins of P1 and P5 are limited to a maximum of 50 mA. This is the remaining capacity of the onboard voltage regulator. GPIO currents also draw from this resource. (See Figure 4-3.)

Table 5-3 shows the connections for the Model B revision 2.0. According to the Raspberry Pi website[14], these pin assignments are not expected to change beyond Rev 2.0 in future revisions. The additional Rev 2.0 header P5 is shown in Table 5-4.

Table 5-3. *Rev 2.0 GPIO Header Connector P1 (Top View)*

Lower Left			Upper Left
3.3 V power, 50 mA max	P1-01	P1-02	5 V power
GPIO 2 (I2C1_SDA1)+R1=1.8k	P1-03	P1-04	*5 V power*
GPIO 3 (I2C1_SCL1)+R2=1.8k	P1-05	P1-06	Ground
GPIO 4 (GPCLK 0/1-Wire)	P1-07	P1-08	GPIO 14 (TXD0)
Ground	P1-09	P1-10	GPIO 15 (RXD0)
GPIO 17 (GEN0)	P1-11	P1-12	GPIO 18 (PCM_CLK/GEN1)
GPIO 27 (GEN2)	P1-13	P1-14	*Ground*
GPIO 22 (GEN3)	P1-15	P1-16	GPIO 23 (GEN4)
3.3 V power, 50 mA max	P1-17	P1-18	GPIO 24 (GEN5)
GPIO 10 (SPI_MOSI)	P1-19	P1-20	*Ground*
GPIO 9 (SPI_MISO)	P1-21	P1-22	GPIO 25 (GEN6))
GPIO 11 (SPI_SCKL)	P1-23	P1-24	GPIO 8 (CE0_N)
Ground	P1-25	P1-26	GPIO 7 (CE1_N)
Lower Right			**Upper Right**

Table 5-4. *Rev 2.0 P5 Header (Top View)*

Lower Left			Upper Left
(Square) 5 V	P5-01	P5-02	3.3 V, 50 mA
GPIO 28	P5-03	P5-04	GPIO 29
GPIO 30	P5-05	P5-06	GPIO 31
Ground	P5-07	P5-08	Ground
Lower Right			**Upper Right**

■ **Note**   Chapter 7 provides more information on identifying your Raspberry Pi. If you have an early pre Rev 2.0 board, be aware that the GPIO pins differ.

Safe Mode

If your Raspbian SD image supports it, a *safe mode* can be activated when needed. The New Out of Box Software (NOOBS) image still appears to support this feature.

Pin P1-05, GPIO 3 is special to the boot sequence for Rev 2.0 models. (This is GPIO 1 on the pre Rev 2.0 Model B.) Grounding this pin or jumpering this to P1-06 (ground) causes the boot sequence to use a safe mode boot procedure. If the pin is used for some other purpose, you can prevent this with configuration parameter avoid_safe_mode=1. Be very careful that you don't accidentally ground a power pin (like P1-01 or P1-02) when you do use it.

If yours fails to respond to safe mode, it may be due to a manufacturing error. See this message:

www.raspberrypi.org/phpBB3/viewtopic.php?f=29&t=12007

In that thread, it is suggested that you check the following:

```
$ vcgencmd otp_dump | grep 30:
30:00000002
```

If you see the value 2, it means that the firmware thinks this is a Rev 1.0 board (even though it may be a Rev 2.0). When that applies, it will not support the safe mode sequence. Newer Rev 2.0 Pis do not have this issue.

When safe mode is invoked by the jumper, the config.txt file is ignored except for the avoid_safe_mode parameter. Additionally, this mode overrides the kernel command line, and kernel_emergency.img is loaded. If this file is unavailable, kernel.img is used instead.

The intent of this feature is to permit the user to overcome configuration problems without having to edit the SD card on another machine in order to make a correction. The booted emergency kernel is a BusyBox image with /boot mounted so that adjustments can be made. Additionally, the /dev/mmcblk0p2 root file system partition can be fixed up or mounted if necessary.

Logic Levels

The logic level used for GPIO pins is 3.3 V and is *not* tolerant of 5 V TTL logic. The Raspberry Pi PCB is designed to be plugged into PCB extension cards or otherwise carefully interfaced to 3 V logic. Input voltage parameters V_{IL} and V_{IH} are described in Chapter 12. This feature of the Pi makes it an interesting case study as we interface it to the outside world.

GPIO Configuration at Reset

The Raspberry Pi GPIO pins can be configured by software control to be input or output, to have pull-up or pull-down resistors, or to assume some specialized peripheral function. After reset, only GPIO 14 and 15 are assigned a special function (UART). After boot up, however, software can even reconfigure the UART pins as required.

When a GPIO pin is configured for output, there is a limited amount of current that it can drive (source or sink). By default, each P1 GPIO is configured to use an 8 mA driver, when the pin is configured as an output. Chapter 12 has more information on the software control of this.

■ **Note**   Raspbian 1-Wire bus is GPIO 4 (GPCLK0) Pin P1-07.

1-Wire Driver

The default GPIO pin used for the 1-Wire driver is GPIO 4. This is hard-coded in the following kernel source file:

arch/arm/mach-bcm2708/bcm2708.c

If you need to change this default, alter the line in bcm2708.c that defines the macro W1_GPIO:

```
#define  W1_GPIO  4
```

Then rebuild your kernel.

Header P5

Be careful with the orientation of this Model B Rev 2.0 header strip. See Figure 5-2: while looking down at P1, with its pin 1 at the lower left, the P5 strip has its pin 1 at the upper left (note the square pad on either side of the PCB).

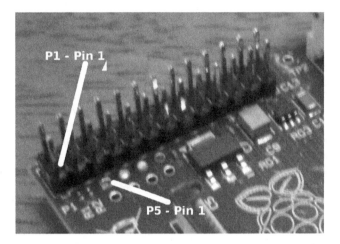

Figure 5-2. P5's pin 1 location on the Rev 2.0 Model B

As a practical matter, I found that the pins for P5 can be soldered into the PCB with some care (they are not included). However, the proximity of P5 to P1 makes it impossible to plug in a header connector to P1 and P5 at the same time. With the pins installed, it is possible to use individual wire plugs on the pins as needed. I ended up plugging in a dual-wire plug on P5-04 and P5-06, which is one row away from P1. These wires were then brought out to connectors on a wood strip for easier access.

By default, GPIO pins 28 through 31 are configured for driving 16 mA. (Chapter 12 has more information about this.)

Reset

In the revision 2.0 Raspberry Pi, a reset circuit was implemented, as shown in Figure 5-4.[11] To complete the reset circuit, attach a push button to pins 1 and 2 of P6, as shown in Figure 5-3.[14]

Figure 5-3. *Model B Rev 2.0 P6*

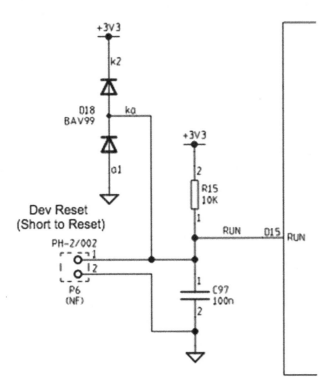

Figure 5-4. *Reset circuit*

To actuate the reset, P6 pin 1 is short-circuited to P6 pin 2. This resets the BCM2835 SoC chip. This is something you will want to avoid using while Raspbian Linux is up and running. Use reset as a last resort to avoid losing file content.

CHAPTER 6

SDRAM

The Model B Rev 2.0 Raspberry Pi has 512 MB of SDRAM, while the older revisions and remaining models have 256 MB. Contrast this to the AVR class ATmega168p, which has 1 KB of static RAM. *SDRAM* is *synchronous dynamic random access memory*, which synchronizes with the system bus for improved performance. It uses a form of pipelining to gain this advantage.

There isn't much about the memory hardware that concerns the average Pi developer. However, in this chapter, you'll examine some useful Raspbian Linux kernel interfaces that inform us how that memory is utilized. You'll also examine how to access the memory-mapped ARM peripherals directly from your Linux application.

/proc/meminfo

The pseudo file /proc/meminfo provides us with information about memory utilization. This information varies somewhat by architecture and the compile options used for that kernel. Let's study an example that is produced by Raspbian Linux, on the Raspberry Pi:

```
$ cat /proc/meminfo
MemTotal:        448996 kB
MemFree:         340228 kB
Buffers:          14408 kB
Cached:           58532 kB
SwapCached:           0 kB
Active:           45948 kB
Inactive:         51564 kB
Active(anon):     24680 kB
Inactive(anon):     820 kB
Active(file):     21268 kB
Inactive(file):   50744 kB
Unevictable:          0 kB
Mlocked:              0 kB
SwapTotal:       102396 kB
SwapFree:        102396 kB
Dirty:                0 kB
Writeback:            0 kB
AnonPages:        24584 kB
Mapped:           20056 kB
Shmem:              932 kB
Slab:              6088 kB
SReclaimable:      2392 kB
```

```
SUnreclaim:       3696 kB
KernelStack:      1216 kB
PageTables:       1344 kB
NFS_Unstable:        0 kB
Bounce:              0 kB
WritebackTmp:        0 kB
CommitLimit:    326892 kB
Committed_AS:   215104 kB
VmallocTotal:   188416 kB
VmallocUsed:       744 kB
VmallocChunk:   186852 kB
```

All of the memory values shown have the units *KB* to the right of them, indicating kilo (1,024) bytes. This next example was taken from a Model A Raspberry Pi, with 256 MB:[63]

```
$cat/proc/meminfo
MemTotal:       190836 kB
MemFree:        151352 kB
Buffers:          7008 kB
Cached:          20640 kB
SwapCached:          0 kB
Active:          14336 kB
Inactive:        18648 kB
Active(anon):     5468 kB
Inactive(anon):      0 kB
Active(file):     8868 kB
Inactive(file): 18648 kB
Unevictable:         0 kB
Mlocked:             0 kB
SwapTotal:           0 kB
SwapFree:            0 kB
Dirty:               0 kB
Writeback:           0 kB
AnonPages:        5348 kB
Mapped:           6512 kB
Shmem:             136 kB
Slab:             3712 kB
SReclaimable:     1584 kB
SUnreclaim:       2128 kB
KernelStack:       944 kB
PageTables:        620 kB
NFS_Unstable:        0 kB
Bounce:              0 kB
WritebackTmp:        0 kB
CommitLimit:     95416 kB
Committed_AS:    57876 kB
VmallocTotal:   188416 kB
VmallocUsed:       704 kB
VmallocChunk:   186852 kB
```

Many of these values are noticeably smaller.

In the sections that follow, a Model B to Model A comparison is provided. In some cases, the comparison isn't meaningful because the values represent activity that has or has not occurred. For example, the value for AnonPages is going to depend on the mix of commands and applications that have run. But values from both models are provided for completeness. Other values such as MemTotal can be meaningfully compared, however.

MemTotal

The MemTotal line indicates the total amount of memory available, minus a few reserved binary regions. Note that memory allocated to the GPU is not factored into MemTotal. Some may choose to allocate the minimum of 16 MB to the GPU to make more memory available.

	Model B	Model A
MemTotal	448,996 KB	190,836 KB

If we break this down a bit further, accounting for memory allocated to the GPU (see Chapter 16 for more details), we find that there is about 9.5 MB (1.9%) of memory that is unaccounted for, as shown in Table 6-1.

Table 6-1. *GPU and Main Memory Breakdown*

Memory	Model B	Comments
MemTotal	448,996 KB	/proc/meminfo
gpu_mem	65,536 KB	/boot/config.txt
Total	514,532 KB	502.5 MB
Unaccounted for	9,756 KB	9.5 MB

MemFree

MemFree normally represents the sum of LowFree + HighFree memory in kilobytes on the Intel x86 platform. For ARM, this simply represents the amount of memory available to user space programs.

	Model B	Model A
MemFree	340,228 KB	151,352 KB

The Model B has 332.25 MB for application programs, which amounts to about 64.9% (Rev 2.0). The Model A values indicate about 57.7% of the memory is available.

Buffers

This value represents temporary buffers used within the kernel for raw disk blocks, and so forth. This value should not get much larger than about 20 MB or so.[27]

	Model B	Model A
Buffers	14,408 KB	7,008 KB

Cached

This value represents the read file content that has been cached (page cache). This does not include the content reported for SwapCached.

	Model B	Model A
Cached	58,532 KB	20,640 KB

SwapCached

The value shown for SwapCached represents memory that was swapped out and is now swapped back in. For efficiency, these memory pages are still represented by swap disk space, should they be needed again.

	Model B	Model A
SwapCached	0 KB	0 KB

The fact that the value is reported as zero is a happy sign that no swapping has occurred, or is no longer pertinent.

Active

The Active memory value represents recently used memory that is not reclaimed, unless absolutely necessary.

	Model B	Model A
Active	45,948 KB	14,336 KB

Inactive

This value represents memory that is not active and is likely to be reclaimed when memory is needed.

	Model B	Model A
Inactive	51,564 KB	18,648 KB

Active(anon)

This value represents memory that is not backed up by a file and is active. Active memory is not reclaimed unless absolutely necessary.

	Model B	Model A
Active(anon)	24,680 KB	5,468 KB

Inactive(anon)

This value represents memory that is not backed up by a file and is not active. Inactive memory is eligible to be reclaimed if memory is required.

	Model B	Model A
Inactive(anon)	820 KB	0 KB

Active(file)

This value represents file-backed memory, which is active. Active memory is reclaimed only if absolutely required.

	Model B	Model A
Active(file)	21,268 KB	8,868 KB

Inactive(file)

This value represents inactive memory that is backed by a file. Inactive memory is eligible for reclamation, when memory is required.

	Model B	Model A
Inactive(file)	50,744 KB	18,648 KB

Unevictable

This amount reflects the total amount of memory that cannot be reclaimed. Memory that is locked, for example, cannot be reclaimed.

	Model B	Model A
Unevictable	0 KB	0 KB

Mlocked

This value reports the amount of locked memory.

	Model B	Model A
Mlocked	0 KB	0 KB

SwapTotal

This value reports the total amount of swap space available in kilobytes.

	Model B	Model A
SwapTotal	102,396 KB	0 KB

SwapFree

This value reports the remaining amount of swap space available in kilobytes.

	Model B	Model A
SwapFree	102,396 KB	0 KB

Dirty

This value represents the kilobytes of memory that have been modified and are waiting to be written to disk.

	Model B	Model A
Dirty	0 KB	0 KB

Writeback

This value reports the amount of memory in kilobytes being written back to disk.

	Model B	Model A
Writeback	0 KB	0 KB

AnonPages

This represents the non-file-backed pages of memory mapped into user space.

	Model B	Model A
AnonPages	24,584 KB	5,348 KB

Mapped

This value reports the files that have been mapped into memory. This may include library code.

	Model B	Model A
Mapped	20,056 KB	6,512 KB

Shmem

This parameter does not appear to be documented well. However, it represents the amount of shared memory in kilobytes.

	Model B	Model A
Shmem	932 KB	136 KB

Slab

This parameter is described as "in-kernel data structures cache."[27]

	Model B	Model A
Slab	6,088 KB	3,712 KB

SReclaimable

This parameter is described as "Part of Slab that might be reclaimed, such as caches."[27]

	Model B	Model A
SReclaimable	2,392 KB	1,584 KB

SUnreclaim

This parameter is described as "Part of Slab that cannot be reclaimed [under] memory pressure."[27]

	Model B	Model A
SUnreclaim	3,696 KB	2,128 KB

KernelStack

This value reports the memory used by the kernel stack(s).

	Model B	Model A
KernelStack	1,216 KB	944 KB

PageTables

This value reports the amount of memory required by the page tables used in the kernel. Clearly, with more memory to manage, there is more memory dedicated to page tables.

	Model B	Model A
PageTables	1,344 KB	620 KB

NFS_Unstable

This value represents "NFS pages sent to the server, but not yet committed to stable storage."[27] This example data suggests that NFS is not being used.

	Model B	Model A
NFS_Unstable	0 KB	0 KB

Bounce

This reports the memory used for "block device bounce buffers."[27]

	Model B	Model A
Bounce	0 KB	0 KB

WritebackTmp

This parameter reports the memory used by FUSE for "temporary writeback buffers."[27]

	Model B	Model A
WritebackTmp	0 KB	0 KB

CommitLimit

The documentation states:

> *Based on the overcommit ratio (*vm.overcommit_ratio*), this is the total amount of memory currently available to be allocated on the system. This limit is only adhered to if strict overcommit accounting is enabled (mode 2 in* vm.overcommit_memory*). The* CommitLimit *is calculated with the following formula:[27]*
> *CommitLimit = (vm.overcommit_ratio × Physical RAM) + Swap*

For example, a system with 1 GB of physical RAM and 7 GB of swap with a vm.overcommit_ratio of 30 would yield a CommitLimit of 7.3 GB. For more details, see the memory overcommit documentation in vm/overcommitaccounting. The formula can be written as follows:

$$C = (R \times r) + S$$

The elements of this formula are described here:

- C is the overcommit limit.

- R is the physical RAM available (MemTotal).

- S is the swap space available (SwapTotal).

- r is the overcommit ratio percent (expressed as a fraction).

The overcommit ratio, r, is not reported in the /proc/meminfo data. To obtain that ratio, we consult another pseudo file. This example was taken from a Rev 2.0 Model B, but it appears to be a value common to all Pis:

```
$ cat /proc/sys/vm/overcommit_ratio
50
```

The value 50 is to be interpreted as r = 0.50 (50%).

Using the overcommit formula, the value for S can be computed for the swap space available:

$$S = C - (R \times r)$$
$$= 326892 - (448996 \times 0.50)$$
$$= 326892 - 262144$$
$$= 102394 KB$$

This fits within 2 KB of the SwapTotal value of 102,396 KB reported by /proc/meminfo.

The overcommit ratio is configurable by the user, by writing a value into the pseudo file. This example changes the ratio to 35%:

```
$ sudo -i
# echo 35 >/proc/sys/vm/overcommit_ratio
# cat /proc/sys/vm/overcommit_ratio
35
```

The CommitLimit values reported by our example Raspberry Pi sessions are shown in Table 6-2 for comparison purposes. A Model B pre Rev 2.0 version is also included here for comparison.

Table 6-2. *Example Model B to Model A Memory Comparisons*

	Model B Rev 2.0	Model B Pre 2.0	Model A
CommitLimit	326,892 KB	127,868 KB	95,416 KB
MemTotal	448,996 KB	124,672 KB	190,836 KB
SwapTotal	102,396 KB	65,532 KB	0 KB
Commit Ratio	50	50	50

With thanks to Dan Braun for providing the Model B Pre 2.0 data.

The value of the Model A commit ratio was calculated here since it wasn't available from the website. But if you calculate the swap space S for it, you arrive at the value of –2 KB, if you assume 50% for the commit ratio. This agrees with the 2 KB difference you saw earlier.

Committed_AS

This parameter is described as follows:

> *The amount of memory presently allocated on the system. The committed memory is a sum of all of the memory which has been allocated by processes, even if it has not been "used" by them as of yet. A process which* malloc()*'s 1 GB of memory, but only touches 300 MB of it will only show up as using 300 MB of memory even if it has the address space allocated for the entire 1 GB. This 1 GB is memory which has been "committed" to by the VM and can be used at any time by the allocating application. With strict overcommit enabled on the system (mode 2 in* vm.overcommit_memory*), allocations which would exceed the* CommitLimit*(detailed above) will not be permitted. This is useful if one needs to guarantee that processes will not fail due to lack of memory once that memory has been successfully allocated.*[27]

	Model B	Model A
Committed_AS	215,104 KB	57,876 KB

VmallocTotal

This represents the total amount of allocated virtual memory address space.

	Model B	Model A
VmallocTotal	188,416 KB	188,416 KB

VmallocUsed

This is the amount of virtual memory that is in use, reported in kilobytes.

	Model B	Model A
VmallocUsed	744 KB	704 KB

VmallocChunk

This value reports the largest size of a vmalloc area, in kilobytes.

	Model B	Model A
VmallocChunk	186,852 KB	186,852 KB

Physical Memory

Let's now turn our attention to the Raspberry Pi's physical memory layout. Normally, physical memory isn't a concern to application programmers, because the operating system and its drivers provide an abstract and often portable way to access them. However, when this support is absent, direct access to a peripheral like the PWM controller is necessary.

Figure 6-1 illustrates the physical addressing used on the Raspberry Pi. The SDRAM starts at physical address zero and works up to the ARM/GPU split point (Chapter 16 defines the split point). The ARM peripherals are mapped to physical memory starting at the address of 0x20000000. This starting address is of keen interest to Pi programmers.

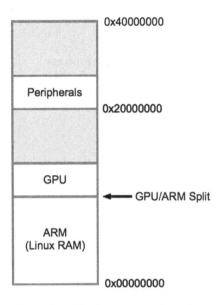

Figure 6-1. *Physical memory layout*

In the region labeled Peripherals, the offsets and addresses indicated in Table 6-3 are of interest to us.

Table 6-3. *Peripheral Offsets for the Raspberry Pi*

Peripheral	Offset	Address	Description	C Offset Macro
Base	0x00000000	0x20000000	Starting address	BCM2708_PERI_BASE
PADS_GPIO	0x00100000	0x20100000	PADS base	PADS_GPIO_BASE
GPIO 00..27	0x0010002C	0x2010002C	GPIO 00..27 pads	PADS_GPIO_00_27
GPIO 28..45	0x00100030	0x20100030	GPIO 28..45 pads	PADS_GPIO_28_45
GPIO 46..53	0x00100034	0x20100034	GPIO 46..53 pads	PADS_GPIO_46_53
Clock	0x00101000	0x20101000	Clock registers	CLK_BASE
GPIO	0x00200000	0x20200000	GPIO registers	GPIO_BASE
GPPUD	0x00200025	0x20200025	Pull-up enable	
GPPUDCLK0	0x00200026	0x20200026	Pull-up clock 0	
GPPUDCLK1	0x00200027	0x20200027	Pull-up clock 1	
PWM	0x0020C000	0x2020C000	PWM registers	PWM_BASE

Throughout this book, you'll see the macros BCM2708_PERI_BASE and GPIO_BASE, for example, used in programs that access the peripherals directly.

Memory Mapping

To gain access to physical memory under Linux, we make use of the /dev/mem character device and the mmap(2) system call. The /dev/mem node is shown here:

```
$ ls -l /dev/mem
crw-r----T 1 root kmem 1, 1 Dec 31 1969 /dev/mem
```

From the ownership information shown, it is immediately obvious that you'll need root privileges to access it. This is sensible given that a process can cause havoc with direct access to the physical memory. Clearly, the Pi developer should exercise caution in what the applications do with it.

The mmap(2) system call API is shown here:

```
#include <sys/mman.h>

void *mmap(
  void      *addr,     /*Address to use */
  size_t    length,    /*Number of bytes to access */
  int       prot,      /*Memory protection */
  int       flags,     /*Option flags */
  int       fd,        /*Opened file descriptor */
  off_t     offset     /*Starting off set */
) ;
```

Rather than look at all the options and flags available to this somewhat complicated system call, let's look at the ones that we use in the following code:

```
static char *map = 0;

static void
gpio_init() {
    int fd;
    char *map;

    fd = open("/dev/mem",O_RDWR|O_SYNC) ;    /*Needs root access */
    if ( fd < 0 ) {
        perror("Opening /dev/mem") ;
        exit(1) ;
    }

    map = (char *) mmap(
        NULL,                 /*Any address */
        BLOCK_SIZE,           /* # of bytes */
        PROT_READ|PROT_WRITE,
        MAP_SHARED,           /*Shared */
        fd,                   /* /dev/mem */
        GPIO_BASE             /*Offset to GPIO */
    ) ;
```

```
    if ( (long)map == -1L ) {
        perror("mmap(/dev/mem)");
        exit(1) ;
    }

    close(fd);
    ugpio = (volatile unsigned *)map;
}
```

The first thing performed in this code is to open the device driver node /dev/mem. It is opened for reading and writing (O_RDWR), and the option flag O_SYNC requests that any write(2) call to this file descriptor result in blocking the execution of the caller until it has completed.

Address

Next, the mmap(2) call is invoked. The address argument is provided with NULL (zero) so that the kernel can choose where to map it into the caller's address space. If the application were to specify a starting address to use and the kernel was not able use it, the system call would fail. The starting address is returned and assigned to the character pointer map in the preceding listing.

Length

Argument 2 is supplied with the macro BLOCK_SIZE in this example. This is the number of bytes you would like to map into your address space. This was defined earlier in the program as 4 KB:

```
#define BLOCK_SIZE (4*1024)
```

While the application may not need the full 4 KB of physical memory mapped, mmap(2) may insist on using a multiple of the page size. This can be verified on the command line as follows:

```
$ getconf PAGE_SIZE
4096
```

A program could determine this as well, by using the sysconf(2) system call:

```
#include <unistd.h>

...
long sz = sysconf(_SC_PAGESIZE);
```

Protection

The third mmap(2) argument is supplied with the flags PROT_READ and PROT_WRITE. This indicates that the application wants both read and write access to the memory-mapped region.

Flags

The flags argument is supplied with the value MAP_SHARED. This permits nonexclusive access to the underlying mapping.

File Descriptor

This argument supplies the underlying opened file to be mapped into memory. In this case, we map a region of physical ARM memory into our application by using the opened device driver node /dev/mem.

Offset

This last argument specifies the location in physical memory where we want to start our access. For the GPIO registers, it is the address 0x20200000.

Return Value

The return value, when successful, will be an application address that points to the physical memory region we asked for. The application programmer need not be concerned with what this address is, except to save and use it for access.

The return value is also used for indicating failure, so this should be checked and handled:

```
if ( (long) map == -1L ) {
    perror("mmap(/dev/mem)");
    exit(1);
}
```

The returned address (pointer) map is cast to a long integer and compared to -1L. This is the magic value that indicates that an error occurred. The error code is found in errno.

Volatile

The last section of this initialization code for GPIO assigns the address map to another variable, ugpio, as follows:

```
ugpio = (volatile unsigned *)map;
```

The value ugpio was defined earlier in the program:

```
static volatile unsigned *ugpio = 0;
```

There are two things noteworthy about this:

- The data type is an unsigned int (32 bits on the Pi).
- The pointed-to data is marked as *volatile*.

Since the Pis registers are 32 bits in size, it is often more convenient to access them as 32-bit words. The unsigned data type is perfect for this. But be careful with *offsets* in conjunction with this pointer, since they will be *word* offsets rather than byte offsets.

The volatile keyword tells the compiler not to optimize access to memory through the pointer variable. Imagine code that reads a peripheral register and reads the same register again later, to see whether an event has occurred. An optimizing compiler might say to itself, "I already have this value in CPU register R, so I'll just use that since it is faster." But the effect of this code is that it will never see a bit change in the peripheral's register because that data was not fetched back into a CPU register. The volatile keyword forces the compiler to retrieve the value even though it would be faster to use the value still found in a register.

Virtual Memory

In the previous section, you looked at how to access physical memory in an application, provided that you had the rights to do so (root or setuid). The Broadcom Corporation PDF manual "BCM2835 ARM Peripherals," page 5, also shows a *virtual* memory layout on the right. This should not be confused with the *physical* memory layout that you examined earlier. Virtual memory can be accessed through /dev/kmem driver node using mmap(2), but we won't be needing that in this book.

Final Thoughts on SDRAM

Some parameters such as Buffers impact the performance of Raspbian Linux on the Pi. From our comparison, we saw that the Model A seems to use about half of the buffering available to the Model B Rev 2.0 Pi. This is reasonable when limited memory has to be divided between operating system and application use.

Another performance area related to memory is how much SDRAM is dedicated to GPU use. This parameter is examined in Chapter 16.

Probably the most important aspect of memory allocation is how much memory is available to the developer's application programs. The value of MemFree is perhaps the most useful metric for this. When exceeding physical memory limits, the swapping parameters then become measurements of interest.

Finally, we took a detailed look at how to access the Raspberry Pi peripherals directly using mmap(2). Until Raspbian Linux gains device drivers for peripherals such as PWM, the direct access technique will be necessary. Even with driver support, there are sometimes valid reasons to access the peripheral registers directly.

CHAPTER 7

CPU

The Raspberry Pi includes an ARM 700 MHz CPU. In this chapter, you'll first look at the versions of the Pi that have been released into the wild. Then after looking briefly at overclocking, you'll examine how the CPU is exploited by the Linux application.

Identification

Several revisions of the Pi have been released and sold. Table 7-1 lists the known revisions and some of the changes related to them.

Table 7-1. *Board Identification*[40, 41]

Code	Model	Rev.	RAM	P1-03	P1-05	P1-13	P5	Manuf.	Comments
0002	B	1.0	256 MB	GPIO0	GPIO1	GPIO21	N	Egoman?	
0003	B	1.0+	256 MB	GPIO0	GPIO1	GPIO21	N	Egoman?	Fuse mod and D14 removed
0004	B	2.0	256 MB	GPIO1	GPIO2	GPIO27	Y	Sony	
0005	B	2.0	256 MB	GPIO1	GPIO2	GPIO27	Y	Qisda	
0006	B	2.0	256 MB	GPIO1	GPIO2	GPIO27	Y	Egoman	
0007	A	2.0	256 MB	GPIO1	GPIO2	GPIO27	Y	Egoman	
0008	A	2.0	256 MB	GPIO1	GPIO2	GPIO27	Y	Sony	
0009	A	2.0	256 MB	GPIO1	GPIO2	GPIO27	Y	Qisda	
000d	B	2.0	512 MB	GPIO1	GPIO2	GPIO27	Y	Egoman	
000e	B	2.0	512 MB	GPIO1	GPIO2	GPIO27	Y	Sony	
000f	B	2.0	512 MB	GPIO1	GPIO2	GPIO27	Y	Qisda	

Once your Raspberry Pi has booted up in Raspbian Linux, you can check the board's identification with the following command:

```
$ cat /proc/cpuinfo
Processor        :  ARMv6-compatible processor rev 7 (v6l)
BogoMIPS         :  697.95
Features         :  swp half thumb fastmult vfp edsp java tls
CPU implementer  :  0x41
CPU  architecture :  7
CPU  variant     :  0x0
CPU  part        :  0xb76
CPU  revision    :  7
Hardware         :  BCM2708
Revision         :  000f
Serial           :  00000000f52b69d9
```

The preceding example reports a revision of 000f, which is a Rev 2.0 Pi.

Overclocking

Raspbian Linux for the Raspberry Pi is conservatively configured for reliability by default. Those with the need for speed can reconfigure it for increased performance but at the risk of less-reliable operation.

Raspbian Linux 3.6.11 provides a `raspi-config` menu of five CPU profiles. The profile None is the default:

Profile	ARM CPU	Core	SDRAM	Overvolt
None	700 MHz	250 MHz	400 MHz	0
Modest	800 MHz	250 MHz	400 MHz	0
Medium	900 MHz	250 MHz	450 MHz	2
High	950 MHz	250 MHz	450 MHz	6
Turbo	1 GHz	500 MHz	600 MHz	6

The `raspi-config` requires root privileges and is started as follows:

```
$ sudo raspi-config
```

The initial menu screen provides an `overclock` selection with the description `Configure overclocking`. Choosing that menu item opens another menu, allowing you to choose a profile.

Choosing a profile from this menu changes the following parameters in `/boot/config.txt`:

Parameter	None	Modest	Medium	High	Turbo
arm_freq=	700	800	900	950	1000
core_freq=	250	250	250	250	500
sdram_freq=	400	400	450	450	600
over_voltage=	0	0	2	6	6

When trading reliability for performance, these factors should be considered as it relates to your application:

- How critical is the application for
  - Correctness/accuracy
  - Uptime
- How does increased performance relate to the results?
  - Improved accuracy (Fourier transforms, real-time processing)
  - Increased number of measurements/sampling points
- What is the impact of failure?
- Will the unit perform reliably in all required temperatures (in an enclosure, outdoors)?

How do these performance profiles affect day-to-day performance? Developers are often concerned about compile times, so I did a simple compile-time test.

The test procedure used is as follows:

1. With `raspi-config`, configure the desired overclocking profile.
2. Reboot.
3. Change to the book's source code top-level directory.
4. Use the command `make clobber`.
5. Use the command `time make`.

Table 7-2 summarizes the results in seconds for compiling all projects for this book, using the different overclocking profiles. The elapsed times did not always improve (Real), but they can vary widely because of how I/O to the SD card occurs. The CPU time otherwise improved, with one small exception between Medium and High "User" CPU time.

Table 7-2. *Profile Compile Tests*

Profile	Real	User	System
None	56.641	23.730	3.520
Modest	37.475	22.330	3.510
Medium	40.127	20.830	3.360
High	49.318	20.980	3.240
Turbo	32.756	15.380	2.650

Everyone has a different appetite for speed. I usually favor reliability over speed, since failure and intermittent problems can cause "wild goose chases" and otherwise waste valuable time. Yet in some situations performance can be important enough to accept the risks. An application performing real-time Fourier transforms on audio might justify Turbo mode, for example.

Execution

Connected with the idea of the CPU is program execution itself. Before you look at program execution, you need to take high-level view of the execution context. Figure 7-1 shows the operating environment that an executing program operates within.

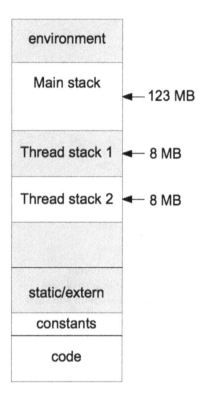

Figure 7-1. *Program execution context*

At the lowest end of the address space is the "text" region containing the program code. This region of virtual memory is read-only, containing read-only program constants in addition to executable code.

The next region (in increasing address) contains blocks of uninitialized arrays, buffers, static C variables, and extern storage.

At the high end of memory are environment variables for the program, like PATH. You can easily check this yourself by using getenv("PATH") and printing the returned address for it. Its address will likely be the highest address in your Raspberry Pi application, except possibly for another environment variable.

Below that, your main program's stack begins and grows downward. Each function call causes a new stack frame to be created below the current one.

If you now add a thread to the program, a new stack has to be allocated for it. Experiments on the Pi show that the first thread stack gets created approximately 123 MB below the main stack's beginning. A second thread has its stack allocated about 8 MB below the first. Each new thread's stack (by default) is allocated 8 MB of stack space.

Dynamically allocated memory gets allocated from the *heap*, which sits between the static/extern region and the bottom end of the stack.

Threads

Before threads were perfected under Linux, many application developers tended to avoid them. Now, however, there is little reason to.

Every attempt was made to keep the project programs in this book simple. This usually meant also avoiding threads. Yet, a few projects would have been more complicated without them. In the example using ØMQ, threads would have been present behind the scenes, even if we didn't see them in our application code.

With that introduction, let's take a crash course on the pthread API as it applies to Raspbian Linux.

pthread Headers

All pthread functions require the following header file:

```
#include <pthread.h>
```

When linking programs compiled to use pthreads, add the linker option:

-lpthread: Link with the pthread library.

pthread Error Handling

The pthread routines return zero when they succeed and *return an error code when they fail.* The value errno is *not* used for these calls.

The reason behind this is likely that it was thought that the traditional Unix errno approach would be phased out in the near future (at the time POSIX threads were being standardized). The original use of errno was as follows:

```
extern int errno;
```

However, this approach didn't work for threaded programs. Imagine two threads concurrently opening files with open(2), which sets the errno value upon failure. Both threads cannot share the same int value for errno.

Rather than change a vast body of code already using errno in this manner, other approaches were implemented to provide each thread with its own private copy of errno. This is one reason that programs today using errno must include the header file errno.h. The header file takes care of defining the thread specific reference to errno.

Because the pthread standard was developing before the errno solution generally emerged, the pthread library returns the error code directly when there is an error and returns zero when the call is a success. If Unix were to be rewritten from scratch today, all system calls would probably work this way.

pthread_create(3)

The function pthread_create(3) is used to create a new thread of execution. The function call looks more daunting than it really is:

```
int pthread_create(
  pthread_t *thread,
  const pthread_attr_t *attr,
  void *( start_routine)(void *),
  void *arg
);
```

The call to pthread_create(3) creates a new stack, sets up registers, and performs other housekeeping. Let's describe the arguments:

thread: This first argument is simply a pointer to a pthread_t variable to receive the created thread's ID value. The ID value allows you to query and control the created thread. If the call succeeds, the thread ID is returned to the calling program.

attr: This is a pointer to a pthread_attr_t attribute object that supplies various options and parameters. If you can accept the defaults, simply supply zero or NULL.

start_routine: As shown in the following code, this is simply the name of a start routine that accepts a void pointer and returns a void pointer.

arg: This generic pointer is passed to start_routine. It may point to anything of interest to the thread function (start_routine). Often this is a structure containing values, or in a C++ program, it can be the pointer to an object. If you don't need an argument value, supply zero (or NULL).

returns: Zero is returned if the function is successful; otherwise, an error number is returned (not in errno).

Error	Description
EAGAIN	Insufficient resources to create another thread, or a system-imposed limit on the number of threads was encountered.
EINVAL	Invalid settings in attr.
EPERM	No permission to set the scheduling policy and parameters specified in attr.

The C language syntax of argument 3 is a bit nasty for beginning C programmers. Let's just show what the function for argument 3 looks like:

```
void *
start_routine(void *arg) {
    ...
    return some_ptr;
}
```

The following is perhaps the simplest example of thread creation possible:

```
static void *
my_thread(void *arg) {
    ...                             // thread execution
    return 0;
}

int
main(int argc, char **argv) {
    pthread_t tid;                  // Thread   ID
    int rc;

    rc = pthread_create(&tid,0,my_thread,0);
    assert(!rc);
```

This example does not use thread attributes (argument 2 is zero). We also don't care about the value passed into my_thread(), so argument 4 is provided a zero. Argument 3 simply needs to tell the system call what function to execute. The value of rc will be zero if the thread is successfully created (tested by the assert(3) macro).

At this point, the main thread and the function my_thread() execute in parallel. Since there is only one CPU on the Raspberry Pi, only one executes at any instant of time. But they both execute concurrently, trading blocks of execution time in a preemptive manner. Each, of course, runs using its own stack.

Thread my_thread() terminates gracefully, by returning.

pthread_attr_t

There are several thread attributes that can be fetched and set. You'll look only at perhaps the most important attribute (stack size) to keep this crash course brief. For the full list of attributes and functions, you can view the man pages for it:

```
$ man pthread_attr_init
```

To initialize a new attribute, or to release a previously initialized pthread attribute, use this pair of routines:

```
int pthread_attr_init(pthread_attr_t *attr);
int pthread_attr_destroy(pthread_attr_t *attr);
```

> attr: Address of the pthread_attr_t variable to initialize/destroy

> returns: Zero upon success, or an error code when it fails (not in errno)

Error	Description
ENOMEM	Insufficient resources (memory)

The Linux implementation of pthread_attr_init(3) may never return the ENOMEM error, but other Unix platforms might.

The following is a simple example of creating and destroying an attribute object:

```
pthread_attr_t attr;

pthread_attr_init(&attr);    // Initialize attr
...
pthread_attr_destroy(&attr); // Destroy attr
```

Perhaps one of the most important attributes of a thread is the stack size attribute:

```
int pthread_attr_setstacksize(pthread_attr_t *attr, size_t stacksize);
int pthread_attr_getstacksize(pthread_attr_t *attr, size_t *stacksize);
```

> attr: The pointer to the attribute to fetch a value from, or to establish an attribute in.

> stacksize: This is a stack size value when setting the attribute, and a pointer to the receiving size_t variable when fetching the stack size.

> returns: Returns zero if the call is successful; otherwise, returns an error number (not in errno).

The following error is possible for pthread_attr_setstacksize(3):

Error	Description
EINVAL	The stack size is less than PTHREAD_STACK_MIN (16,384) bytes.

The Linux man page further states:

On some systems, pthread_attr_setstacksize() can fail with the error EINVAL if stack size is not a multiple of the system page size.

The following simple example obtains the system default stack size and increases it by 8 MB:

```
pthread_attr_t attr;
size_t         stksiz;

pthread_attr_init(&attr);                       // Initialize attr
pthread_attr_getstacksize (&attr,&stksiz);      // Get stack size
stksiz  += 8 * 1024 * 1024;                     // Add 8 MB
pthread_attr_setstacksize(&attr,stksiz);        // Set stack size
```

The system default is provided by the initialization of attr. Then it is a matter of "getting" a value out of the attr object, and then putting in a new stack size in the call to pthread_attr_setstacksize().

Note that this set of operations has simply prepared the attributes object attr for use in a pthread_create() call. The attribute takes effect in the new thread, when the thread is actually created:

```
pthread_attr_t attr;

...
rc = pthread_create(&tid,&attr,my_thread,0);
```

pthread_join(3)

In the earlier pthread_create() example, the main program creates my_thread() and starts it executing. At some point, the main program is going to finish and want to exit (or return). If the main program exits before my_thread() completes, the entire process and the threads in it are destroyed, even if they have not completed.

To cause the main program to wait until the thread completes, the function pthread_join(3) is used:

```
int pthread_join(pthread_t thread, void **retval);
```

> thread: Thread ID of the thread to be joined with.
>
> retval: Pointer to the void * variable to receive the returned value. If you are uninterested in a return value, this argument can be supplied with zero (or NULL).
>
> returns: The function returns zero when successful; otherwise, an error number is returned (not in errno).

The following example has added pthread_join(3), so that the main program does not exit until my_thread() exits.

```
int
main(int argc,char **argv) {
        pthread_t tid;                          // Thread ID
        void *retval = 0;                       // Returned value pointer
        int rc;

        rc = pthread_create(&tid,0,my_thread,0);
        assert(!rc);
        rc = pthread_join(tid,&retval);          // Wait for my_thread()
        assert(!rc);
        return 0;
}
```

pthread_detach(3)

The function pthread_join(3) causes the caller to wait until the indicated thread returns. Sometimes, however, a thread is created and never checked again. When that thread exits, some of its resources are retained to allow for a join operation on it. If there is never going to be a join, it is better for that thread to be forgotten when it exits and have its resources immediately released.

The pthread_detach(3) function is used to indicate that no join will be performed on the named thread. This way, the named thread becomes configured to release itself automatically, when it exits.

```
int pthread_detach(pthread_t thread);
```

The argument and return values are as follows:

> thread: The thread ID of the thread to be altered, so that it will not wait for a join when it completes. Its resources will be immediately released upon the named thread's termination.

> returns: Zero if the call was successful; otherwise, an error code is returned (not in errno).

Error	Description
EINVAL	Thread is not a joinable thread.
ESRCH	No thread with the ID thread could be found.

The pthread_detach function simply requires the thread ID value as its argument:

```
pthread_t tid;              // Thread ID
int rc;

rc = pthread_create(&tid,0,my_thread,0);
assert(!rc);
pthread_detach(tid);        // No joining with this thread
```

pthread_self(3)

Sometimes it is convenient in a piece of code to find out what the *current* thread ID is. The pthread_self(3) function is the right tool for the job:

```
pthread_t pthread_self(void);
```

An example of its use is shown here:

```
pthread_t tid;

tid = pthread_self();
```

pthread_kill(3)

The pthread_kill(3) function allows the caller to send a signal to another thread. The handling of thread signals is beyond the scope of this text. But there is one very useful application of this function, which you'll examine shortly:

```
#include <signal.h>

int pthread_kill(pthread_t thread, int sig);
```

Notice that the header file for signal.h is needed for the function prototype and the signal definitions.

thread: This is the thread ID that you want to signal (or test).

sig: This is the signal that you wish to send. Alternatively, supply zero to test whether the thread exists.

returns: Returns zero if the call is successful, or an error code (not in errno).

Error	Description
EINVAL	An invalid signal was specified.
ESRCH	No thread with the ID thread could be found.

One useful application of the pthread_kill(3) function is to test whether another thread exists. If the sig argument is supplied with zero, no actual signal is delivered, but the error checking is still performed. If the function returns zero, you know that the thread still *exists*.

But what does it mean when the thread exists? Does it mean that it is still *executing*? Or does it mean that it has not been reclaimed as part of a pthread_join(3), or as a consequence of pthread_detach(3) cleanup?

It turns out that when the thread *exists*, it means that it is still executing. In other words, it *has not returned* from the thread function that was started. If the thread has returned, it is considered to be incapable of receiving a signal.

Based on this, you know that you will get a zero returned when the thread is still executing. When error code ESRCH is returned instead, you know that the thread has completed.

Mutexes

While not strictly a CPU topic, mutexes cannot be separated from a discussion on threads. A *mutex* is a locking device that allows the software designer to stop one or more threads while another is working with a shared resource. In other words, one thread receives exclusive access. This is necessary to facilitate inter-thread communication. I'm simply going to describe the mutex API here, rather than the theory behind the application of mutexes.

pthread_mutex_create(3)

A mutex is initialized with the system call to pthread_mutex_init(3):

```
int pthread_mutex_init(
    pthread_mutex_t         *mutex,
    const pthread_mutexattr_t *attr
);
```

> mutex: A pointer to a pthread_mutex_t object, to be initialized.

> attr: A pointer to a pthread_mutexattr_t object, describing mutex options. Supply zero (or NULL), if you can accept the defaults.

> returns: Returns zero if the call is successful; otherwise, returns an error code (not in errno).

Error	Description
EAGAIN	The system lacks the necessary resources (other than memory) to initialize another mutex.
ENOMEM	Insufficient memory exists to initialize the mutex.
EPERM	The caller does not have the privilege to perform the operation.
EBUSY	The implementation has detected an attempt to reinitialize the object referenced by mutex, a previously initialized, but not yet destroyed, mutex.
EINVAL	The value specified by attr is invalid.

An example of mutex initialization is provided here:

```
pthread_mutex_t mutex;
int rc;

rc = pthread_mutex_init(&mutex,0);
assert (!rc);
```

pthread_mutex_destroy(3)

When the application no longer needs a mutex, it should use pthread_mutex_destroy(3) to release its resources:

```
pthread_mutex_t mutex ;
int rc;


...
rc = pthread_mutex_destroy(&mutex);
assert(!rc);
```

> mutex: The address of the mutex to release resources for
>
> returns: Returns zero when successful, or an error code when it fails (not in errno)

Error	Description
EBUSY	Mutex is locked or in use in conjunction with a pthread_cond_wait(3) or pthread_cond_timedwait(3).
EINVAL	The value specified by mutex is invalid.

pthread_mutex_lock(3)

When a thread needs exclusive access to a resource, it must lock the resource's mutex. As long as the cooperating threads follow the same procedure of locking first, they cannot both access the shared object at the same time.

```
int pthread_mutex_lock(pthread_mutex_t *mutex);
```

> mutex: A pointer to the mutex to lock.
>
> returns: Returns zero if the mutex was successfully locked; otherwise, an error code is returned (not in errno).

Error	Description
EINVAL	The mutex was created with the protocol attribute having the value PTHREAD_PRIO_PROTECT, and the calling thread's priority is higher than the mutex's current priority ceiling. Or the value specified by the mutex does not refer to an initialized mutex object.
EAGAIN	Maximum number of recursive locks for mutex has been exceeded.
EDEADLK	The current thread already owns the mutex.

The following shows the function being called:

```
pthread_mutex_t mutex;
int rc;


...
rc = pthread_mutex_lock(&mutex);
```

pthread_mutex_unlock(3)

When exclusive access to a resource is no longer required, the mutex is unlocked:

```
int pthread_mutex_unlock(pthread_mutex_t *mutex);
```

> mutex: A pointer to the mutex to be unlocked.
>
> returns: Returns zero if the mutex was unlocked successfully; otherwise, an error code is returned (not in errno).

Error	Description
EINVAL	The value specified by mutex does not refer to an initialized mutex object.
EPERM	The current thread does not own the mutex.

A simple example of unlocking a mutex is provided here:

```
pthread_mutex_t mutex;
int rc;

...
rc = pthread_mutex_unlock(&mutex);
```

Condition Variables

Sometimes mutexes alone are not enough for efficient scheduling of CPU between different threads. Mutexes and condition variables are often used together to facilitate inter-thread communication. Some beginners might struggle with this concept, if they are seeing it for the first time.

Why do we need condition variables when we have mutexes?

Consider what is necessary in building a software queue that can hold a maximum of eight items. Before we can queue something, we need to first see if the queue is full. But we cannot test that until we have the queue locked—otherwise, another thread could be changing things under our own noses.

So we lock the queue but find that it is full. What do we do now? Do we simply unlock and try again? This works but it wastes CPU resources. Wouldn't it be better if we had some way of being alerted when the queue was no longer full?

The condition variable works in concert with a mutex and a "signal" (of sorts). In pseudo code terms, a program trying to queue an item on a queue would perform the following steps:

1. Lock the mutex. We cannot examine anything in the queue until we lock it.

2. Check the queue's capacity. Can we place a new item in it? If so:

   a. Place the new item in the queue.

   b. Unlock and exit.

3. If the queue is full, the following steps are performed:

   a. Using a condition variable, "wait" on it, with the associated mutex.

   b. When control returns from the wait, return to step 2.

How does the condition variable help us? Consider the following steps:

1. The mutex is locked (1).

2. The wait is performed (3a). This causes the kernel to do the following:

    a. Put the calling thread to sleep (put on a wait queue)

    b. Unlock the mutex that was locked in step 1

Unlocking of the mutex in step 2b is necessary so that another thread can do something with the queue (hopefully, take an entry from the queue so that it is no longer full). If the mutex remained locked, no thread would be able to move.

At some future point in time, another thread will do the following:

1. Lock the mutex

2. Find entries in the queue (it was currently full), and pull one item out of it

3. Unlock the mutex

4. Signal the condition variable that the "waiter" is using, so that it can wake up

The waiting thread then awakens:

1. The kernel makes the "waiting" thread ready.

2. The mutex is successfully relocked.

Once that thread awakens with the mutex locked, it can recheck the queue to see whether there is room to queue an item. Notice that *the thread is awakened only when it has already reacquired the mutex lock*. This is why condition variables are paired with a mutex in their use.

pthread_cond_init(3)

Like any other object, a condition variable needs to be initialized:

```
int pthread_cond_init(
  pthread_cond_t          *cond,
  const pthread_condattr_t  *attr
);
```

cond: A pointer to the pthread_cond_t structure to be initialized.

attr: A pointer to a cond variable attribute if one is provided, or supply zero (or NULL).

returns: Zero is returned if the call is successful; otherwise, an error code is returned (not in errno).

Error	Description
EAGAIN	The system lacked the necessary resources.
ENOMEM	Insufficient memory exists to initialize the condition variable.
EBUSY	The implementation has detected an attempt to reinitialize the object referenced by cond, a previously initialized, but not yet destroyed, condition variable.
EINVAL	The value specified by attr is invalid.

pthread_cond_destroy(3)

When a condition (cond) variable is no longer required, its resources should be released with the following call:

```
int pthread_cond_destroy(pthread_cond_t *cond);
```

cond: Condition variable to be released.

returns: Zero if the call was successful; otherwise, returns an error code (not in errno).

Error	Description
EBUSY	Detected an attempt to destroy the object referenced by cond while it is referenced by pthread_cond_wait() or pthread_cond_timedwait() in another thread.
EINVAL	The value specified by cond is invalid.

pthread_cond_wait(3)

This function is one-half of the queue solution. The pthread_cond_wait(3) function is called with the mutex already locked. The kernel will then put the calling thread to sleep (on the wait queue) to release the CPU, while at the same time unlocking the mutex. The calling thread remains blocked until the condition variable cond is signaled in some way (more about that later).

When the thread is awakened by the kernel, the system call returns with the mutex locked. At this point, the thread can check the application condition (like queue length) and then proceed if things are favorable, or call pthread_cond_wait(3) again to wait further.

```
int pthread_cond_wait(pthread_cond_t *cond, pthread_mutex_t *mutex);
```

cond: Pointer to the condition variable to be used for the wake-up call.

mutex: Pointer to the mutex to be associated with the condition variable.

returns: Returns zero upon success; otherwise, an error code is returned (not in errno).

Error	Description
EINVAL	The value specified by cond, mutex is invalid. Or different mutexes were supplied for concurrent pthread_cond_timedwait() or pthread_cond_wait() operations on the same condition variable.
EPERM	The mutex was not owned by the current thread at the time of the call.

The following code snippet shows how a queuing function would use this. (Initialization of mutex and cond is assumed.)

```
pthread_mutex_t mutex;
pthread_cond_t cond;

...
pthread_mutex_lock(&mutex);
```

```
while ( queue.length >=max_length )
    pthread_cond_wait(&cond,&mutex);

// queue the item
...
pthread_mutex_unlock(&mutex);
```

The while loop retries the test to see whether the queue is "not full." The while loop is necessary when multiple threads are inserting into the queue. Depending on timing, another thread could beat the current thread to queuing an item, making the queue full again.

pthread_cond_signal(3)

When an item is taken off the queue, a mechanism needs to wake up the thread attempting to put one entry into the full queue. One wake-up option is the pthread_cond_signal(3) system call:

```
int pthread_cond_signal(pthread_cond_t *cond);
```

> cond: A pointer to the condition variable used to signal one thread.

> returns: Returns zero if the function call was successful; otherwise, an error number is returned (not in errno).

Error	Description
EINVAL	The value cond does not refer to an initialized condition variable.

It is *not* an error if no other thread is waiting. This function does, however, wake up one waiting thread, if one or more are waiting on the specified condition variable.

This call is preferred for *performance* reasons if signaling one thread will "work." When there are special conditions whereby some threads may succeed and others would not, you need a *broadcast* call instead. When it can be used, waking *one* thread saves CPU cycles.

pthread_cond_broadcast(3)

This is the broadcast variant of pthread_cond_signal(3). If multiple waiters have different tests, a broadcast should be used to allow *all* waiters to wake up and consider the conditions found.

```
int pthread_cond_broadcast(pthread_cond_t *cond);
```

> cond: A pointer to the condition variable to be *signaled*, waking *all* waiting threads.

> returns: Zero is returned when the call is successful; otherwise, an error number is returned (not in errno).

Error	Description
EINVAL	The value cond does not refer to an initialized condition variable.

It is *not* an error to broadcast when there are no waiters.

CHAPTER 8

■ ■ ■

USB

The USB port has become ubiquitous in the digital world, allowing the use of a large choice of peripherals. The Model B Raspberry Pi supports two USB 2 ports, and the Model A just one.

This chapter briefly examines some power considerations associated with USB support and powered hubs. The remainder of this chapter examines the device driver interface available to the Raspbian Linux developer. Figure 8-1 serves as a chapter reference schematic of the Raspberry USB interface.

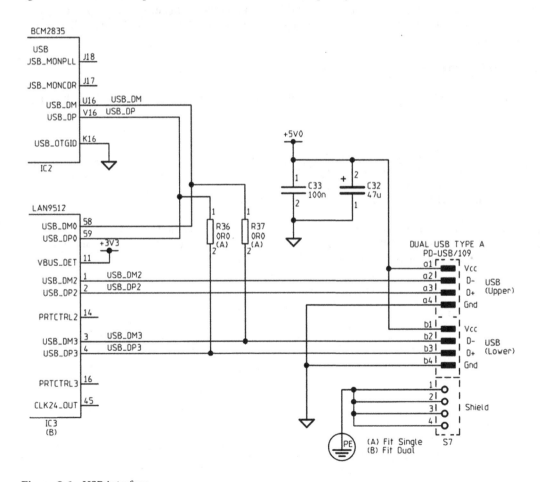

Figure 8-1. *USB interface*

Power

Early models of the Raspberry Pi limited each USB port to 100 mA because of the polyfuses included. Revision 2.0 models did away with these, leaving you with more options.

Even with the polyfuses removed, the end user should remember that the USB ports are powered by the input to the Raspberry Pi PCB. This is supplied through fuse F3 (see Figure 4-3, shown previously in Chapter 4). This limits the maximum USB current to 500 mA for the Model A (which is the limit for one USB port anyway) and 300 mA for the Model B. Exceeding these limits could cause fuse F3 to blow.

■ **Note** Wireless USB adapters consume between 350 mA and 500 mA.

Powered Hubs

Whether you have a Model A or Model B Raspberry Pi, you'll want to use a powered USB hub for high-current peripherals. This is particularly true for wireless network adapters, since they often require up to 500 mA.

A USB hub requires coordination with the Linux kernel and thus requires Raspbian Linux driver support. A number of hubs have been reported not to work. The following web page is a good resource listing hubs that are known work with Raspbian Linux:

```
http://elinux.org/RPi_Powered_USB_Hubs
```

With the powered USB hub plugged in, you can list the USB devices that have registered with the kernel by using the lsusb command:

```
# lsusb
Bus 001 Device 001: ID 1d6b:0002 Linux Foundation 2.0 root hub
Bus 001 Device 002: ID 0424:9512 Standard Microsystems Corp.
Bus 001 Device 003: ID 0424:ec00 Standard Microsystems Corp.
Bus 001 Device 004: ID 0451:2077 Texas Instruments, Inc. TUSB2077 Hub
```

The first three listed are the usual suspects from the Pi's own hardware. The last line shows that a TUSB2077 Hub has been registered. Figure 8-2 shows my Belkin USB hub on a busy workbench. If your hub fails to appear in this report, it likely means that there is no driver support for it.

Figure 8-2. *A powered USB hub*

USB API Support

USB devices are normally supported by device drivers and appear as generic peripherals like keyboards, mice, or storage. The USB Boarduino is a little different, using the FTDI chipset, and supported by a driver.

Once the Boarduino is plugged in, the lsusb command lists it, thanks to the FTDI chipset driver:

```
$ lsusb
...
Bus 001 Device 008: ID 0403:6001 Future Technology Devices \
        International, Ltd FT232 USB-Serial (UART) IC
```

The supporting driver makes the Boarduino available as a serial device:

```
$ ls -l /dev/ttyUSB0
Crw-rw—T 1 root dialout 188, 0 Dec 31 1969 /dev/ttyUSB0
```

The serial device support allows the AVR device to be programmed by avrdude. A Raspberry Pi application can also communicate with the AVR device's application. If you want to use network-like packets, the SLIP serial protocol, for example, can be used to communicate over that link. The "Serial API" section of Chapter 11 covers the Linux API for serial communications.

libusb

Although USB devices are supported by drivers and appear as generic devices, in some situations a user space program needs to communicate with specialized hardware. While Raspbian Linux has libusb installed, the developer will want to install the developer package for it:

```
# apt-get install libusb-dev
```

The USB API is fairly large, complex and beyond the scope of this text. But the curious developer can read more about the `libusb` API at the website:

`http://libusb.sourceforge.net/doc/index.html`

In this chapter, you'll examine just the beginnings of a `libusb` program, so that you can get a flavor of how the API works.

Include Files

The main `include` file for Raspbian `libusb` support is as follows:

`#include <usb.h>`

The next few pages show a simple USB program, which enumerates USB buses and devices. Once a device is located, an attempt is made to "claim" it and then release it (it will print CLAIMED if successful). However, when all of your USB devices are fully supported by drivers, none will be claimed. This list can be checked against the `lsusb` command output.

The next example program was run on a Raspberry Pi with the following USB devices reported by `lsusb`:

```
$ lsusb
Bus 001 Device 002: ID 0424:9512 Standard Microsystems Corp.
Bus 001 Device 001: ID 1d6b:0002 Linux Foundation 2.0 root hub
Bus 001 Device 003: ID 0424:ec00 Standard Microsystems Corp.
Bus 001 Device 004: ID 05ac:1002 Apple, Inc. Extended Keyboard Hub [Mitsumi]
Bus 001 Device 005: ID 0451:2077 Texas Instruments, Inc. TUSB2077 Hub
Bus 001 Device 006: ID 05ac:0204 Apple, Inc.
Bus 001 Device 007: ID 045e:0040 Microsoft Corp. Wheel Mouse Optical
```

The example program was compiled by the provided make file in the `libusb` subdirectory and invoked as follows:

```
$ ./tusb
Device: 007 045e:0040    class 0.0 protocol 0 device 768, manuf 1, serial 0
  0.0.0 class 3
Device: 006 05ac:0204    class 0.0 protocol 0 device 290, manuf 1, serial 0
  0.0.0 class 3
  0.1.0 class 3
Device: 005 0451:2077    class 9.0 protocol 0 device 256, manuf 0, serial 0
  0.0.0 class 9
Device: 004 05ac:1002    class 9.0 protocol 0 device 290, manuf 1, serial 0
  0.0.0 class 9
Device: 003 0424:ec00    class 255.0 protocol 1 device 512, manuf 0, serial 0
  0.0.0 class 255
Device: 002 0424:9512    class 9.0 protocol 2 device 512, manuf 0, serial 0
  0.0.0 class 9
  0.0.1 class 9
Device: 001 1d6b:0002    class 9.0 protocol 1 device 774, manuf 3, serial 1
  0.0.0 class 9
```

These are easily compared by noting the device name, such as 007, which is reported by lsusb to be the Microsoft mouse.

```
1    /***************************************************************
2     * tusb.c - Scan list of USB devices and test claim/release.
3     ***************************************************************/
4
5    #include <stdio.h>
6    #include <stdlib.h>
7    #include <errno.h>
8    #include <usb.h>
9    #include <assert.h>
10
11   /***************************************************************
12    * See http://libusb.sourceforge.net/doc/index.html for API
13    ***************************************************************/
14
15   int
16   main(int argc, char **argv) {
17       struct usb_bus *busses, *bus;
18       struct usb_device *dev;
19       struct usb_device_descriptor *desc;
20       usb_dev_handle *hdev;
21       int cx, ix, ax, rc;
22
23       usb_init();
24       usb_find_busses();
25       usb_find_devices();
26
27       busses = usb_get_busses();
28
29       for ( bus=busses; bus; bus = bus->next ) {
30           for ( dev=bus->devices; dev; dev = dev->next ) {
31               desc = &dev->descriptor;
32
33               printf("Device: %s %04x:%04x ",
34                   dev->filename,
35                   desc->idVendor,
36                   desc->idProduct);
37               printf("  class %u.%d protocol %u",
38                   desc->bDeviceClass,
39                   desc->bDeviceSubClass,
40                   desc->bDeviceProtocol);
41               printf(" device %u, manuf %u, serial %u\n",
42                   desc->bcdDevice,
43                   desc->iManufacturer,
44                   desc->iSerial Number);
45
46               hdev = usb_open(dev);
47               assert(hdev);
48
```

```
49              rc = usb_claim_interface(hdev,0);
50              if ( !rc ) {
51                  puts("  CLAIMED..");
52                  rc = usb_release_interface(hdev, 0);
53                  puts("  RELEASED..");
54                  assert(!rc);
55              }
56          usb_close(hdev);
57
58          /*Configurations */
59          for ( cx=0; cx <dev->descriptor.bNumConfigurations;  ++cx ) {
60              /*Interfaces */
61              for ( ix=0; ix < dev->config[cx].bNumInterfaces;  ++ix ) {
62                  /*Alternates */
63                  for ( ax=0; ax < dev->config[cx].interface[ix].num_altsetting; ++ax ) {
64                      printf("  %d.%d.%d class %u\n",
65                          cx,ix,ax,
66                          dev->config[cx].interface[ix].altsetting[ax].bInterfaceClass);
67                  }
68              }
69          }
70      }
71  }
72
73      return 0;
74  }
75
76  /*End tusb.c */
```

CHAPTER 9

Ethernet

Networking has become an important part of everyday life, whether wireless or by wire. Having a network adapter on your Raspberry Pi allows you to connect to it and do things on it from the comfort of your desktop or laptop computer. It also allows your application on the Pi to reach out to the outside world. Even when the Raspberry Pi is deployed as part of an embedded project, the network interface continues to be important. Remote logging and control are just two examples.

Wired Ethernet

The standard Raspbian SD card image provides a wired network connection, using DHCP to automatically assign an IP address to it. If you are using the HDMI output and keyboard devices to do work on the Pi, the dynamically assigned IP address is not a bother. But if you would like to eliminate the attached display and keyboard, connecting over the network is attractive. The only problem is the potentially changing IP address. (DHCP will not always use a different IP address, since the address is leased for a time.) It is difficult to contact your Raspberry Pi from a laptop until you know its IP address. As you saw in Chapter 3, you can use the nmap command to scan for it, but this is inconvenient:

```
$ sudo nmap -sP 192.168.0.1-254

Starting Nmap 6.25 (http://nmap.org) at 2013-04-14 19:12 EDT
. . .
Nmap scan report for mac (192.168.0.129)
Host is up.
Nmap scan report for rasp (192.168.0.132)
Host is up (0.00071s latency).
MAC Address: B8:27:EB:2B:69:E8 ( Raspberry Pi Foundation )
Nmap done : 254 IP addresses (6 hosts up) scanned in 6.01 seconds
$
```

If you use your Pi at school or away from your own premises, using DHCP may still be the best option for you. If you are plugging it into different networks as you travel, DHCP sets up your IP address properly and *takes care of the name server configuration*. However, if you are using your unit at home, or your school can assign you a valid IP address to use, a static IP address simplifies access.

■ **Note**   Be sure to get approval and an IP address assigned to prevent network conflicts.

/etc/network/interfaces

As supplied by the standard Raspbian image, the /etc/network/interfaces file looks like this:

```
$ cat /etc/network/interfaces
auto lo

iface lo inet loopback
iface eth0 inet dhcp

allow-hotplug wlan0
iface wlan0 inet manual
wpa-roam/etc/wpa_supplicant/wpa_supplicant.conf
iface default inet dhcp
$
```

The wired Ethernet interface (Model B) is named eth0. The line starting with iface eth0 indicates that your network interface eth0 is using DHCP. If this is what you want, leave it as is.

Changing to Static IP

If you haven't booted up your Raspberry Pi with the network cable plugged in, now is a good time to do that. This may save you time later, when we review the name server settings.

Next, before you start changing it, save a backup of the /etc/network/interfaces file in case you want to change it back:

```
$ sudo -i
# cd /etc/network
# cp interfaces interfaces.bak
```

Next, edit the line in /etc/network/interfaces that begins with iface eth0 so that it reads like the following:

```
iface eth0 inet static
    address    192.168.0.177
    gateway    192.168.0.1
    netmask    255.255.255.0
    network    192.168.0.0
    broadcast  192.168.0.255
```

In this example, we have established a fixed IP address of 192.168.0.177, along with the appropriate settings for gateway, netmask, network, and broadcast address. If the network is not your own, get a network administrator to help you with the correct values to use.

There is one other file that needs to be checked and potentially edited:

```
$ cat /etc/resolv.conf
domain myfastisp.net
search myfastisp.net
nameserver 192.168.0.1
```

If you've booted up your Raspberry Pi previously while it was using DHCP (with network cable plugged in), these values may already be suitably configured. Otherwise, you'll need to edit them to get the name service to work. In this example, the Internet Service Provider is myfastisp.net, and name service requests are forwarded through the firewall router at 192.168.0.1.

Test Static IP Address

Once you have configured things, the simplest thing to do is to reboot your Raspberry Pi to make the new settings take effect (use sudo /sbin/reboot or sudo /sbin/shutdown -r now).

Once you've rebooted and logged in, check your IP address:

```
$ ifconfig eth0
eth0 Link encap : Ethernet HWaddr b8:27:eb:2b:69:e9
     inet addr:192.168.0.177   Bcast: 192.168.0.255   Mask: 255.255.255.0
     UP BROADCAST RUNNING MULTICAST MTU: 1500 Metric: 1
     RX packets: 1046 errors: 0 dropped : 3 overruns: 0 frame: 0
     TX packets: 757 errors: 0 dropped: 0 over runs : 0 carrier: 0
     collisions:0 txqueuelen :1000
     RX bytes: 74312 (72.5 KiB) TX bytes: 86127 (84.1 KiB)
```

In the preceding example, the inet addr matches our configured static IP address. Let's now check that the names are resolving. Normally, I would recommend nslookup or dig for this, but neither comes preinstalled on Raspbian. So let's just use ping:

```
$ ping -c1 google.com
PING google.com (74.125.226.4) 56 (84) bytes of data.
64 bytes from yyz06s05-in-f4.1e100.net (74.125.226.4): . . .

--- google.com ping statistics ---
1 packets transmitted, 1 received, 0% packet loss, time 0ms
rtt min/avg/max/mdev = 11.933/11.933/11.933/0.000 ms
$
```

In this example, we see that google.com was looked up and translated to the IP address 74.125.226.4. From this, we conclude that the name service is working. The -c1 option on the ping command line causes only one ping to be performed. Otherwise, ping will keep trying, and you may need to ^C to interrupt its execution.

If the name google.com does not resolve, you'll need to troubleshoot /etc/resolv.conf. As a last resort, you might switch back to using DHCP (interfaces.bak) and reboot. If the /etc/resolv.conf file is updated with new parameters, you might try again.

USB Adapters

If you have a USB Ethernet adapter (non-wireless), you can set up networking for that also. The following line added to /etc/network/interfaces will cause it to use DHCP:

```
iface usb0 inet dhcp
```

For a fixed usb0 IP address, configure as we did earlier (for eth0). For example:

```
iface usb0 inet static
  address   192.168.0.178
  gateway   192.168.0.1
  netmask   255.255.255.0
  network   192.168.0.0
  broadcast 192.168.0.255
```

This provides interface usb0 with a fixed address of 192.168.0.178.

/etc/hosts File

If you have a static IP address for your Raspberry Pi, why not update your Linux, OS X, or Windows hosts file (typically, C:\Windows\system32\drivers\etc\hosts) with a hostname for it? For example, your hosts file could have the following line added:

```
$ cat /etc/hosts
. . .
192.168.0.177 rasp raspi rpi pi # My Raspberry Pi
```

Now you can use a hostname of rasp, raspi, rpi, or pi to access your Raspberry Pi on the network.

Wireless Ethernet

If you haven't already done so, review the "Powered USB Hubs" section of Chapter 8. Wi-Fi adapters can require 350 mA to 500 mA of current draw.

The following web page lists good information about the various brands of Wi-Fi adapters available and their level of support:

```
http://elinux.org/RPi_USB_Wi-Fi_Adapters
```

I have a NetGear WN111(v2) RangeMax Next Wireless adapter available. Apparently, this adapter uses one of the following chips:

- Atheros AR9170

- Atheros AR9101

Since the AR9170 shows up in the supported list for the D-Link DWA-160, there is a reasonable chance of driver support for it. After plugging it into the powered USB hub and rebooting, the console log shows that it is being "*seen*":

```
$ dmesg
. . .
[3.867883] usb 1_1.3.2: New USB device found, idVendor=0846, idProduct=9001
[3.893138] usb 1_1.3.2: New USB device strings: Mfr=16, Product=32, SerialNumber=
[3.923115] usb 1_1.3.2: Product: USB2.0 WLAN
[3.930064] usb 1_1.3.2: Manufacturer : ATHER
[3.963095] usb 1_1.3.2: SerialNumber : 12345
[4.393875] cfg80211: Calling CRDA to update world regulatory domain
[4.663403] usb 1_1.3.2: reset full_speed USB device number 5 using dwc_otg
[4.953470] usbcore: registered new interface driver carl9170
[6.687035] usb 1_1.3.2: firmware not found.
[7.703098] usb 1_1.3.2: kill pending tx urbs.
```

But there is a troubling error message: "firmware not found." Also visible in the log, we see that the driver is named carl9170. Further research reveals that it also requires a firmware file named carl9170-1.fw. While this file is available from other sources, the simplest way to install this file is to install it from Raspbian sources:

```
$ sudo apt-get install firmware-linux
```

The firmware file being sought and installed is as follows:

```
$ ls -l /lib/firmware/carl9170-1.fw
-rw-r--r--1 root root 13388 Jan 14 17:04 /lib/firmware/carl9170-1.fw
```

Rebooting again, the missing firmware message is gone. The lsusb report also confirms the device is ready:

```
# lsusb
Bus 001 Device 001: ID 1d6b :0002 Linux Foundation 2.0 root hub
Bus 001 Device 002: ID 0424:9512 Standard Microsystems Corp.
Bus 001 Device 003: ID 0424: ec00 Standard Microsystems Corp.
Bus 001 Device 004: ID 0451:2077 Texas Instruments, Inc. TUSB2077 Hub
Bus 001 Device 005: ID 0846:9001 NetGear, Inc. WN111(v2) RangeMax Next Wireless \
            [Atheros AR9170+AR9101]
#
```

The hardware driver support is now in place. The device now needs network configuration.

Configuration

You could edit the configuration files by hand if you knew all the possible keywords necessary for your particular wireless authentication protocol. The following Linux raspberrypi 3.2.27+ files are involved:

Pathname	Description
/etc/network/interfaces	Main configuration file for networks
/etc/wpa_supplicant/wpa_supplicant.conf	Authentication information

You'll find a variety of advice on how to configure these on the Internet. But the quickest path to success is to just use the wpa_gui dialog box from the Raspberry Pi desktop. Once you've done it this way, directly editing the configuration files can be performed later if you need to tweak it further.

Figure 9-1 shows how to locate the wpa_gui dialog box from your Pi desktop. Once wpa_gui is started, click the Manage Networks tab, shown in Figure 9-2. If you've made prior attempts at configuring wlan0, delete them all from this menu. Then click the Scan button at the bottom right.

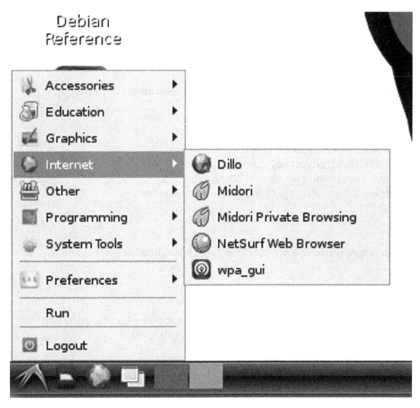

Figure 9-1. *wpa_gui dialog box*

Figure 9-2. *The Manage Networks tab*

After clicking Scan, your wireless network should eventually appear in the scan list, as shown in Figure 9-3.

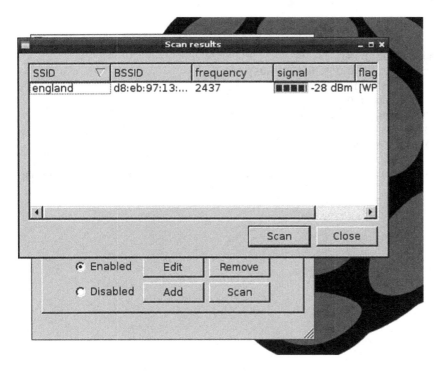

Figure 9-3. *Results of a wireless network scan*

Double-click the line representing your network. This brings up a new dialog box that allows you to fill in the remaining authentication parameters:

Parameter	Example
Authentication	WPA-Personal (PSK)
Encryption	CCMP
PSK	Pass phrase

Enter settings that apply to your network. After completing the data input, click the Add button. As you exit the dialog box, *be sure to select Save Configuration from the File menu.*

■ **Caution**   Don't forget to pull down Save Configuration from the File menu before you exit the setup application. This is easily forgotten, and no reminder of unsaved changes is provided.

After saving the new Wi-Fi configuration, reboot. After the Pi comes back up, log in and check the network interfaces. Look for interface wlan0:

```
$ ifconfig
. . .
wlan0 Link encap: Ethernet HWaddr 00:22:3f:8d: 78: f9
      inet addr:192.168.0.61 Bcast:192.168.0.255 Mask:255.255.255.0
      UP BROADCAST RUNNING MULTICAST MTU: 1500 Metric: 1
      RX packets: 10514 errors: 0 dropped: 0 overruns: 0 frame : 0
      TX packets: 121 errors: 0 dropped : 0 over runs: 0 carrier: 0
      collisions:0 txqueuelen:1000
      RX bytes: 767287 (749.3 KiB) TX bytes: 9188 (8.9 KiB)
```

The preceding example shows that the wlan0 is available and has a DHCP-assigned IP address. You can now ping or ssh to this access point.

■ ■ ■

## CHAPTER 10

SD Card Storage

The file system is central to the Unix system design, from which Linux borrows. The necessary mass storage requirements have traditionally been fulfilled through hard disk subsystems. However, as Linux hosts become as small as cell phones, flash memory technology has replaced the bulky mechanical drive.

SD Card Media

The standard SD card is 32 mm long, 24 mm wide, and 2.1 mm thick. Figure 10-1 illustrates the connections available on the underside of the SD card. The schematic excerpt shown later will document how the connections are made to this media.

Figure 10-1. *SD card pinout*

SD Card Interface

In the Raspberry Pi, the SD card is interfaced to the SoC through GPIO pins 46 through 53, seen in Figure 10-2. The SoC senses the insertion of an SD card through the closing of a socket switch (pins 10 and 11 of the socket). Thus GPIO 47 is brought to ground potential when the socket is occupied.

Looking at the wiring in Figure 10-2, it might be assumed that all data transfers are 4 bits wide (GPIO 50 through GPIO 53). However, as the following sections will describe, this depends on the SD card media used.

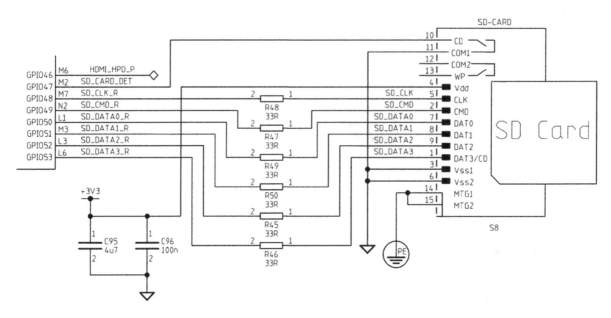

Figure 10-2. *SD card circuit*

SD Card Basics

The SD card includes an internal controller, also known as a Flash Storage Processor (FSP). In this configuration, the Linux host merely provides a command and waits for the response. The FSP takes care of all erase, programming, and read operations necessary to complete the command. In this way, Flash card designs are permitted to increase in complexity as new performance and storage densities are implemented.

The SD card manages data with a sector size of 512 bytes. This was intentionally made the same as the IDE magnetic disk drive for compatibility with existing operating systems. Commands issued by the host include a sector address to allow read/writes of one or more sectors.

▪ **Note** Operating systems may use a multiple of the 512-byte sector.

Commands and data are protected by CRC codes in the FSP. The FSP also automatically performs a read after write to verify that the data is written correctly.[21] If the data write is found defective, the FSP automatically corrects it, replacing the physical sector with another if necessary.

The SD card soft error rate is much lower than a magnetic disk drive. In the rare case when errors are discovered, the last line of defense is a correcting ECC, which allows for data recovery. These errors are corrected in the media to prevent future unrecoverable errors. All of this activity is transparent to the host.

Raspbian Block Size

The block size used by the operating system may be a multiple of the media's sector size. To determine the physical block size used under Raspbian, we first discover how the root file system is mounted (the following listing has been trimmed with ellipses):

```
$ mount
/dev/root on/type ext4 (rw, noatime, . . . )
. . .
/dev/mmcblk0p1 on/boot type vfat (rw, relatime , . . . )
$
```

From this we deduce that the device used for the root file system is /dev/root. The pathname given is a symbolic link, so we need to determine the real device pathname:

```
$ ls -dl /dev/root
lrwxrwxrwx 1 root root 9 Jan 12 19:33/dev/root -> mmcblk0p2
$
```

From this, we deduce that the actual device pathname is /dev/mmcblk0p2. The naming convention used tells us the following:

Component	Name	Number	Type
Prefix	/dev/mmcblk		MMC block
Device number	0	0	
Partition number	p2	2	

From the earlier mount command output, notice that the /boot file system was mounted on /dev/mmcblk0p1. (No symbolic link was used in this case.) From this we understand that the /boot file system is from partition 1 of the same SD card device.

Using the root device information, we consult the /sys pseudo file system to find out the physical sector size. Here we supply mmcblk0 as the third-level pathname qualifier to query the device:

```
$ cat /sys/block/mmcblk0/queue/physical_block_size
  512
$ cat /sys/block/mmcblk0/queue/logical_block_size
  512
$
```

The result shown informs us that the Raspbian Linux used in this example uses a block (sector) size of 512 bytes, both physically and logically. This precisely matches the SD card's sector size. Since the /boot file system uses the same physical device as root, this also applies to that partition.

Disk Cache

While we're examining mounted SD card file systems, let's also check the type of device node used:

```
$ ls -l /dev/mmcblk0p?
brw-rw---T 1 root floppy 179, 1 Dec 31 1969  /dev/mmcblk0p1
brw-rw---T 1 root floppy 179, 2 Jan 12 19:33 /dev/mmcblk0p2
$
```

The example output shows a b at the beginning of the brw-rw—T field. This tells us that the disk device is a *block* device as opposed to a *character* device. (The associated character device would show a c instead.) Block devices are important for file systems because they provide a disk cache capability to vastly improve the file system performance. The output shows that both the root (partition 2) and the /boot (partition 1) file systems are mounted using block devices.

Capacities and Performance

SD cards allow a configurable data bus width within limits of the media. All SD cards start with one data bit line until the capabilities of the memory card are known:

> *The SD bus allows dynamic configuration of the number of data lines. After power-up, by default, the SD card will use only DAT0 for data transfer. After initialization, the host can change the bus width (number of active data lines). This feature allows [an] easy trade-off between hardware cost and system performance.*[18]

After the capabilities of the media are known, the data bus can be expanded under software control, as supported. Given that SD cards with memory capacities up to 2 GB operate with a 1-bit data bus, it is highly desirable to use a 4 GB or larger card on the Raspberry Pi, even if the extra storage is not required. More-advanced cards also offer greater transfer speeds by use of higher data clock rates.

Table 10-1 summarizes SD card capabilities.[19]

Table 10-1. *SD Card Capabilities*

Standard	Description	Greater Than	Up To	Data Bus
SDSC	Standard capacity	0	2 GB	1-bit
SDHC	High capacity	2 GB	32 GB	4-bit
SDXC	Extended capacity	32 GB	2 TB	4-bit

Transfer Modes

There are three basic data transfer modes used by SD cards:[18]

- SPI Bus mode
- 1-bit SD mode
- 4-bit SD mode

SPI Bus Mode

The SPI Bus mode is used mainly by consumer electronics using small microcontrollers supporting the SPI bus. Examining Table 10-2 reveals that data is transmitted 1 bit at a time in this mode (pin 2 or 7).

Table 10-2. *SPI Bus Mode*

Pin	Name	I/O	Logic	Description	SPI
1	nCS	I	PP	Card select (negative true)	CS
2	DI	I	PP	Data in	MOSI
3	VSS	S	S	Ground	
4	VDD	S	S	Power	
5	CLK	I	PP	Clock	SCLK
6	VSS	S	S	Ground	
7	DO	O	PP	Data out	MISO
8	NC			Memory cards	
	nIRQ	O	OD	Interrupt on SDIO cards	
9	NC			Not connected	

The various SD card connections are used in different ways, as documented by the Table 10-2 mnemonics in the columns I/O and Logic. Table 10-3 is a legend for these and also applies to later Tables 10-4 and 10-5.

Table 10-3. *Legend for I/O and Logic*

Notation	Meaning	Notes
I	Input	
O	Output	Relative to card
I/O	Input or output	
PP	Push/pull logic	
OD	Open drain	
S	Power supply	
NC	Not connected	Or logic high

1-bit SD Mode

Table 10-4 lists the pins and functions of the SD card when it is in 1-bit SD mode. The data traverses pin 7 (DAT0) while the clock is supplied on pin 5. Pin 2 is used to send commands and receive responses. This mode uses a proprietary transfer format.

Table 10-4. *1-bit SD Mode*

Pin	Name	I/O	Logic	Description
1	NC			No connection
2	CMD	I/O	PP/OD	Command/response
3	VSS	S	S	Ground
4	VDD	S	S	Power
5	CLK	I	PP	Clock
6	VSS	S	S	Ground
7	DAT0	I/O	PP	Data 0
8	NC	NC		Memory cards
	nIRQ	O	OD	SDIO cards
9	NC			No connection

4-bit SD Mode

This is the mode used when the data bus width is more than a single bit and supported by SDHC and SDXC cards. Higher data clock rates also improve transfer rates. Table 10-5 lists the pin assignments.

Table 10-5. *4-bit SD Mode*

Pin	Name	I/O	Logic	Description
1	DAT3	I/O	PP	Data 3
2	CMD	I/O	PP/OD	Command/response
3	VSS	S	S	Ground
4	VDD	S	S	Power
5	CLK	I	PP	Clock
6	VSS	S	S	Ground
7	DAT0	I/O	PP	Data 0
8	DAT1	I/O	PP	Data 1
	nIRQ	O	OD	SDIO cards share with interrupt
9	DAT2	I/O	PP	Data 2

Wear Leveling

Unfortunately, Flash memory is subject to *wear* for each *write* operation performed (as each write requires erasing and programming a block of data). The design of Flash memory requires that a large block of memory be erased and rewritten, even if a single sector has changed value. For this reason, wear leveling is used as a technique to extend the life of the media. Wear leveling extends life by moving data to different physical blocks while retaining the same logical address.

▪ **Note**   ScanDisk calls the block of Flash memory being erased and rewritten a *zone*.

Some cards use wear leveling.[18] Indeed the SanDisk company indicates that their products do use wear leveling.[20] However, the type of wear leveling supported by SanDisk is limited to zones within the media. Each SanDisk zone has 3% extra capacity, from which writes can be wear leveled within. If the zone size is 4 MB and is overprovisioned by 3%, this leaves about 245 spare sectors within each zone. Thus each 4 MB zone holds 8,192 active sectors at any given instant, rotated among 245 spares.

▪ **Note**   SanDisk indicates that the 4 MB zones may change with future memory capacities.

Other manufacturers may not implement wear leveling at all or use a lower level of overprovisioning. Wear leveling is not specified in the SD card standard, so no manufacturer is compelled to follow SanDisk's lead.

Note that wear leveling applies to read/write file systems. If the file system is mounted read-only, no erase and program operations are occurring inside the card. So no "erase wear" is taking place. But do take into account all of the mounted partitions on the same media.

If you are using your Raspberry Pi for educational purposes, you can probably ignore the issue. However, using known brands like SanDisk can provide you with additional quality assurance. Consider also the advantage of documented overprovisioning and wear leveling characteristics.

▪ **Caution**   Some brands of SD cards have been reported not to work with the Raspberry Pi, so the brand/product issue cannot be totally ignored.

CHAPTER 11

■ ■ ■

UART

The Raspberry Pi has a UART interface to allow it to perform serial data communications. The data lines used are 3.3 V logic-level signals and should *not* be connected to TTL logic (+5 V) (they also are *not RS-232 compatible*). To communicate with equipment using RS-232, you will need a converter module.

RS-232 Converter

While an industrious person could build their own RS-232 converter, there is little need to do so when cheap converters are available.

Figure 11-1 shows a MAX232CSE chip interface that I use. (This unit supports only the RX and TX lines.) When searching for a unit, be sure that you get one that works with 3 V logic levels. Some units work only with TTL (+5 V) logic, which would be harmful to the Pi. The MAX232CSE chip will support 3 V operation when its VCC supply pin is connected to +3 V.

Figure 11-1. *MAX232CSE interface*

■ **Note**   Throughout this text, we'll refer to *3 V*, knowing that it is precisely 3.3 V.

Figure 11-2 is a schematic excerpt of the UART section of the Raspberry Pi. The UART connections are shown as TXD0 and RXD0.

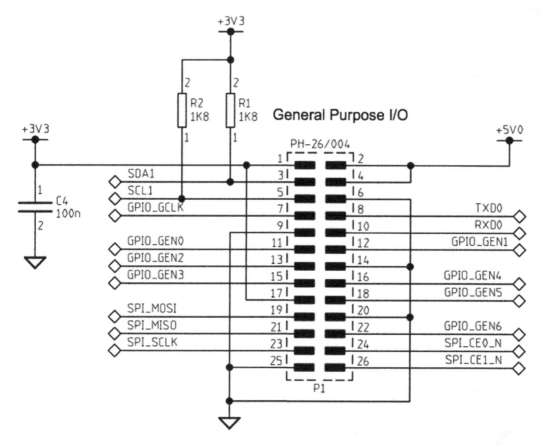

Figure 11-2. *UART interface*

Also when selecting a converter, consider whether you need only the data lines, or the data lines *and the hardware flow control signals*. Some units support only the RX and TX lines. For hardware flow control, you'll also want the CTS and DTR signals. A full RS-232 converter would also include DTR, DSR, and CD signals.

DTE or DCE

When choosing your RS-232 converter, keep in mind that there are two types of serial connections:

DCE: Data communications equipment (female connector)

DTE: Data terminal equipment (male connector)

A normal USB serial adapter (for a laptop, for example) will present a DTE (male) connector. The wiring of this cable is such that it expects to plug into to a DCE (female) connection. When this holds true for your Raspberry Pi's adapter, the laptop's serial adapter can plug straight into the DCE (female) connector, *eliminating* the need for a crossover cable or null modem.

Consequently, for your Pi, choose a RS-232 converter that provides a female (DCE) connector. Likewise, make sure that you acquire for the laptop/desktop a cable or USB device that presents a male (DTE) connection. Connecting DTE to DTE or DCE to DCE requires a crossover cable, and depending on the cable, a "gender mender" as well. It is best to get things "straight" right from the start.

Assuming that you used a DCE converter for the Pi, connect the RS-232 converter's 3 V logic TX to the Pi's TXD0 and the RX to the Pi's RXD0 data lines.

All this business about DCE and DTR has always been rather confusing. If you also find this confusing, there is another practical way to look at it. Start with the connectors and the cable(s) that you plan to use. Make sure they mate at both ends and that the serial cable is known to be a *straight cable* (instead of a *crossover*). Once those physical problems are taken care of, you can get the wiring correct. Connect the TX to RX, and RX to TX. In other words, *you* wire the crossover in your own wiring between the RS-232 adapter and the Raspberry Pi. The important thing to remember is that somewhere the transmitting side needs to send a signal into the RX (receiving) side, in both directions.

■ **Note**   A straight serial cable will connect pin 2 to pin 2, and pin 3 to pin 3 on a DB9 or DB25 cable. A crossover cable will cross these two, among other signal wire changes.

RS-232

RS-232 is the traditional name for a series of standards related to serial communication. It was first introduced by the Radio Sector of the EIA in 1962.[46] The first data terminals were teletypewriters (DTE) communicating with modems (DCE). Early serial communications were plagued by incompatibilities until later standards evolved.

A serial link includes two data lines, with data being transmitted from a terminal and received by the same terminal. In addition to these data lines are several handshaking signals (such as RTS and CTS). By default, these are not provided for by the Raspberry Pi.

Figure 11-3 shows a serial signal transmission, with time progressing from left to right. RS-232 equipment expects a signal that varies between –15 V and +15 V.

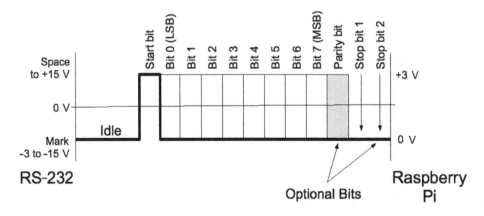

Figure 11-3. *Serial signal*

The standard states that the signal is considered to be in a *mark state*, when the voltage is between –3 and –15 V. The signal is considered in a *space state* if the voltage is between +3 and +15 V. The RS-232 data line is in the mark state when the line is idle.

Start Bit

When an asynchronous character of data is to be sent, the line first shifts to a space level for the duration of 1 bit. This is known as the *start bit* (0). Data bits immediately follow.

Asynchronous lines do not use a clock signal like synchronous links. The asynchronous receiver must have a clock matching the same baud rate as the transmitter. The receiver samples the line 16 times in the bit cell time to determine its value. Sampling helps to avoid a noise pulse from triggering a false data read.

Data Bits

Data bits immediately follow the start bit, least significant bit first. A space is a 0 data bit, while mark represents a 1 bit. Early teletype equipment used 5 data bits sending characters in the 5-bit Baudot code.[47] For this reason, serial ports can be configured for 5, 6, 7, or 8 data bits. Before the ASCII character set was extended to 8 bits, it was common to use 7-bit serial data.

Parity Bit

An optional parity bit can be generated when transmitting or can be detected on the receiving side. The parity can be odd, even, or stick (mark or space). The most commonly used setting today is No Parity, which saves 1-bit time for faster communication. Older equipment often used parity to guard against errors from noisy serial lines. Odd parity is preferred over even because it forces at least one signal transition in the byte's transmission. This helps with the data reliability.

Mark or space parity is unusual and has limited usefulness. Mark parity could be used along with 2 stop bits to effectively provide 3 stop bits for very slow teletypewriter equipment. Mark or space parity reduces the effective throughput of data without providing any benefit, except possibly for diagnostic purposes. Table 11-1 summarizes the various parity configurations.

Table 11-1. *RS-232 Parity Settings*

Parity	X	Notes
None	N	No parity bit
Even	E	1 if even number of data 1-bits
Odd	O	1 if odd number of data 1-bits
Mark	M	Always at mark level (1)
Space	S	Always at space level (0)

Stop Bit(s)

Asynchronous communication requires synchronizing the receiver with the transmitter. For this reason, 1 or more stop bits exist so that the receiver can synchronize with the leading edge of the next start bit. In effect, each stop bit followed by a start bit provides built-in synchronization.

Many UARTs support 1, 1.5, or 2 stop bits. The Broadcom SoC supports 1 or 2 stop bits only. The use of 2 stop bits was common for teletypewriter equipment and probably rarely used today. Using 1 stop bit increases the overall data throughput. Table 11-2 summarizes the stop-bit configurations.

Table 11-2. *Stop-Bit Configuration*

Stop Bits	Description
1	1 stop bit
1.5	1.5 stop bits (†)
2	2 stop bits

†Unsupported by the Raspberry Pi

Baud Rate

The *baud rate* is calculated from bits per second, which includes the start, data, parity, and stop bits. A link using 115200 baud, with no parity and 1 stop bit, provides the following data byte rate:

$$D_{rate} = \frac{B}{s+d+p+S}$$
$$= \frac{115200}{1+8+0+1}$$
$$= 11,520 \text{ bytes/sec}$$

where
B is the baud rate.
s is the start bit (always 1).
d is the number of data bits (5, 6, 7, or 8).
p is the parity bit (0 or 1).
S is the stop bit (1, 1.5, or 2).
The 115200 baud link allows 11,250 bytes per second. If a parity bit is added, the throughput is reduced:

$$D_{rate} = \frac{115200}{1+8+1+1}$$
$$= 10,472.7 \text{ bytes/sec}$$

The addition of a parity bit reduces the transmission rate to 10,472.7 bytes per second.
Table 11-3 lists the standard baud rates that a serial link can be configured for on the Raspberry Pi.

Table 11-3. *Standard Baud Rates*

Rate	Notes
75	Teletypewriters
110	Teletypewriters
300	Low-speed (acoustic) modem
1200	
2400	
4800	
9600	
19200	
38400	
57600	
115200	Raspberry Pi console

Break

With asynchronous communication, it is also possible to send and receive a *break signal*. This is done by stretching the start bit beyond the data bits and the stop bit(s), and eventually returning the line to the mark state. When the receiver sees a space instead of a mark for the stop bit, it sees a *framing error*.

Some UARTs distinguish between a framing error and a break by noting how long the line remains in the space state. A simple framing error can happen as part of noisy serial line communications (particularly when modems were used) and normally attributed to a received character error. Without break detection, it is possible to assume that a break has been received when several framing errors occur in a sequence. Short sequences of framing errors, however, can also just indicate a mismatch in baud rates between the two end points.

Flow Control

Any link that transmits from one side to a receiver on the other side has the problem of flow control. Imagine a factory assembly line where parts to be assembled arrive at the worker's station faster than he can assemble them. At some point, the conveyor belt must be temporarily stopped, or some parts will not get assembled. Alternatively, if the conveyor belt is reduced in speed, the assembly worker will always be able to keep up, but perhaps at a slower than optimal pace.

Unless the serial link receiver can process every character of data as fast as it arrives, it will need flow control. The simplest approach is to simply reduce the baud rate, so that the receiver can always keep up. But this isn't always satisfactory and leads to a reduced overall throughput. A logging application might be able to write the information quickly, except when writes occur to an SD card, for example.

A better approach is to signal to the transmitter to stop sending when the receiver is bogged down. Once the receiver catches up, it can then tell the transmitter to resume transmission. Note that this problem exists for both sides of a serial link:

- Data transmitted to the terminal (DTE)
- Data transmitted to the data communications equipment (DCE)

Two forms of flow control are used:

- Hardware flow control
- Software flow control

Hardware Flow Control

Hardware flow control uses additional signal lines to regulate the flow of data. The RS-232 standards have quite an elaborate set of signals defined, but the main signals needed for flow control are shown in Table 11-4. Unlike the data line, these signals are inactive in the space state and active in the mark state.

Table 11-4. *Hardware Flow Controls*

DTE	Direction	DCE	Description	Active
RTS	→	RTS	Request to send(†)	Low
CTS	←	CTS	Clear to send(†)	
DSR	←	DSR	Data set ready	Low
DTR	→	DTR	Data terminal ready	

† Primary flow control signals

The most important signals are the ones marked with a dagger in Table 11-4. When CTS is active (mark), for example, the DCE (Pi) is indicating that it is OK to send data. If the DCE gets overwhelmed by the volume of data, the CTS signal will change to the inactive (space) state. Upon seeing this, the DTE (laptop) is required to stop sending data. (Otherwise, loss of data may occur.)

Similarly, the laptop operating as the DTE is receiving data from the DCE (Pi). If the laptop gets overwhelmed with the volume of incoming data, the RTS signal is changed to the inactive state (space). The remote end (DCE) is then expected to cease transmitting. When the laptop has caught up, it will reassert RTS, giving the DCE permission to resume.

The DTR and DSR signals are intended to convey the readiness of the equipment at each end. If the terminal was deemed not ready (DTR), DSR is not made active by the DCE. Similarly, the terminal will not assert DTR unless it is ready. In modern serial links, DTR and DSR are often assumed to be true, leaving only CTS and RTS to handle flow control.

Where flow control is required, hardware flow control is considered more reliable than software flow control.

Software Flow Control

To simplify the cabling and the supporting hardware for serial communications, the hardware flow controls can be omitted/ignored. In its place, a data protocol is used instead.

Initially, each end of the link assumes readiness for reception of data. Data is sent until an XOFF character is received, indicating that transmission should stop. The receiver sends the XON character when it is ready to resume reception again. These software flow control characters are shown in Table 11-5.

Table 11-5. *Software Flow Control Characters*

Code	Meaning	ASCII	Hex	Keyboard
XOFF	Pause transmission	DC3	13	Control-S
XON	Resume transmission	DC1	11	Control-Q

In a terminal session, the keyboard commands can be used to control the serial connection. For example, if information is displaying too fast, the user can type Ctrl-S to cause the transmission to stop. Pressing Ctrl-Q allows it to resume.

The disadvantages of software flow control include the following:

1. Line noise can prevent the receiver from seeing the XOFF character and can lead to loss of data (causing data overrun).

2. Line noise can prevent the remote end from seeing the XON character and can fail to resume transmission (causing a link "lockup").

3. Line noise can cause a false XON/XOFF character to be received (data loss or link lockup).

4. The delay in the remote end seeing a transmitted XOFF character can cause loss of data if the receiving buffer is full.

5. The XON and XOFF characters cannot be used for data in the transmission.

Problems 1 to 3 can cause link lockups or data loss to occur. Problem 4 is avoidable if the buffer notifies the other end early enough to prevent a buffer overflow. Problem 5 is an issue for binary data transmission.

Raspberry Pi UARTs

The Raspberry Pi supports two UARTs:

UART	Driver	Node	GPIO	ALT
UART0	drivers/tty/serial/amba- pl011.c	/dev/ttyAMA0	14 & 15	0
UART1	The mini has no driver.		14 & 15	5

Some websites have incorrectly stated that the mini UART is the one being used. But this does not jibe with the Broadcom documentation, nor the Raspbian Linux device driver. The Broadcom *BCM2835 ARM Peripherals* manual states that the mini UART is UART1. UART1 is available only as alternate function 5 for GPIO 14 and 15. Raspbian Linux boots up using alternate function 0 for GPIO 14 and 15, providing the UART0 peripheral instead. Finally, the source code for the device driver references PL011 in the naming throughout.

ARM PL011 UART

By default, UART0 is provided after reset and boot-up, on GPIO 14 (TX) and 15 (RX), configured as alternate function 0 (Table 11-6). UART0 is the full UART, referred to as the ARM PL011 UART. Broadcom refers the interested reader to the *ARM PrimeCell UART (PL011) Revision r1p5 Technical Reference Manual* for more information.

Table 11-6. UART0 Pins

Function	GPIO	P1/P5	ALT	Direction	Description
TXD	14	P1-08	0	Out	DTE transmitted data
RXD	15	P1-10	0	In	DTE received data
RTS	17	P1-11	3	Out	Request to send
CTS	30	P5-05	3	In	Clear to send

RTS/CTS Access

Hardware flow controls CTS and RTS are available on GPIO 30 and 17, respectively, when configured. By default these are GPIO inputs, but this can be changed. To gain access to the UART's CTS and RTS signals, configure GPIO 30 and 17 to *alternate function 3*. Table 11-6 summarizes the connections that are used by the UART.

The following short C program shows how to gain access to these signals. The listing for the included source file gpio_io.c is given in the "Direct Register Access" section of Chapter 12.

```
1       /******************************************************************
2        * rtscts.c          Configure GPIO 17 & 30 for RTS & CTS
3        ******************************************************************/
4
5       #include <stdio.h>
6       #include <stdlib.h>
7       #include <fcntl.h>
8       #include <unistd.h>
9       #include <errno.h>
10      #include <setjmp.h>
11      #include <sys/mman.h>
12      #include <signal.h>
13
14      #include "gpio_io.c"     /*GPIO routines */
15
16      static inline void
17      gpio_setalt(intgpio, unsigned alt) {
18              INP_GPIO(gpio);
19              SET_GPIO_ALT(gpio, alt);
20      }
21
22      int
23      main(int argc, char **argv) {
24
25              gpio_init();                    /*Initialize GPIO access */
26              gpio_setalt(17, 3);             /*GPIO 17 ALT = 3 */
27              gpio_setalt(30, 3);             /*GPIO 3 0 ALT = 3 */
28              return 0;
29      }
30
31      /*End rtscts.c */
```

PL011 UART Features

The Broadcom *BCM2835 ARM Peripherals* manual states that the following features are *unsupported*:

- *No* Infrared Data Association (IrDA) support

- *No* Serial InfraRed (SIR) protocol encoder/decoder (endec)

- *No* direct memory access (DMA)

- *No* support for signals DCD, DSR, DTR, and RI

The following features *are* supported, however:

- Separate 16×8 transmit and 16×12 receive FIFO buffers

- Programmable baud rate generator

- False start-bit detection

- Line-break generation and detection

- Support of control functions CTS and RTS

- Programmable hardware flow control

- Fully programmable serial interface characteristics:

    - Data can be 5, 6, 7, or 8 bits.

    - Even, odd, mark, space, or no-parity bit generation and detection.

    - 1 or 2 stop-bit generation.

    - Baud rate generation, DC up to UARTCLK/16.

Broadcom also states that there are some differences between its implementation of the UART and the 16C650 UART. But these are mostly device driver details:

- Receive FIFO trigger levels are 1/8, 1/4, 1/2, 3/4, and 7/8.

- Transmit FIFO trigger levels are 1/8, 1/4, 1/2, 3/4, and 7/8.

- The internal register map address space and the bit function of each register differ.

- 1.5 stop bits is *not* supported.

- *No* independent receive clock.

The only real concern to the application developer is that the 1.5 stop-bits configuration option is not available, which is rarely used these days anyway.

If you need the RS-232 DCD, DSR, DTR, and RI signals, these can be implemented using GPIO input and output pins (along with the appropriate RS-232 line-level shifters). These are relatively slow-changing signals, which can easily be handled in user space. The one limitation of this approach, however, is that the hang-up TTY controls provided by the device driver will be absent. To change that, the device driver source code could be modified to support these signals using GPIO. The Raspbian Linux module of interest for this is as follows:

```
drivers/tty/serial/amba-pl011.c
```

Exclusive Serial Line Use

As outlined in Chapter 19's "Available Consoles" section, the serial device /dev/ttyAMA0 is easily applied as a serial console device. However, some Raspberry Pi application developers will want to use that serial interface for application purposes, instead of a console. Without taking measures for exclusive access, the console will write to your serial peripheral and respond to its input as well (as root console commands).

Even if you turned off the console, there can still be unwanted interaction from a login prompt.

Procedure

Use the following steps to configure exclusive serial port access:

1. Eliminate console references to `console=ttyAMA0,...` in the files:

    a. `/boot/cmline.txt`

    b. `/boot/config.txt` (check option `cmdline="..."`)

2. Eliminate the kernel debugging option `kgdboc=ttyAMA0,...` as outlined for the console in step 1.

3. Eliminate the login prompt caused by the `/etc/inittab` entry. Look for `ttyAMA0` and comment the line out. The line will look something like `T0:23:respawn:/sbin/getty -L ttyAMA0 115200 vt100`.

With these steps accomplished, reboot. The device `/dev/ttyAMA0` should be available exclusively for your application to use.

Verification

To check that `/etc/inittab` has not launched a getty process, use the following after rebooting:

```
$ ps aux | grep ttyAMA0
```

No entries should appear.

To check that you have eliminated all kernel console references to the device, you can use the following:

```
$ grep ttyAMA0 /proc/cmdline
```

Serial API

The Linux operating system provides access to serial port functions through a family of system and library calls. Most of these require that you have an open file descriptor for the serial device driver being used. For the Raspberry Pi, this will usually be the device `/dev/ttyAMA0`. Full information can be had from these man pages:

- `tcgetattr(3)`
- `tty_ioctl(4)`-`ioctl(2)` equivalents to `tcgetattr(3)`

The bulk of the developer work for serial ports is configuration of the serial driver:

- Physical characteristics: baud rate, data bits, parity, and stop bits
- Driver processing characteristics: raw or cooked mode, for example

Once the driver is configured, the software developer is able to use the usual `read(2)`/`readv(2)`, `write(2)`/`writev(2)`, `select(2)`, or `poll(2)` system calls.

For an example program using some of this API, see the "Software" section of Chapter 27.

Header Files

Programs involved in altering TTY settings will want to include the following include files:

```
#include <termios.h>
#include <unistd.h>
```

open(2)

Most of the serial operations in this section require an open file descriptor to the TTY device being used. For the Raspberry Pi UART, you'll want to specify /dev/ttyAMA0.

```
int fd;

fd = open("/dev/ttyAMA0",O_RDWR); /* Open for reading and writing */
if ( fd < 0 ) {
    perror("Opening/dev/ttyAMA0");
```

You may need to take special measures to gain access to the device, since by default it will be protected. Note the permissions and user/group ownership:

```
$ ls -l /dev/ttyAMA0
crw-rw---1 root tty 204, 64 Feb 9 13:12  /dev/ttyAMA0
```

struct termios

Many of the serial port configuration options require the use of the structure termios:

```
struct termios {
    tcflag_t  c_iflag;      /* input mode flags */
    tcflag_t  c_oflag;      /* output mode flags */
    tcflag_t  c_cflag;      /* control mode flags */
    tcflag_t  c_lflag;      /* local mode flags */
    cc_t      c_line;       /* line discipline */
    cc_t      c_cc[NCCS];   /* control characters */
    speed_t   c_ispeed;     /* input speed */
    speed_t   c_ospeed;     /* output speed */
};
```

The tables in the following sections describe the C language macros used for the members of the termios structure:

- Table 11-7 lists the macros for member c_iflag.
- Table 11-8 lists the macros for member c_oflag.
- Table 11-9 lists the macros for member c_cflag.
- Table 11-10 lists the macros for member c_lflag.
- Table 11-11 lists the macros for member c_cc.

Table 11-7. *Input (c_iflag) Flags*

Flag	Set	Description	Flag	Description
BRKINT	T	Break causes SIGINT else 0x00	ISTRIP	Strip off eighth bit
	F	Break reads as 0x00	INLCR	Translate NL to CR
IXANY		Any character will resume	IUTF8	Input is UTF8 charset
IXOFF		Enable input XON/XOFF	ICRNL	Translate CR to NL
IXON		Enable output XON/XOFF	IGNBRK	Ignore break
IGNPAR		Ignore framing and parity errors	IGNCR	Ignore CR
IUCLC		Translate uppercase to lowercase		
INPCK		Enable parity checking		
PARMRK	T	Prefix framing/parity error with \377		
	F	Don't prefix with \377 (byte reads 0)		

Table 11-8. *Output (c_oflag) Flags*

Flag	Description	Flag	Description
CR0	CR delay mask 0	OFDEL	Fill character is DEL else NUL
CR1	CR delay mask 1	OFILL	Use fill characters instead of timed delay
CR2	CR delay mask 2	OLCUC	Translate lowercase to uppercase
CR3	CR delay mask 3	ONLCR	Translate NL to CR-NL
CRDLY	CR delay: apply CR0-CR3	ONLRET	Don't output CR
FF0	FF delay mask 0	ONOCR	Don't output CR at column 0
FF1	FF delay mask 1	OPOST	Enable output processing
FFDLY	FF delay: apply FF0-FF1	TAB0	Tab delay mask 0
NL0	NL delay mask 0	TAB1	Tab delay mask 1
NL1	NL delay mask 1	TAB2	Tab delay mask 1
NLDLY	NL delay: apply NL0-NL1	TAB3	Tab delay mask 2
OCRNL	Translate CR to NL	TABDLY	Tab delay: apply TAB0-TAB3

Table 11-9. *Control (c_cflag) Flags*

Flag	Baud	Flag	Baud	Flag	Description
B0	Hang-up	B115200	115,200	CLOCAL	Ignore modem controls
B50	50	B230400	230,400	CMSPAR	Stick parity
B75	75	B460800	460,800	CREAD	Enable receiver
B110	110	B500000	500,000	CRTSCTS	Enable RTS/CTS flow
B134	134	B576000	576,000	CS5	5 data bits
B150	150	B921600	921,600	CS6	6 data bits
B200	200	B1000000	1,000,000	CS7	7 data bits
B300	300	B1152000	1,152,000	CS8	8 data bits
B600	600	B1500000	1,500,000	CSIZE	Data bits mask
B1200	1,200	B2000000	2,000,000	CSTOPB	2 stop bits (else 1)
B1800	1,800	B2500000	2,500,000	HUPCL	Modem control hang-up
B2400	2,400	B3000000	3,000,000	PARENB	Enable parity
B4800	4,800	B3500000	3,500,000	PARODD	Odd or stick = 1 parity
B9600	9,600	B4000000	4,000,000	CBAUD	Rate mask
B19200	19,200			CBAUDEX	Extended mask
B38400	38,400			CIBAUD	Input rate mask
B57600	57,600			EXTA	External A
				EXTB	External B

Table 11-10. *Local (c_lflag) Flags*

Flag	Description	Flag	Description
ECHOCTL	Echo controls as ^X	ECHO	Echo input
IEXTEN	Enable input processing	ECHOE	Erase previous char
PENDIN	Reprint upon reading	ECHOK	Erase line on kill
ECHOKE	Erase each char on kill	ISIG	Generate signals
ECHONL	Echo NL even if !ECHO	NOFLSH	No flush on signal
ECHOPRT	Print chars during erase	TOSTOP	Send SIGTTOU
ICANON	Enable canonical mode	XCASE	Terminal is uppercase

Table 11-11. *Special (c_cc) Characters*

Macro	Description	Macro	Description
VEOF	End-file (^D)	VQUIT	Quit (^\)
VEOL	End line (NUL)	VREPRINT	Reprint (^R)
VEOL2	End line 2	VSTART	XON (^Q)
VERASE	Erase (^H)	VSTOP	XOFF (^S)
VINTR	Interrupt (^C)	VSUSP	Suspend (^Z)
VKILL	Kill (^U)	VTIME	Time-out decsecs
VLNEXT	Literal next (^V)	VWERASE	Word erase (^W)
VMIN	Min chars to read		

tcgetattr(3)

Before you make changes to the serial port settings, you will want to retrieve the current settings in case you later need to restore them. This also greatly simplifies configuration, allowing you to change only the settings that need changing.

Use the tcgetattr(3) function to fetch the current serial device settings:

```
int tcgetattr(int fd, struct termios *termios_p);
```

where

fd is the open TTY file descriptor.
termios_p is the struct to be filled with current setting information.

```
struct termios term;
int rc;

rc = tcgetattr(fd,&term);
if ( rc < 0 ) {
    perror("tcgetattr(3)");
```

tcsetattr(3)

When the termios structure has been defined with the serial parameters you wish to use, the tcsetattr(3) call is used to set them in the device driver:

```
int tcsetattr(
  int fd,
  int optional_actions,
  const struct termios *termios_p
);
```

where

fd is the open TTY file descriptor to change.
optional_actions is one of three actions (listed in the following table).
termios_p is a pointer to the new settings to be applied.

The three choices for optional_actions are as follows:

optional_actions	Meaning
TCSANOW	The change occurs immediately.
TCSADRAIN	Change occurs after all output has been sent.
TCSAFLUSH	As TCSADRAIN, but pending input is discarded.

The following shows an example of use:

```
struct termios term;
int rc;

...
rc = tcsetattr(fd,TCSADRAIN,&term);
if ( rc < 0 ) {
    perror("tcsetattr(3)");
```

tcsendbreak(3)

A break signal can be transmitted to the remote end by calling the tcsendbreak(3) function:

```
int tcsendbreak(int fd, int duration);
```

where
  fd is the open TTY file descriptor.
  duration is the amount of time to use to represent a break.
  When the argument duration is zero, it sends a break signal lasting between 0.25 and 0.5 seconds. When the argument is nonzero, the man page states that some implementation-defined amount of time is used instead.

```
int rc;

rc = tcsendbreak(fd,0);
if ( rc < 0 ) {
    perror("tcsendbreak(3)");
```

tcdrain(3)

The function tcdrain(3) can be used to block the execution of the calling program until all of the output characters have been transmitted out of the UART:

```
int tcdrain(int fd);
```

where
  fd is the open TTY file descriptor. An example follows:

```
int rc;

rc = tcdrain(fd);
if ( rc < 0 ) {
    perror("tcdrain(3)");
```

tcflush(3)

The tcflush(3) call can be used to flush pending input or output data from the serial port buffers.

```
int tcflush(int fd, int queue_selector);
```

where
fd is the open TTY file descriptor.
queue_selector determines which queue(s) are to be flushed.
The following values are used for the queue_selector argument:

queue_selector	Description
TCIFLUSH	Flushes unread incoming data
TCOFLUSH	Flushes untransmitted output data
TCIOFLUSH	Flushes both unread and untransmitted data

The following example flushes pending input data:

```
int rc;

rc = tcflush(fd,TCIFLUSH);
```

tcflow(3)

Various flow control operations can be performed by calling the tcflow(3) function:

```
int tcflow(int fd, int action);
```

where
fd is the open TTY file descriptor.
action is the flow control action required (as shown in the following table).
The valid choices for action are as follows:

action	Description
TCOOFF	Suspends output (transmission stops)
TCOON	Resumes output
TCIOFF	Immediately sends a STOP character to stop the remote device
TCION	Transmits a START character to resume the remote device

The following example shows the program immediately suspending output:

```
int rc;

rc = tcflow(fd,TCOOFF);
if ( rc < 0 ) {
    perror("tcflow (3)");
```

cfmakeraw(3)

The cfmakeraw(3) function is a *convenience routine* to establish raw mode, where no special data conversions or mappings occur. The caller should first call upon tcgetattr(3) to define the initial termios structure settings. Then cfmakeraw(3) can be used to adjust those settings for raw mode:

```
void cfmakeraw(struct termios *termios_p);
```

where
    termios_p is a pointer to a struct populated with the serial device's current settings, to be altered.
    Note that *no file descriptor is provided* since this function doesn't actually change anything beyond the data structure that was passed to it. After calling cfmakeraw(3), the user will need to use cfsetattr(3) to inform the driver of the changes.

```
struct termios term;
int rc;

rc = cfgetattr(fd,&term);          /*Get settings */
cfmakeraw(&term);                  /* Alter settings for raw mode */
rc = tcsetattr(fd,TCSADRAIN,&term); /* Apply the settings */
```

Calling cfmakeraw(3) is equivalent to manually applying the following changes:

```
struct termios term;
...
term.c_iflag &= ~(IGNBRK | BRKINT | PARMRK | ISTRIP
                 | INLCR  | IGNCR  | ICRNL  | IXON);
term.c_oflag &= ~OPOST;
term.c_lflag &= ~(ECHO   | ECHONL | ICANON | ISIG | IEXTEN);
term.c_cflag &= ~(CSIZE  | PARENB);
term.c_cflag |=CS8;
```

This is a good place to pause and discuss what raw mode is. There are two forms of serial I/O supported by Linux (and Unix generally):
    Cooked mode: The input, output, and echoing functions are modified/performed by the kernel.
    Raw mode: The input/output data is sent to/from the application unchanged by the kernel.
    The serial port developer, wishing to communicate with a serial device or AVR class microcontroller, will be very interested in raw mode. Using raw mode, the data you transmit is sent unmodified to its destination. Likewise, the data received is received as it was originally transmitted. Cooked mode, which is the norm, is a very different beast.
    The original purpose of serial lines for Unix was the handling of user interaction using terminal I/O (this is still true for the serial port console). Many terminal processing functions were considered common enough among applications to centralize them in the kernel. This saved the application from having to deal with these physical aspects and lead to consistency in their handling. This terminal handling is affectionately known as *cooked mode*.
    The main areas of cooked mode processing are as follows:
    Input processing: The type of kernel processing performed on serial input data (like backspace processing)
    Output processing: The type of kernel processing performed on serial output data (like converting a sent line feed into a carriage return and line-feed pair)
    Local processing: Involving input *and* output, processing features such as echo
    Control processing: Other serial controls

We can get a sense of how raw mode differs from cooked mode by looking at what cfmakeraw(3) changes. Looking at

```
term.c_iflag &= ~ (IGNBRK | BRKINT | PARMRK | ISTRIP
                 | INLCR  | IGNCR  | ICRNL  | IXON);
```

we see that the following input processing features are disabled:

Flag	Description	Setting
IGNBRK	Ignore break	Disabled
BRKINT	Break reads as 0x00	Disabled
PARMRK	Don't prefix with \377 (byte reads 0)	Disabled
ISTRIP	Strip off eighth bit	Disabled
INLCR	Translate NL to CR	Disabled
IGNCR	Ignore CR	Disabled
ICRNL	Translate CR to NL	Disabled
IXON	Enable output XON/XOFF	Disabled

Disabling ISTRIP prevents the kernel from stripping the high-order bit in the byte. Disabling INLCR, ICRNL prevents the substitution of NL or CR characters (for input). Disabling IGNCR prevents the kernel from deleting the CR character from the input stream. Disabling IXON disables software flow control so that the characters XON and XOFF can be read by the application program.

Looking at the output processing changes,

```
term.c_oflag &= ~OPOST;
```

we see that the following change applies:

Flag	Description	Setting
OPOST	Enable output processing	Disabled

This disables all output processing features with one flag.

Local processing includes both input and output. The following local processing flags are changed:

```
term.c_lflag &= ~(ECHO | ECHONL | ICANON | ISIG| IEXTEN);
```

From this, we see that these local processing features are disabled:

Flag	Description	Setting
ECHO	Echo input	Disabled
ECHONL	Echo NL even if !ECHO	Disabled
ICANON	Enable canonical mode	Disabled
ISIG	Generate signals	Disabled
IEXTEN	Enable input processing	Disabled

109

Disabling ICANON means that all special nonsignal characters defined in c_cc are disregarded (like VERASE). Disabling ISIG means that there will be no signals sent to your application for characters like VINTR. Disabling IEXTEN disables other c_cc character processing like VEOL2, VLNEXT, VREPRINT, VWERASE, and the IUCLC flag. Disabling ECHO and ECHONL disables two aspects of character echoing.

Finally, the following control aspects are changed:

```
term.c_cflag &= ~ (CSIZE | PARENB);
term.c_cflag |= CS8;
```

meaning that:

Flag	Description	Setting
CSIZE	Data bits mask	Masked-out data bits
PARENB	Generate/detect parity	Disabled
CS8	8 data bits	Set to 8-bit data

The CSIZE masking is used to reset the data bits field to zeros. This allows the CS8 bit pattern to be or-ed in later, setting the data bits value to 8 bits. Disabling the PARENB flag causes parity generation on output to be disabled, and disables parity checking on input. If your raw link requires parity generation and checking, you'll need to undo this particular change in your own code.

You can see from this list that a plethora of special processing is altered to go from cooked mode to raw mode. It is no wonder that this support routine was made available.

cfgetispeed(3)

The current *input* baud rate for the line can be queried by the cfgetispeed(3) function:

```
speed_t cfgetispeed(const struct termios *termios_p);
```

where

termios_p is the pointer to the structure containing the terminal configuration.

Because the termios structure has been extended and modified over the years, this function provides a more portable way to extract the input baud rate, including the more recently added higher baud rates.

```
struct termios term;
speed_t baud_rate;
baud_rate = cfgetispeed(&term);
```

cfgetospeed(3)

The current *output* baud rate can be extracted from the termios structure with

```
speed_t cfgetospeed(const struct termios *termios_p);
```

where

termios_p is the pointer to the structure containing the terminal configuration.

Because the termios structure has been extended and modified over the years, this function provides a portable way to extract the output baud rate, including the more recently added higher baud rates.

cfsetispeed(3)

The cfsetispeed(3) function permits a portable way to establish an input baud rate in the termios structure:

```
int cfsetispeed(struct termios *termios_p, speed_t speed);
```

where

termios_p is the pointer to the TTY configuration structure to be modified.
speed is the input baud rate to apply.
Note that this function only updates the termios data structure and has no direct effect on the device being used.

```
struct termios term;
int rc;

rc = cfsetispeed(&term,115200);
if ( rc < 0 ) {
    perror("cfsetispeed(3)");
```

cfsetospeed(3)

The cfsetospeed(3) function sets the output baud rate in the termios structure:

```
int cfsetospeed(struct termios *termios_p, speed_t speed);
```

where

termios_p is the pointer to the TTY configuration structure being modified.
speed is the output baud rate to apply.
Note that this function only updates the termios data structure with no direct effect on the device being used.

```
struct termios term;
int rc;

rc = cfsetospeed(&term,9600);
if ( rc < 0 ) {
perror("cfsetospeed(3)");
```

cfsetspeed(3)

Most serial communication uses a common baud rate for transmitting and receiving. For this reason, this is the preferred function to invoke for establishing both the input and output baud rates:

```
int cfsetspeed(struct termios *termios_p, speed_t speed);
```

where

termios_p is the pointer to the TTY configuration structure to be modified.
speed is the input and output baud rate to apply.
Note that this function only updates the termios data structure with no direct effect on the device being used.

```
struct termios term;
int rc;

rc = cfsetspeed(&term,9600);
if ( rc < 0 ) {
perror("cfsetsspeed(3)");
```

read(2)

The read(2) system call can be used for reading from the serial port, in addition to normal Linux files and other devices:

```
#include <unistd.h>
```

```
ssize_t read(int fd, void *buf, size_t count);
```

where
    fd is the open file descriptor to read from.
    buf is the buffer to read the data into.
    count is the maximum number of bytes to read.
    returns an int, where
        -1 indicates an error, with the error code found in errno.
        0 indicates that the serial port has been closed with the end-of-file character.
        >0 indicates the number of bytes read.
    The errors that pertain to blocking calls on a serial port include the following:

Error	Description
EBADF	fd is not a valid file descriptor.
EFAULT	buf is outside your accessible address space.
EINTR	The call was interrupted by a signal before any data was read.

More will be said about EINTR near the end of this chapter.
The following example reads up to 256 bytes into the array buf, from the serial port open on the file unit fd:

```
int fd;          /*Opened serial port */
char buf[256];
int rc;

rc = read(fd,buf,sizeof buf);
if ( rc < 0 ) {
    fprintf(stderr,"%s: reading serial port.\n",strerror(errno));
    ...
} else if ( !rc ) {
    /*End file */
} else {
    /*Process rc bytes in buf[] */
}
```

write(2)

To transmit data on a serial link, you can use the write(2) system call:

```
#include <unistd.h>

ssize_t write(int fd, const void *buf, size_t count);
```

where
>   fd is the file unit of the opened serial port.
>   buf is the buffer containing the bytes to be transmitted.
>   count is the number of bytes to transmit.
>   returns an int, where
>>   -1 indicates that an error has occurred, with the error found in errno.
>>   0 indicates no bytes were transmitted (end-of-file, port was closed).
>>   >0 indicates the number of bytes transmitted.
>   The possible errors related to blocking calls for serial port writes include the following:

Error	Description
EBADF	fd is not a valid file descriptor or is not open for writing.
EFAULT	buf is outside your accessible address space.
EINTR	The call was interrupted by a signal before any data was written.

Normally, only an error (-1) or a value of count is returned. If the serial port was opened for *nonblocking* I/O, the returned count can be *less* than the requested count (this mode of operation is not discussed here). In blocking mode (which we are assuming here), the call will return only when the full count requested has been written. Any failure would otherwise result in an error being returned instead.

The following is an example of its use, as it pertains to a serial port:

```
int fd;
char buf[256];
int rc, n;

strcpy(buf,"Hello World!\n");
n = strlen(buf);

rc = write(fd,buf,n);
if ( rc < 0 ) {
    fprintf(stderr,"%s: writing serial link.\n",strerror(errno));
    ...
}
assert(rc == n);
```

readv(2) and writev(2)

An often neglected option for reading and writing are the readv(2) and writev(2) system calls. These tend to be more useful for programs that work with packets than for interactive terminal sessions. These are presented because the serial port application developer may want to use a protocol that has more than one buffer containing headers, data, and trailer. Using the scatter-gather routines can enhance your code communicating with an AVR class microcontroller. The use of an I/O vector here is similar in concept to the I/O vectors used by I2C I/O operations in the ioctl(2,I2C_RDWR) system call (see Chapter 14).

```
#include <sys/uio.h>

ssize_t readv(int fd, const struct iovec *iov, int iovcnt);
ssize_t writev(int fd, const struct iovec *iov, int iovcnt);
```

where
> fd is the open serial port file descriptor for reading/writing.
> iov is the I/O vector directing the reading/writing.
> iovcnt is the I/O vector count.
> returns an int, where
>> -1 indicates an error, leaving the error code in errno, see read(2) or write(2).
>> 0 indicates that an end-of-file condition occurred.
>> >n indicates the actual number of bytes read/written.
> The I/O vector is shown here:

```
struct iovec {
    void    *iov _base;    /*Starting address */
    size_t  iov_len;       /*Number of bytes to transfer */
};
```

In the following example, a simple terminal writev(2) system call is used to piece together three pieces of information, to be transmitted to the terminal:

- The text Hello

- The person's name provided in the argument name

- The text !\n\r at the end

One of the advantages of the writev(2) call is its ability to take separate buffers of data and transmit them as a whole in one I/O operation:

```
void
fun(int serport, const char *name) {
    struct iovec iov[3];
    int rc;

    iov[0].iov_base = "Hello";
    iov[0].iov_len = 6;
    iov[1].iov_base = (void *)name;
    iov[1].iov_len = strlen(name);
    iov[2].iov_base = "!\n\r";
    iov[2].iov_len = 3;

    rc = writev(serport,iov,3);
    if ( rc < 0 ) {
        fprintf(stderr,"%s: writev(2)\n",strerror(errno));
        abort();
    }
}
```

Each segment to be transmitted is described by one iov[x] member, each consisting of a buffer pointer and the number of bytes. The writev(2) system call is told how many iov[] entries to use in its third calling argument.

Error EINTR

One error code that afflicts many device I/O system calls is the EINTR error, "Interrupted system call." This error code applies to read(2), readv(2), write(2), and writev(2) on devices that may "block" execution until the required data has been fully read/written. (This also applies to ioctl(2) when I2C I/O is performed.) The EINTR error is not returned for I/O to disk because these I/O calls don't block for a long time (the I/O is to/from a file system disk memory buffer). The application developer should otherwise plan on handling this error.

The EINTR error is the Unix way of working with signals. Consider what happens when your application is waiting for a single keystroke from the user at a terminal (or reading a packet from an AVR class device):

```
rc = read(fd,buf,n);        /*Block until n bytes read */
```

Until that read is satisfied (or the file descriptor is closed), execution will stop there. In the meantime, another process or thread may signal your application to do something, perhaps to shut down and exit. A signal handler like the following is invoked when the signal is handled:

```
static void
sigint_handler(int signo) {
    is_signaled = 1;        /*Please exit this program */
}
```

At this point, your application is in the middle of a system call, waiting to read from the serial port. The system call's registers are saved on the stack frame, and your application has entered into the kernel. The handling of the signal means that the kernel calls your signal handler, placing another stack frame on your current stack.

Because a signal can arrive at any time, there are many things you can't do from within a signal handler. For example, you must not invoke malloc(3) or other non-reentrant functions. Otherwise, you risk doing another malloc(3) inside an interrupted malloc(3), which leads to disaster. The important point here is that a very limited number of safe things can be performed from inside a signal handler.

One thing that *is* safe to do in a signal handler is to set a global variable of some kind, like the is_signaled variable in the example. One problem remains: how does the code blocked in the read(2) call respond to this notification? When the signal handler returns, the application will continue to block trying to read from the serial port.

The Unix solution to this problem is to have the kernel return an error code EINTR after a signal handler receives a signal. In this manner, the read(2) call returns an error, allowing the application program to test whether it received a signal. The following code shows how the simple read(2) call is replaced with a loop that checks whether the signal handler was called:

```
do  {
    rc = read(fd, buf, n);      /*Block until n bytes read */
    if ( is_signaled )
        longjmp(shutdown,1);    /*Shutdown this server */
} while ( rc == -1 && errno == EINTR );

if ( rc == -1 ) {               /*Check for non EINTR errors */
    fprintf(stderr,"%s: read(2)\n",strerror(errno));
    abort();
}
```

In this code snippet, we see that the read(2) call is performed as part of a loop. As long as an error is returned *and the* errno *value is* EINTR, we check for any interesting events (like is_signaled) and repeat the call. If any other type of error occurs or we succeed, we drop out of the loop.

This is the basic template that should be used for any call that might receive EINTR, even if you don't plan to handle signals in your application. Otherwise, you may find that your Pi application may run for weeks and then one day when you least expect it, fail because of a received EINTR error.

CHAPTER 12

■ ■ ■

GPIO

General-purpose I/O is a topic near to the hearts of Raspberry Pi owners, because this is the interface to the outside world. The BCM2835 is flexibly designed to allow I/O pins to be reconfigured under software control. GPIO 14 can be an input, an output, or operate as a serial port TX data line, for example. This makes the Raspberry Pi very adaptable.

One of the challenges related to the Pi's GPIO interface is that it uses a weak CMOS 3 V interface. The GPIO pins are susceptible to static electricity damage, and the I/O pins are weak drivers (2 to 16 mA). Additionally, GPIO power must be budgeted from the total spare current capacity of 50 mA. Using adapter boards overcomes these problems but adds considerably to the cost. This then provides a fertile area for coming up with cheap and effective roll-your-own solutions.

Pins and Designations

Figures 12-1 and 12-2 show the schematic GPIO connections for the Raspberry Pi. You will notice that the GPIO pins are also designated with the GENx designation. (Gen 7 to 10 was not available prior to version 2.) This may have been an early attempt to follow the Arduino lead of naming their pins digital0 or analog4, for example, in a generic way. It appears, however, that this naming convention has not really caught on among Pi users. Despite this, these names are cross-referenced in Table 12-1. These are probably the preferred first choices when shopping for GPIO pins to use, since they are less likely to be required for special (alternate) functions like UART or SPI.

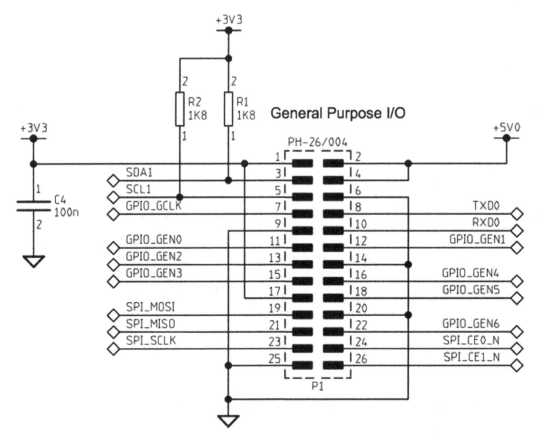

Figure 12-1. *GPIO P1 header*

Table 12-1. *Rev 2.0 GEN and GPIO Designations*

GENx	GPIOy	Header
GEN0	GPIO 17	P1-11
GEN1	GPIO 18	P1-12
GEN2	GPIO 27	P1-13
GEN3	GPIO 22	P1-15
GEN4	GPIO 23	P1-16
GEN5	GPIO 24	P1-18
GEN6	GPIO 25	P1-22
GEN7	GPIO 28	P5-03
GEN8	GPIO 29	P5-04
GEN9	GPIO 30	P5-05
GEN10	GPIO 31	P5-06

A couple of GPIO pins have pull-up resistors. Figure 12-1 shows that GPIO pins 2 (SDA1) on P1-03, and GPIO 3 (SCL1) on P1-05, have an 1.8 $k\Omega$ pull-up resistor. This should be taken into account if you use these for something other than I2C.

The layouts of headers P1 and P5, where the GPIO pins are made accessible, are documented in Chapter 5.

▪ **Note** P5 was not present prior to version 2, but both Models A and B now include it (without header pins).

Configuration After Reset

Upon reset, most GPIO pins are configured as general-purpose inputs with the exceptions noted in Table 12-2. (Figure 12-2 applies to version 2, Models A and B.) The Pull-up column indicates how the internal pull-up resistor is initially configured. The pull-up resistors apply when the GPIO is configured as an input pin.

Table 12-2. *Rev 2.0 Configuration After Reset*

GPIO	Pull-up	Config	ALT
0	High	Input	
1	High	Input	
2	High	SDA1	0
3	High	SCL1	0
4	High	Input	
5	High	GPCLK1	0
6	High	Output	
7	High	Input	
8	High	Input	
9	Low	Input	
10	Low	Input	
11	Low	Input	
14	Low	TXD0	0
15	Low	RXD0	0
16	Low	Output	
17	Low	Input	
18	Low	Input	
21	Low	Input	
22	Low	Input	
23	Low	Input	
24	Low	Input	

(*continued*)

Table 12-2. (*continued*)

GPIO	Pull-up	Config	ALT
25	Low	Input	
27	Low	Output	
28	-	Input	
29	-	Input	
30	Low	Input	
31	Low	Input	
40	Low	PWM0	0
45	-	PWM1	0

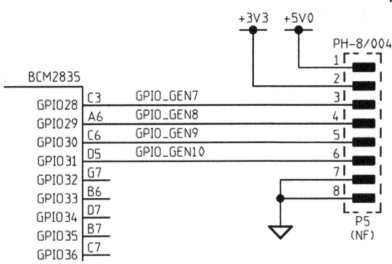

Figure 12-2. *GPIO P5 header*

Pull-up Resistors

As noted earlier, GPIO pins 2 and 3 have an external resistor tied to the +3.3 V rail. The remaining GPIO pins are pulled high or low by an internal 50 $k\Omega$ resistor in the SoC.[56, 48] The internal pull-up resistor is rather weak, and effective at only giving an unconnected GPIO input a defined state. A CMOS input should not be allowed to float midway between its logic, high or low. When pull-up resistance is needed for an external circuit, it is probably best to provide an external pull-up resistor, rather than rely on the weak internal one.

Configuring Pull-up Resistors

The pull-up configuration of a GPIO pin can be configured using the SoC registers GPPUP and GPPUDCLK0/1. (The "Physical Memory" section of Chapter 6 has the physical addresses for these registers.)

The GPPUP register is laid out as follows:

Bits	Field	Description	Type	Reset
GPPUP Register				
31-2	-	Unused	R	0
		GPIO pin pull-up/down		
1-0	PUD	00 Off—disable pull-up/down	R/W	0
		01 Pull-down enable		
		10 Pull-up enable		
		11 Reserved		

The GPPUDCLK0 register is laid out as follows:

Bits	Field	Description	Type	Reset
GPPUDCLK0 Register				
31-0	PUDCLKn	n = 0..31	R/W	0
		0 No effect		
		1 Assert clock		

Finally, the GPPUDCLK1 register is formatted this way:

Bits	Field	Description	Type	Reset
GPPUDCLK1 Register				
31-22	-	Reserved	R	0
21-0	PUDCLKn	n = 32..53	R/W	0
		0 No effect		
		1 Assert clock		

According to the Broadcom documentation, the general procedure for programming the pull-up resistor is this:

1. Write the pull-up configuration desired in the rightmost 2 bits of the 32-bit GPPUP register. The configuration choices are as follows:

    00: Disable pull-up control.

    01: Enable pull-down control.

    10: Enable pull-up control.

2. Wait 150 cycles to allow the preceding write to be registered.

3. Write a 1-bit to every GPIO position, in the group of 32 GPIO pins being configured. GPIOs 0–31 are configured by register GPPUDCLK0.

4. Wait another 150 cycles to allow step 3 to register.

5. Write 00 to GPPUP to remove the control signal.

121

6. Wait another 150 cycles to allow step 5 to register.

7. Finally, write to GPPUDCLK0/1 to remove the clock.

The Broadcom procedure may seem confusing because of the word *clock*. Writing to GPPUP and GPPUDCLK0/1 registers by using the preceding procedure is designed to provide a pulse to the internal pull-up resistor flip-flops (their data clock input). First a state is established in step 1, and then the configured 1 bits are clocked high in step 3 (for selected GPIO pins). Step 5 establishes a zero state, which is then sent to the flip-flop clock inputs in step 7.

The documentation also states that the current settings for the pull-up drivers *cannot* be read. This makes sense when you consider that the state is held by these internal flip-flops that were changed by the procedure. (There is no register access available to read these flip-flops.) Fortunately, when configuring the state of a particular GPIO pin, you change only the pins you select by the GPPUDCLK0/1 register. The others remain unchanged.

The program pullup.c, shown next, provides a simple utility to change the pull-up resistor settings. The program listing for gpio_io.c is provided in the "Direct Register Access" section of Chapter 12. The source for timed_wait.c is found in the "Source Code" section of Chapter 25.

After compiling, the following example changes the GPIO 7 pull-up to high and GPIO 8 to low:

```
$ ./pullup 7=low 8=high
```

```
1   /********************************************************************
2    * pullup.c : Change the pull-up resistor setting for GPIO pin
3    ********************************************************************/
4
5   #include <stdio.h>
6   #include <stdlib.h>
7   #include <fcntl.h>
8   #include <unistd.h>
9   #include <errno.h>
10  #include <setjmp.h>
11  #include <sys/mman.h>
12  #include <signal.h>
13
14  #include "gpio_io.c"                    /*GPIO routines */
15  #include "timed_wait.c"                 /*Delay */
16
17  /********************************************************************
18   * 0x7E200094  GPPUD          GPIO  Pin   Pull-up/down Enable
19   * 0x7E200098  GPPUDCLK0 GPIO  Pin   Pull-up/down Enable Clock 0
20   ********************************************************************/
21
22  #define GPIO_GPPUD          *(ugpio+37)
23  #define GPIO_GPPUDCLK0      *(ugpio+38)
24
25  static inline void
26  gpio_setpullup(int gpio, int pull) {
27          unsigned mask = 1 << gpio;        /*GPIOs 0 to 31 only */
28          unsigned pmask = pull >=0 ? ( 1 << !! pull) : 0;
29
30          GPIO_GPPUD = pmask ;              /*Select pull-up setting */
31          timed_wait (0, 500, 0) ;
32          GPIO_GPPUDCLK0 = mask ;           /*Set the GPIO of interest */
33          timed_wait (0, 500, 0) ;
34          GPIO_GPPUD = 0 ;                  /*Reset pmask */
```

```
35            timed_wait (0, 500, 0);
36            GPIO_GPPUDCLK0 = 0 ;                  /*Set the GPIO of interest */
37            timed_wait (0, 500, 0);
38 }
39
40  /*************************************************************************
41   * Command line arguments are of the form <gpio>={low , high or none },
42   * for example : ./pull-up 7=high 8=low
43   *
44   * Only the first character of the argument after '=' is checked.
45   *************************************************************************/
46  int
47  main(int argc, char **argv) {
48            int x, gpio, p;
49            char arg [64];
50
51            gpio_init();
52
53            for ( x=1; x<argc; ++x ) {
54                    if ( sscanf (argv [x] ,"%d=%s", &gpio, arg) != 2 )
55                            goto errxit;
56                    if ( *arg == 'n' )
57                            p = -1;
58                    else if ( *arg == ' l ' || *arg == 'h ' )
59                            p = *arg == 'h ' ? 1 : 0;
60                    else goto errxit;
61                    if ( gpio < 0 || gpio > 31 )  {
62                            fprintf (stderr,"%s : GPIO must be <= 31\n",
63                                    argv[x]) ;
64                            return 1;
65                    }
66                    gpio_setpullup(gpio, p);
67            }
68            return 0;
69
70  errxit : fprintf (stderr,"Argument '%s ' must be in the form\n"
71                  " <gpio>=<arg> where arg is h, l or n.\ n",
72                  argv [ x ] ) ;
73            return 1;
74 }
75
76 /*End pullup.c */
```

The default drive strengths after booting are listed next, along with the GPIO addresses for the corresponding GPIO pads:

Address	GPIO Pads	Reset Drive Strength
0x2010002C	GPIO 0 to 27	8 mA
0x20100030	GPIO 28 to 45	16 mA
0x20100034	GPIO 46 to 53	8 mA

Table 12-3 summarizes the GPIO Pads Control register. Note that to be successful setting values in this register, the field labeled PASSWRD must receive the value 0x5A. This is a simple measure to avoid having the values trashed by an accidental write to this location.

Table 12-3. *GPIO Pads Control*

Bits	Field	Description		I/O	Reset
31:24	PASSWRD	0x5A	Must be 0x5A when writing	W	0x00
23:05	Reserved	0x00	Write as zero, read as don't care	R/W	
04:04	SLEW	Slew rate			
		0	Slew rate limited	R/W	1
		1	Slew rate not limited		
03:03	HYST	Enable input hysterisis			
		0	Disabled	R/W	1
		1	Enabled		
02:00	DRIVE	Drive strength		R/W	3
		0	2 mA		
		1	4 mA		
		2	6 mA		
		3	8 mA (default except 28 to 45)		
		4	10 mA		
		5	12 mA		
		6	14 mA		
		7	16 mA (GPIO 28 to 45)		

Testing Pull-up State

If you want to test the state of the pull-up resistors, the following procedure can be used:

1. Make sure no connection is attached so that the input can float.

2. Configure the GPIO pin as an input.

3. Configure the GPIO as active high (that is, not *active low*).

4. Read the input value.

    a. A reading of 1 means that the input was pulled high.

    b. A reading of 0 means that the input was pulled low.

Note that GPIO pins 2 and 3 are pulled up by external resistors, while others may be connected to other circuits (GPIO 6). This will affect your readings for those pins. Note also that pins configured for alternate functions may be *outputs* and will be driven.

When the input GPIO is configured with no pull-up, you *might* see random values, but this is unreliable. An input voltage can float above or below a threshold and remain there for a time.

The script presented in the "GPIO Input Test" section of Chapter 12 can be used to test a GPIO input (^C to exit the script).

Logic Levels

GPIO pins use 3 V logic levels. The precise BCM2835 SoC logic-level specifications are as follows:

Parameter	Volts	Description
V_{IL}	≤ 0.8	Voltage, input low
V_{IH}	≥ 1.3	Voltage, input high

As we work through several projects in this book, we'll be making frequent references to these parameters. You might want to commit these voltage levels to memory or mark the page with a tab. The voltage levels between V_{IL} and V_{IH} are considered to be ambiguous or undefined, and must be avoided.

Drive Strength

How much drive can a GPIO pin provide in terms of current drive? The design of the SoC is such that each GPIO pin can safely sink or source up to 16 mA without causing it harm.[28] The drive strength is also software configurable from 2 mA up to 16 mA.[29] The boot-up default is to use the drive strength of 8 mA.[28] However, as our test program pads.c will show, the GPIO outputs 28 to 45 were found configured for 16 mA (GPIO 28 to 31 are available on header P5).

Table 12-3 shows the SoC registers for reading and configuring the drive strength of the GPIO pins. There are three registers, affecting GPIO pins in three groups of 28 (two groups affect user-accessible GPIOs). The slew rate, hysteresis, and drive strength settings all apply at the group level. The drive strength is configured through a 3-bit value from 2 mA to 16 mA, in increments of 2 mA. When writing to these registers, the field PASSWRD must contain the hexadecimal value 0x5A, as a guard against accidental changes.

To visualize how the Raspberry Pi controls drive strength, examine Figure 12-3. The control lines Drive0 through Drive2 are enabled by bits in the DRIVE register. With these three control lines disabled (zero), only the bottom 2 mA amplifier is active (this amplifier is always enabled for outputs). This represents the weakest drive-strength setting.

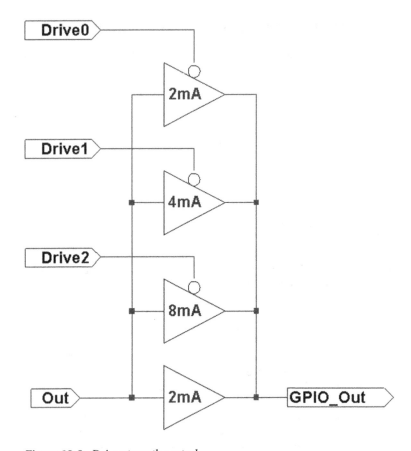

Figure 12-3. *Drive-strength control*

With Drive0 set to a 1, the top amplifier is enabled, adding another 2 mA of drive, for a total of 4 mA. Enabling Drive1 adds a further 4 mA of drive, totaling 8 mA. Enabling Drive2 brings the total drive capability to 16 mA.

It should be mentioned that these drive capabilities are *not current limiters* in any way. What they do is apply more amplifier drive in order to meet the logic-level requirements (next section). If the GPIO output is wired up to a light load like a CMOS chip or MOSFET transistor where little current is drawn, then the minimum drive of 2 mA suffices. The single GPIO 2 mA buffer can effortlessly establish a logic high in its proper voltage range as well as bring the voltage to a logic low when required.

When the GPIO output is loaded with a higher current load, the single 2 mA buffer may not be enough to keep the logic level within spec. By applying more amplifier drive, the output voltage levels are coerced into the correct operating range.

Input Pins

A GPIO input pin should experience voltages only between 0 and the 3.3 V maximum. Always exercise caution when interfacing to other circuits that use higher voltages like TTL logic, where 5 V is used. The SoC is not tolerant of overvoltages and can be damaged.

While there exist protection diodes for protecting against negative input swings, these are weak and intended only to bleed away negative static charges. Be sure to design your input circuits so that the GPIO input never sees a negative input potential.

Output Pins

As an output GPIO pin, the user bears full responsibility for current limiting. There is *no* current limiting provided. When the output pin is in the high state, as a voltage source, it tries to supply 3.3 V (within the limits of the transistor).

If this output is shorted to ground (worst case), then as much current as can be supplied will flow. This will lead to permanent damage.

The outputs also work to the specifications listed earlier, but the attached load can skew the operating voltage range. An output pin can *source* or *sink* current. The amount of current required and the amount of *output drive* configured alters the operating voltage profile. As long as you keep within the current limits for the configured drive capability, the voltage specifications should be met.

Figure 12-4 illustrates how a GPIO port sources current into its load (R_{load}). Current flows from the +3.3 V supply, through transistor M_1, out the GPIO pin, and into R_{load} to ground. Because of this, it takes a high (logic 1) to send current into the load. This makes the circuit an "active high" configuration.

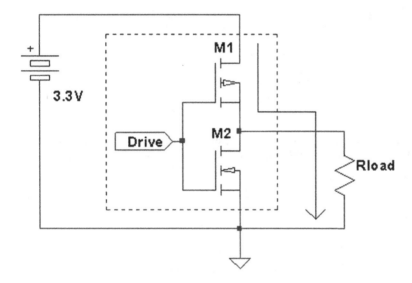

Figure 12-4. *GPIO output high*

Figure 12-5 shows how the GPIO output sinks current instead. Because R_{load} is connected to the +3.3 V supply, current flows through R_{load}, into the GPIO output pin, and through the bottom transistor M_2 to ground. To send current through the load, a low (logic 0) is written to the output port. This is the *active low* configuration.

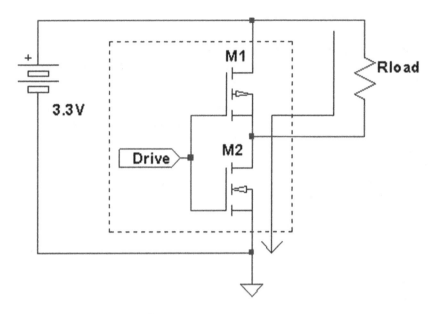

Figure 12-5. *GPIO output low*

Figure 12-6 shows the active high configuration's R_{load} circuit element substituted with an *LED* and limiting resistor *R*. Since there is no current limiting provided by the GPIO port, resistor *R* must be provided to do this.

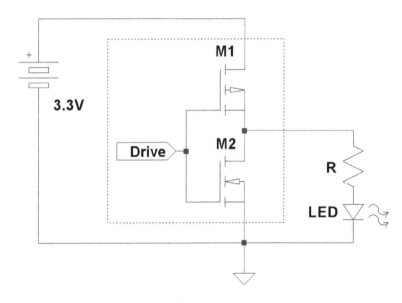

Figure 12-6. *GPIO driving an LED*

Driving LEDs

When an LED is hooked up to the GPIO output port, R_{load} becomes the LED and *the limiting resistor* (in series). The math is complicated slightly by the fact that the LED is a diode. As a diode, it has a voltage drop, which should be subtracted from the supply voltage. For red LEDs, the voltage drop is usually between 1.63 and 2.03 V.[30]

Knowing the current draw you want for the LED, the resistor R can be calculated from the following:

$$R = \frac{V_{CC} - V_{LED}}{I_{LED}}$$

where

V_{CC} is the supply voltage (+3.3 V).

V_{LED} is the voltage drop for the LED.

I_{LED} is the required current draw for the LED.

For V_{LED} it is best to assume the worst case and assume the lower voltage drop of 1.63 V. Assuming we need 8 mA to get reasonable brightness from the LED, we can calculate the resistance of the limiting resistor:

$$R = \frac{3.3 - 1.63}{0.008}$$
$$= 208.75\Omega$$

Since resistors come in standard values, we round up to a standard 10% component of 220 Ω.

■ **Note**   Rounding resistance down would lead to higher current. It is better to err on the side of less current.

The LED and the 220 Ω limiting resistor can be wired according to Figure 12-4 (and shown in Figure 12-6). When wired this way, a high is written to the GPIO output port to make current flow through the LED.

The sense of the GPIO port can be altered by the sysfs file active_low (see Table 12-5 later in this chapter). Putting the GPIO pin 7 into active low mode reverses the logic sense, as follows:

```
# echo 1  >/sys/class/gpio/gpio7/active_low
```

With this mode in effect, writing a 1 to GPIO pin 7 causes the pin to go "low" on the output and causes the LED to go off:

```
# echo 1  >/sys/class/gpio/gpio7/value
```

If the LED was wired according to Figure 12-5, it would turn on instead.

Driving Logic Interfaces

For LEDs, the requirements of the interface are rather simple. The interface is a success if the LED is lit when the output port is in one state, and the LED is dark in the other. The precise voltage appearing at the GPIO output pin in these two states is of little concern, as long as the maximum current limits are respected.

When interfacing to logic, the output *voltage* is critical. For the receiving logic, the output level must be at least V_{IH} to reliably register a 1 bit (for the BCM2835, this is 1.3 V). Likewise, the output should present less than V_{IL} to reliably register a 0 in the receiver (for the BCM2835, this is 0.8V). Any voltage level between these limits is *ambiguous* and can cause the receiver to randomly see a 0 or a 1.

There are a fairly large number of approaches to interfacing between different logic families. A good source of information is provided by the document "Microchip 3V Tips 'n Tricks."[31]

Another document titled "Interfacing 3V and 5V Applications, AN240" describes the issues and challenges of interfacing between systems.[32] It describes, for example, how a 5 V system can end up raising the 3 V supply voltage if precautions are not taken.

Approaches to interfacing include direct connections (when safe), voltage-dividing resistors, diode resistor networks, and the more-complex op-amp comparators.

When choosing an approach, remember to consider the necessary switching speed of the interface required.

Driving Bi-color LEDs

This is a good point to inject a note about driving bi-color LEDs. Some of these are configured so that one LED is forward biased while the other is reversed biased. This has the advantage of needing only the usual two LED leads. To change colors, you simply change the polarity of the power going into the pair.

To drive these and choose a color, you need a way to reverse the current. This is normally done using the H-Bridge driver, which is explored in Chapter 28. There a bipolar stepper motor is driven by the H-Bridge driver. The LED, however, requires considerably less current, and so this is an easy assignment. If you choose a bi-color LED requiring 10 mA or less, you can drive it directly from a pair of GPIO outputs.

Figure 12-7 illustrates the bi-color LED driving arrangement. Compare this configuration with the H-Bridge in Chapter 28's Figure 28-1. Do you see the similarity?

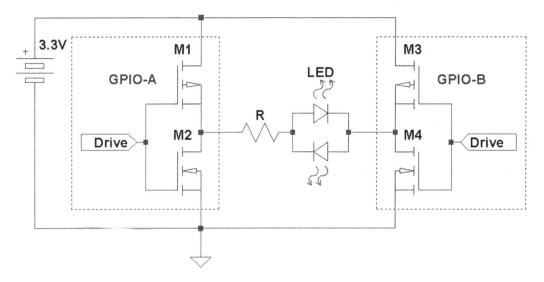

Figure 12-7. *Driving a bi-colored LED*

The pair of GPIO outputs form an H-Bridge because each of the outputs themselves are a pair of CMOS driving transistors—an upper and lower half. It is this pairing that makes them capable of both sourcing and sinking a current. By using two GPIO outputs, you form an H-Bridge driver.

To light the bi-color LED in one color, make one GPIO high (source), while the other is made low (sink). Then the current will flow through the LED from the first GPIO output into the second. To reverse the current and see the other color, make the first GPIO low and the other high. Now the current flows from the second GPIO output into the first.

Testing Drive Strength

There's nothing like finding out for yourself the configured parameters of your Raspberry Pi. The program pads.c (next) dumps out the GPIO Pads Control registers so that you can verify the actual parameters in effect.

Each GPIO pin defaults to setting 3 (for 8 mA).[28] Running the pads.c program on my Rev 2.0 Raspberry Pi showed that the GPIO group from 28 to 45 was configured for *16 mA*. GPIO pins 28 to 31 are available on header P5.

The following example session shows the output for my Raspberry Pi:

```
$ sudo ./pads
07E1002C  :    0000001B  1  1  3
07E10030  :    0000001F  1  1  7
07E10034  :    0000001B  1  1  3
```

The last four fields on each output line are as follows:

1. The word value in hexadecimal
2. The configured slew rate setting
3. The configured hysteresis setting
4. The drive-level code

What this suggests is that GPIO 28 through 31 could be used, if you have higher current driving requirements.

If you have a requirement to change these settings from within a C program, the program pads.c can be easily modified. Use the macro GETPAD32 (line 16) for inspiration.

```
1   /*********************************************************************
2    * pads . c : Examine GPIO Pads Control
3    *********************************************************************/
4   #include <stdio.h>
5   #include <stdlib.h>
6   #include <fcntl.h>
7   #include <sys/mman.h>
8   #include <unistd.h>
9
10  #define BCM2708_PERI_BASE 0 x20000000
11  #define PADS_GPIO_BASE (BCM2708_PERI_BASE + 0 x100000 )
12  #define PADS_GPIO_00_27 0x002C
13  #define PADS_GPIO_28_45 0x0030
14  #define PADS_GPIO_46_53 0x0034
15
16  #define GETPAD32(offset)  ( *(unsigned *) ((char *) (pads)+offset))
17
18  #define BLOCK_SIZE  (4*1024)
19
20  volatile unsigned *pads ;
21
22  void
23  initialize(void) {
24      int mem_fd = open("/dev/mem",O_RDWR|O_SYNC);
25      char *pads_map;
26
```

```
27        if ( mem_fd <= 0 )  {
28            perror("Opening/dev/mem");
29            exit(1);
30        }
31
32        pads_map = (char *)mmap(
33            NULL,              /*Any address */
34            BLOCK_SIZE,        /*Map length */
35            PROT_READ|PROT_WRITE,
36            MAP_SHARED,
37            mem_fd,            /*File to map */
38            PADS_GPIO_BASE  /*Offset to registers */
39        );
40
41        if  ( (long)pads_map == -1L )  {
42            perror("mmap failed.");
43            exit(1);
44        }
45
46        close(mem_fd);
47        pads = (volatile unsigned *)pads_map;
48  }
49
50  int
51  main(int argc,char **argv) {
52       int x;
53       union {
54           struct {
55               unsigned    drive : 3;
56               unsigned    hyst  : 1;
57               unsigned    slew : 1;
58               unsigned    reserved : 13;
59               unsigned    passwrd  : 8;
60           } s;
61           unsigned  w;
62        } word;
63
64       initialize();
65
66       for ( x=PADS_GPIO_00_27; x<=PADS_GPIO_46_53; x += 4 ) {
67           word.w = GETPAD32(x) ;
68           printf("%08X : %08X %x %x %x\n" ,
69               x+0x7E10000, word.w,
70               word.s.slew, word.s. hyst, word.s.drive) ;
71       }
72
73       return 0;
74  }
75
76  /*End */
```

GPIO Current Budget

Gert van Loo states that "the Raspberry-Pi 3V3 supply was designed with a maximum current of ~3 mA per GPIO pin."[29] He correctly concludes that if "you load each pin with 16 mA, the total current is 272 mA."

From this, we can calculate the designed current budget for GPIO pins:

1. Gert is referring to 17 GPIO pins ($\frac{272mA}{16mA} = 17$)
2. The Pi is designed for $17 \times 3\ mA = 51mA$

This is consistent with the 50 mA capacity figure we arrived at in Chapter 4. This is the remaining current capacity available from pins P1-01, P1-17, and P5-02.

Consequently, when budgeting your 3.3 V supply current, factor in the following:

> *GPIO*: Current used for each GPIO *output* pin assigned (2 mA to 16 mA)

> *+3.3 V*: All current going to circuits powered from P1-01, P1-17, and P5-02.

> *MAX232CSE*: If you attached a RS-232 adapter, allow for about 15 mA.

To save on your power budget, configure unused GPIO pins as inputs.

Configuration

Each GPIO pin is affected by several configuration choices:

- General-purpose input, output, or alternate function
- Input event detection method
- Input pull-up/pull-down resistors
- Output drive level

Alternate Function Select

When a GPIO pin is configured, you must choose whether it is an input, an output, or an alternate function (like the UART). The complete list of choices is shown in Table 12-4. The exact nature of what *alternate function x* means depends on the pin being configured.

Table 12-4. *Alternate Function Selection*

Code	Function Selected	ALT
000	GPIO pin is an input.	
001	GPIO pin is an output.	
100	GPIO pin is alternate function 0.	0
101	GPIO pin is alternate function 1.	1
110	GPIO pin is alternate function 2.	2
111	GPIO pin is alternate function 3.	3
011	GPIO pin is alternate function 4.	4
010	GPIO pin is alternate function 5.	5

The values shown in the table's Code column are used in the configuration register itself. The alternate function numbers are listed in the ALT column. Keeping these two straight can be confusing when programming. Once the function has been selected, the configuration is then fine-tuned according to its peripheral type.

Output Pins

When a pin is configured for output, the remaining elements of configuration consist of the following:

- Logic sense
- Output state

The output state of the GPIO pins can either be set by the kernel as a 32-bit word (affects 32 GPIOs at a time) or individually set or cleared. Having individual set/clear operations allows the host to change individual bits without disturbing the state of others (or having to know their state).

Input Pins

Input pins are more complex because of the additional hardware functionality offered. This requires that the input GPIO pin be configured for the following:

- Detect rising input signals (synchronous/asynchronous)
- Detect falling input signals (synchronous/asynchronous)
- Detect high-level signals
- Detect low-level signals
- Logic sense
- Interrupt handling (handled by driver)
- Choose no pull-up; use a pull-up or pull-down resistor

Once these choices have been made, it is possible to receive data related to input signal changes, or simply query the pin's current state.

Alternate Function

When an alternate function such as the UART is chosen, many aspects of the pin's configuration are predetermined. Despite this, each pin used by the peripheral should be preconfigured for input or output according to its function. These details are normally provided by the supporting driver.

Sysfs GPIO Access

In this section, we're going to access the GPIO pins through the /sys pseudo file system. This is the GPIO *driver* interface. Because it provides file system objects, it is possible to control GPIO pins from the command line (or shell).

The C/C++ programmer might be quick to dismiss this approach, because it might seem too slow. However, for input pins, the driver provides the advantage of providing a reasonable edge-level detection that is not possible when accessing the GPIO registers directly. The driver is able to receive interrupts when a GPIO state changes. This information can in turn be passed onto the application program using poll(2) or select(2).

Everything that you need for GPIO access is rooted in the top-level directory:

/sys/class/gpio

At this directory level, two main control pseudo files are maintained by the driver. These are write-only:

export: Requests the kernel to export control of the requested GPIO pin by writing its number to the file

unexport: Relinquishes control of the GPIO pin by writing its number to the file

---

■ **Note** Even root gets the permission denied if you try to read these files.

Normally, the kernel manages the GPIO pins, especially if they are used for resources that need them (like the UART). In order for an application to manipulate a GPIO pin, it must first request that the kernel relinquish control of the requested pin. From a userspace perspective, the operation is like opening a file. The script or program should be prepared for failure in the event that a GPIO pin is busy.

CORRECT USE OF SUDO

It is tempting to perform some operations from a nonroot account, using sudo like this:

```
$ sudo echo 17 >/sys/class/gpio/export
-bash: /sys/class/gpio/export: Permission denied
```

This does not work because the I/O redirection is performed by the shell *before* the sudo command begins. Change to interactive mode first and then the operation will succeed:

```
$ sudo -i
# echo 17 >/sys/class/gpio/export
```

export

The export pseudo file allows you to request a GPIO pin from the kernel. For example, if you want to manipulate GPIO pin 17, you request it from the kernel by writing its pin number to the pseudo file:

```
$  sudo -i
#  echo 17  >/sys/class/gpio/export
```

After a successful run, list the directory /sys/class/gpio:

```
#  ls
export  gpio17  gpiochip0  unexport
#
```

A new subdirectory (a symlink to a directory, actually) named gpio17 appears. This tells you that the kernel has given up control of GPIO 17 and has provided you this file system object to manipulate. At this point, you can consider the GPIO 17 as available.

unexport

Some applications may require a GPIO pin for only a short time. When the application is finished with the pin, the application can release the pin back to the kernel. This is done by writing to the unexport pseudo file:

```
$  sudo  -i
#  echo  17  >/sys/class/gpio/unexport
```

After this command completes, the pseudo object gpio17 disappears from the /sys/class/gpio directory. This confirms that the GPIO is now being managed by the driver and makes it impossible for userspace programs to mess with it (except for direct register access).

gpioX

Once you have a file system object like /sys/class/gpio/gpio17 to work with, you can configure it and perform I/O. The main objects that you'll see are outlined in Table 12-5. The ones normally used by shell programs are simply as follows:

> direction: To set the I/O direction
>
> value: To read or write the I/O bit
>
> active_low: To alter the sense of logic

Table 12-5. */sys/class/gpio/gpioX Objects*

Object	Type	R/W	Values	Description
direction	File	R/W	in	Input pin
			out	Output pin
			high	Output & high
			low	Output & low
value	File	R/W	0 or 1	Read or write
edge	File	R/W	None	No edge
			Rising	Rising edge
			Falling	Falling edge
			Both	Rising or falling
active_low	File	R/W	0	Normal sense
			1	Active low
uevent	File			
subsystem	Symlink			Symlink to self
power	Directory	R		

The values used for direction are worth expanding on:

Value	Description
in	GPIO becomes an input port.
out	GPIO becomes an output port (with some prior state).
high	GPIO becomes output, but in a 1 state (high).
low	GPIO becomes output, but in a 0 state (low).

The high and low options look like convenience frills, but they're not. Consider configuring an output and setting it to 1:

```
# echo out >/sys/class/gpio/gpio7/direction
# echo 1 >/sys/class/gpio/gpio7/value
```

Some time will pass before the execution of the second command takes place to establish the correct output level. If the GPIO output state was previously left in a zero state, the GPIO 7 pin will reflect a 0 (low) until the second command completes. For electronic devices operating in nanosecond time frames, this can be a problem.

To provide glitch-free configuration, the following can be done instead:

```
# echo high >/sys/class/gpio/gpio7/direction
```

This way, the driver takes the necessary steps to establish the correct output level prior to making the pin an output.

The settings of the file named edge affect how a C program (for example) would process poll(2) on the file named value (reading). A poll(2) system call could block the execution of the program until the required event occurred (like a rising edge).

Active Low

Sometimes it is desirable to have the logic inverted for the GPIO pin being used. For example, when driving an LED in the circuit configuration of Figure 12-5, a logic low is required to light the LED.

Value	Description
0	Noninverted logic
1	Inverted logic

Inverting the logic allows you to light the LED with a logic 1:

```
# echo 1 >/sys/class/gpio/gpio7/active_low
# echo 1 >/sys/class/gpio/gpio7/value
```

Conversely, if you don't want inverted logic, you should be certain to establish that by writing a 0:

```
# echo 0 >/sys/class/gpio/gpio7/active_low
```

Chip Level

You will also notice the presence of a subdirectory named gpiochipN in /sys/class/gpio, where *N* is a numeric digit. The following main pseudo files exist within that directory:

> base: The value read should be the same value *N*, which is the first GPIO managed by this chip.

> label: The label (for example, bcm2708_gpio) of the chip, which is not necessarily unique. Used for diagnostic purposes.

> ngpio: The value read indicates how many GPIOs this chip manages, starting with the value read from base.

GPIO Tester

If you decided to build yourself a prototype board with the Raspberry Pi mounted on it, you may find this simple shell script useful for checking the wiring of the GPIO breakout clips. Or perhaps you just want to verify that the connection brought out to the breadboard is the correct one. Simply supply the GPIO pin number that you want to blink, on the command line:

```
$ cat ./gp
#!/bin/bash

GPIO="$1"
SYS=/sys/class/gpio
DEV=/sys/class/gpio/gpio$GPIO

if [ ! -d $DEV ] ; then
    # Make pin visible
    echo $GPIO >$SYS/export
fi

# Set pin to output
echo out >$DEV/direction

function put() {
    # Set value of pin (1 or 0)
    echo $1 >$DEV/value
}

while true ; do
    put 1
    echo "GPIO $GPIO: on"
    sleep 1
    put 0
    echo "GPIO $GPIO: off $(date)"
    sleep 1
done

# End
```

To exercise GPIO 25 (GEN6), use this command (project file `scripts/gp`):

```
# ./gp 25
```

When testing with an LED and alligator clip lead, ground yourself to the ground pin first (or better still, a good ground like a water tap). Static electricity can be especially bad in the winter months. It not only can cause your Pi to reset but also can inflict internal damage. After discharging yourself to the ground pin, apply the lead and allow time enough for 1-second-on and 1-second-off events.

▦ **Note** Cats are especially bad for static electricity.

GPIO Input Test

To test out the GPIO input capability, a simple script is presented next (and is available in the `scripts` subdirectory as a file named input). By default, it assumes 0 for the *active low* setting, meaning that normal logic applies to the input values. If, on the other hand, a 1 is used, inverted logic will be applied. Using the script named input, apply one of the following commands to start it (^C to end it):

```
# ./input 0     # Normal "active high" logic
. . .
# ./input 1     # Use active low logic
```

The script, of course, can be modified, but as listed, it reads an input on GPIO 25 (GEN6) and presents what it has read to GPIO 24 (GEN5). It additionally reports what has been read to standard output. If the output (GPIO 24) is wired to an LED, the input status will be visible in the LED (use Figure 12-6 as a guide for wiring).

The script has its limitations, one of which is that the `sleep(1)` command is used. This causes it to have a somewhat sluggish response. If you don't like that, you can comment out the `else` and `sleep` commands. As a consequence, it will hog the CPU, however, but be more responsive.

```
#!/bin/bash

ALO="${1:-0}"   # 1=active low, else 0
INP=25          # Read from GPIO 25 (GEN6)
OUT=24          # Write t o GPIO 24 (GEN5)

set -eu
trap "close_all" 0

function close_all() {
  close $INP
  close $OUT
}
function open() { # pin direction
  dev=$SYS/gpio$1
  if [ ! -d $dev ] ; then
    echo $1 >$SYS/export
  fi
```

```
    echo $2 >$dev/direction
    echo none >$dev/edge
    echo $ALO >$dev/active_low
}
function close() { # pin
  echo $1 >$SYS/unexport
}
function put() { # pin value
  echo $2 >$SYS/gpio$1/value
}
function get() { # pin
  read BIT <$SYS/gpio$1/value
  echo $BIT
}
count=0
SYS=/sys/class/gpio

open $INP in
open $OUT out
put $OUT 1
LBIT=2

while true ; do
  RBIT=$(get $INP)
  if [ $RBIT -ne $LBIT ] ; then
    put $OUT $RBIT
    printf "%04d Status : %d\n" $count $RBIT
    LBIT=$RBIT
    let count=count+1
  else
    sleep 1
  fi
done

# End
```

The following is an example session:

```
# ./input
0000 Status : 0
0001 Status : 1
0002 Status : 0
0003 Status : 1
^C
#
```

When GPIO 25 is grounded, 0 should be read, as reported in line 0000 of the example. If you then apply a high (for example, from the +3.3 V supply), a 1 should be reported.

Floating Potentials

The beginning student may be puzzled about "glitches" seen by some GPIO inputs (28 or 29). When a GPIO input without a pull-up resistor is unattached, the line can "float," or change over time, due to static electrical buildup. Unless a pull-up or pull-down resistor is attached (or configured), the pin can assume *intermediate* voltages. A voltage in the range of $V_{IL} = 0.8\ V$ to $V_{IH} = 1.3\ V$ is ambiguous to the Pi. Input voltages in this range may read randomly as 1s or 0s.

■ **Caution**   If you are using a loose wire or alligator clip to apply high or low signals to an input GPIO pin, be very careful to avoid static electricity, which can cause damage. Use a ground strap or hold onto the Pi's ground to bleed any static away, while changing connections. Static electricity may also cause your Raspberry Pi to reset. A real ground, like a water tap, is best for bleeding off static.

When using a button or switch, for example, use a pull-up resistor to +3.3 V (or configure the SoC to use one). In this manner, high is immediately seen by the input when the switch or button is temporarily unconnected.

■ **Note**   A switch is temporarily disconnected while changing its poles.

Reading Events

One of the shortcomings of the input script is that it must poll the input pin's value continuously, to see if the value has changed. In a multiprocessing environment like Linux, it is rude to burn the CPU like this (hence the compromise with the sleep command). A better design would have the program wait for a change on the input pin, allowing other processes to use the CPU while it waits.

The GPIO driver within the kernel is, in fact, able to do that, though not usable by shell commands. The C program evinput.c is an example program that takes advantage of this capability and is presented next. It uses the poll(2) system call to accomplish this. The basic procedure used is this:

1.   The GPIO pin X is configured for input.

2.   The value of /sys/class/gpio/gpioX/edge has been configured for the edge(s) to be reported (see Table 12-5).

3.   When querying the input pin, the open file descriptor for /sys/class/gpio/gpioX/value is provided to the poll(2) call (line 111).

4.   The time-out is specified as –1 in argument 3, so poll(2) will wait forever, if necessary.

5.   When there is new data for the GPIO input, poll(2) returns and rc will be greater than zero, breaking out of the loop.

6.   The program must rewind to the beginning of the pseudo file with lseek(2) (line 118).

7.   Finally, the text is read from the value file in line 119.

Step 6 can be omitted if you only need notification. However, to read the correct data, a rewind to the start of the pseudo file is required.

The program shown also checks whether the signal handler was called. If it sees that variable is_signaled has been set, the routine gpio_poll() returns –1 to indicate to the caller that a program exit is needed (lines 112 to 113).

Test Run

A test was performed using a GPIO output pin (27) wired to the input pin (17). In one session, GPIO output pin 27 was changed from 0 to 1 and back. The events were captured in the other session, running ./evinput.

■ **Note** If the reader compiles the programs using the included makefile for each program, the programs are automatically built to use setuid root. Doing this allows them to run with root privileges, without needing to use the sudo command.

The following is a session output obtained from the ./evinput run. The output pauses after reporting the first line (line 4). Following that, new lines appear whenever the input pins change state.

```
1  $ ./evinput 17
2  Monitoring for GPIO input changes:
3
4  GPIO 17 changed: 0
5  GPIO 17 changed: 1
6  GPIO 17 changed: 0
7  GPIO 17 changed: 1
8  ^C
9  $
```

Input GPIO pin 17 was changed from this separate session, using output GPIO 27 (recall that it is wired to GPIO 17 for this test):

```
1  # cd /sys/class/gpio
2  # echo 27 >export
3  # ls
4  export gpio27 gpiochip0 unexport
5  # cd gpio27
6  # ls
7  active_low direction edge power subsystem uevent value
8  # echo out >direction
9  # echo 0 >value
10 ## s t a r t e d . / evinput 17 he r e . . .
11 # echo 1 >value
12 # echo 0 >value
13 # echo 1 >value
```

From the sessions shown, GPIO 17 was set low in the preceding line 9. After that, the ./evinput program was started and the first line is reported (line 4 in the evinput session). As the input pin changed state in lines 11+ (in the preceding code), the input events were being reported in lines 5+ (evinput session).

Checking the system with the top command, you'll see that ./evinput does not consume CPU. Yet the program is indeed responsive to the input change events. This leaves the CPU for all of your other processes that you may need to run.

```
1    / **********************************************************************
2     *  evinput.c : Event driven GPIO input
3     *
4     *  ./evinput gpio#
5     **********************************************************************/
6
7    #include <stdio.h>
8    #include <stdlib.h>
9    #include <fcntl.h>
10   #include <unistd.h>
11   #include <string.h>
12   #include <errno.h>
13   #include <signal.h>
14   #include <assert.h>
15   #include <sys/poll.h>
16
17   static int gpio_inpin = -1;          / * GPIO input pin */
18   static int is_signaled = 0;          / * Exit program if signaled */
19
20   typedef enum {
21           gp_export=0,                 / * /sys/class/gpio/export */
22           gp_unexport,                 / * /sys/class/gpio/unexport */
23           gp_direction,                / * /sys/class/gpio%d/direction */
24           gp_edge,                     / * /sys/class/gpio%d/edge */
25           gp_value                     / * /sys/class/gpio%d/value */
26   } gpio_path_t;
27
28   /*
29    * Internal : Create a pathname for type in buf.
30    * /
31   static const char *
32   gpio_setpath(int pin, gpio_path_t type, char * buf, unsigned bufsiz) {
33           static const char * paths[] = {
34                   "export", "unexport", "gpio%d/direction",
35                   "gpio%d/edge", "gpio%d/value"};
36           int slen;
37
38           strncpy (buf, "/sys/class/gpio/", bufsiz);
39           bufsiz -= (slen = strlen(buf));
40           snprintf(buf+slen, bufsiz, paths[type], pin);
41           return buf;
42   }
43
44   /*
45    * Open /sys/class/gpio%d/value for edge detection :
46    */
47   static int
```

```
48   gpio_open_edge(int pin, const char * edge)  {
49            char buf [128];
50            FILE *f;
51            int fd;
52
53            /*Export pin : /sys/class/gpio/export */
54            gpio_setpath(pin, gp_export, buf, size of buf);
55            f = fopen(buf, "w");
56            assert(f);
57            fprintf(f,"%d\n", pin);
58            fclose(f);
59
60            /*Direction :  /sys/class/gpio%d/direction */
61            gpio_setpath(pin, gp_direction, buf, size of buf);
62            f = fopen(buf, "w");
63            assert(f);
64            fprintf(f,"in\n");
65            fclose(f);
66
67            /*Edge :  /sys/class/gpio%d/edge */
68            gpio_setpath(pin, gp_edge, buf, size of buf);
69            f = fopen (buf, "w");
70            assert(f);
71            fprintf(f,"% s\n", edge);
72            fclose(f);
73
74            /*Value :  /sys/class/gpio%d/value */
75            gpio_setpath(pin, gp_value, buf, size of buf);
76            fd = open(buf,O_RDWR);
77            return fd;
78   }
79
80   /*
81    *  Close (unexport) GPIO pin :
82    * /
83   static void
84   gpio_close(int pin) {
85            char buf[128];
86            FILE *f;
87
88            / * Unexport :    /sys/class/gpio/unexport */
89            gpio_setpath(pin, gp_unexport, buf, size of buf);
90            f = fopen(buf, "w");
91            assert(f);
92            fprintf(f,"%d\n", pin);
93            fclose(f);
94   }
95
96   /*
97    * This routine will block until the open GPIO pin has changed
98    * value. This pin should be connected to the MCP23017 /INTA
99    * pin.
```

144

```
100 */
101 static int
102 gpio_poll(int fd) {
103         struct pollfd polls;
104         char buf [32];
105         int rc, n;
106
107         polls.fd = fd;                      /* /sys/class/gpio17/value */
108         polls.events = POLLPRI;             /*Exceptions * /
109
110         do      {
111                 rc = poll(&polls, 1, -1);           /*Block */
112                 if ( is_signaled )
113                         return -1;                  /*Exit if ^C received */
114         } while ( rc < 0 && errno == EINTR );
115
116         assert (rc > 0);
117
118         lseek(fd, 0, SEEK_SET);
119         n = read(fd, buf, size of buf) ;    /*Read value */
120         assert(n > 0);
121         buf[n] = 0;
122
123         rc = sscanf(buf,"% d",&n);
124         assert(rc==1);
125         return n;                           /*Return value */
126 }
127
128 /*
129  * Signal handler to quit the program  :
130  * /
131 static void
132 sigint_handler(int signo) {
133         is_signaled = 1;                    /*Signal to exit program */
134 }
135
136 /*
137  * Main program :
138  */
139 int
140 main(int argc, char ** argv)  {
141         int fd, v;
142
143         /*
144          * Get GPIO input pin to use :
145          */
146         if (argc != 2) {
147 usage:  fprintf(stderr, "Usage: %s <gpio_in_pin>\n", argv[0]);
148                 return 1;
149         }
```

```
150            if ( sscanf(argv[1], "%d",&gpio_inpin) != 1 )
151                    goto usage;
152            if ( gpio_inpin < 0 || gpio_inpin >=32 )
153                    goto usage;
154
155            signal (SIGINT, sigint_handler) ;          /*Trap on SIGINT */
156            fd = gpio_open_edge(gpio_inpin, "both");   /*GPIO input */
157
158            puts("Monitoring for GPIO input changes: \n");
159
160            while ( (v = gpio_poll (fd)) >=0 ) {        /*Block until input changes */
161                    printf("GPIO %d changed: %d\n", gpio_inpin, v);
162            } while ( !is_signaled );                   /*Quit if ^C' d */
163
164            putchar('\n');
165            close(fd);                                  /*Close gpio%d/value */
166            gpio_close(gpio_inpin);                     /*Unexport gpio * /
167            return 0;
168 }
169
170 / *  End event.c * /
```

Direct Register Access

It is possible to access the GPIO registers directly. The module gpio_io.c shows the code that can be used for this. It requires the program to invoke gpio_init() upon startup, which then makes the registers available. The code as presented is intended to be #included into the module using it. (Normally, it would be compiled as a separate module.) The API made available is outlined in the following subsections.

These routines are used in several examples and projects within this book, including the following:

> pullup: Change the pull-up register setting.

> bipolar: Drive a bipolar stepper motor (Chapter 28).

> rtscts: Change the ALT function (Chapter 11).

> valt: View ALT function settings (subdir valt in source code).

> unipolar: Drive a unipolar stepper motor (Chapter 27).

> dht11: Humidity and temperature sensor (Chapter 22).

> pwm: Pulse width modulation (Chapter 30).

gpio_init( )

This function call opens access to the GPIO registers. This will require root privileges, which is why many programs in this book were compiled with setuid root. The operation of this routine is to gain access to the physical memory space, so that the GPIO registers can be accessed. This procedure is covered in the "Memory Mapping" section of Chapter 6.

```
void gpio_init(void);
```

gpio_config( )

This function call allows the caller to configure a pin as input or output:

```
typedef enum {
    Input = 0,        /*GPIO is an Input */
    Output            /*GPIO is an Output */
} direction_t;

void gpio_config(int gpio,direction_t output);
```

> The arguments are as follows:
>
> > gpio: The GPIO pin to be configured
> >
> > output: The value Input or Output

gpio_write( )

This function permits the caller to set the output GPIO pin to a 1 or a 0.

```
void gpio_write(int gpio,int bit);
```

> The arguments are as follows:
>
> > gpio: The GPIO pin to write to
> >
> > bit: The value of the output bit (1 or 0)
>
> Only the least significant bit of argument bit is used.

gpio_read( )

This function reads the requested GPIO pin and returns the bit (0 or 1).

```
int gpio_read(int gpio);
```

> The single argument gpio is used to specify the GPIO pin to be read.

gpio_io.c

The following pages show the program listing for gpio_io.c:

```
1   /*****************************************************************
2    * gpio_io.c :     GPIO Access Code
3    *****************************************************************/
4
5   #define BCM2708_PERI_BASE           0x20000000
6   #define GPIO_BASE                   (BCM2708_PERI_BASE + 0x200000)
7   #define BLOCK_SIZE (4*1024)
8
```

```
9    /*GPIO setup macros. Always use INP_GPIO (x) before using OUT_GPIO(x)
10      or SET_GPIO_ALT(x, y )  */
11   #define INP_GPIO (g) *(ugpio + ((g)/10)) &= ~(7 <<(((g) % 10)*3))
12   #define OUT_GPIO(g) *(ugpio + ((g)/10)) |=  (1 <<(((g) % 10)*3))
13   #define SET_GPIO_ALT(g,a)  \
14      *(ugpio + (((g)/10))) |= (((a) <=3?(a) + 4 : (a)==4?3:2)<<(((g)%10)*3))
15
16   #define GPIO_SET *(ugpio+7)   /* sets bits   */
17   #define  GPIO_CLR *(ugpio+10) /* clears  bits   */
18   #define  GPIO_GET *(ugpio+13) /* gets  all  GPIO input levels  */
19
20   typedef enum {
21      Input = 0,              /*GPIO is an Input*/
22      Output                 /*GPIO is an Output*/
23   } direction_t;
24
25   static volatile unsigned *ugpio;
26
27   /*********************************************************************
28    * Perform initialization to access GPIO registers:
29    * Sets up pointer ugpio.
30    *********************************************************************/
31   static void
32   gpio_init() {
33      int fd;
34      char *map;
35
36      fd = open("/dev/mem",O_RDWR|O_SYNC);     /*Needs root access */
37      if ( fd < 0 ) {
38          perror("Opening/dev/mem");
39          exit(1);
40      }
41
42      map = (char * ) mmap(
43          NULL,                  /*Any address */
44          BLOCK_SIZE,            /* # of bytes */
45          PROT_READ| PROT_WRITE,
46          MAP_SHARED,            /*Shared */
47          fd,                    /* /dev/mem */
48          GPIO_BASE              /*Offset to GPIO */
49      ) ;
50
51      if ( (long)map == 1L ) {
52          perror("mmap(/dev/mem)");
53          exit(1);
54      }
55
56      close(fd);
57      ugpio = (volatile unsigned *)map;
58   }
59
```

```
60   /*******************************************************************
61    * Configure GPIO as Input or Output
62    *******************************************************************/
63   static inline void
64   gpio_config (int gpio, direction_t output) {
65       INP_GPIO (gpio);
66       if ( output ) {
67           OUT_GPIO(gpio);
68       }
69   }
70
71   /*******************************************************************
72    * Write a bit to the GPIO pin
73    *******************************************************************/
74   static inline void
75   gpio_write(int gpio, int bit) {
76       unsigned sel = 1  << gpio;
77
78       if ( bit ) {
79           GPIO_SET = sel;
80       } else  {
81           GPIO_CLR = sel;
82       }
83   }
84
85   /*******************************************************************
86    * Read a bit from a GPIO pin
87    *******************************************************************/
88   static inline int
89   gpio_read(int gpio)  {
90       unsigned sel = 1 << gpio;
91
92       return (GPIO_GET) & sel ? 1 : 0 ;
93   }
94
95   / * End gpio_io.c */
```

GPIO Transistor Driver

The GPIO pins on the Pi are often going to be pressed into driving something in the outside world. GPIO pins 28 to 31 can drive up to 16 mA, maximum. The remaining GPIO pins are configured to drive up to 8 mA. These are fairly weak interfaces to the outside world.

Sometimes all that is needed is a simple one-transistor buffer. The 2N2222A transistor is cheap and drives a fair amount of current. Figure 12-8 shows a simple driver circuit attached to a GPIO output pin.

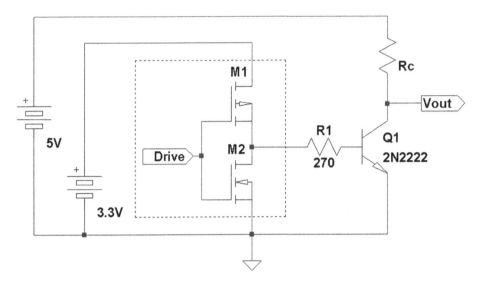

Figure 12-8. *2N2222A driver*

The GPIO output driver sees only a diode-like path to ground through the base of transistor Q_1. Resistor R_1 is chosen to limit that current.

The resistor shown as R_c in the figure represents the load, like a high-current LED in series with a current-limiting resistor. Alternatively, it may be a resistor chosen so that the V_{out} represents a stiffer output voltage.

In the diagram, the resistor R_c is connected to the +5 V power supply. This is safe because current *cannot* flow from the collector into the base of Q_1. This prevents 5 V from flowing into the GPIO pin (that junction is *reversed* biased). Thus Q_1 allows you to convert the 3.3 V GPIO output into a 5 V TTL signal, for example. The 2N2222A transistor has an absolute maximum V_{CE} of 30 V. This allows you to drive even higher voltage loads, provided that you stay within the transistor's current and power ratings.

Driver Design

The transistor driver circuit is limited by the power-handling capability of Q_1 and the maximum collector current. Looking at the datasheet, the maximum power listed for Q_1 is 0.5 W at 25ºC. When the transistor is turned on (saturated), the voltage across Q_1 (V_{CE}) is between 0.3 V and 1 V (see $V_{CE(sat)}$ in the datasheet). The remainder of the voltage is developed across the load. If we assume the worst case of 1 V for V_{CE} (leaving 4 V across the load), we can compute the maximum current for I_C:

$$I_C = \frac{P_{Q1}}{V_{CE}}$$

$$= \frac{1}{0.3}$$

$$= 3.3A$$

Clearly, this calculated current exceeds the listed absolute maximum current I_C of 600 mA. So we use the maximum current for I_C = 600 mA instead. For safety, we use the minimum of these maximum ratings. While this transistor is clearly capable of driving up to 600 mA of current, let's design our driver for a modest current flow of 100 mA.

The next thing to check is the H_{FE} of the part. The parameter value required is the *lowest* H_{FE} value for the amount of collector current flowing (H_{FE} drops with increasing I_C current). A STMicroelectronics datasheet shows its 2N2222A part as having an $H_{FE} = 40$, $I_C = 500\ mA$, with $V_{CE} = 10\ V$. They also have a more favorable H_{FE} value of 100, for 150 mA, but it is best to err on the side of safety. We can probably assume a safe compromise of $H_{FE} = 50$.

The H_{FE} parameter is important because it affects how much current is required to drive Q_1's base. The input base current is calculated as follows:

$$I_B = \frac{I_C}{H_{FE}}$$

$$= \frac{100mA}{50}$$

$$= 2mA$$

This value tells us that the GPIO pin will need to supply up to 2 mA of drive into Q_1's base. With 2 mA of drive, Q_1 will be able to conduct up to 100 mA in the collector circuit. A current of 2 mA is easily accommodated by any GPIO pin. Note that if you were to design closer to the design limits of this transistor (500 mA in this example), you should probably allow an additional 10% of base current "overdrive" to make certain that the transistor goes into saturation.

Current flow into the base of Q_1 creates a voltage drop of $V_{BE} = 0.7\ V$, from the input base lead to ground. So to calculate the resistor value R_1 we take the V_{R1} divided by the current. The highest voltage coming from GPIO is going to be slightly less than the 3.3 V power supply rail. It is safe to assume that $GPIO_{HIGH} = 3\ V$. The voltage appearing across R_1 is thus $GPIO_{HIGH}-V_{BE}$.

$$R_1 = \frac{GPIO_{HIGH} - V_{BE}}{I_B}$$

$$= \frac{3 - 0.7}{0.002}$$

$$= 1,150\Omega$$

The nearest 10% standard resistor value is $R_1 = 1.2\ k\Omega$. Using this resistor value as a check, let's compute backward what our actual drive capability is from Q_1. First we need to recompute I_B now that we know R_1:

$$I_B = \frac{GPIO_{HIGH} - V_{BE}}{R_1}$$

$$= \frac{3 - 0.7}{1200}$$

$$= 1.9mA$$

This tells us that the GPIO output pin will not have to source more than 1.9 mA of current, using $R_1 = 1.2\ k\Omega$. Now let's calculate the maximum drive we can reliably expect in the collector circuit of Q_1:

$$I_C = I_B \times H_{FE}$$

$$= 0.0019 \times 50$$

$$= 95mA$$

■ **Note** This discussion glibly avoids the effects of components being within ±10% tolerance.

This computes that the designed 2N2222A driver circuit is capable of driving up to 95 mA.

To obtain even more performance out of that driver (if you need it), you could choose a resistor closer to the actual value desired (1150 Ω). It turns out that a 1% resistor can be had at exactly 1.15 $k\Omega$:

$$I_C = I_B \times H_{FE}$$
$$= 0.002 \times 50$$
$$= 100mA$$

Be careful that your design does not stress the transistor beyond its maximum ratings (power and current). You might be willing to risk the cheap transistor, but keep in mind that the poor little thing might be holding back a higher voltage (like a river dam). If the transistor is destroyed, the high voltage may come crashing into the base circuit and cause damage to the Pi's GPIO pin. So be nice to Q_1!

Substitution

You don't have to use my choice of the 2N2222A transistor for driving a load. Substitute what you have or what you plan to order. Today's DMMs can measure the transistor H_{FE}, so that makes planning easier when using junk box parts.

Another critical factor in selecting a part is the power capability of the transistor. You should probably know exactly what that limit is, unless you are driving an extremely light load. Finally, it is important to know what the maximum voltage ratings are for the selected transistor, if you plan to drive voltages higher than 3 V. You need to be able to count on it holding back those higher voltages in the collector circuit to prevent damage to the Pi.

Inductive Loads

Inductive loads like relays and motors present a special problem. They generate a high reverse voltage when current is switched off or interrupted. When the relay coil is turned off, the magnetic field collapses around the coil of wire. This induces a high voltage, which can damage the Pi (and can also provide a mild electric shock).

Electric motors exhibit a similar problem. As the DC current sparks and stutters at the commutator inside the motor, high reverse voltage spikes are sent back into the driving circuit. This is due to the magnetic field collapsing around the motor windings.

Consequently, inductive loads need a reverse-biased diode across the load to short out any induced currents. The diode conducts only when the back electromotive force (EMF) is generated by the inductive load.

Figure 12-9 shows diode D_1 reverse biased across the relay coil winding L_1 (or motor). The diode bleeds away any reverse current that might be generated. Use a diode with sufficient current-carrying capability (matching at least the current in Q_1).

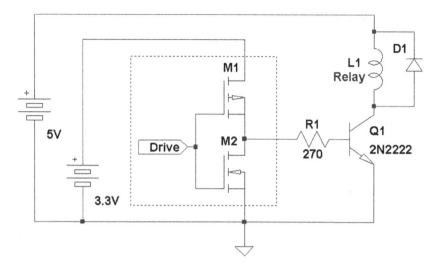

Figure 12-9. *Driver for inductive load*

Since there is no current-limiting resistor used in series with L_1, whether motor or relay, make sure that no more current than I_{Cmax} will flow. For relays, you need a coil resistance greater than or equal to 50 Ω, when driven from approximately 5 V. Otherwise, you risk burning out driver Q_1 (assuming the 2N2222A with its power limit of 0.5 watts at 5 V). You can drive lower resistance coils, if you designed your driver to handle the additional current. For example, a 500 mA driver can handle coil resistances as low as 10 ohms (at 5 V).

The 2N2222A transistor is probably suitable for only the smallest of electric motors. Depending on how it is used, a motor can stall and thus greatly increase its current demands. Motors also have high startup currents. If the motor is started and stopped frequently, the driving transistor may be overworked.

Driver Summary

This section on the transistor driver should not be thought of as your only choice in driver solutions. It was presented because it is simple and cheap and can fill the need for many small loads, like high-current LEDs or panel lightbulbs. Simple and cheap may be essential for robot building when many drivers are required.

While students may use the Gertboard for labs, we still need to provide a substitute when the Raspberry Pi is integrated into something that was built (like a robot). It might be wise to stock up on a few good transistor types for this purpose.

Utility gpio

For this book, I have avoided using instances of "magic package X." However, the `wiringPi` project is popular enough that no chapter on GPIO would be complete without mentioning it. The `wiringPi` project provides a handy utility for displaying and changing GPIO functionality. The package can be downloaded from here:

```
https://projects.drogon.net/raspberry-pi/wiringpi/download-and-install
```

This page lists instructions for obtaining, compiling, and installing the package. Once installed, the gpio command is available:

```
$ gpio -h
gpio : Usage : gpio -v
       gpio -h
       gpio [-g ] <read/write /wb/pwm/ clock/mode> ...
       gpio [-p ] <read/write /wb> ...
       gpio readall
       gpio unexportall/exports ...
       gpio export/edge/unexport ...
       gpio drive <group> <value>
       gpio pwm-bal/pwm-ms
       gpio pwmr <range>
       gpio pwmc <divider>
       gpio load spi / i2c
       gpio gbr <channel>
       gpio gbw <channel> <value>
```

There are many options and functions within this utility. I'll just demonstrate some quick examples of the most useful ones. Once installed, the full details of the utility can be found by this command:

```
$ man 1 gpio
```

Displaying GPIO Settings

The following command can be used to display your GPIO settings:

```
$ gpio readall
```

wiringPi	GPIO	Name	Mode	Value
0	17	GPIO 0	IN	High
1	18	GPIO 1	IN	Low
2	27	GPIO 2	OUT	Low
3	22	GPIO 3	IN	Low
4	23	GPIO 4	IN	Low
5	24	GPIO 5	IN	Low
6	25	GPIO 6	IN	Low
7	4	GPIO 7	IN	Low
8	2	SDA	ALT0	High
9	3	SCL	ALT0	High
10	8	CE0	IN	Low
11	7	CE1	IN	Low
12	10	MOSI	IN	Low
13	9	MISO	IN	Low
14	11	SCLK	IN	Low
15	14	TxD	ALT0	High
16	15	RxD	ALT0	High

```
|    17    |   28   |  GPIO8  |  IN  |  Low |
|    18    |   29   |  GPIO9  |  IN  |  Low |
|    19    |   30   |  GPIO10 |  IN  |  Low |
|    20    |   31   |  GPIO11 |  IN  |  Low |
+----------+--------+---------+------+------+
```

Reading GPIO

As a convenience, the gpio command allows you to read values from the command line:

```
$ gpio export 27 in
$ gpio -g read 27
0
$ gpio unexportall
```

Use the -g option to specify that the pin number is a GPIO pin number. (I found the need for the -g option irksome.)

Writing GPIO

Like the read function, the gpio command can write values:

```
$ gpio export 27 out
$ gpio -g write 27 1
$ gpio -g read 27
1
$ gpio -g write 27 0
$ gpio -g read 27
0
$ gpio unexportall
```

Use the -g option to specify GPIO pin numbers for the read/write commands.

Modify Drive Levels

The gpio command also enables you to alter the drive levels of the three available pads. The following changes pad 1 to drive level 6 (from 7):

```
$ gpio drive 1 6
```

Use the pads program shown earlier in this chapter to verify the current settings:

```
$ gpio drive 1 6
$ ./pads
07E1002C : 0000001B 1 1 3
07E10030 : 0000001E 1 1 6
07E10034 : 0000001B 1 1 3
```

This kind of change should not be made lightly. If you don't have a sound reason to change these drive levels, it is recommended that you don't.

CHAPTER 13

■ ■ ■

1-Wire Driver

The 1-Wire protocol was developed by Dallas Semiconductor Corp. initially for the iButton.[37] This communication protocol was attractive enough to be applied to other devices and soon adopted by other manufacturers. This chapter provides an overview of the 1-Wire protocol and how it is supported in the Raspberry Pi.

1-Wire Line and Power

The 1-Wire protocol actually uses two wires:

- *Data*: The single wire used for data communication

- *Ground*: The ground or "return" wire

The 1-Wire protocol was designed for communication with low–data content devices like temperature sensors. It provides for low-cost remote sensing by supplying power over the same wire used for data communications. Each sensor can accept power from the data line while the data line is in the high state (which is also the line's idle state). The small amount of power that is siphoned off charges the chip's internal capacitor (usually about 800 pF).[37]

When the data line is active (going low), the sensor chips continue to run off of their internal capacitors (in parasitic mode). Data communications cause the data line to fluctuate between low and high. So whenever the line level returns high again, even for an instant, the capacitor recharges.

The device also provides an optional V_{DD} pin, allowing power to be supplied to it directly. This is sometimes used when parasitic mode doesn't work well enough. This, of course, requires an added wire, which adds to the cost of the circuit. We'll be focusing on the parasitic mode in this chapter. In parasitic mode, V_{DD} is connected to the ground.

Line Driving

The data line is driven by *open collector* transistors in the master and slave devices. The line is held high by a *pull-up* resistor when the driver transistors are all in the Off state. To initiate a signal, one transistor turns on and thus pulls the line down to ground potential.

Figure 13-1 shows a simplified schematic of the master attached to the bus. Some voltage V (typically, +5 V) is applied to the 1-Wire bus through the pull-up resistor R_{pullup}. When the transistor M_2 is in the Off state, the voltage on the bus remains high because of the pull-up resistor. However, when the master device activates transistor M_2, current is caused to flow from the bus to the ground, acting like a signal short-circuit. Slave devices attached to the bus will see a voltage near zero.

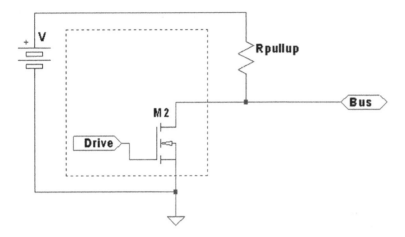

Figure 13-1. *1-Wire driver circuit*

■ **Note**   The Raspbian Linux 1-Wire bus uses GPIO 4 (GPCLK0) pin P1-07.

Likewise, when a slave is signaled to respond, the master listens to the bus while the slave activates its driving transistor. Whenever all driving transistors are off, the bus returns to the high idle state.

The master can request that all slave devices reset. After the master has made this request known, it relinquishes the bus and allows it to return to the high state. All slave devices that are connected to the bus respond by bringing the line low after a short pause. Multiple slaves will bring the line low at the same time, but this is permitted. This informs the master that at least one slave device is attached to the bus. Additionally, this procedure puts all slaves into a known reset state.

Master and Slave

The master device is always in control of the 1-Wire bus. Slaves speak only to the master, and only when requested. There is never slave-to-slave device communication.

If the master finds that communication becomes difficult for some reason, it may force a bus reset. This corrects for an errant slave device that might be jabbering on the line.

Protocol

This section presents a simplistic introduction to the 1-Wire communication protocol. Knowing something about how the signaling works is not only interesting, but may be helpful for troubleshooting. More information is available on the Internet.[38]

Reset

Figure 13-2 provides a simplified timing diagram of the reset procedure for the 1-Wire protocol. When the master driver begins, it must reset the 1-Wire bus to put all the slave devices into a known state.

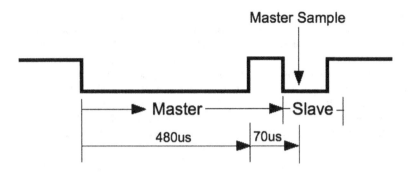

Figure 13-2. *1-Wire reset protocol*

For reset, the bus is brought low and held there for approximately 480 μsec. Then the bus is released, and the pull-up resistor brings it high again. After a short time, slave devices connected to the bus start responding by bringing the line low and holding it for a time. Several slaves can participate in this at the same time. The master samples the bus at around 70 μsec after it releases the bus. If it finds the line low, it knows that there is at least one slave connected and responding.

Soon after the master sampling point, all slaves release the bus again and go into a listening state. They do not respond again until the master specifically addresses a slave device. For simplicity, we'll omit the discovery protocol used.

■ **Note**   Each slave has a guaranteed unique address.

Data I/O

The data protocol is shown in Figure 13-3. Whether writing a 0 or 1 bit, the sending device brings the bus line low. This announces the start of a data bit.

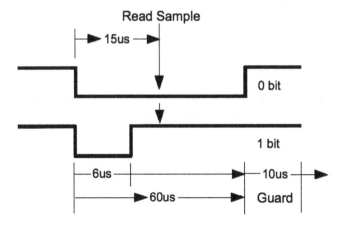

Figure 13-3. *1-Wire read/write of 1 data bit*

When a 0 is being transmitted, the line is held low for approximately 60 μsec. Then the bus is released and allowed to return high. When a 1 bit is being transmitted, the line is held low for only about 6 μsec before releasing the bus. Another data bit is not begun until 70 μsec after the start of the previous bit. This leaves a guard time of 10 μsec between bits. The receiver then has ample time to process the bit and gains some signal noise immunity.

The receiver notices a data bit is coming when the line drops low. It then starts a timer and samples the bus at approximately 15 μsec. If the bus is still in the low state, a 0 data bit is registered. Otherwise, the data bit is interpreted as a 1. Having registered a data bit, the receiver then waits further until the line returns high (in the case of a 0 bit). The receiver remains idle until it notices the line going low again, announcing the start of the next bit.

The sender can be either the master or the slave, but the master always has control. Slaves do not write data to the bus unless the master has specifically requested it.

Slave Support

Table 13-1 lists the slave devices that are supported by Raspbian Linux. The module names listed are found in the kernel source directory arch/arm/machbcm2708/slave.

Table 13-1. *1-Wire Slave Driver Support*

Device	Module	Description
DS18S20	w1_therm.c	Precision digital thermometer
DS18B20		Programmable resolution thermometer
DS1822		Econo digital thermometer
DS28EA00		9- to 12-bit digital thermometer with PIO
bq27000	w1_bq27000.c	Highly accurate battery monitor
DS2408	w1_ds2408.c	Eight-channel addressable switch
DS2423	w1_ds2423.c	4 KB RAM with counter
DS2431	w1_ds2431.c	1 KB EEPROM
DS2433	w1_ds2433.c	4 KB EEPROM
DS2760	w1_ds2760.c	Precision Li+ battery monitor
DS2780	w1_ds2780.c	Stand-alone fuel gauge

Reading Temperature

The support for the usual temperature sensors is found in the kernel module w1_therm. When you first boot your Raspbian Linux, that module may not be loaded. You can check for it with the lsmod command:

```
$ lsmod
Module          Size    Used by
snd_bcm2835     12808   1
snd_pcm         74834   1 snd_bcm2835
snd_seq         52536   0
snd_timer       19698   2 snd_seq, snd_pcm
snd_seq_device  6300    1 snd_seq
snd             52489   7 snd_seq_device, snd_timer,
                          snd_seq, snd_pcm, snd_bcm2835
snd_page_alloc  4951    1 snd_pcm
```

The module w1_therm is not loaded according to the example. This module also depends on the driver module wire. Another thing you can check is the pseudo file system:

```
$ ls -l /sys/bus/w1
ls: cannot access /sys/bus/w1 : No such file or directory
```

Having not found the pathname /sys/bus/w1, we have confirmation that the device driver is not loaded. Loading module w1_therm will bring in most of its module dependents:

```
$ sudo modprobe w1_therm
$ lsmod
Module              Size    Used by
w1_therm            2705    0
wire                23530   1 w1_therm
cn                  4649    1 wire
snd_bcm2835         12808   1
snd_pcm             74834   1 snd_bcm2835
...
```

After the wire module is loaded, you'll see the /sys/bus/w1/devices directory. One more module is needed:

```
$ sudo modprobe w1_gpio
$ lsmod
Module              Size    Used by
w1_gpio             1283    0
w1_therm            2705    0
wire                23530   2 w1_therm,w1_gpio
cn                  4649    1 wire
snd_bcm2835         12808   1
...
$ cd /sys/bus/w1/devices
$ ls
w1_bus_master1
```

Once module w1_gpio is loaded, there is a bus master driver for GPIO pin 4 (the default GPIO for the 1-Wire bus) at the ready. The bus master makes its presence known by creating directory w1_bus_master1. Change to that directory and list it to see the associated pseudo files within it. Table 13-2 lists the initial set of pseudo files and symlinks found there.

Table 13-2. *w1_bus_masterX Files*

File	Type	Read Content
driver	Symlink	
power	Directory	
subsystem	Symlink	
uevent	File	DRIVER=w1_master_driver
w1_master_add	File	Write device ID xx-xxxxxxxxxxxx to add slave
w1_master_attempts	File	88
w1_master_max_slave_count	File	10
_master_name	File	w1_bus_master1
w1_master_pointer	File	0xd7032148
w1_master_pullup	File	1
w1_master_remove	File	Write device ID xx-xxxxxxxxxxxx to remove slave
w1_master_search	File	–1
w1_master_slave_count	File	0
w1_master_slaves	File	Not found
w1_master_timeout	File	10

Bus Master

The bus master driver scans for new slave devices every 10 seconds (according to w1_master_timeout). File w1_master_attempts indicates how many scans have been performed to date. File w1_master_slave_count shows how many slaves have been detected out of a maximum of w1_master_max_slave_count. Reading w1_master_slaves provides a list of slaves found or not found.

The following is an example output session produced while two DS18B20 temperature sensors were connected to the bus:

```
$ cd /sys/bus/w1/devices/w1_bus_master1
$ cat w1_master_slaves
28-00000478d75e
28-0000047931b5
$
```

Slave Devices

Figure 13-4 shows the pinout of the Dallas DS18B20 slave device. This temperature sensor is typical of many 1-wire slave devices.

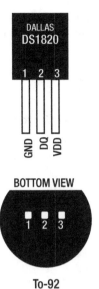

PIN DESCRIPTION

GND - Ground
DQ - Data In/Out
V_{DD} - Power Supply Voltage

Figure 13-4. *DS18B20 pin-out*

Slave devices are identified by a pair of digits representing the product family, followed by a hyphen and serial number in hexadecimal. The ID 28-00000478d75e is an example. You might also want to try different devices, like the similar DS18S20. Figure 13-5 illustrates the DS18B20 attached to the Raspberry Pi.

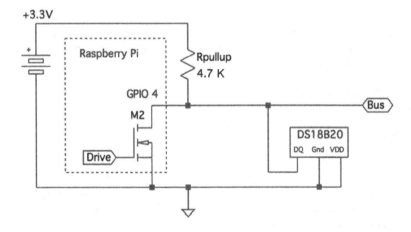

Figure 13-5. *1-Wire with DS18B20 slave circuit*

When things are working correctly, the bus master detects slave devices automatically as part of its periodic scan. If the device you've attached is not showing up within 10 seconds or so, you may want to try forcing it. You can force adding a slave device entry as follows:

```
# cd /sys/bus/w1/devices/w1_bus_master1
# echo 28-0000028f6667 >w1_master_add
```

Upon doing this, subdirectory 28-0000028f6667 will appear, at least until the driver gives up trying to communicate with it (the following line with the ellipsis is abbreviated):

```
# ls -ltr  ./28-0000028f6667
total 0
-rw-r--r--  1  root  root  4096  Jan  30  18:56  uevent
lrwxrwxrwx  1  root  root     0  Jan  30  18:56  subsystem -> ../../../bus/w1
-r--r--r--  1  root  root  4096  Jan  30  18:56  w1_slave
Drwxr-xr-x  2  root  root     0  Jan  30  18:56  powerr
-r--r--r--  1  root  root  4096  Jan  30  18:56  name
-r--r--r--  1  root  root  4096  Jan  30  18:56  id
lrwxrwxrwx  1  root  root     0  Jan  30  18:56  driver -> .../w1_slave_driver
```

If you want to remove a slave device, you can use the w1_master_remove file. The device will reappear in 10 seconds or so (due to a scanning period), if the device is still physically connected to the bus.

```
# echo  28-0000028f6667 >w1_master_remove
```

The following example shows how two DS18B20 temperature sensors show up on the 1-Wire bus:

```
$ cd /sys/bus/w1/devices
$ ls
28-00000478d75e 28-0000047931b5 w1_bus_master1
$
```

Reading the Temperature

The slave device's temperature can be read by reading its w1_slave pseudo file. In this example, we read two DS18B20 temperature sensors that are supposed to be accurate to ±0.5 °C. Reading these two sensors together should show fairly good agreement (they were in close proximity of each other):

```
$ cat 28-00000478d75e/w1_slave 28-0000047931b5/w1_slave
14 01 4b 46 7f ff 0c 10 b4 : crc=b4 YES
14 01 4b 46 7f ff 0c 10 b4 t=17250
14 01 4b 46 7f ff 0c 10 b4 : crc=b4 YES
14 01 4b 46 7f ff 0c 10 b4 t=17250
$
```

Each sensor brings back two lines of data from the device driver. We see that both sensors agree exactly—that the temperature is 17.250°C. This speaks well for their accuracy. The DS18B20 device also supports a wide temperature range (-55°C to +125°C), which make them good as outdoor sensors.

If the read hangs at this point, it may be that the sensor hasn't fully registered yet. This can happen if you forced adding it, but the driver was unable to communicate with it.

1-Wire GPIO Pin

Raspbian Linux has its driver support for the 1-Wire bus on GPIO 4 (P1-07). This pin is hard-coded in the kernel driver. If you want to change this, look for the definition of W1_GPIO in the source file:

arch/arm/mach-bcm2708/bcm2708.c

Change the definition of W1_GPIO to the pin you require (found near line 73):

```
// use GPIO 4 for the one-wire GPIO pin, if enabled
#define W1_GPIO 4
```

Then, of course, you'll need to rebuild and install the new kernel.

CHAPTER 14

■ ■ ■

I2C Bus

The I2C bus, also known as the two-wire interface (TWI), was developed by Philips circa 1982 to allow communication with lower-speed peripherals.[49] It was also economical because it required only two wires (excluding ground and power connections). Since then, other standards have been devised, building upon this framework, such as the SMBus. However, the original I2C bus remains popular as a simple, cost-effective way to connect peripherals.

I2C Overview

Figure 14-1 shows the I2C bus in the Raspberry Pi context. The Raspberry Pi provides the I2C bus using the BCM2835 as the bus master. Notice that the Pi also provides the external pull-up resistors R_1 and R_2, shown inside the dotted lines.

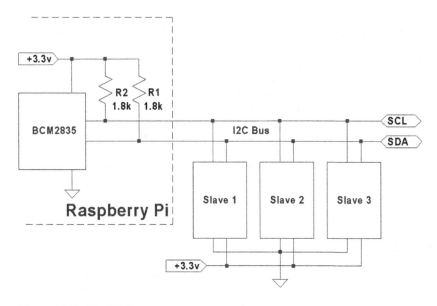

Figure 14-1. *The I2C bus*

The two I2C bus lines are provided on the header strip P1:

P1	Rev	1.0		Rev	2.0 +	
	GPIO	I2C	Bus	GPIO	I2C	Bus
P1-03	0	SDA0	I2C-0	2	SDA1	I2C-1
P1-05	1	SCL0		3	SCL1	

Note that the original Raspberry Pi provided I2C bus 0, but switched to using bus 1 with Rev 2.0 and later units.

The design of the I2C bus is such that multiple peripherals are attached to the SDA and the SCL lines. Each slave (peripheral) has its own unique 7-bit address. For example, the MCP23017 GPIO extender peripheral might be configured with the address of 0x20. Each peripheral is called upon by the master by using this address. All nonaddressed peripherals are expected to remain quiet so that communication can proceed with the selected slave device.

SDA and SCL

The two bus lines used for I2C are as follows:

Line	P1	Idle	Description
SDA	P1-03	High	Serial data line
SCL	P1-05	High	Serial clock line

Both masters and slaves take turns at "grabbing the bus" at various times. Master and slave use open-drain transistors to drive the bus. It is because all participants are using open-drain drivers that pull-up resistors must be used (provided by the Pi). Otherwise, the data and clock lines would float between handoffs.

The open-drain driver design allows all participants to drive the bus lines—just not at the same time. Slaves, for example, turn off their line drivers, allowing the master to drive the signal lines. The slaves just listen, until the master calls them by address. When the slave is required to answer, the slave will then assert its driver, thus grabbing the line. It is assumed by the slave that the master has already released the bus at this point. When the slave completes its own transmission, it releases the bus, allowing the master to resume.

The idle state for both lines is high. The high state for the Raspberry Pi is +3.3 V. Other systems may use +5 V signaling. When shopping for I2C peripherals, you'll want to choose ones that will operate at the 3 V level. Otherwise, 5 V peripherals can sometimes be used with careful planning or with use of signal adapters. The DS1307 Real-Time clock project is one such a case that is covered in Chapter 25.

Multimaster and Arbitration

The I2C protocol does support the idea of multiple masters. This complicates things, because two masters may grab the bus and transmit at the same time. When this happens, a process of arbitration is used to resolve the clash.

Each transmitting master simultaneously monitors what it sees on the bus that it is driving. If a discrepancy is seen between what it is transmitting and what it is sensing on the bus line, it knows that it must release the bus and cease. The first node to notice conflict is required to release the bus. The other that has not noticed any discrepancy is free to continue its transmission, since its message has not been affected. If it too sees a problem, it will also cease and retry later.

Not all devices support this arbitration. Ones that do are usually advertised as having *multimaster support*. Multimaster arbitration is not covered in this book, since this is an advanced I2C topic.

Bus Signaling

The start and stop bits are special in the I2C protocol. The start bit is illustrated in Figure 14-2. Notice the SDA line transition from high to low, while the clock remains in the high (idle) state. The clock will follow by going low after 1/2 bit time following the SDA transition. This special signal combination informs all connected devices to "listen up," since the next piece of information transmitted will be the device address.

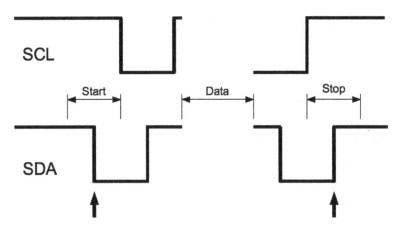

Figure 14-2. *I2C start/stop signaling*

The stop bit is also special in that it allows slave devices to know whether more information is coming. When the SDA line transitions from low to high midway through a bit cell, it is interpreted as a *stop bit*. The stop bit signals the end of the message.

There is also the concept of a *repeated start*, often labeled in diagrams as *SR*. This signal is electrically identical to the start bit, except that it occurs within a message in place of a stop bit. This signals to the peripheral that more data is being sent or required as part of another message.

Data Bits

Data bit timings are approximately as shown in Figure 14-3. The SDA line is expected to stabilize high or low according to the data bit being sent, prior to the SCL line going high. The receiver clocks in the data on the falling edge of SCL, and the process repeats for the next data bit. Note that most significant bits are transmitted first.

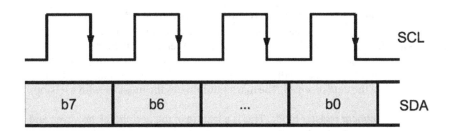

Figure 14-3. *I2C Data bit transmission*

Message Formats

Figure 14-4 displays two example I2C messages that can be used with the MCP23017 chip (Chapter 23). The simplest message is the write register request.

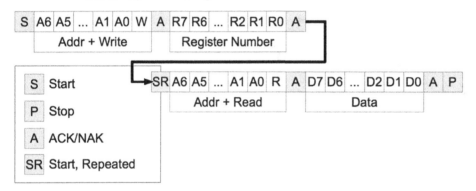

Figure 14-4. *Example I2C messages*

The diagram shows each message starting with the S (start) bit and ending with a P (stop) bit. After the start bit, each message begins with a byte containing the 7-bit peripheral address and a read/write bit. Every peripheral must read this byte in order to determine whether the message is addressed to it.

The addressed peripheral is expected to return an ACK/NAK bit after the address is sent. If the peripheral fails to respond for any reason, the line will go high due to the pull-up resistor, indicating a NAK. The master, upon seeing a NAK, will send a stop bit and terminate the transmission.

When the peripheral ACKs the address byte, the master then continues to write when the request is a write. The first example shows the MCP23017 8-bit register number being written next. This indicates which of the peripheral's registers is to be written to. The peripheral will then ACK the register number, allowing the master to follow with the data byte to be written into the selected register. This too must be ACKed. If the master has no more data to send, the P (stop) bit is sent to end the transmission. Otherwise, more data bytes could follow with the sequence ending with the stop bit.

The second example in Figure 14-4 shows how a message may be composed of both write and read messages. The initial sequence looks like the write, but this only writes a register number into the peripheral. Once the register number is ACKed, the master then sends an SR (start, repeated) bit. This tells the peripheral that no more write data is coming and to expect a peripheral address next. Since the address transmitted specifies the same peripheral, the same peripheral responds with an ACK. This request is a read, so the peripheral continues to respond with 8 bits of the requested read data, with the master ACKing the data received. The master terminates the message with a P (stop) to indicate that no more data is to be read.

Many peripherals will support an *auto-increment* register mode. This is a feature of the peripheral, however, and not all devices support this. Once a peripheral's register has been established by a write, successive reads or writes can occur in auto-increment mode, with the register being incremented with each byte transferred. This results in more-efficient transfers.

Which I2C Bus?

Before we look at the I2C software API provided by Raspbian Linux, you should first determine which I2C bus you'll be working with. Early Raspberry Pi revisions provided I2C bus 0 on header strip P1, while later units changed this to bus 1. This will matter to both commands and programs communicating with I2C peripherals.

The "Identification" section of Chapter 7 discusses how to identify your Pi by displaying the firmware code from /proc/cpuinfo. What is displayed as a Revision is actually more of a firmware code. The following is a quick check example:

```
$ grep Revision /proc/cpuinfo
Revision        : 000f
```

From this information, use the firmware code (revision) number to determine which I2C bus to use:

Revision	I2C Bus	SDA	SCL
		P1-03	P1-05
0002	0	GPIO-0	GPIO-1
0003	0		
0004+	1	GPIO-2	GPIO-3

I2C Bus Speed

Unlike the SPI bus, the I2C bus operates at a fixed speed within Raspbian Linux. The SoC document claims I2C operation up to 400 kHz, but the reported clock rate during the Raspbian Linux boot is 100 kHz:

```
$ dmesg | grep -i i2c
[1005.08] i2c /dev entries driver
[1026.43] bcm2708_i2c bcm2708_i2c.0: BSC0 Controller at. . . (baudrate 100k)
[1026.43] bcm2708_i2c bcm2708_i2c.1: BSC1 Controller at . . .(baudrate 100k)
```

Don't be alarmed if the preceding grep command doesn't provide any output. Later versions of Raspbian didn't load bcm2708_i2c at boot time. You should see the same messages in the /var/log/syslog after you manually load the module as shown here:

```
$ sudo modprobe i2c_bcm2708
$ tail /var/log/syslog
. . .
Mar 12 20:16:55 raspberrypi kernel: [168.845802] bcm2708_i2c bcm2708_i2c.0: \
  BSC0 Controller at 0x20205000 (irq 79) (baudrate 100k)
Mar 12 20:16:55 raspberrypi kernel: [168.846423] bcm2708_i2c bcm2708_i2c.1: \
  BSC1 Controller at 0  x20804000 (irq 79) (baudrate 100k)
```

Tools

Working with I2C peripherals is made easier with the use of utilities. These I2C utilities are easily installed using the following command:

```
$ sudo apt-get install i2c-tools
```

The i2c-tools package includes the following utilities:

i2cdetect: Detects peripherals on the I2C line

i2cdump: Dumps values from an I2C peripheral

i2cset: Sets I2C registers and values

i2cget: Gets I2C registers and values

Each of these utilities has a man page available for additional information. We'll be using some of these commands in this chapter and in later parts of this book.

I2C API

In this section, we'll look at the bare-metal C language API for the I2C bus transactions. An application using this API is provided in Chapter 23's "MCP23017 GPIO Extender" section.

Kernel Module Support

Access to the I2C bus is provided through the use of kernel modules. If lsmod indicates that the drivers are not loaded, you can load them at the command line:

```
$ sudo modprobe i2c-dev
$ sudo modprobe i2c-bcm2708
```

Once these modules are loaded, i2cdetect should be able to see bus-level support. On Revision 2.0 and later Raspberry Pis, the i2c-0 bus is for internal use. The user bus is shown as i2c-1. On early Pis this is reversed.

```
$ i2cdetect -l
i2c-0    unknown        bcm2708_i2c.0        N/A
i2c-1    unknown        bcm2708_i2c.1        N/A
```

After the driver support is available, the device nodes should appear under /dev:

```
$ ls -l /dev/i2c*
crw-rw---T 1 root root 89, 0 Feb 18 23:53  /dev/i2c-0
crw-rw---T 1 root root 89, 1 Feb 18 23:53  /dev/i2c-1
```

Header Files

The following header files should be included in an I2C program:

```
#include <sys/ioctl.h>
#include <linux/i2c-dev.h>
```

open(2)

Working with I2C devices is much like working with files. You'll open a file descriptor, do some I/O operations with it, and then close it. The one difference is that you'll want to use ioctl(2) calls instead of the usual read(2)/write(2) calls.

```
#include <sys/types.h>
#include <sys/stat.h>
#include <fcntl.h>

int open(const char *pathname, int flags, mode_t mode);
```

where

> pathname is the name of the file/directory/driver that you need to open/create.
>
> flags is the list of optional flags (use O_RDWR for reading and writing).
>
> mode is the permission bits to create a file (omit argument, or supply zero when not creating).
>
> returns -1 (error code in errno) or open file descriptor >=0 .

Error	Description
EACCES	Access to the file is not allowed.
EFAULT	The pathname points outside your accessible address space.
EMFILE	The process already has the maximum number of files open.
ENFILE	The system limit on the total number of open files has been reached.
ENOMEM	Insufficient kernel memory was available.

To work with an I2C bus controller, your application must open the driver, made available at the device node:

```
int fd;

fd = open("/dev/i2c-1",O_RDWR);
if ( fd < 0 ) {
    perror("Opening /dev/i2c-1");
```

Note that the device node (/dev/i2c-1) is owned by root, so you'll need elevated privileges to open it or have your program use setuid(2).

ioctl(2,I2C_FUNC)

In I2C code, a check is normally performed to make sure that the driver has the right support. The I2C_FUNC ioctl(2) call allows the calling program to query the I2C capabilities. The capability flags returned are documented in Table 14-1.

```
long funcs;
int rc;

rc = ioctl(fd,I2C_FUNCS,&funcs);
if ( rc < 0 ) {
    perror("ioctl(2,I2C_FUNCS)");
    abort();
}

/* Check that we have plain I2C support */
assert(funcs & I2C_FUNC_I2C);
```

Table 14-1. I2C_FUNC bits

Bit Mask	Description
I2C_FUNC_I2C	Plain I2C is supported (non SMBus)
I2C_FUNC_10BIT_ADDR	Supports 10-bit addresses
I2C_FUNC_PROTOCOL_MANGLING	*Supports:*
	I2C_M_IGNORE_NAK
	I2C_M_REV_DIR_ADDR
	I2C_M_NOSTART
	I2C_M_NO_RD_ACK

The assert() macro used here checks that at least plain I2C support exists. Otherwise, the program aborts.

ioctl(2,I2C_RDWR)

While it is possible to use ioctl(2,I2C_SLAVE) and then use read(2) and write(2) calls, this tends not to be practical. Consequently, the use of the ioctl(2,I2C_RDWR) system call will be promoted here instead. This system call allows considerable flexibility in carrying out complex I2C I/O transactions.

The general API for any ioctl(2) call is as follows:

```
#include <sys/ioctl.h>

int ioctl(int fd, int request, argp);
```

where

> fd is the open file descriptor.

> request is the I/O command to perform.

> argp is an argument related to the command (type varies according to request).

> returns -1 (error code in errno), number of msgs completed (when request = I2C_RDWR).

Error	Description
EBADF	fd is not a valid descriptor.
EFAULT	argp references an inaccessible memory area.
EINVAL	request or argp is not valid.

When the request argument is provided as I2C_RDWR, the argp argument is a pointer to struct i2c_rdwr_ioctl_data. This structure points to a list of messages and indicates how many of them are involved.

```
struct i2c_rdwr_ioctl_data {
    struct i2c_msg   *msgs;      /* ptr to array of simple messages */
    int              nmsgs;      /* number of messages to exchange */
};
```

The individual I/O messages referenced by the preceding structure are described by struct i2c_msg:

```
struct i2c_msg {
    __u16         addr;    /* 7/10 bit slave address */
    __u16         flags;   /* Read/Write & options */
    __u16         len;     /* No. of bytes in buf */
    __u8          *buf;    /* Data buffer */
};
```

The members of this structure are as follows:

addr: Normally this is the 7-bit slave address, unless flag I2C_M_TEN and function I2C_FUNC_10BIT_ADDR are used. Must be provided for each message.

flags: Valid flags are listed in Table 14-2. Flag I2C_M_RD indicates the operation is a read. Otherwise, a write operation is assumed when this flag is absent.

buf: The I/O buffer to use for reading/writing this message component.

len: The number of bytes to read/write in this message component.

Table 14-2. *I2C Capability Flags*

Flag	Description
I2C_M_TEN	10-bit slave address used
I2C_M_RD	Read into buffer
I2C_M_NOSTART	Suppress (Re)Start bit
I2C_M_REV_DIR_ADDR	Invert R/W bit
I2C_M_IGNORE_NAK	Treat NAK as ACK
I2C_M_NO_RD_ACK	Read will not have ACK
I2C_M_RECV_LEN	Buffer can hold 32 additional bytes

An actual ioctl(2,I2C_RDWR) call would be coded something like the following. In this example, a MCP23017 *register* address of 0x15 is being written out to peripheral address 0x20, followed by a read of 1 byte:

```
int fd;
struct i2c_rdwr_ioctl_data msgset;
struct i2c_msg iomsgs[2];
static unsigned char reg_addr[] = {0x15};
unsigned char rbuf[1];
int rc;

iomsgs[0].addr   = 0x20;            /* MCP23017-A */
iomsgs[0].flags  = 0;               /* Write operation. */
iomsgs[0].buf    = reg_addr;
iomsgs[0].len    = 1;
```

```
iomsgs[1].addr   = iomsgs[0].addr;   /* Same MCP23017-A */
iomsgs[1].flags  = I2C_M_RD;         /* Read operation */
iomsgs[1].buf    = rbuf;
iomsgs[1].len    = 1;

msgset.msgs      = iomsgs;
msgset.nmsgs     = 2;

rc = ioctl(fd,I2C_RDWR,&msgset);
if ( rc < 0 ) {
    perror("ioctl (2, I2C_RDWR)");
```

The example shown defines iomsgs[0] as a write of 1 byte, containing a register number. The entry iomsgs[1] describes a read of 1 byte from the peripheral. These two messages are performed in one ioctl(2) transaction. The flags member of iomsgs[x] determines whether the operation is a read (I2C_M_RD) or a write (0).

■ **Note**   Don't confuse the peripheral's internal register with the peripheral's I2C address.

Each of the iomsgs[x].addr members must contain a valid I2C peripheral address. Each message can potentially address a different peripheral, though there are no examples of this in this book. The ioctl(2) will return an error with the first message failure. For this reason, you may not always want to combine multiple messages in one ioctl(2) call, especially when different devices are involved.

The returned value, when successful, is the number of struct i2c_msg messages successfully performed.

CHAPTER 15

SPI Bus

The Serial Peripheral Interface bus, known affectionately as *spy*, is a synchronous serial interface that was named by Motorola.[39] The SPI protocol operates in full-duplex mode, allowing it to send and receive data simultaneously. Generally speaking, SPI has a speed advantage over the I2C protocol but requires more connections.

SPI Basics

Devices on the SPI bus communicate on a master/slave basis. Multiple slaves coexist on a given SPI bus, with each slave being selected for communication by a slave select signal (also known as chip select). Figure 15-1 shows the Raspberry Pi as the master communicating with a slave. Additional slaves would be connected as shown with the exception that a different slave select signal would be used.

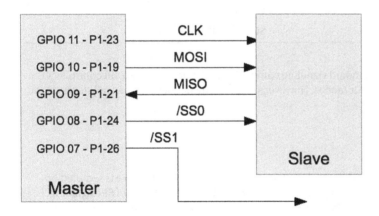

Figure 15-1. *SPI interface*

Data is transmitted from the master to the slave by using the MOSI line (master out, slave in). As each bit is being sent out by the master, the slave sends data bits on the MISO line (master in, slave out). Bits are shifted out of the master and into the slave. Simultaneously, bits are shifted out of the slave and into the master. Both transfers occur to the beat of the system clock (CLK).

Many SPI devices support only 8-bit transfers, while others are more flexible. The SPI bus is a de facto standard, meaning that there is no standard for data transfer width and SPI mode.[39] The SPI controller can also be configured to transmit the most significant or the least significant bit first. All of this flexibility can result in confusion.

SPI Mode

SPI operates in one of four possible clock signaling modes, based on two parameters:

Parameter	Description
CPOL	Clock polarity
CPHA	Clock phase

Each parameter has two possibilities, resulting in four possible SPI modes of operation. Table 15-1 lists all four modes available. Note that a given mode is often referred to by using a pair of numbers like *1,0* or simply as mode *2* (for the same mode, as shown in the table). Both types of references are shown in the Mode column.

Table 15-1. *SPI Modes*

CPOL	CPHA	Mode		Description
0	0	0,0	0	Noninverted clock, sampled on rising edge
0	1	0,1	1	Noninverted clock, sampled on falling edge
1	0	1,0	2	Inverted clock, sampled on rising edge
1	1	1,1	3	Inverted clock, sampled on falling edge
		Clock Sense		**Description**
		Noninverted		Signal is idle low, active high
		Inverted		Signal is idle high, active low

Peripheral manufacturers did not define a standard signaling convention in the beginning, so SPI controllers allow configuration to accommodate any of the four modes. However, once a mode has been chosen, all slaves on the same bus must agree.

Signaling

The clock polarity determines the idle clock level, while the phase determines whether the data line is sampled on the rising or falling clock signal. Figure 15-2 shows mode 0,0, which is perhaps the preferred form of SPI signaling. In Figure 15-2, the slave is selected first, by bringing the $\overline{SS}$ (slave select) active. Only one slave can be selected at a time, since there must be only one slave driving the MISO line. Shortly after the slave is selected, the master drives the MOSI line, and the slave simultaneously drives the MISO line with the first data bit. This can be the most or least significant bit, depending on how the controller is configured. The diagram shows the least significant bit first.

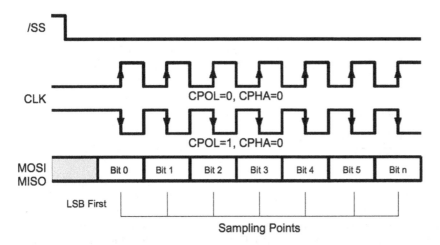

Figure 15-2. *SPI signaling, modes 0 and 2*

In mode 0,0 the first bit is clocked into the master and slave when the clock line falls from high to low. This clock transition is positioned midway in the data bit cell. The remaining bits are successively clocked into master and slave simultaneously as the clock transitions from high to low. The transmission ends when the master deactivates the slave select line. When the clock polarity is reversed (CPOL = 1, CPHA = 0), the clock signal shown in Figure 15-2 is simply inverted. The data is clocked at the same time in the data cell, but on the rising edge of the clock instead.

Figure 15-3 shows the clock signals with the phase set to 1 (CPHA = 1). When the clock is noninverted (CPOL = 0), the data is clocked on the rising edge. Note that the clock must transition to its nonidle state one-half clock cycle earlier than when the phase is 0 (CPHA = 0). When the SPI mode is 1,1, the data is clocked in on the falling edge of the clock.

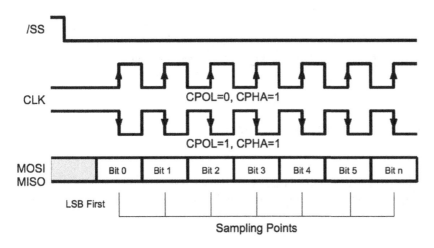

Figure 15-3. *SPI signaling modes 1 and 3*

While the four different modes can be confusing, it is important to realize that the data is sampled at the same times within the data bit cells. The data bit is always sampled at the midpoint of the data cell. When the clock phase is 0 (CPHA = 0), the data is sampled on the trailing edge of the clock, whether falling or rising according to CPOL. When the clock phase is 1 (CPHA = 1), the data is sampled on the leading edge of the clock, whether rising or falling according to CPOL.

Slave Selection

While some protocols address their slaves by using transmitted data, the SPI bus simply uses a dedicated line for each slave. The Raspberry Pi dedicates the GPIO pins listed in Table 15-2 as slave select lines (also known as chip enable lines).

Table 15-2. *Raspberry Pi Built-in Chip Enable Pins*

GPIO	Chip Enable	P1
8	$\overline{CE0}$	P1-24
7	$\overline{CE1}$	P1-26

The Raspbian Linux kernel driver supports the use of only these two chip enable lines. However, the driver is designed such that you don't have to use them, or only these. It is possible, for example, to add a third GPIO pin as a slave select. The application simply takes responsibility for activating the slave select GPIO line prior to the data I/O and deactivates it after. When the driver is controlling the two slave selects, this is done automatically.

Driver Support

Raspbian Linux supports SPI through the spi_bcm2708 kernel module. As a loadable kernel module, it may not be loaded by default. Check for it by using the lsmod command:

```
$ lsmod
Module              Size    Used by
spidev              5136    0
spi_bcm2708         4401    0
...
```

If you would like the module loaded by default after a reboot, edit the /etc/modprobe.d file raspi-blacklist.conf. In the file, look for the line

```
blacklist spi-bcm2708
```

and change that to a comment line, by putting a # character in front, as follows:

```
# blacklist spi-bcm2708
```

With that module un-blacklisted, the module will automatically be loaded with each new reboot.
The kernel module can be manually loaded by using modprobe command:

```
$ sudo modprobe spi_bcm2708
```

This loads the module and its dependents. Once the kernel module support is present, the device driver nodes should appear:

```
$ ls /dev/spi*
/dev/spidev0.0  /dev/spidev0.1
$
```

These two device nodes are named according to which slave select should be activated, as shown in Table 15-3.

Table 15-3. *SPI Device Nodes*

Pathname	Bus	Device	GPIO	$\overline{SS}$
/dev/spidev0.0	0	0	8	$\overline{CE0}$
/dev/spidev0.1	0	1	7	$\overline{CE1}$

If you open either of these device nodes by applying the option SPI_NO_CS, the node chosen makes no difference. Macro SPI_NO_CS indicates that slave select will be performed by the application instead of the driver, if any select is used at all. (When only one slave device is attached, the peripheral can be permanently selected.)

SPI API

The bare-metal API for SPI involves calls to ioctl(2) to configure the interface and further calls to ioctl(2) for simultaneous read and write. The usual read(2) and write(2) system calls can be used, when a one-sided transfer is being performed.

Header Files

The header files needed for SPI programming are as follows:

```
#include <fcntl.h>
#include <unistd.h>
#include <stdint.h>
#include <sys/ioctl.h>
#include <linux/types.h>
#include <linux/spi/spidev.h>
```

The spidev.h include file defines several macros and the struct spi_ioc_transfer. Table 15-4 lists the main macros that are declared. The macros SPI_CPOL and SPI_CPHA are used in the definitions of the values SPI_MODE_x. If you prefer, it is possible to use SPI_CPOL and SPI_CPHA in place of the mode macros.

Table 15-4. *SPI Macro Definitions*

Macro	Supported	Description
SPI_CPOL	Yes	Clock polarity inverted (CPOL = 1)
SPI_CPHA	Yes	Clock phase is 1 (CPHA = 1)
SPI_MODE_0	Yes	SPI Mode 0,0 (CPOL = 0, CPHA = 0)
SPI_MODE_1	Yes	SPI Mode 0,1 (CPOL = 0, CPHA = 1)
SPI_MODE_2	Yes	SPI Mode 1,0 (CPOL = 1, CPHA = 0)
SPI_MODE_3	Yes	SPI Mode 1,1 (CPOL = 1, CPHA = 1)
SPI_CS_HIGH	Yes	Chip select is active high
SPI_LSB_FIRST	No	LSB is transmitted first
SPI_3WIRE	No	Use 3-Wire data I/O mode
SPI_LOOP	No	Loop the MOSI/MISO data line
SPI_NO_CS	Yes	Do not apply Chip Select
SPI_READY	No	Enable extra Ready signal

Communicating with an SPI device consists of the following system calls:

open(2): Opens the SPI device driver node

read(2): Reads with 0 bytes being transmitted

write(2): Writes data while discarding received data

ioctl(2): For configuration and bidirectional I/O

close(2): Closes the SPI device driver node

In SPI communication, the use of read(2) and write(2) is unusual. Normally, ioctl(2) is used to facilitate simultaneous read and write transfers.

Open Device

In order to perform SPI communication through the kernel driver, you need to open one of the device nodes by using open(2). The general format of the device pathname is

```
/dev/spidev<bus>.<device>
```

as we saw earlier. The following is a code snippet opening bus 0, device 0.

```
int fd;

fd = open("/dev/spidev0.0",O_RDWR);
if ( fd < 0 ) {
    perror("Unable to open SPI driver");
    exit(1);
}
```

SPI communication involves both reading and writing, so the driver is opened for read and write (O_RDWR).

SPI Mode Macros

Before SPI communications can be performed, the mode of communication needs to be configured. Table 15-5 lists the C language macros that can be used to configure the SPI mode to be used.

Table 15-5. *SPI Mode Macros*

Macro	Effect	Comments
SPI_CPOL	CPOL = 1	Or use SPI_MODE_x
SPI_CPHA	CPHA = 1	Or use SPI_MODE_x
SPI_CS_HIGH	SS is active high	Unusual
SPI_NO_CS	Don't assert select	Not used/application controlled

These bit values are simply or-ed together to specify the options that are required. The use of SPI_CPOL implies CPOL = 1. Its absence implies CPOL = 0. Similarly, the use of SPI_CPHA implies CPHA = 1 (otherwise, CPHA = 0). The options SPI_MODE_x use the SPI_CPOL and SPI_CPHA macros to define them. You don't need to use them both in your code. The mode definitions are shown here:

```
#define SPI_MODE_0 (0|0)
#define SPI_MODE_1 (0|SPI_CPHA)
#define SPI_MODE_2 (SPI_CPOL|0)
#define SPI_MODE_3 (SPI_CPOL|SPI_CPHA)
```

The unsupported options are not shown, though one or more of these could be supported in the future.

■ **Note** The mode values SPI_LOOP, SPI_LSB_FIRST, SPI_3WIRE, and SPI_READY are not currently supported in the wheezy release of Raspbian Linux.

The following is an example that defines SPI_MODE_0:

```
uint8_t mode = SPI_MODE_0;
int rc;

rc = ioctl(fd,SPI_IOC_WR_MODE,&mode);
if ( rc < 0 ) {
    perror("Can't set SPI write mode.");
```

If you'd like to find out how the SPI driver is currently configured, you can read the SPI mode with ioctl(2) as follows:

```
uint8_t mode;
int rc;

rc = ioctl(fd,SPI_IOC_RD_MODE,&mode);
if ( rc < 0 ) {
    perror("Can't get SPI read mode.");
```

Bits per Word

The SPI driver also needs to know how many bits per I/O word are to be transmitted. While the driver will likely default to 8 bits, it is best not to depend on that. This can be configured with the following ioctl(2) call:

```
uint8_t bits = 8;
int rc;

rc = ioctl(fd, SPI_IOC_WR_BITS_PER_WORD,&bits);
if ( rc < 0 ) {
    perror ("Can't set bits per SPI word.");
```

■ **Note**   The SPI driver in the Raspbian wheezy release supports only 8-bit transfers.

The currently configured value can be fetched with ioctl(2) as follows:

```
uint8_t bits;
int rc;

rc = ioctl(fd,SPI_IOC_RD_BITS_PER_WORD,&bits);
if ( rc == -1 ) {
    perror("Can't get bits per SPI word.");
```

When the number of bits is not an even multiple of eight, the bits are assumed to be right-justified. For example, if the word length is set to 4 bits, the least significant 4 bits are transmitted. The higher-order bits are ignored.

Likewise, when receiving data, the least significant bits contain the data. All of this is academic on the Pi, however, since the driver supports only byte-wide transfers.

Clock Rate

To configure the data transmission rate, you can set the clock rate with ioctl(2) as follows:

```
uint32_t speed = 500000; /* Hz */
int rc;

rc = ioctl(fd,SPI_IOC_WR_MAX_SPEED_HZ,&speed);
if ( rc < 0 ) {
    perror("Can't configure SPI clock rate.");
```

The current configured clock rate can be fetched by using the following ioctl(2) call:

```
uint32_t speed; /* Hz */
int rc;

rc = ioctl(fd,SPI_IOC_RD_MAX_SPEED_HZ,&speed);
if ( rc < 0 ) {
    perror("Can't get SPI clock rate.");
```

Data I/O

SPI communication involves transmitting data while simultaneously receiving data. For this reason, the read(2) and write(2) system calls are usually inappropriate. The ioctl(2) call can, however, perform a simultaneous read and write.

The SPI_IOC_MESSAGE(n) form of the ioctl(2) call uses the following structure as its argument:

```
struct spi_ioc_transfer {
    __u64   tx_buf;         /* Ptr to tx buffer */
    __u64   rx_buf;         /* Ptr to rx buffer */
    __u32   len;            /* # of bytes */
    __u32   speed_hz;       /* Clock rate in Hz */
    __u16   delay_usecs;    /* Delay in microseconds */
    __u8    bits_per_word;  /* Bits per "word" */
    __u8    cs_change;      /* Apply chip select */
    __u32   pad;            /* Reserved */
};
```

The tx_buf and rx_buf structure members are defined as a 64-bit unsigned integers (__u64). For this reason, you must cast your buffer pointers when making assignments to them:

```
uint8_t tx[32], rx[32];
struct spi_ioc_transfer tr;

tr.tx_buf = (unsigned long) tx;
tr.rx_buf = (unsigned long ) rx;
```

On the Raspberry Pi, you will see example code that simply casts the pointers to unsigned long. The compiler automatically promotes these 32-bit values to a 64-bit value. This is safe on the Pi because the pointer value is a 32-bit value.

If you do not wish to receive data (maybe because it is "don't care" data), you can null out the receive buffer:

```
uint8_t tx[32];
struct spi_ioc_transfer tr;

tr.tx_buf = (unsigned long) tx;
tr.rx_buf = 0;                      /* ignore received data */
```

Note that to receive data, the master must always transmit data to shift data out of the slave peripheral. If any byte transmitted will do, you can omit the transmit buffer. Zero bytes will then be automatically transmitted by the driver to shift the slave data out onto the MISO line.

It is also permissible to transmit from the buffer you're receiving into:

```
uint8_t io[32];
struct spi_ioc_transfer tr;

tr.tx_buf = (unsigned long) io;     /* Transmit buffer */
tr.rx_buf = (unsigned long) io;     /* is also recv buffer */
```

The len structure member indicates the number of bytes for the I/O transfer. Receive and transmit buffers (when both used) are expected to transfer the same number of bytes.

The member speed_hz defines the clock rate that you wish to use for this I/O, in Hz. This overrides any value configured in the mode setup, for the duration of the I/O. The value will be automatically rounded down to a supported clock rate when necessary.

When the value speed_hz is 0, the previously configured clock rate is used (SPI_IOC_WR_MAX_SPEED_HZ).

When the delay_usecs member is nonzero, it specifies the number of microseconds to delay between transfers. It is applied at the end of a transfer, rather than at the start. When there are multiple I/O transfers in a single ioctl(2) request, this allows time in between so that the peripheral can process the data.

The bits_per_word member defines how many bits there are in a "word" unit. Often the unit is 1 byte (8 bits), but it need not be (but note that the Raspbian Linux driver supports only 8 bits).

An application might use 9 bits to transmit the 8-bit byte and a parity bit, for example. The bits communicated on the SPI bus are taken from the least significant bits of the buffer bytes. This is true even when transmitting the most significant bit first.

When the bits_per_word value is 0, the previously configured value from SPI_IOC_WR_BITS_PER_WORD is used. (See drivers/spi/spi-bcm2708.c in the function bcm2708_process_transfer()).

■ **Note** The Raspbian wheezy driver requires that bits_per_word is the value 8 or 0.

The cs_change member is treated as a Boolean value. When 0, no chip select is performed by the driver. The application is expected to do what is necessary to notify the peripheral that it is selected (usually a GPIO pin is brought low). Once the I/O has completed, the application then must normally unselect the slave peripheral.

When the cs_change member is true (non-zero), the slave selected will *depend on the device pathname that was opened*. The bus and the slave address are embedded in the device name:

/dev/spidev<bus>.<device>

When cs_change is true, the driver asserts $\overline{GPIO8}$ for spidev0.0 and asserts $\overline{GPIO7}$ for spidev0.1 prior to I/O and then deactivates the same upon completion. Of course, using these two nodes requires two different open(2) calls.

The SPI_IOC_MESSAGE(n) macro is used in the ioctl(2) call to perform one or more SPI I/O operations. The macro is unusual because it requires an argument *n*. (Perhaps someone will take it upon themselves someday to clean this interface up to work like I2C.) This specifies how many I/O transfers you would like to perform. An array of spi_ioc_transfer structures is declared and configured for each transfer required, as shown in the next example:

```
struct spi_ioc_transfer io[3];    /* Define 3 transfers */
int rc;

io[0].tx_buf = . . . ;            /* Configure I/O */
...
io[2].bits_per_word = 8;

rc = ioctl(fd,SPI_IOC_MESSAGE(3),& io[0]);
```

The preceding example will perform three I/O transfers. Since the application never gets to perform any GPIO manipulation between these I/Os, this applies to communicating with one particular slave device.

The following example code brings all of the concepts together, to demonstrate one I/O. The spi_ioc_transfer structure is initialized so that 32 bytes are transmitted and simultaneously 32 are received.

```
uint8_t tx[32], rx[32];
struct spi_ioc_transfer tr;
int rc;

tr.tx_buf        = (unsigned long) tx;
tr.rx_buf        = (unsigned long) rx;
tr.len           = 32;
tr.delay_usecs   = delay;
tr.speed_hz      = speed;
tr.bits_per_word = bits;

rc = ioctl(fd,SPI_IOC_MESSAGE(1),&tr);
if ( rc < 1 ) {
    perror("Can't send spi message");
```

Here a single I/O transmission occurs, with data being sent from array tx and received into array rx.

The return value from the ioctl(2) call returns the number of bytes transferred (32 in the example). Otherwise, -1 is returned to indicate that an error has occurred.

Close

Like all Unix I/O operations, the device is closed when the open file descriptor is no longer required:

```
close(fd);
```

Write

The write(2) system call can be used, if the received data is unimportant. Note, however, that no delay is applied with this call.

Read

The read(2) system call is actually inappropriate for SPI since the master must transmit data on MOSI in order for the slave to send bits back on the MISO line. However, when read(2) is used, the driver will automatically send out 0 bits as necessary to accomplish the read. (Be careful that your peripheral will accept 0 bytes without unintended consequences.) Like the write(2) call, no delay is provided.

SPI Testing

When developing your SPI communication software, you can perform a simple loopback test to test your framework. Once the framework checks out, you can then turn your attention to communicating with the actual device.

While the Raspbian Linux driver does not support the SPI_LOOP mode bit (in the wheezy release), you can still physically loop your SPI bus by connecting a wire from the MOSI output back to the MISO input pin (connect GPIO 10 to GPIO 9).

A simple program, shown next, demonstrates this type of loopback test. It will write out 4 bytes (0x12, 0x23, 0x45, and 0x67) to the SPI driver. Because you have wired the MOSI pin to the MISO input, anything transmitted will also be received.

When the program executes, it will report the number of bytes received and four hexadecimal values:

```
$ sudo ./spiloop
rc=4 12 23 45 67
$
```

If you remove the wire between MOSI and MISO, and connect the MISO to a high (+3.3 V), you should be able to read 0xFF for all of the received bytes. If you then connect MISO to ground, 0x00 will be received for each byte instead. (Be certain to apply to the correct pin, since applying high or low to an output can damage it, and do not apply +5 V.)

```
1   /*********************************************
2    * spiloop.c - Example loop test
3    * Connect MOSI (GPIO 10) to MISO (GPIO 9)
4    *********************************************/
5   #include <stdio.h>
6   #include <errno.h>
7   #include <stdlib.h>
8   #include <stdint.h>
9   #include <fcntl.h>
10  #include <unistd.h>
11  #include <sys/ioctl.h>
12  #include <linux/types.h>
13  #include <linux/spi/spidev.h>
14
15  static int fd = -1;
16
17  static void
18  errxit(const char *msg) {
19          perror(msg);
20          exit(1);
21  }
22
23  int
24  main(int argc, char ** argv) {
25          static uint8_t tx[] = {0x12, 0x23, 0x45, 0x67};
26          static uint8_t rx[] = {0xFF, 0xFF, 0xFF, 0xFF};
27          struct spi_ioc_transfer ioc = {
28                  .tx_buf = (unsigned long) tx,
29                  .rx_buf = (unsigned long) rx,
30                  .len = 4,
31                  .speed_hz = 100000,
32                  .delay_usecs = 10,
33                  .bits_per_word = 8,
34                  .cs_change = 1
35          } ;
36          uint8_t mode = SPI_MODE_0;
37          int rc;
38
```

```
39          fd = open("/dev/spidev0.0",O_RDWR);
40          if ( fd < 0 )
41                  errxit("Opening SPI device.");
42
43          rc = ioctl(fd,SPI_IOC_WR_MODE,&mode);
44          if ( rc < 0 )
45                  errxit("ioctl (2) setting SPI mode.");
46
47          rc = ioctl(fd,SPI_IOC_WR_BITS_PER_WORD,&ioc.bits_per_word);
48          if ( rc < 0 )
49                  errxit("ioctl (2) setting SPI bits perword.");
50
51          rc = ioctl(fd,SPI_IOC_MESSAGE(1),&ioc);
52          if ( rc < 0 )
53                  errxit("ioctl (2) for SPI I/O");
54          close(fd);
55
56          printf("rc=%d %02X %02X %02X %02X\n",
57                  rc, rx[0], rx[1], rx[2], rx[3]);
58          return 0;
59 }
```

CHAPTER 16

Boot

When the power is first applied to the Raspberry Pi, or it has been reset (see the "Reset" section of Chapter 5), a *boot sequence* is initiated. As you will see in this chapter, it is the GPU that actually brings up the ARM CPU.

The way that the Raspberry Pi is designed, it *must* be booted from firmware found on the SD card. It cannot boot from any other source. RISC code for the GPU is provided by the Raspberry Pi Foundation in the file bootcode.bin.

After the second-stage boot loader has been executed, it is possible that other operating systems or ARM boot loaders such as U-Boot can be initiated.

Booting ARM Linux

Generally speaking, Linux under the ARM architecture needs a small amount of assistance to get started. The following are some of the minimal things that the boot loader needs to do:[25]

1. Initialize and configure memory (with MMU, cache, and DMA disabled)

2. Load the kernel image into memory

3. Optionally, load an initial RAM disk image

4. Initialize and provide boot parameters to the loaded kernel (ATAG list)

5. Obtain/determine the Linux machine type (MACH_TYPE)

6. Execute the kernel image with the correct starting register values (r1 = machine number, r2 points to the ATAG list)

7. Additionally, the boot loader is expected to perform some initialization of a serial and/or video console.

In the Raspberry Pi, this boot-loading assistance comes from the embedded GPU in the SoC. The GPU supports a small RISC core that is able to run from initial code found in its ROM. From this small amount of code, the GPU is able to initialize itself and the SD card hardware. From the media on the SD card, it is able to bootstrap itself the rest of the way. For this reason, the Raspberry Pi must always bootstrap from an SD card.

Boot Sequence

This section looks at the startup sequence in greater detail. The participating hardware components, the files and data elements are considered. The boot procedure consists of the following sequence of events:

1. At power-up (or reset), the ARM CPU is offline.[23]

2. A small RISC core in the GPU begins to execute SoC ROM code (first-stage boot loader).

3. The GPU initializes the SD card hardware.

4. The GPU looks at the first FAT32 partition in the SD media. (There remains some question about specific limitations as Broadcom has documented this—for example, can it boot from a first FAT16 partition?)

5. The second-stage boot-loader firmware named bootcode.bin is loaded into the GPU.

6. The GPU control passes to the loaded bootcode.bin firmware (SDRAM is initially disabled).

7. The file start.elf is loaded by the GPU into RAM from the SD card.

8. An additional file, fixup.dat, is used to configure the SDRAM partition between GPU and ARM CPU.

9. The file config.txt is examined for configuration parameters that need to be processed.

10. Information found in cmdline.txt is presumably also passed to start.elf.

11. The GPU allows the ARM CPU to execute the program start.elf.

12. The module start.elf runs on the ARM CPU, with information about the kernel to be loaded.

13. The kernel is loaded, and execution control passes to it.

Boot Files

The FAT32 partition containing the boot files is normally mounted as /boot, after Raspbian Linux has come up. Table 16-1 lists the files that apply to the boot process. The text files can be edited to affect new configurations. The binary files can also be replaced by new revisions of the same.

Table 16-1. /boot Files

File Name	Purpose	Format
bootcode.bin	Second-stage boot loader	Binary
fixup.dat	Configure split of GPU/CPU SDRAM	Binary
config.txt	Configuration parameters	Text
cmdline.txt	Command-line parameters for kernel	Text
start.elf	ARM CPU code to be launched	Binary
kernel.img	Kernel to be loaded	Binary
	Name can be overridden with kernel= parameter in config.txt	

config.txt

The config.txt file permits you to configure many aspects of the boot process. Some options affect physical devices, and others affect the kernel being loaded.

Composite Video Settings

The composite video output from the Raspberry Pi is primarily configured by three basic parameters:

- sdtv_mode
- sdtv_aspect
- sdtv_disable_colourburst

Standard Definition Video

The parameter sdtv_mode determines the video mode (TV standard) of the composite video output jack.

sdtv_mode	Description
0	Normal NTSC (default)
1	Japanese NTSC (no pedestal)
2	Normal PAL
3	Brazilian PAL 525/60

Composite Aspect Ratio

The sdtv_aspect parameter configures the composite video aspect ratio.

sdtv_aspect	Description
1	4:3 (default)
2	14:9
3	16:9

Color Burst

By default, color burst is enabled. This permits the generation of color out of the composite video jack. Setting the video for monochrome may be desirable for a sharper display.

sdtv_disable_colourburst	Description
0	Color burst enabled (default)
1	Color burst disabled (monochrome)

High-Definition Video

This section covers config.txt settings that affect HDMI operation.

HDMI Safe Mode

The hdmi_safe parameter enables support of automatic HDMI configuration for optimal compatibility.

hdmi_safe	Description
0	Disabled (default)
1	Enabled

When hdmi_safe=1 (enabled), the following settings are implied:

- hdmi_force_hotplug=1
- config_hdmi_boost=4
- hdmi_group=1
- hdmi_mode=1
- disable_overscan=0

HDMI Force Hot-Plug

This configuration setting allows you to force a hot-plug signal for the HDMI display, whether the display is connected or not. The NOOBS distribution enables this setting by default.

hdmi_force_hotplug	Description
0	Disabled (non-NOOBS default)
1	Use HDMI mode even when no HDMI monitor is detected (NOOBS default)

HDMI Ignore Hot-Plug

Enabling the hdmi_ignore_hotplug setting causes it to appear to the system that no HDMI display is attached, even if there is. This can help force composite video output, while the HDMI display is plugged in.

hdmi_ignore_hotplug	Description
0	Disabled (default)
1	Use composite video even if an HDMI display is detected

HDMI Drive

This mode allows you to choose between DVI (no sound) and HDMI mode (with sound, when supported).

hdmi_drive	Description
1	Normal DVI mode (no sound)
2	Normal HDMI mode (sound will be sent if supported and enabled)

HDMI Ignore EDID

Enabling this option causes the EDID information from the display to be ignored. Normally, this information is helpful and is used.

hdmi_ignore_edid	Description
Unspecified	Read EDID information
0xa5000080	Ignore EDID information

HDMI EDID File

When hdmi_edid_file is enabled, the EDID information is taken from the file named edid.txt. Otherwise, it is taken from the display, when available.

hdmi_edid_file	Description
0	Read EDID data from device (default)
1	Read EDID data from edid.txt file

HDMI Force EDID Audio

Enabling this option forces the support of all audio formats even if the display does not support them. This permits pass-through of DTS/AC3 when reported as unsupported.

hdmi_force_edid_audio	Description
0	Use EDID-provided values (default)
1	Pretend all audio formats are supported

Avoid EDID Fuzzy Match

Avoid fuzzy matching of modes described in the EDID.

avoid_edid_fuzzy_match	Description
0	Use fuzzy matching (default)
1	Avoid fuzzy matching

HDMI Group

The hdmi_group option defines the HDMI type.

hdmi_group	Description
0	Use the preferred group reported by the EDID (default)
1	CEA
2	DMT

HDMI Mode

This option defines the screen resolution to use in CEA or DMT format (see the parameter hdmi_group in the preceding subsection "HDMI Group"). In Table 16-2, the modifiers shown have the following meanings:

H means 16:9 variant of a normally 4:3 mode.

2x means pixel doubled (higher clock rate).

4x means pixel quadrupled (higher clock rate).

R means reduced blanking (fewer bytes are used for blanking within the data stream, resulting in lower clock rates).

Table 16-2. *HDMI Mode Settings*

Group	CEA			DMT		
Mode	Resolution	Refresh	Modifiers	Resolution	Refresh	Notes
1	VGA			640×350	85 Hz	
2	480 p	60 Hz		640×400	85 Hz	
3	480 p	60 Hz	H	720×400	85 Hz	
4	720 p	60 Hz		640×480	60 Hz	
5	1080 i	60 Hz		640×480	72 Hz	
6	480 i	60 Hz		640×480	75 Hz	

(*continued*)

Table 16-2. (*continued*)

Group	CEA			DMT		
Mode	Resolution	Refresh	Modifiers	Resolution	Refresh	Notes
7	480 i	60 Hz	H	640×480	85 Hz	
8	240 p	60 Hz		800×600	56 Hz	
9	240 p	60 Hz	H	800×600	60 Hz	
10	480 i	60 Hz	4x	800×600	72 Hz	
11	480 i	60 Hz	4x H	800×600	75 Hz	
12	240 p	60 Hz	4x	800×600	85 Hz	
13	240 p	60 Hz	4x H	800×600	120 Hz	
14	480 p	60 Hz	2x	848×480	60 Hz	
15	480 p	60 Hz	2x H	1024×768	43 Hz	Don't use
16	1080 p	60 Hz		1024×768	60 Hz	
17	576 p	50 Hz		1024×768	70 Hz	
18	576 p	50 Hz	H	1024×768	75 Hz	
19	720 p	50 Hz		1024×768	85 Hz	
20	1080 i	50 Hz		1024×768	120 Hz	
21	576 i	50 Hz		1152×864	75 Hz	
22	576 i	50 Hz	H	1280×768		R
23	288 p	50 Hz		1280×768	60 Hz	
24	288 p	50 Hz	H	1280×768	75 Hz	
25	576 i	50 Hz	4x	1280×768	85 Hz	
26	576 i	50 Hz	4x H	1280×768	120 Hz	R
27	288 p	50 Hz	4x	1280×800		R
28	288 p	50 Hz	4x H	1280×800	60 Hz	
29	576 p	50 Hz	2x	1280×800	75 Hz	
30	576 p	50 Hz	2x H	1280×800	85 Hz	
31	1080 p	50 Hz		1280×800	120 Hz	R
32	1080 p	24 Hz		1280×960	60 Hz	
33	1080 p	25 Hz		1280×960	85 Hz	
34	1080 p	30 Hz		1280×960	120 Hz	R
35	480 p	60 Hz	4x	1280×1024	60 Hz	
36	480 p	60 Hz	4x H	1280×1024	75 Hz	
37	576 p	50 Hz	4x	1280×1024	85 Hz	

(*continued*)

Table 16-2. (*continued*)

Group	CEA			DMT		
Mode	Resolution	Refresh	Modifiers	Resolution	Refresh	Notes
38	576 p	50 Hz	4x H	1280×1024	120 Hz	R
39	1080 i	50 Hz	R	1360×768	60 Hz	
40	1080 i	100 Hz		1360×768	120 Hz	R
41	720 p	100 Hz		1400×1050		R
42	576 p	100 Hz		1400×1050	60 Hz	
43	576 p	100 Hz	H	1400×1050	75 Hz	
44	576 i	100 Hz		1400×1050	85 Hz	
45	576 i	100 Hz	H	1400×1050	120 Hz	R
46	1080 i	120 Hz		1440×900		R
47	720 p	120 Hz		1440×900	60 Hz	
48	480 p	120 Hz		1440×900	75 Hz	
49	480 p	120 Hz	H	1440×900	85 Hz	
50	480 i	120 Hz		1440×900	120 Hz	R
51	480 i	120 Hz	H	1600×1200	60 Hz	
52	576 p	200 Hz		1600×1200	65 Hz	
53	576 p	200 Hz	H	1600×1200	70 Hz	
54	576 i	200 Hz		1600×1200	75 Hz	
55	576 i	200 Hz	H	1600×1200	85 Hz	
56	480 p	240 Hz		1600×1200	120 Hz	R
57	480 p	240 Hz	H	1680×1050		R
58	480 i	240 Hz		1680×1050	60 Hz	
59	480 i	240 Hz	H	1680×1050	75 Hz	
60				1680×1050	85 Hz	
61				1680×1050	120 Hz	R
62				1792×1344	60 Hz	
63				1792×1344	75 Hz	
64				1792×1344	120 Hz	R
65				1856×1392	60 Hz	
66				1856×1392	75 Hz	
67				1856×1392	120 Hz	R
68				1920×1200		R

(*continued*)

Table 16-2. (*continued*)

Group	CEA			DMT		
Mode	Resolution	Refresh	Modifiers	Resolution	Refresh	Notes
69				1920×1200	60 Hz	
70				1920×1200	75 Hz	
71				1920×1200	85 Hz	
72				1920×1200	120 Hz	R
73				1920×1440	60 Hz	
74				1920×1440	75 Hz	
75				1920×1440	120 Hz	R
76				2560×1600		R
77				2560×1600	60 Hz	
78				2560×1600	75 Hz	
79				2560×1600	85 Hz	
80				2560×1600	120 Hz	R
81				1366×768	60 Hz	
82	1080 p	60 Hz				
83				1600×900		R
84				2048×1152		R
85	720 p	60 Hz				
86				1366×768		R

HDMI Boost

The config_hdmi_boost parameter allows you to tweak the HDMI signal strength.

config_hdmi_boost	Description
0	Non-NOOBS default
1	
2	
3	
4	Use if you have interference issues (NOOBS default setting)
5	
6	
7	Maximum strength

HDMI Ignore CEC Init

When this option is enabled, the CEC initialization is not sent to the device. This avoids bringing the TV out of standby and channel switch when rebooting.

hdmi_ignore_cec_init	Description
0	Normal (default)
1	Don't send initial active source message

HDMI Ignore CEC

When this option is enabled, the assumption made is that CEC is not supported at all by the HDMI device, even if the device does have support. As a result, no CEC functions will be supported.

hdmi_ignore_cec	Description
0	Normal (default)
1	Disable CEC support

Overscan Video

A few options control the overscan support of the composite video output. When overscan is enabled, a certain number of pixels are skipped at the sides of the screen as configured.

Disable Overscan

The disable_overscan option can disable the overscan feature. It is enabled by default:

disable_overscan	Description
0	Overscan enabled (default)
1	Overscan disabled

Overscan Left, Right, Top, and Bottom

These parameters control the number of pixels to skip at the left, right, top, and bottom of the screen.

Parameter	Pixels to Skip
overscan_left=0	At left
overscan_right=0	At right
overscan_top=0	At top
overscan_bottom=0	At bottom

Frame Buffer Settings

The Linux frame buffer support is configured by a few configuration options described in this section.

Frame Buffer Width

The default is to define the width of the frame buffer as the display's width minus the overscan pixels.

framebuffer_width	Description
default	Display width overscan
framebuffer_width=n	Set width to *n* pixels

Frame Buffer Height

The default is to define the height of the frame buffer as the display's height minus the overscan pixels.

framebuffer_height	Description
default	Display height overscan
framebuffer_height=n	Set height to *n* pixels

Frame Buffer Depth

This parameter defines the number of bits per pixel.

framebuffer_depth	Description
8	Valid, but default RGB palette makes an unreadable screen
16	Default
24	Looks better but has corruption issues as of 6/15/2012
32	No corruption, but requires framebuffer_ignore_alpha=1, and shows wrong colors as of 6/15/2012

Frame Buffer Ignore Alpha

The alpha channel can be disabled with this option. As of this writing, this option must be used when using a frame buffer depth of 32 bits.

framebuffer_ignore_alpha	Description
0	Alpha channel enabled (default)
1	Alpha channel disabled

General Video Options

The display can be flipped or rotated in different ways, according to the display_rotate option. You should be able to do both a flip and a rotate by adding the flip values to the rotate value.

▪ **Note**   I was unable to get the flip options to work on Linux Raspberry Pi 3.2.27+ #250. It is possible that a newer version of the boot-loader bootcode.bin may be needed. But as of 2014, this remains an issue.

The 90º and 270º rotations require additional memory on the GPU, so these options won't work with a 16 MB GPU split.

display_rotate	Description
0	0º (default)
1	90º
2	180º
3	270º
0x1000	Horizontal flip
0x2000	Vertical flip

While the flip options are documented, I was unable to get them to work. The rotations, however, were confirmed as working.

Licensed Codecs

The following options permit you to configure the purchased license key codes for the codecs they affect.

Option	Notes
decode_MPG2=0x12345678	License key for hardware MPEG-2 decoding
decode_WVC1=0x12345678	License key for hardware VC-1 decoding

Testing

The following test option enables image/sound tests during boot. This is intended for manufacturer testing.

test_mode	Description
0	Disable test mode (default)
1	Enable test mode

Memory

This section summarizes configuration settings pertaining to memory.

Disable GPU L2 Cache

The `disable_l2cache` option allows the ARM CPU access to the GPU L2 cache to be disabled. This needs the corresponding L2 disabled in the kernel.

disable_l2cache	Description
0	Enable GPU L2 cache access (default)
1	Disable GPU L2 cache access

GPU Memory (All)

The gpu_mem option allows configuration of the GPU memory for all Raspberry Pi board revisions (unless gpu_mem_256 or gpu_mem_512 is supplied).

gpu_mem	Description
gpu_mem=64	Default is 64 MB
gpu_mem=128	128 MB

GPU Memory (256)

The gpu_mem_256 option allows configuration of the GPU memory for the 256 MB Raspberry Pi boards. When specified, it overrides the gpu_mem option setting.

gpu_mem_256	Description
unspecified	Defined by gpu_mem option
gpu_mem_256=128	128 MB (example)

GPU Memory (512)

The gpu_mem_512 option configures the GPU memory allocated for the 512 MB Raspberry Pi boards. When specified, it overrides the gpu_mem option setting.

gpu_mem_512	Description
unspecified	Defined by gpu_mem option
gpu_mem_512=128	128 MB (example)

Boot Options

Several options in this section affect the boot process. Many options pertain to the kernel being started, while others affect file systems and devices.

Disable Command-Line Tags

The disable_commandline_tags option permits the user to prevent start.elf from filling in ATAGS memory before launching the kernel. This prevents the cmdline.txt file from being supplied to the kernel at boot time.

disable_commandline_tags	Description
0	Enable ATAGS (default)
1	Disable command line in ATAGS

Command Line

The cmdline option allows you to configure the kernel command-line parameters within the config.txt file, instead of the cmdline.txt file.

cmdline	Description
unspecified	Command line is taken from cmdline.txt
cmdline="command"	Command line is taken from parameter

Kernel

By default, start.elf loads the kernel from the file named kernel.img. Specifying the kernel parameter allows the user to change the file's name.

kernel	Description
unspecified	kernel="kernel.img" (default)
kernel="plan9.img"	kernel="plan9.img"

Kernel Address

This parameter determines the memory address where the kernel image is loaded into.

kernel_address	Description
0x00000000	Default

RAM File System File

The ramfsfile parameter names the file for the RAM FS file, to be used with the kernel.

ramfsfile	Description
unspecified	No RAM FS file used
ramfsfile="ramfs.file"	File ramfs.file is used

RAM File System Address

The ramfsaddr parameter specifies where the RAM file system image is to be loaded into memory.

ramfsaddr	Description
0x00000000	Default address

Init RAM File System

This option is a convenience option, which combines the options ramfsfile and ramfsaddr.

initramfs	Arg 1	Arg 2	Description
initramfs	initram.gz	0x00800000	Example

Device Tree Address

The device_tree_address option defines where the device tree address is loaded.

device_tree_address	Description
0x00000000	Default

Init UART Baud

The init_uart_baud option allows the user to reconfigure the serial console to use a baud rate that is different from the default.

init_uart_baud	Description
115200	Default baud rate

Init UART Clock

The init_uart_clock parameter permits the user to reconfigure the UART to use a different clock rate.

init_uart_clock	Description
3000000	Default

Init EMMC Clock

The init_emmc_clock parameter allows the user to tweak the EMMC clock, which can improve the SD card performance.

init_emmc_clock	Description
100000000	Default

Boot Delay

The boot_delay and boot_delay_ms options allow the user to reconfigure the delay used by start.elf prior to loading the kernel. The actual delay time used is computed from the following:

$$D = 1000 \times b + m$$

where

- D is the computed delay in milliseconds.
- b is the boot_delay value.
- m is the boot_delay_ms value.

boot_delay (b)	Description
1	Default

The boot_delay_ms augments the boot_delay parameter.

boot_delay_ms (m)	Description
0	Default

Avoid Safe Mode

A jumper or switch can be placed between pins P1-05 (GPIO 1) and P1-06 (ground) to cause start.elf to initiate a *safe mode* boot. If GPIO 1 is being used for some other I/O function, the safe mode check should be disabled.

avoid_safe_mode	Description
0	Default (check P1-05 for safe mode)
1	Disable safe mode check

Overclocking

According to the Raspberry Pi Configuration Settings file, Revision 14 (http://elinux.org/RPi_config.txt) the ARM CPU, SDRAM, and GPU have their own clock signals (from a PLL). The GPU core, H.264, V3D, and ISP all share the same clock.

The following commands can be used to check your CPU, once you have a command-line prompt. The /proc/cpuinfo pseudo file will give you a BogoMIPS figure:

```
$ cat /proc/cpuinfo
Processor       : ARMv6-compatible processor rev 7 ( v6l )
BogoMIPS        : 697.95
Features        : swp half thumb fastmult vfp edsp java tls
CPU implementer : 0x41
CPU architecture : 7
CPU variant     : 0x0
CPU part        : 0xb76
CPU revision    : 7
Hardware        : BCM2708
Revision        : 000f
Serial          : 00000000 f52b69e9
$
```

The vcgencmd can be used to read the ARM CPU clock frequency:

```
$ vcgencmd measure_clock arm
frequency (45)=700074000
$
```

To configure for overclocking, you start with the phase-locked loop (PLL). The PLL frequency is computed as follows:

$$p = floor\left(\frac{2400}{2c}\right)(2c)$$

where

- p is the computed PLL frequency.
- c is the core frequency.

From this, the GPU frequency multiple m is computed from a trial GPU frequency t as follows:

$$m = \frac{p}{t}$$

The value m is then rounded to the nearest *even* integer value, and the *final* GPU frequency g is computed as follows:

$$g = \frac{p}{m}$$

If we take an example where the core frequency c is 500 MHz, then p is determined as follows:

$$P = floor\left(\frac{2400}{2 \times 500}\right) \times (2 \times 500)$$

$$= 2000$$

Further, if we are targeting a GPU frequency of 300 MHz, we compute m:

$$m = \frac{2000}{300} = 6.666$$

The value m is rounded to the nearest *even* integer:

$$m = 6$$

The final GPU frequency becomes

$$g = \frac{p}{m} = \frac{2000}{6} = 333.33$$

The example GPU clock is 333.33 MHz.

Table 16-3 lists the standard clock profiles, as provided by the Raspberry Pi Foundation. Additionally, it is stated that if the SoC reaches `temp_limit`, the overclock settings will be disabled. The value of `temp_limit` is configurable.

Table 16-3. *Standard Clock Profiles*

Profile	ARM CPU	Core	SDRAM	Over Voltage
None	700 MHz	250 MHz	400 MHz	0
Modest	800 MHz	300 MHz	400 MHz	0
Medium	900 MHz	333 MHz	450 MHz	2
High	950 MHz	450 MHz	450 MHz	6
Turbo	1000 MHz	500 MHz	500 MHz	6

Warranty and Overclocking

At one time, overclocking could void your warranty. Also note that Internet forum users have reported SD card corruption when trying out overclocked configurations (though several improvements to SD card handling have been made). Be sure to back up your SD card. The following combination of parameters may set a permanent bit in your SoC chip and void your warranty. While the Raspberry Pi announcement (`www.raspberrypi.org/introducing-turbo-mode-up-to-50-more-performance-for-free/`) speaks of overclocking without voiding the warranty, it is subject to some conditions like using the `cpufreq` driver. The following conditions may put your warranty in jeopardy:

- `ver_voltage > 0`, and at least one of the following:
- `force_turbo = 1`
- `current_limit_override = 0x5A000020`
- `temp_limit > 85`

Force Turbo Mode

The documentation indicates that force_turbo has no effect if other overclocking options are in effect.

By default, force_turbo is disabled. When disabled, it disables some other configuration options such as h264_freq. However, enabling force_turbo also enables h264_freq, v3d_freq, and isp_freq.

force_turbo	Description
0 (default)	Enables dynamic clocks and voltage for the ARM core, GPU core, and SDRAM. In this mode, settings for h264_freq, v3d_freq, and isp_freq are ignored.
1	Disables dynamic clocks and voltage for the ARM core, GPU core, and SDRAM. Configuration option values h264_freq, v3d_freq, and isp_freq apply when specified.

Initial Turbo

The initial_turbo option is described in config.txt as "enables turbo mode from boot for the given value in seconds (up to 60)." This is somewhat confusing.

What is meant is that turbo mode will be enabled after a delay of a configured number of seconds after boot. By default, if turbo mode is enabled, it is enabled immediately (after examining config.txt).

The initial_turbo option allows the boot process to proceed at normal clock rates until the process has progressed to a certain point. Some people on Internet forums that experience SD card corruption from overclocking will suggest the initial_turbo option as a solution.

initial_turbo	Description
0	No timed turbo mode (default)
60	Maximum number of seconds after boot before enabling turbo mode

Temperature Limit

The temp_limit configuration option allows the user to override the default safety limit. Increasing this value beyond 85°C voids your warranty.

When the SoC temperature exceeds temp_limit, the clocks and voltages are set to default values for safer operation.

temp_limit	Description
85	Temperature limit in Celsius (default)
> 85	Voids your warranty

ARM CPU Frequency

The parameter arm_freq sets the clock frequency of the ARM CPU in MHz. This option applies in non-turbo and turbo modes.

arm_freq	Description
700	Default ARM CPU frequency, in MHz
> 700	May void warranty—check related conditions

Minimum ARM CPU Frequency

This option can be used when using dynamic clocking of the ARM CPU. This sets the lowest clock speed for the ARM.

arm_freq_min	Description
700	Default ARM CPU frequency in MHz
> 700	May void warranty—check related conditions

GPU Frequency

The gpu_freq option determines the following other values:

Parameter	MHz
core_freq	Core frequency
h264_freq	H.264 frequency
isp_freq	Image sensor pipeline frequency
v3d_freq	3D video block frequency

The gpu_freq parameter has the following default value:

gpu_freq	Description
250	Default GPU frequency (MHz)

Core Frequency

The core_freq option allows the user to configure the GPU processor core clock. This parameter also affects the ARM performance, since it drives the L2 cache.

core_freq	Description
250	Default in MHz

Minimum Core Frequency

When dynamic clocking is used, this sets the minimum GPU processor core clock rate. See also the core_freq option. Like the core_freq option, this parameter affects the ARM performance, since it drives the L2 cache.

core_freq_min	Description
250	Default in MHz

H.264 Frequency

This parameter configures the frequency of the video block hardware. This parameter applies when force_turbo mode is enabled.

h264_freq	Description
250	Default in MHz

ISP Frequency

This parameter configures the image sensor pipeline clock rate and applies when force_turbo mode is enabled.

isp_freq	Description
250	Default in MHz

V3D Frequency

The v3d_freq configures the 3D block frequency in MHz. This parameter applies when force_turbo mode is enabled.

v3d_freq	Description
250	Default in MHz

SDRAM Frequency

The sdram_freq parameter allows the user to configure frequency of the SDRAM.

sdram_freq	Description
400	Default in MHz

Minimum SDRAM Frequency

When dynamic clocks are used, the sdram_freq_min allows the user to configure a minimum clock rate in MHz.

sdram_freq_min	Description
400	Default in MHz

Avoid PWM PLL

The avoid_pwm_pll configuration parameter allows the user to unlink the core_freq from the rest of the GPU. A Pi configuration note states, "analog audio should still work, but from a fractional divider, so lower quality."

avoid_pwm_pll	Description
0	Linked core_freq (default)
1	Unlinked core_freq

Voltage Settings

The configuration parameters in this subsection configure voltages for various parts of the Raspberry Pi.

Current Limit Override

When supplied, the switched-mode power supply current limit protection is disabled. This can be helpful with overclocking if you are encountering reboot failures.

current_limit_override	Description
Unspecified	Default (limit in effect)
0x5A000020	Disables SMPS current limit protection

Over Voltage

The ARM CPU and GPU core voltage can be adjusted through the over_voltage option. Use the values shown in Table 16-4.

Over Voltage Minimum

The over_voltage_min option can be used when dynamic clocking is employed, to prevent the voltage dropping below a specified minimum. Use the values from Table 16-4.

Table 16-4. *Voltage Parameter Values*

Parameter	Voltage	Notes
-16	0.8 V	
-15	0.825 V	
-14	0.85 V	
-13	0.875 V	
-12	0.9 V	
-11	0.925 V	
-10	0.95 V	
-9	0.975 V	
-8	1.0 V	
-7	1.025 V	
-6	1.05 V	
-5	1.075 V	
-4	1.1 V	
-3	1.125 V	
-2	1.15 V	
-1	1.175 V	
0	1.2 V	Default
1	1.225 V	
2	1.25 V	
3	1.275 V	
4	1.3 V	
5	1.325 V	
6	1.35 V	
7	1.375 V	Requires force_turbo=1
8	1.4 V	Requires force_turbo=1

Over Voltage SDRAM

The over_voltage_sdram configuration option is a convenient way to set three options at once:

- over_voltage_sdram_c: SDRAM controller voltage
- over_voltage_sdram_i: SDRAM I/O voltage adjust
- over_voltage_sdram_p: SDRAM physical voltage adjust

Raspberry Pi documentation says the over_voltage_sdram option "sets over_ voltage_sdram_c, over_voltage_sdram_i, over_voltage_sdram_p together." Use the values shown in Table 16-4.

SDRAM Controller Voltage

Use the over_voltage_sdram_c option to set the voltage for the SDRAM controller. Use the values shown in Table 16-4. See also the over_voltage_sdram option.

SDRAM I/O Voltage

Use the over_voltage_sdram_i option to set the voltage for the SDRAM I/O subsystem. Use the values shown in Table 16-4. See also the over_voltage_sdram option.

SDRAM Physical Voltage

The over_voltage_sdram_p option adjusts the "physical voltage" for the SDRAM subsystem. Use the values shown in Table 16-4. See also the over_voltage_sdram option.

cmdline.txt

The cmdline.txt file is used to supply command-line arguments to the kernel. The Raspbian values supplied in the standard image are broken into multiple lines here for easier reading (note that the NOOBS distribution may show a different device for the root file system):

```
$ cat /boot/cmdline.txt
dwc_otg.lpm_enable=0 \
 console=ttyAMA0,115200 \
 kgdboc=ttyAMA0,115200 \
 console=tty1 \
 root=/dev/mmcblk0p2 \
 rootfstype=ext4 \
 elevator=deadline \
 rootwait
$
```

This file is provided as a convenience, since the parameters can be configured in the config.txt file, using the cmdline="text" option. When the config.txt option is provided, it supersedes the cmdline.txt file.

Once the Raspbian Linux kernel comes up, you can review the command-line options used as follows (edited for readability):

```
$ cat /proc/cmdline
 dma.dmachans=0x7f35 \
 bcm2708_fb.fbwidth=656 \
 bcm2708_fb.fbheight=416 \
 bcm2708.boardrev=0xf \
 bcm2708.serial=0xf52b69e9 \
 smsc95xx.macaddr=B8:27:EB:2B:69:E9 \
 sdhci-bcm2708.emmc_clock_freq=100000000 \
 vc_mem.mem_base=0x1c000000 \
 vc_mem. mem_size=0x20000000 \
 dwc_otg.lpm_enable=0 \
 console=ttyAMA0,115200 \
```

```
kgdboc=ttyAMA0,115200 \
console=tty1 \
root=/dev/mmcblk0p2 \
rootfstype=ext4 \
elevator=deadline \
rootwait
$
```

Additional options can be seen prepended to what was provided in the `cmdline.txt` file. Options of the format `name.option=values` are specific to kernel-loadable modules. For example, the parameter `bcm2708_fb.fbwidth=656` pertains to the module `bcm2708_fb`.

There are too many Linux kernel parameters to describe here (entire books have been written on this topic), but some of the most commonly used ones are covered in the following subsections.

Serial console=

The Linux console parameter specifies to Linux what device to use for a console. For the Raspberry Pi, this is normally specified as follows:

```
console=ttyAMA0,115200
```

This references the serial device that is made available after boot-up as `/dev/ttyAMA0`. The parameter following the device name is the baud rate (115200).

The general form of the serial console option is as follows:

```
console=ttyDevice,bbbbpnf
```

The second parameter is the options field:

Zone	Description	Value	Raspbian Notes
bbbb	Baud rate	115200	Can be more than four digits
p	Parity	n	No parity
		o	Odd parity
		e	Even parity
n	Number of bits	7	7 data bits
		8	8 data bits
f	Flow control	r	RTS
		omitted	No RTS

Virtual console=

Linux supports a virtual console, which is also configurable from the `console=` parameter. Raspbian Linux specifies the following:

```
console=tty1
```

This device is available from /dev/tty1, after the kernel boots up. The tty parameters used for this virtual console can be listed (edited here for readability):

```
$ sudo -i
# stty -a </dev/tty1
speed 38400 baud ; rows 26; columns 82; line = 0;
intr = ^C; quit = ^\; erase = ^?; kill = ^U; \
eof = ^D; eol = <undef>; eol2 = <undef>; swtch = <undef>;
start = ^Q; stop = ^S ; susp = ^Z; rprnt = ^R; werase = ^W; \
lnext = ^V; flush = ^O; min = 1; time = 0;
-parenb -parodd cs8 hupcl -cstopb cread -clocal -crtscts
-ignbrk brkint -ignpar -parmrk -inpck -istrip -inlcr \
-igncr icrnl ixon -ixoff -iuclc -ixany imaxbel iutf8
opost -o lcuc -ocrnl onlcr -onocr -onlret -ofill -ofdel \
nl0 cr0 tab0 bs0 vt0 ff0
isig icanon iexten echo echoe echok -echonl -noflsh \
-xcase -tostop -echoprt -echoctl echoke
#
```

kgdboc=

The kgdboc parameter was named after the idea "kgdb over console." This allows you to use a serial console as your primary console as well as use it for kernel debugging. The primary console, however, need not be a serial console for kgdboc to be used.[27]

The Raspbian image supplies this:

```
kgdboc=ttyAMA0,115200
```

This allows kernel debugging to proceed through serial device /dev/ttyAMA0, which is the only serial device supported on the Raspberry Pi.

root=

The Linux kernel needs to know what device holds the root file system. The standard Raspbian image supplies the following:

```
root=/dev/mmcblk0p2
```

This points the kernel to the SD card (mmcblk0), partition 2 (non-NOOBS distribution). See also the rootfstype parameter.

The general form of the root= parameter supports three forms:

- root=MMmm: Boot from major device MM, minor mm (hexadecimal).

- root=/dev/nfs: Boot a NFS disk specified by nfsroot (see also nfs-root= and ip=).

- root=/dev/name: Boot from a device named /dev/name.

rootfstype=

In addition to specifying the device holding the root file system, the Linux kernel sometimes needs to know the file system type. This is configured through the rootfstype parameter. The standard Raspbian image supplies the following:

```
rootfstype=ext4
```

This example indicates that the root file system is the ext4 type.

The Linux kernel can examine the device given in the root parameter to determine the file system type. But there are scenarios where the kernel cannot resolve the type or gets confused. Otherwise, you may want to force a certain file system type. Another situation is when MTD is used for the root file system. For example, when using JFFS2, it must specified.

elevator=

This option selects the I/O scheduler scheme to be used within the kernel. The standard Raspbian image specifies the following:

```
elevator=deadline
```

To find out the I/O scheduler option being used and the other available choices (in your kernel), we can consult the /sys pseudo file system:

```
$ cat /sys/block/mmcblk0/queue/scheduler
noop [deadline] cfq
$
```

The name mmcblk0 is the name of the device that your root file system is on. The output shows in square brackets that the deadline I/O scheduler is being used. The other choices are noop and cfq. These I/O schedulers are as follows:

Name	Description	Notes
noop	No special ordering of requests	
cfq	Completely fair scheduler	Older
deadline	Cyclic scheduler, but requests have deadlines	Newest

The deadline I/O scheduler is the newest implementation, designed for greater efficiency and fairness. The deadline scheduler uses a cyclic elevator, except that it additionally logs a deadline for the request. A cyclic elevator is one where the requests are ordered according to sector numbers and head movement (forward and backward). The deadline scheduler will use the cyclic elevator behavior, but if it looks like the request is about to expire, it is given immediate priority.

rootwait=

This option is used when the device used for the root file system is a device that is started asynchronously with other kernel boot functions. This is usually needed for USB and MMC devices, which may take extra time to initialize. The rootwait option forces the kernel to wait until the root device becomes ready.

Given that the root file system is on the SD card (a MMC device), the Raspbian image uses the following:

```
rootwait
```

nfsroot=

The nfsroot option permits you to define a kernel that boots from an NFS mount (assuming that NFS support is compiled into the kernel). The square brackets show placement of optional values:

```
nfsroot=[server-ip:]root-dir[,nfs-options]
```

Field	Description
server-ip	NFS server IP number (default uses ip=)
root-dir	Root dir on NFS server. If there is a %s present, the IP address will be inserted there.
nfs-options	NFS options like ro, separated by commas

When unspecified, the default of /tftpboot/client_ip_address will be used. This requires that root=/dev/nfs be specified and optionally ip= may be added.

To test whether you have NFS support in your kernel, you can query the /proc file system when the system has booted:

```
$ cat /proc/filesystems
nodev    sysfs
nodev    rootfs
nodev    bdev
nodev    proc
nodev    cgroup
nodev    tmpfs
nodev    devtmpfs
nodev    debugfs
nodev    sockfs
nodev    pipefs
nodev    anon_inodefs
nodev    rpc_pipefs
nodev    configfs
nodev    devpts
         ext3
         ext2
         ext4
nodev    ramfs
         vfat
         msdos
nodev    nfs
nodev    nfs4
nodev    autofs
nodev    mqueue
```

From this example, we see that both the older NFS (nfs) and the newer NFS4 file systems are supported.

ip=

This option permits the user to configure the IP address of a network device, or to specify how the IP number is assigned. See also the `root=` and `nfsroot=` options.

```
ip=client-ip:server-ip:gw-ip:netmask:hostname:device:autoconf
```

Table 16-5 describes the fields within this option. The `autoconf` *value* can appear by itself, without the intervening colons if required. When `ip=off` or `ip=none` is given, no autoconfiguration takes place. The autoconfiguration protocols are listed in Table 16-6.

Table 16-5. *ip= Kernel Parameter*

Field	Description	Default
ip-client	IP address of the client	Autoconfigured
ip-server	IP address of NFS server, required only for NFS root	Autoconfigured
gw-ip	IP address of server if on a separate subnet	Autoconfigured
netmask	Netmask for local IP address	Autoconfigured
hostname	Hostname to provide to DHCP	Client IP address
device	Name of interface to use	When more than one is available, autoconf
autoconf	Autoconfiguration method	Any

Table 16-6. *Autoconfiguration Protocols*

Protocol	Description
off or none	Don't autoconfigure
on or any	Use any protocol available (default)
dhcp	Use DHCP
bootp	Use BOOTP
rarp	Use RARP
both	Use BOOTP or RARP but not DHCP

Emergency Kernel

In the event that your Raspberry Pi does not boot up properly, an emergency kernel is provided in /boot as file `kernel_emergency.img`. This kernel includes a BusyBox root file system to provide recovery tools. Through use of `e2fsck`, you'll be able to repair your normal Linux root file system. If necessary, you'll be able to mount that file system and make changes with the BusyBox tools.

To activate the emergency kernel, mount your SD card in a Linux, Mac, or Windows computer. Your computer should see the FAT32 partition, allowing you to rename files and edit configurations. Rename your current `kernel.img` to something like `kernel.bak` (you likely want to restore this kernel image later). Then rename `kernel_emergency.img` as `kernel.img`.

If you have used special configuration options in `config.txt` and `cmdline.txt`, you should copy these to `config.bak` and `cmdline.bak`, respectively. Then remove any special options that might have caused trouble (especially overclocking options). Alternatively, you can restore original copies of these two files, as provided by the standard Raspbian image download.

■ **Note**   Your FAT32 partition (`/boot`) probably has about 40 MB of free disk space (for a standard Raspbian disk image). Renaming large files, rather than copying them, saves disk space. Consequently, renaming kernel images is preferred over copying. Small files like `config.txt` or `cmdline.txt` can be copied as required.

The entire procedure is summarized here:

1. Rename `kernel.img` to `kernel.bak` (retain the normal kernel).

2. Rename `kernel_emergency.img` to `kernel.img`.

3. Copy `config.txt` to `config.bak`.

4. Copy `cmdline.txt` to `cmdline.bak`.

5. Edit or restore `config.txt` and `cmdline.txt` to original or safe configurations.

Step 5 requires your own judgment. If you have customized hardware, there may be some nonstandard configuration settings that you need to keep (see the previous "Avoid Safe Mode" section). The idea is to simply give your emergency kernel as much chance for success as possible. Disabling all overclocking options is also recommended.

■ **Caution**   After changes, make sure you properly unmount the SD card media (Linux/Mac) or "safely remove USB device" in Windows. Pulling the SD card out before all of the disk data has been written will corrupt your FAT32 partition, adding to your troubles. This may even cause loss of files.

With the kernel exchanged and the configuration restored to safe options, it should now be possible to boot the emergency kernel. Log in and rescue.

To restore your system back to its normal state, you'll need to follow these steps:

1. Rename `kernel.img` to `kernel_emergency.img` (for future rescues).

2. Rename `kernel.bak` to `kernel.img` (reinstate your normal kernel).

3. Restore/alter your `config.txt` configuration, if necessary.

4. Restore/alter your `cmdline.txt` configuration, if necessary.

At this point, you can reboot with your original kernel and configuration.

CHAPTER 17

Initialization

After the Linux kernel is booted, the first executing userland process ID number (PID) is 1. This process, known as init, is initially responsible for spawning all other required processes required by the system. The init process continues to execute after the system is up, running as a daemon (in the background). It should never be terminated by the user (when attempted on Raspbian Linux, the kill request was ignored).

Run Levels

The init process maintains a concept of a run level for the system. The current run level can be checked at the command line:

```
$ runlevel
N 2
$
```

The N shown here is the previous run level that was in effect. This N means that there was no prior run level. The 2 shown at the right is the current run-level number.

Raspbian Linux supports the run levels shown in Table 17-1. According to the action defined in Raspbian Linux's /etc/inittab file, it changes to run level 2 by default (see the /etc/inittab line with the initdefault action, which is described later). If problems are encountered, such as a corrupted root file system, the run level is taken to *single-user mode* (1). This allows the user at the console to repair the problem and resume the transition to a multiuser run level (normally 2) afterward.

Table 17-1. *Raspbian Run Levels*

Run Level	Meaning	Notes
S or s	Used at initial boot	Reserved
0	Halt	Reserved
1	Single-user mode	Reserved
2	Multiuser mode	Default
3	Multiuser mode	
4	Multiuser mode	

(*continued*)

Table 17-1. (*continued*)

Run Level	Meaning	Notes
5	Multiuser mode	
6	Initiate reboot	Reserved
7	Undocumented	See man 8 init
8	Undocumented	
9	Undocumented	

/etc/inittab

Once the init process has begun and performed its own initialization, it starts reading from configuration file /etc/inittab. This small file has a simple format composed of four fields, separated by colons:

```
id:runlevels:action:process
```

Lines beginning with a # are ignored as comments. Table 17-2 describes the four fields.

Table 17-2. /etc/inittab Fields

Field	Name	Description
1	id	A *unique* 1- to 4-character name for the entry
2	runlevel(s)	Lists the run levels for which the specified action should be performed
3	action	Describes the action required
4	process	Command-line text for the process

inittab Action initdefault

The /etc/inittab file should have one (and only one) entry, with an action named initdefault. This identifies what the initial run level should be after booting. The run level value is taken from the runlevels field of this entry. The Raspbian Linux image uses the following:

```
# The default runlevel.
id:2:initdefault:
```

This specifies that run level 2 is entered after the Linux kernel has booted. The name in the id field is not important here and simply must be unique within the file. The process field is also ignored for this entry. If the /etc/inittab file lacks the initdefault entry, init will ask for a run level from the console.

Field 3 of the inittab line specifies an action. The possible action choices are described in Table 17-3.

Table 17-3. *init Actions*

Action	Description	Notes
respawn	Restart whenever process terminates.	
wait	The process is started once when the run level is entered, and init will wait for its termination.	
once	Process is started when run level is entered.	
boot	Executed during system boot.	Ignores run levels, after sysinit entries
bootwait	Executed during system boot, but waits for the process to complete.	Ignores run levels, after sysinit entries
off	This does nothing (treat as a comment).	
ondemand	Execute upon demand: a, b, or c.	No run-level change
initdefault	Specifies the initial run level to use.	
sysinit	Execute during system boot.	Prior to boot/bootwait Ignores run levels
powerwait	Execute process when power goes down.	Waits for termination
powerfail	Execute process when power goes down.	Does not wait
powerokwait	Execute process when power restored.	
powerfailnow	Execute process when UPS signals near exhaustion of battery.	
ctrlaltdel	Execute process when init sees SIGINT.	SIGINT triggered by Ctrl-Alt-Delete.
kbrequest	Execute process after special key press.	

General Startup Sequence

Ignoring special events like power on demand and keyboard events, the general /etc/inittab processing follows this sequence:

1. /etc/inittab is searched for the initdefault action.

2. The user is prompted at the console for a run level, if none is found in /etc/inittab or the file is missing.

3. The init process sets the run level.

4. The sysinit entries are performed.

5. The boot and bootwait entries are performed.

6. All other entries that include the established run level are performed.

Step 4: sysinit

The standard Raspbian image uses the following for step 4:

```
# Boot-time system configuration/initialization script.
# This is run first except when booting in emergency (-b) mode.
si::sysinit:/etc/init.d/rcS
```

The preceding sysinit entry specifies that script /etc/init.d/rcS is to be run. This is a simple script that redirects the execution to yet another script:

```
#!/bin/sh
#
# rcS
#
# Call all S??* scripts in /etc/rcS.d/ in numerical/alphabetical order
#

exec /etc/init.d/rc S
```

From this we see that execution continues with /etc/init.d/rc with argument 1 set to S. This script is responsible for starting and stopping services on run-level changes. This particular inittab entry is used at initial boot-up and is used to invoke all startup scripts in /etc/rcS.d/S*.

Each of the /etc/rcS.d/S* scripts get invoked with one argument, start. Normally, the script would invoke /etc/rcS.d/K* scripts first (kill scripts that we will discuss later), but upon initial boot, there is no prior run level.

Step 5: boot/bootwait

Under Raspbian Linux, there are no boot or bootwait entries to perform.

Step 6: runlevel

The last step of the initialization involves changing from the non-run-level N to the run level 2, which was declared by the initdefault entry. The Raspbian inittab declares that the /etc/init.d/rc script is run with a run-level argument for each of these run-level changes:

```
l0:0:wait:/etc/init.d/rc 0
l1:1:wait:/etc/init.d/rc 1
l2:2:wait:/etc/init.d/rc 2
l3:3:wait:/etc/init.d/rc 3
l4:4:wait:/etc/init.d/rc 4
l5:5:wait:/etc/init.d/rc 5
l6:6:wait:/etc/init.d/rc 6
```

The first part of starting a new run level is to run the stop (kill) scripts at the *new* run level, provided that there was a previous run level. At boot time, there is no current level (it is N). So at startup, these scripts are ignored.

If, however, the system had been in single-user mode (for example) and the system was changed to run level 2, these kill scripts would be invoked:

```
$ ls -lL /etc/rc2.d/K*
-rwxr-xr-x 1 root root 2610 Jul  25 2011 /etc/rc2.d/K01lightdm
-rwxr-xr-x 1 root root 6491 Jul  21 2012 /etc/rc2.d/K05nfs-common
-rwxr-xr-x 1 root root 2344 Jun 15 2012 /etc/rc2.d/K05rpcbind
```

The script /etc/init.d/rc first iterates through these kill scripts (in sort order). When the current level has a stop (kill) script, the following logic applies:

1. If the previous run level *did* have a matching stop (kill) script, and

2. If the previous level *didn't* have a start script,

3. *Then there is no need to execute the stop (kill) script.*

Otherwise, the corresponding kill script is necessary and is performed.

At startup, or after a run-level change, the startup scripts for the new run level (2 in this example) are performed. When the current level has a start script, then the following logic applies:

1. If the previous run level *also* has a matching start script, and

2. The current level *doesn't* have a stop (kill) script,

3. *Then there is no need to stop and restart the script.*

Otherwise, the start script is invoked.

For all run levels except 0 and 6, the action being performed by the /etc/init.d/rc script is to *start* services (except where kill scripts apply). Entering run level 0 (halt) or 6 (reboot) is a bit different, since the script must be *stopping* services.

The following is an example list of startup scripts used by the Raspberry Pi when entering run level 2 after booting:

```
$ ls -lL /etc/rc2.d/S*
-rwxr-xr-x 1 root root 1276 Aug 31 2012  /etc/rc2.d/S01bootlogs
-rwxr-xr-x 1 root root 4698 May  1 2012   /etc/rc2.d/S01ifplugd
-rwxr-xr-x 1 root root  995 Aug 31 2012   /etc/rc2.d/S01motd
-rwxr-xr-x 1 root root 3054 Sep 26 2012  /etc/rc2.d/S01rsyslog
-rwxr-xr-x 1 root root  714 Jun  28 2012  /etc/rc2.d/S01sudo
-rwxr-xr-x 1 root root 3169 May 10 2011  /etc/rc2.d/S01triggerhappy
-rwxr-xr-x 1 root root 3033 Jul   9 2012  /etc/rc2.d/S02cron
-rwxr-xr-x 1 root root 2832 Sep 29 2012  /etc/rc2.d/S02dbus
-rwxr-xr-x 1 root root 2148 Jun   9 2012  /etc/rc2.d/S02dphys-swapfile
-rwxr-xr-x 1 root root 1814 Dec 26 2009  /etc/rc2.d/S02ntp
-rwxr-xr-x 1 root root 4395 Dec 13 06:43 /etc/rc2.d/S02rsync
-rwxr-xr-x 1 root root 3881 Feb 24 2012  /etc/rc2.d/S02ssh
-rwxr-xr-x 1 root root 1313 Jun  30 2012 /etc/rc2.d/S04plymouth
-rwxr-xr-x 1 root root  782 Mar 16 2012 /etc/rc2.d/S04rc.local
-rwxr-xr-x 1 root root 1074 Mar 16 2012 /etc/rc2.d/S04rmnologin
```

Like many Linux distributions, Raspbian Linux places the actual script files in the directory /etc/init.d. The names found in /etc/rc2.d, for example, are symlinks to the actual files.

It should also be noted that these scripts are run in the order determined by the pair of digits following the S or K prefix. This is a natural consequence of the way the shell sorts file names when listing files.

inittab Action wait

The wait init action is useful for entries that you want to run individually when the new run level is first entered. The init process will not resume with further entries until the launched process has terminated (whether launched successfully or not). Presumably, there is an implied order based on line sequence found in the file. An important attribute of this type of entry is that it is performed only *once* upon starting the run level.

inittab Action once

The once action is very similar to the wait action, except that the init process will *not* wait for the started process to terminate (perhaps it doesn't). Entries marked once are started only once per entry of a given run level, but init then proceeds with immediately processing other entries.

inittab Action respawn

The respawn option is often used for processes that manage terminal lines (gettys). The following example is taken from the standard Raspbian /etc/inittab:

```
# Spawn a getty on Raspberry Pi serial line
T0:23:respawn:/sbin/getty -L ttyAMA0 115200 vt100
```

This entry is used whenever init enters run levels 2 or 3. It launches program /sbin/getty to prompt the user for login on the serial console device (/dev/ttyAMA0 in this example). Other command-line parameters help the getty program to configure the terminal and login environment. When the user logs out of his session, the getty process terminates. When init notices that the process has terminated, it starts /sbin/getty again because of the respawn action. In this way, the terminal line is readied for the next user login.

■ **Caution** When using the respawn action for your own application, be careful that it doesn't fail frequently. Otherwise, init will churn by repeatedly restarting your process after it fails. You may eventually get a message on the console with init temporarily suspending the entry. This reduces the hogging of system resources from frequent respawning. But this suspension is temporary.

Changing Run Levels

The preceding sections outlined the startup procedure. Let's now examine what happens when you change run levels.

telinit

The /sbin/telinit executable is linked to the init program file /sbin/init. This form of the command is used to inform the executing init process to request a change of run levels:

```
# telinit x
```

where *x* is the new run level to enter. The run level may be specified only as one of the choices described in Table 17-4.

Table 17-4. *telinit Run Levels*

Level	Description
0-6	Run level 0, 1, 2, 3, 4, 5, or 6
a, b, c	Invoke inittab entries with a, b, or c
Q or q	Tell init to reexamine /etc/inittab
S or s	Change to single-user mode
U or u	Tell init to reexecute itself

Any unrecognized level is silently ignored.

Change of Run Level

Let's use an example to keep the references concrete. If you were in run level 1 and directed the system to change to run level 2 with

```
# telinit  2
```

the following happens:

1. /etc/init.d/rc executes all K* (kill) scripts for run level 2 (the level you are changing to), with an argument of stop.

2. /etc/init.d/rc executes all S* (start) scripts for run level 2, with the argument start.

3. Except where previously noted (redundant stop and start script executions are omitted)

Another way to think about this is that all K* symlinks at a particular run level identify services that *should not be running* at that level. Similarly, the S* symlinks identify services that *should be running* at that level.

Single-User Mode

Changing to single-user mode works the same as for any other level, except that most of the scripts are designed to be kill scripts to stop services (/etc/rc1.d/K*), rather than to start them.

The concept of single-user mode is that only one user will be using the system, without unnecessary services running in the background. This run level is normally used to repair the file systems or to reconfigure the system.

Halt and Reboot

Changing to level 0 (halt) or 6 (reboot) requires stopping all services. As a result, in this case only the kill scripts are performed with the argument stop. In the file

```
/usr/share/doc/sysv-rc/README.runlevels
```

you will find this remark:

In the future, the /etc/rc6.d/SXXxxxx scripts MIGHT be moved to /etc/rc6.d/K1XXxxxx for clarity.

Creating a New Service

If you had a dedicated application for your Raspberry Pi, you might want to assign it to a dedicated run level, perhaps 4. In this manner, you could still perform maintenance and perhaps even development in run level 2. When it was time to start the dedicated application, you'd use telinit to change to run level 4. You could even have /etc/inittab cause a reboot directly into level 4, by the following entry:

```
id:4:initdefault:
```

Rebooting directly to your custom run level 4 would be useful for solar applications to handle restarts due to power fluctuations.

To arrange the startup/kill scripts, you would need the following:

1. Kill scripts at the following locations (symlinks to /etc/init.d/service). These apply when you change from level 4 to one of the other levels, where you don't want the service running.

    a. /etc/rc2.d/KXXservice

    b. /etc/rc3.d/KXXservice

    c. /etc/rc5.d/KXXservice

    d. Note that single-user mode by default will not have other services left running.

2. You will need a startup script for run level 4:

    a./etc/rc4.d/SXXservice

In the preceding script, XX is a sequence number (00 to 99) that positions where in the list of scripts it gets executed.

Also note that the symlinks

- /etc/rc2.d/KXXservice

- /etc/rc2.d/SXXservice

point to the same file in /etc/init.d/service. The K* symlinks are invoked with the argument stop, while the S* symlinks are invoked with start. This means that your single /etc/init.d/service script file should stop or start based on this command-line argument.

The advantage of running your dedicated application from its own run level includes the following:

- Less competition for CPU resources from unused daemons

- Increased security by not running services that permit external login attempts

- Restricted physical access—login only via the serial port console (when configured)

- Automatic restart of your application after a power failure

With run levels 3, 4, and 5 to work with, you can configure a mix of different dedicated application profiles.

vcgencmd

Apart from the usual Linux commands that display status, the Raspberry Pi includes a custom command named vcgencmd, which can report voltages and temperatures. This chapter documents the known features of the command.

The executable file behind the command is /usr/bin/vcgencmd.

vcgencmd Commands

There is no man page for this command, but the list of all supported options can be displayed with the commands option. The command output has been broken over several lines for readability:

```
$ vcgencmd commands
commands="vcos, ap_output_control, ap_output_post_processing, \
pm_set_policy, pm_get_status, pm_show_stats, pm_start_logging, \
pm_stop_logging, version, commands, set_vll_dir, \
led_control, set_backlight, set_logging, get_lcd_info, \
set_bus_arbiter_mode, cache_flush, otp_dump, codec_enabled, \
measure_clock, measure_volts, measure_temp, get_config, \
hdmi_ntsc_freqs, render_bar, disk_notify, inuse_notify, \
sus_suspend, sus_status, sus_is_enabled, \
sus_stop_test_thread, egl_platform_switch, mem_validate, \
mem_oom, mem_reloc_stats, file, vctest_memmap, vctest_start, \
vctest_stop, vctest_set, vctest_get"
```

At the time of this writing, some of these options remained undocumented. A summary list of options is itemized in Table 18-1.

Table 18-1. *Summary of vcgencmd Command-Line Options*

Option Name	Argument(s)	Description
ap_output_control		
ap_output_post_processing		
cache_flush		Flushes GPU's L1 cache
codec_enabled	codec	Reports status of codec
commands		Lists options

(continued)

Table 18-1. (*continued*)

Option Name	Argument(s)	Description
disk_notify		
egl_platform_switch		
file		
get_config		
get_lcd_info		Returns height, width, and depth of the display frame buffer
hdmi_ntsc_freqs		
inuse_notify		
led_control		
measure_clock	clock	Reports frequency
measure_temp		Reports SoC temperature
measure_volts	device	Reports voltage
mem_oom		Reports Out of Memory events
mem_reloc_stats		Reports relocatable memory stats
mem_validate		
otp_dump		
pm_get_status		
pm_set_policy		
pm_show_stats		
pm_start_logging		
pm_stop_logging		
render_bar		
set_backlight		
set_bus_arbiter_mode		
set_logging		

Option measure_clock

This firmware access option provides the user with clock rate information, according to the argument appearing after measure_clock. Valid values for *<clock>* are listed in Table 18-2.

```
vcgencmd  measure_clock  <clock>
```

Table 18-2. *Valid Arguments for the* measure_clock *Option*

Clock	Description
arm	ARM CPU
core	Core
dpi	Display Pixel Interface
emmc	External MMC device
h264	h.264 encoder
hdmi	HDMI clock
isp	Image Sensor Pipeline
pixel	Pixel clock
pwm	Pulse Width Modulation
uart	UART clock
v3d	Video 3D
vec	

The following shell script is often used to list all available clocks:

```
$ for src in arm core h264 isp v3d uart pwm emmc pixel vec hdmi dpi ; do
     echo -e "$src : $(vcgencmd measure_clock $src)" ;
done
```

Here is the example output:

```
arm    :    frequency (45)=700074000
core   :    frequency (1)=250000000
h264   :    frequency (28)=250000000
isp    :    frequency (42)=250000000
v3d    :    frequency (43)=250000000
uart   :    frequency (22)=3000000
pwm    :    frequency (25)=0
emmc   :    frequency (47)=100000000
pixel  :    frequency (29)=108000000
vec    :    frequency (10)=0
hdmi   :    frequency (9)=163683000
dpi    :    frequency (4)=0
```

Option measure_volts

The measure_volts option allows the various subsystem voltages to be reported:

```
$ for id in core sdram_c sdram_i sdram_p ; do
  echo -e "$id: $(vcgencmd measure_volts $id)" ;
done
core:      volt=1.20V
sdram_c:   volt=1.20V
sdram_i:   volt=1.20V
sdram_p:   volt=1.23V
```

Table 18-3 provides a legend for the output report lines.

Table 18-3. *Valid Device Names for measure_volts*

Device	Description
core	Core
sdram_c	SDRAM controller
sdram_i	SDRAM I/O
sdram_p	SDRAM physical

Option measure_temp

The measure_temp option allows the user to retrieve the SoC temperature, in degrees Celsius.

```
$ vcgencmd measure_temp
temp=36.3 °C
```

In this example, the relatively idle core was reported to be 36.3°C.

Option codec_enabled

The codec_enabled option reports the operational status of the codecs supported by the Raspberry Pi. Valid codec names are listed in Table 18-4. The codec support can be summarized with the following command:

```
$ for id in H264 MPG2WCV1 ; do
  echo -e "$id: $(vcgencmd codec_enabled $id)";
done
H264:    H264=enabled
MPG2:    MPG2=disabled
WCV1:    WCV1=disabled
```

Table 18-4. *vcgencmd CODEC Names*

Name	Description
H264	h.264 CODEC
MPG2	MPEG-2 CODEC
WVC1	VC1 CODEC

Option version

The version option reports the GPU firmware version:

```
$ vcgencmd version
Oct 25 2012 16:37:21
Copyright (c) 2012 Broadcom
version 346337 (release)
```

Option get_lcd_info

While get_lcd_info was undocumented at the time of this writing, it appears to provide LCD/monitor width and height, and pixel depth:

```
$ vcgencmd get_lcd_info
720 480 24
```

Option get_config

The get_config option is useful in scripts that need to query your Raspberry Pi's configuration, as defined in /boot/config.txt. See Chapter 16 for the options that can be queried. For example, a script can query whether avoid_safe_mode is in effect:

```
$ vcgencmd get_config avoid_safe_mode
avoid_safe_mode=0
```

CHAPTER 19

■ ■ ■

Linux Console

The Raspbian Linux console is configured (or assumed) by the kernel command line. See the console option described in Chapter 16.

Available Consoles

The list of consoles is available through the /proc/consoles pseudo file:

```
$ cat /proc/consoles
tty1                    -WU (EC p  )     4:1
ttyAMA0                 -W- (E  p  )   204:64
```

The organization and flags displayed are described in Tables 19-1 and 19-2. The major and minor numbers are confirmed in the following example session output:

```
$ ls -l /dev/tty1 /dev/ttyAMA0
crw-rw---- 1 root tty    4,   1 Jan 21 00:06  /dev/tty1
crw-rw---- 1 root tty  204, 64 Jan 21 00:06  /dev/ttyAMA0
```

Table 19-1. /proc/consoles Fields

Field	Parameter	Example	Description
1	device	tty1	/dev/tty1
			R = read
2	operations	-WU-	W = write
			U = unblank
3	flags	(EC p)	See flags in Table 19-2
4	major:minor	4:1	Device major/minor

Table 19-2. *The Meaning of Flags Displayed in Parentheses*

Flag	Meaning
E	The console is enabled.
C	Is the preferred console.
B	Primary boot console.
p	Used for printk buffer.
b	Not a TTY, but is a Braille device.
a	Safe to use when CPU is offline.

Serial Console

If you wired up a serial console to your Raspberry Pi, you can use a utility such as PuTTY (http://www.chiark.greenend.org.uk/~sgtatham/putty/download.html) on your laptop or desktop computer to connect to it. The serial console sees the following first few lines at boot (long lines are edited):

```
Uncompressing Linux... done, booting the kernel.
[    0.000000] Initializing cgroup subsys cpu
[    0.000000] Linux version 3.2.27+  (dc4@dc4-arm-01) \
(gcc version 4.7.2 20120731 (prerelease) \
(crosstool -NG linaro -1.13.1+bzr2458 - Linaro GCC 2012.08 )) \
#250 PREEMPT Thu Oct 18 19:03:02 BST 2012
[    0.000000] CPU: ARMv6-compatible processor [410fb767] \
revision 7 (ARMv7), cr=00c5387d
[    0.000000]  CPU : PIPT /VIPT nonaliasing data cache, \
VIPT nonaliasing instruction cache
[    0.000000]  Machine:  BCM2708
```

Using the dmesg command, you can see almost the same thing:

```
$ dmesg | head -5
[    0.000000] Initializing cgroup subsys cpu
[    0.000000] Linux version 3.2.27+ (dc4@dc4-arm-01) \
(gcc version 4.7.2 20120731 (prerelease) \
(crosstool -NG linaro -1.13.1+bzr2458 - Linaro GCC 2012.08)) \
#250 PREEMPT Thu Oct 18 19:03:02 BST 2012
[    0.000000] CPU: ARMv6-compatible processor [410fb767] \
revision 7 (ARMv7), cr=00c5387d
[    0.000000] CPU:PIPT/VIPT nonaliasing data cache, \
VIPT nonaliasing instruction cache
[    0.000000] Machine:BCM2708
```

The difference is that the initial Uncompressing Linux console output is missing. Additionally, any debug messages that a new kernel might display can be capturable on a serial console.

CHAPTER 20

■ ■ ■

Cross-Compiling

Embedded computers often lack the necessary resources for developing and compiling software. The Raspberry Pi is rather special in this regard since it already includes the gcc compiler and the needed linking tools (under Raspbian Linux). But while the code can be developed and built on the Raspberry Pi, it may not always be the most suitable place for software development. One reason is the lower performance of the SD card.

To compile *native* code for the Raspberry Pi, you need a compiler and linker that knows how to generate ARM binary executables. Yet it must run on a host with a different architecture (for example, Mac OS X). Hence the reason it is called a *cross*-compiler. The cross-compiler will take your source code on the local (build) platform and generate ARM binary executables, to be installed on your target Pi.

There are prebuilt cross-compile tools available, including the Raspberry Pi Foundation's own tools (git://github.com/raspberrypi/tools.git), but these can be problematic for some versions of Linux. Running the cross-compiler on a different Linux release than it was built for may cause the software to complain about missing or incompatible shared libraries. But if you find that you can use a prebuilt release, it will save considerable time.

In this chapter, you'll walk through how to build your own cross-compiler. This may permit you to get the job done using your existing Linux release.

Terminology

Let's first cover some terminology used in this chapter:

> *build*: Also called the *local* platform, this is the platform that you perform the compiling on (for example, Mac OS X).

> *target*: The destination platform, which is the Raspberry Pi (ARM) in this chapter.

Let's now consider some of the cross-compiling issues before you take the plunge. There are two main problem areas in cross-compiling:

- All C/C++ include files and libraries for the Raspberry Pi (ARM) must be available on your build platform.

- The cross-compiler and related tools must generate code suitable for the target platform.

So before you decide that you want to build a cross-compiler environment, are you prepared to

- Provide all matching C/C++ header files from the ARM platform?

- Provide all ARM libraries needed, including libraries for third-party products like sqlite3 that you intend to link with?

- Provide sufficient disk space for the cross-compiler and tools?

The crosstool-NG software will mitigate some of these issues. For example, the correct Linux headers are chosen by the configuration step shown later in this chapter.

Disk space solves many issues by holding a copy of your Raspberry Pi's root file system on your build platform. Simple programs won't require this (for example, a Hello World). But software linking to libraries may require this. Even if you're strapped for disk space, you may be able to mount the Raspbian SD card on the build platform, thus gaining access to the Raspberry Pi's root file system.

Operating System

The procedure used for building a cross-compiler environment is somewhat complex and fragile. Using the crosstool-NG software simplifies things considerably. Despite this advantage, it is best to stick with proven cross-compiler platforms and configurations.

You might be tempted to say, "The source code is open, and so it should work on just about any operating system." (You might even say, "I'll fix the problems myself.") The reality is not quite so simple. I use the Mac Ports collection (`www.macports.org`) for a number of things and quickly discovered the limitations of building a crosstool-NG on Mac OS X. For example, I found that objcopy was not supported when `./configure` was run for the cross-compiler. Unless you are willing to spend time on Internet forums and wait for answers, I suggest you take a more pragmatic approach—build your cross-compiling environment on a recent and stable Ubuntu or Debian environment.

This chapter uses Ubuntu 14.04 LTS hosted in VirtualBox 4.3.12 (`www.virtualbox.org`) on a Mac OS X Mavericks MacBook Pro, running an Intel i7 processor. Current versions of Ubuntu are recommended. Ubuntu 12.10 was the version tested and used by the process documented at this link:

`www.kitware.com/blog/home/post/426`

Host, Guest, Build, and Target

At this point, a short note is in order because these terms can get confusing, especially for those performing this for the first time. Let's list the environment terms, which will be referred to throughout the remainder of this chapter:

- *Host* environment

- *Guest* environment

- *Build/local* environment

- *Target* environment

So many environments! The terms *host* and *guest* environments enter the picture when you are using a virtual machine like VirtualBox. VirtualBox is used to *host* another operating system on top of the one you are using. For example, you might be running Mac OS X on your laptop. In this example, the OS X environment *hosts* Ubuntu Linux within VirtualBox. The Ubuntu Linux operating system is thus referred to as the *guest* operating system.

The term *build* (or *local*) environment refers to the Linux environment that is executing the cross-compiler and tools. These Linux tools produce or manipulate code for the *target* environment (your Raspberry Pi's ARM CPU).

Platform Limitations

Many people today are using 64-bit platforms similar to my own MacBook Pro, with an Intel i7 processor. This may present a problem if you want to build a cross-compiler for the Raspberry Pi, which is a 32-bit platform. Many people building a cross-compiler on a 64-bit platform have encountered software problems building for a 32-bit platform.

For this reason, if you are using a 64-bit platform, you'll probably want to choose a VirtualBox solution. This will allow you to run a 32-bit operating system to host the cross-compiler. On the other hand, if you are already running a 32-bit operating system, creating a native cross-compiler for the Pi is a real possibility.

Without VirtualBox (Native)

If you are already using a Linux development environment like Debian or Ubuntu, the term *host* is equivalent to the build (or local) environment. The host and guest environments are likewise equivalent, though it is probably more correct to say there is no guest operating system in this scenario. This simpler scenario leaves us with just two environments:

Host/guest/build: Native environment running the cross-compiler tools

Target: The destination execution environment (Raspberry Pi)

Using VirtualBox (Ubuntu/Linux)

If you do not have a suitable Linux environment, one can be hosted on the platform you have. You can host Linux from Windows, Mac OS X, Solaris, or another distribution of Linux. VirtualBox can be downloaded from the following:

`www.virtualbox.org`

When VirtualBox is used, the *host* environment is the environment that is running VirtualBox (for example, Mac OS X). The *guest* operating system will be Ubuntu (recommended) or Debian. This leaves us with three environments in total:

Host: Or native, running VirtualBox (for example, Windows)

Guest/build: Ubuntu/Debian development environment within VirtualBox

Target: The destination execution environment (your Raspberry Pi)

Planning Your Cross-Development Environment

The main consideration at this point is normally disk space. If you are using VirtualBox, limited memory can be another factor. If you are using Linux or Mac OS X, check your mounted disks for available space (or Windows tools as appropriate):

```
$ df -k
Filesystem          1024-blocks      Used          Available      Capacity    Mounted on
/dev/disk0s2        731734976        154168416     577310560      22%         /
devfs               186              186           0              100%        /dev
map -hosts          0                0             0              100%        /net
map auto_home       0                0             0              100%        /home
map -static         0                0             0              100%        /Volumes/oth
$
```

In the preceding example output, we see that the root file system has plenty of space. But your file system may be laid out differently. Symlinks can be used when necessary to graft a larger disk area onto your home directory.

If you're using VirtualBox, create virtual disks with enough space for the Linux operating system and your cross-compiler environment. You may want to put your Linux software on one virtual disk with a minimum size of about 8–10 GB (allow it to grow larger).

Allow a minimum of 10 GB for your cross-compiler environment (and allow it to grow). 9 GB is just barely large enough to host the cross-compiler tools and allow you to compile a Hello World type of program. But you must also factor in additional space for the Raspberry Linux kernel, its include files, and all other third-party libraries that you might need to build with (better still, a copy of the Raspberry Pi's root file system).

Within your development Ubuntu/Debian build environment, make sure your cross-compiler and build area are using the disk area that has available space. It is easy to glibly create a directory someplace convenient and find out later that the space that you thought you were going to use wasn't available.

Building the Cross-Compiler

At this point, I'll assume that you've set up and installed Ubuntu in VirtualBox, if necessary. Otherwise, you are building your cross-compiler tools on an existing Ubuntu/Debian system, with disk space sufficient for the job.

We will be using the basic recipe outlined from this web resource:

"Cross-Compiling for Raspberry Pi," `www.kitware.com/blog/home/post/426`

Download crosstool-NG

The released crosstool-NG downloads are found at this site:

```
http://crosstool-ng.org/download/crosstool-ng/
     current release: crosstool-ng-1.19.0.tar.bz2
```

It is normal practice to download the newest stable version of software. I am using 1.19.0 in this text because it was current at the time of writing.

Staging Directory

I'll assume that you've symlinked to your disk area with sufficient available disk space. In other words, the symlink named ~/devel points to the development area to be used. This can be just a subdirectory if you have sufficient disk space there.

In directory ~/devel, create a subdirectory named staging (~/devel/staging) and change it to the following:

```
$ cd ~/devel       # Dir is ~/devel
$ mkdir staging
$ cd ./staging     # Dir is ~/devel/staging
$ pwd
/home/myuserid/devel/staging
$
```

Unpack the Tarball

Assuming the tarball `crosstool-ng-1.19.0.tar.bz2` was downloaded to your home directory, you would perform the following (change the option j if the suffix is not `.bz2`):

```
$ tar xjvf ~/crosstool-ng-1.19.0.tar.bz2
. . .
$
```

After the unpacking completes, you should have a subdirectory named `crosstoolng-1.19.0` in your `staging` directory.

Create /opt/x-tools

You can choose a different location if you like, but I'm going to assume that the crosstool-NG software is going to install into `/opt/x-tools`. We'll also assume your user ID is `fred` (substitute your own).

```
$ sudo mkdir -p /opt/x-tools
$ sudo chown fred /opt/x-tools
```

Once your installation is complete later, you can change the ownership back to `root` for protection.

Install Package Dependencies

The crosstool-NG build depends on several packages provided by Ubuntu/Debian as optionally installed software:

bison: GNU yacc

flex: GNU lex

subversion: Subversion source control package

libtool: Library tool

texinfo: Install the texinfo package

gawk: GNU awk (gawk)

gperf: Perfect hash function generator

automake: Tool for generating GNU standards-compliant Makefiles

Save time by making sure these packages are installed before proceeding to the next step. Package dependencies often change over time. Depending on your host system, you may find that additional packages (such as libncurses5-dev, for example) are also needed. If more packages are needed, the configure step usually identifies them.

Configure crosstools-NG

With the package dependencies installed, you are now in a position to make the crosstool-NG software:

```
$ cd ~/devel/staging/crosstool-ng-1.19.0
$ ./configure --prefix=/opt/x-tools
```

If this completes without errors, you are ready to build and install the crosstool-NG software. If it reports that you are missing package dependencies, install them now and repeat.

make crosstool-ng

At this point, you should have no trouble building crosstool-NG. Perform the following make command:

```
$ cd ~/devel/staging/crosstool-ng-1.19.0
$ make
```

This takes very little time and seems trouble free.

make install

Once the crosstool-NG package has been compiled, it is ready to be installed into /opt/x-tools. From the same directory:

```
$ sudo make install
```

If you still own the directory /opt/x-tools from earlier (recall sudo chown fred /opt/x-tools), you won't need to use sudo in the preceding step. After make install is performed, you will have the crosstool-NG command ct-ng installed in the directory /opt/x-tools/bin.

PATH

To use the newly installed ct-ng command, you will need to adjust your PATH environment variable:

```
$ PATH="/opt/x-tools/bin:$PATH"
```

The website also indicates that you might have to unset environment variable LD_LIBRARY_PATH, if your platform has it defined. If so, then unset it as follows:

```
$ unset LD_LIBRARY_PATH
```

Now you should be able to run ct-ng to get version info (note that there are no hyphens in front of version in the following command). Seeing the version output confirms that your ct-ng command has been installed and is functional:

```
$ ct-ng version
This is crosstool-NG version 1.19.0

Copyright (C) 2008  Yann E. MORIN <yann.morin.1998@free.fr>
This is free software; see the source for copying conditions.
There is NO warranty; not even for MERCHANTABILITY or FITNESS FOR A PARTICULAR PURPOSE.
```

Cross-Compiler Configuration

The command ct-ng simplifies the work necessary to configure and build the cross-compiler tool chain. From here, we are concerned with building the cross-compiler tools themselves. When that process is completed, you will have populated the cross-compiler tools into the directory /opt/x-tools/arm-unknown-linux-gnueabi.

Before `ct-ng` can build your cross-compiler, it must first be configured:

```
$ cd ~/devel/staging
$ ct-ng menuconfig
```

If you get a "command not found" error message, check that the PATH variable is set properly.

Paths and Misc Options

When the command starts up, the menu configuration screen is presented.

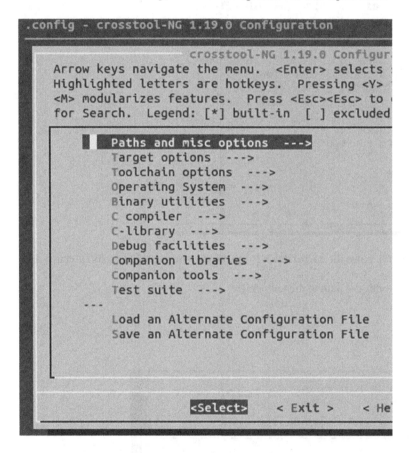

Press Enter, to open the Paths and Misc Options submenu.

Once in the Paths and Misc Options menu, as shown next, use the cursor key to move down to Try Features Marked as Experimental. Once that line is highlighted, press the spacebar to put an asterisk inside the square brackets, to select the option (pressing space again toggles the setting).

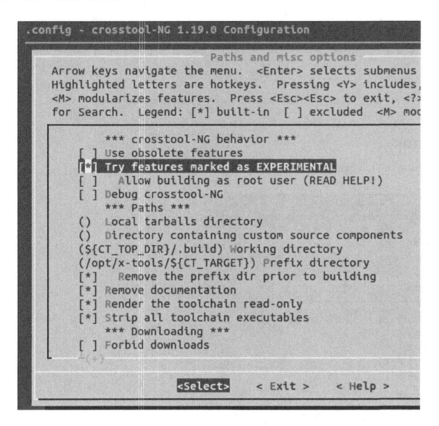

After doing that, while in the same menu, move the cursor down to the middle entry labelled Prefix Directory and press Enter to select it.

For the procedure used in this book, modify the path to the following:

```
/opt/x-tools/${CT_TARGET}
```

as illustrated here:

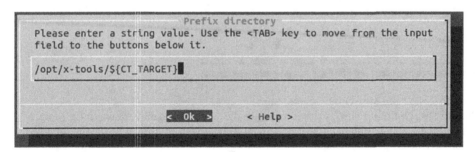

Once the pathname is established, press Enter on the OK button shown. This returns you to the Paths and Misc Options menu.

Then select the Exit button shown at the bottom, and press Enter again.

Target Options

From the main menu, select Target Options with the cursor and press Enter to open that menu. Then choose Target Architecture and press Enter. In that menu, choose Arm and use the Select button at the bottom. This returns you to the Target Options menu.

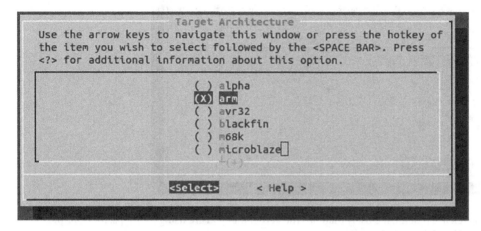

While in the Target Options menu (shown next), verify the Endianness setting by reviewing the status in brackets. It should read Little Endian. If not, enter that menu and change it to *Little endian*. Below the Endianness menu item is the Bitness option. It should already indicate 32-bit. If not, select it and change the setting to 32-bit.

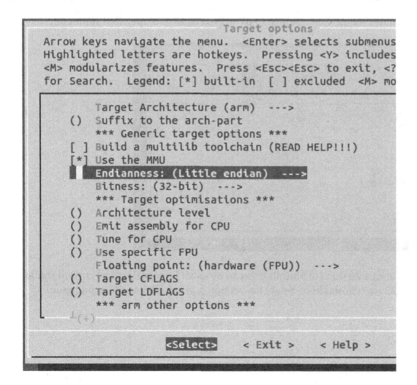

Finally, exit this submenu with the Exit button.

Operating System

At the main menu again, choose Operating System and then choose Linux Kernel Version.

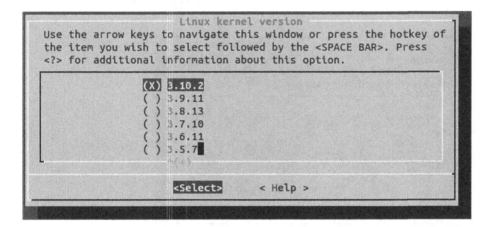

It is best to choose the release that most closely matches the kernel that you are using (perhaps, for example, 3.10.2). Once you have chosen, exit back to the main menu.

Binary Utilities

At the main menu, open the Binary Utilities menu. Cursor down to Binutils Version and open that submenu:

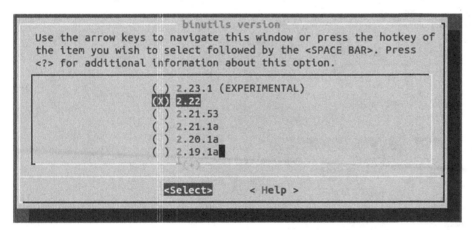

In this menu, you are presented various versions of binutils that can be used. Choose the most current stable (nonexperimental) version. Version 2.22 was chosen here. Select the version and exit back to the main menu.

C Compiler

At the main menu, open the C Compiler submenu. Here it is recommended that you enable the Show Linaro Versions option.

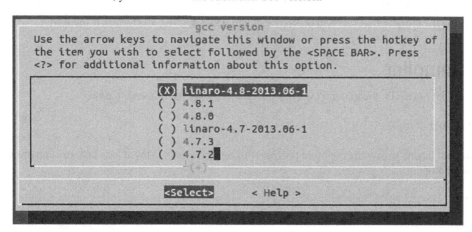

Once that is enabled, you can select the submenu Gcc Version:

The preceding figure shows linaro-4.8.2013.06-1 being chosen (which I had good results with). Newer versions are always becoming available. Choose the compiler and then choose the Select button at the bottom.

Then choose Exit once again to return to the main menu.

Save Configuration

Unless you have a reason to change anything else, exit the menu again to cause the Save prompt to appear:

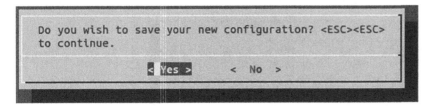

Upon selecting Yes, the command exits with the following session output showing in the terminal window:

```
$ ct-ng menuconfig
  IN    config.gen/arch.in
  IN    config.gen/kernel.in
  IN    config.gen/cc.in
  IN    config.gen/libc.in
  IN    config/config.in
#
# configuration saved
#
```

At this point, it is worth mentioning that you may want to save your configuration somewhere outside the current directory. The configuration is saved in a file named .config and can be copied elsewhere. The following is a suggestion:

```
$ cp .config ~/ct-ng.config.bak
```

Saving the file outside the current directory will prevent accidental loss if ct-ng distclean is invoked.

Build Cross-Compiler

Check the ownership of /opt/x-tools. If you don't own this directory, change the ownership now:

```
$ sudo chown -R fred /opt/x-tools
```

This will save you from having to execute the build process with root privileges. Now at long last, you can initiate the building of the cross-compiler:

```
$ cd ~/devel/staging
$ ct-ng build
```

Allow a good block of time for this job. This is not something that can be pushed through in a hurry. Ideally, you can just leave the command to run and check for successful completion in an hour or so. However, it is not uncommon for different software problems to arise at this stage. I once spent an entire Saturday troubleshooting this step. If you do encounter problems, read the next section for some troubleshooting tips.

If all goes well, ct-ng compiles and installs tools into /opt/x-tools without any further interaction. In the following session, Retrieving needed toolchain components is rather brief, because this was a session rerun with the components cached somewhere. Your download times will be longer when doing this for the first time.

```
[INFO]   Performing some trivial sanity checks
[INFO]   Build started 20140103.102402
[INFO]   Building environment variables
[INFO]   =================================================================
[INFO]   Retrieving needed toolchain components' tarballs
[INFO]   Retrieving needed toolchain components' tarballs: done in 0.13s (at 00:04)
[INFO]   =================================================================
[INFO]   Extracting and patching toolchain components
[INFO]   Extracting and patching toolchain components: done in 3.96s (at 00:08)
[INFO]   =================================================================
[INFO]   Installing GMP for host
[INFO]   Installing GMP for host: done in 37.57s (at 00:46)
[INFO]   =================================================================
[INFO]   Installing MPFR for host
[INFO]   Installing MPFR for host: done in 18.16s (at 01:04)
[INFO]   =================================================================
[INFO]   Installing PPL for host
[INFO]   Installing PPL for host: done in 268.27s (at 05:32)
[INFO]   =================================================================
[INFO]   Installing CLooG/PPL for host
[INFO]   Installing CLooG/PPL for host: done in 6.45s (at 05:39)
[INFO]   =================================================================
[INFO]   Installing MPC for host
[INFO]   Installing MPC for host: done in 7.97s (at 05:47)
[INFO]   =================================================================
[INFO]   Installing binutils for host
[INFO]   Installing binutils for host: done in 53.52s (at 06:40)
[INFO]   =================================================================
[INFO]   Installing pass -1 core C compiler
[INFO]   Installing pass -1 core C compiler: done in 222.36s (at 10:23)
[INFO]   =================================================================
[INFO]   Installing kernel headers
[INFO]   Installing kernel headers: done in 4.54s (at 10:27)
[INFO]   =================================================================
[INFO]   Installing C library headers & start files
[INFO]   Installing C library headers & start files: done in 31.26s (at 10:58)
[INFO]   =================================================================
[INFO]   Installing pass -2 core C compiler
[INFO]   Installing pass -2 core C compiler: done in 512.54s (at 19:31)
[INFO]   =================================================================
[INFO]   Installing C library
[INFO]   Installing C library: done in 805.58s (at 32:57)
[INFO]   =================================================================
[INFO]   Installing final compiler
[INFO]   Installing final compiler: done in 484.58s (at 41:01)
[INFO]   =================================================================
[INFO]   Cleaning -up the toolchain's directory
[INFO]   Stripping all toolchain executables
```

```
[INFO]   Cleaning -up the toolchain's directory: done in 3.86s (at 41:05)
[INFO]   Build completed at 20130103.110507
[INFO]   (elapsed: 41:04.93)
[INFO]   Finishing installation (may take a few seconds )...
[41:05]  /
```

The overall time for my build was 41 minutes (reported to be 83 minutes on a Windows 8 Intel i5 using VirtualBox). My build was performed in VirtualBox running on Mac OS X Mavericks, using the Intel i7 processor (2.8 GHz). On the same Mac, I found that the times approximately doubled when the VirtualBox disk images were located on a USB 2.0 disk drive. From these figures, you can estimate your build time.

Troubleshooting

The session output that you get from this build process is very terse. As such, you don't always get a clear idea of what the real failure was. For this reason, you'll often need to check the build.log file:

```
$ less build.log
```

Using less, you can navigate to the end of the build.log file by typing a capital G.

One failure that frequently occurs in the beginning is a *failed download*. While the build process does retry downloads and tries different download methods, it can still fail. All that you need to do is to start the build again. It will download only the remaining files needed. Sometimes it will succeed on the second or third retry attempt.

Sometimes a component will fail in its *configuration phase*. Check the build.log file first to determine precisely which component is involved. Next you will want to examine the config.log file for that particular component. For example, let's say the isl component failed. Dive down into the .build subdirectory until you find its config.log file:

```
$ cd .build/arm-unknown-linux-gnueabi/build/build-isl-host-i686-build_pc-linux-gnu
$ less config.log
```

Navigate to the end of config.log and work backward a few pages. Eventually, you will see text describing the command that was tried and the error message produced. In one instance, I was able to determine that the custom compiler option that I added (-fpermissive) was causing the failure. The solution then was to remove that option and try again.

Some errors will occur only with certain version choices. At one time, I was receiving errors related to PPL and needed a patch to correct it. Google is your friend (the following patch is an example):

```
http://patchwork.ozlabs.org/patch/330733/
```

I found that saving that patch to a file and applying it to the sources corrected the issue. Later, when I decided to start over with a different choice of compiler, this patch became unnecessary (the software was downloaded fresh again).

In getting through these issues, you can simply make corrections and then rerun the ct-ng build command. It is recommended that you plan for a later rebuild of everything again (after a clean), once the problems are solved. This will ensure that you have a good build without dependency issues.

If, after a correction, you run into the same problem, you may need to do a clean step first and start over. Depending on how deep you think the problem may be, choose one of the following:

- ct-ng clean
- ct-ng distclean (Be careful; see the following text.)

The `ct-ng clean` command will usually be enough, forcing the next build to start fresh. Any downloaded files and configuration will remain and are reused.

The `ct-ng distclean` command is much more drastic, since it removes all of the downloaded content *and your configuration files.* I copied the `.config` file to `.config.bak` and discovered to my horror that `.config.bak` had been removed! So if you back up the `.config` file, copy it *outside* the current directory for safety.

Above all, keep your head. It's difficult to troubleshoot these issues if you feel time pressure or get angry over the time invested. When under time pressure, leave it for another day when you can deal with it leisurely and thoughtfully. Each redo takes considerable time. Wherever possible, eliminate the guesswork.

With each problem, take a deep breath, patiently look for clues, and pay attention to the details in the error messages. Remember that line in the movie *Apollo 13*: "Work the problem, people!"

## CHAPTER 21

Cross-Compiling the Kernel

While normally not possible on embedded platforms, it *is* possible to build kernels on your Raspberry Pi with its luxurious root file system. Despite this, cross-compiling on desktop systems is preferred for faster compile times. This chapter examines the procedure for building your Raspbian kernel.

It is assumed that you have the cross-compiler tools and environment ready. Either the tool set built in Chapter 20 or an installed prebuilt tool chain will do. In this chapter, I assume that the cross-compiler prefix is as follows (ending in a hyphen):

/opt/x-tools/arm-unknown-linux-gnueabi/bin/arm-unknown-linux-gnueabi-

Substitute as appropriate, if your tools are installed differently.

Image Tools

According to the "RPi Buying Guide" from eLinux.org, "The way the memory addresses are arranged in the Broadcom SoC, you will need to prepare the compiled image for use." Consequently, an image tool must be used so that the built kernel image can be modified for booting by the Raspberry Pi.

Note You can read more of the "RPi Buying Guide" at
http://s3.amazonaws.com/szmanuals/8d4eb934fa27c2cbecd2a7f3b6922848.

Let's begin by creating and changing to a work directory:

```
$ mkdir ~/work
$ cd ~/work
```

The tools can be downloaded from here:

```
$ wget https://github.com/raspberrypi/tools/archive/master.tar.gz
```

They can also be fetched from the Git repository:

```
$ git clone --depth 1 git@github.com:raspberrypi/tools.git
```

Save time with the -depth 1 option to avoid downloading older versions that you are uninterested in. The git command will produce a subdirectory named tools. After git has completed, the following additional git steps are recommended:

```
$ rm -fr ./tools/.git      # Delete unneeded .git subdirectory
$ mv tools tools-master     # Rename for consistency in this chapter
$ tar czvf master.tar.gz    # create master.tar.gz as if we downloaded it
```

Whether you simply downloaded master.tar.gz or created it in the preceding step (after using git), unpack the tarball into /opt as follows:

```
$ cd /opt
$ sudo tar xzf ~/work/master.tar.gz
```

This creates the subdirectory /opt/tools-master.

■ **Note** If you have trouble using git from VirtualBox, there may be networking issues involved (reconfiguration may correct this). The simplest workaround is to simply use git outside VirtualBox and upload the master.tar.gz file with scp.

If you need to save space and you don't need to use the other tools included, remove them:

```
$ cd /opt/tools-master
$ ls
arm-bcm2708  configs  mkimage  pkg  sysidk  usbboot
```

If you are using the cross-compiler from Chapter 20, you won't need the arm-bcm2708 subdirectory:

```
$ cd /opt/tools-master
$ sudo rm -fr arm-bcm2708
```

To use the image tool, you'll need Python installed, so install it now, if needed.

Download Kernel

The first thing needed is the Raspbian kernel sources. If you want the "bleeding edge" in development, the git command is the best way to acquire the source code.

While you could clone the entire Linux project, this will result in a long download. The following method is suggested as a quick way to obtain the kernel release of interest from git (change 3.10.y to the release that you want to fetch):

```
$ mkdir ~/work/linux
$ cd ~/work/linux
$ git init
$ git fetch -depth 1 git@github.com:raspberrypi/linux.git \
      rpi-3.10.y:refs/remotes/origin/rpi-3.10.y
$ git checkout origin/rpi-3.10.y
```

The source tarball can be fetched more easily with the wget command. Here is an example download:

```
$ wget https://github.com/raspberrypi/linux/archive/rpi-3.10.y.tar.gz
```

If you get an error message about an untrusted certificate (ERROR: The certificate of 'github.com' is not trusted), add the –no-check-certificate option:

```
$ wget --no-check-certificate \
  https://github.com/raspberrypi/linux/archive/rpi-3.10.y.tar.gz
```

In this chapter, I assume that you have downloaded the tarball. Once the download is complete, unpack the sources somewhere convenient. I also assume that you're going to use ~/work/rasp as your working directory:

```
$ mkdir -p ~/work/rasp
$ cd ~/work/rasp
$ tar xzf ~/rpi-3.10.y.tar.gz
```

This should leave you a subdirectory named rpi-3.10.y that you can change to the following:

```
$ cd ~/work/rasp/linux-rpi-3.10.y
```

Edit Makefile

It is possible to put the ARCH= and CROSS-COMPILE= definitions on the make command line like this:

```
$ make ARCH=arm CROSS-COMPILE=/opt/x-tools/arm-unknown-\
linux-gnueabi/bin/arm-unknown-linux-gnueabi-
```

However, this is tedious and error prone. You could use an alias or some other workaround, but the best approach is probably just to edit these parameters in the top-level Makefile.

Using an editor of your choice, look for a line in the top-level Makefile that starts with ARCH=, as shown here:

```
ARCH            ?= $ (SUBARCH)
CROSS_COMPILE   ?= $ (CONFIG_CROSS_COMPILE:"%"=%)
```

The safest thing to do is to duplicate these pair of lines and comment out the first pair, keeping them around in their original form. Then modify the second pair as shown:

```
#ARCH            ?= $ (SUBARCH)
#CROSS_COMPILE   ?= $ (CONFIG_CROSS_COMPILE:"%"=%)

ARCH            ?= arm
CROSS_COMPILE   ?= /opt/x-tools/arm-unknown-linux-gnueabi/bin/arm-unknown-linux-gnueabi-
```

The CROSS_COMPILE prefix should match everything up to but not including the command name gcc shown next (edited to fit). If you've not already done so, edit the PATH variable so that the cross-compiler tools are searched first:

```
PATH="/opt/x-tools/arm-unknown-linux-gnueabi/bin:$PATH"
```

Now verify that your compiler is being located:

```
$ type arm-unknown-linux-gnueabi-gcc
arm-unknown-linux-gnueabi-gcc is hashed \
    (/opt/x-tools/arm-unknown-linux-gnueabi/bin/arm-unknown-linux-gnueabi-gcc)
```

make mrproper

In theory, this step shouldn't be necessary. But the kernel developers want you to do it anyway, in case something was accidentally left out of place. Keep in mind that this step also removes the .config file. So if you need to keep it, make a copy of it.

```
$ make mrproper
```

■ **Caution**   The command `make mrproper` cleans up everything, including your kernel .config file. You may want to copy .config to .config.bak.

Kernel Config

Before building your kernel, you need a configuration. The downloaded kernel source does not include your Pi's kernel settings. If you want to build the kernel with the same configuration as the one you are using, grab your configuration from your running Pi:

```
$ scp pi@rasp:/proc/config.gz .
```

Then uncompress the configuration and move it into place:

```
$ gunzip <config.gz >~/work/rasp/linux-rpi-3.10.y/.config
```

Alternatively, because there may be new options that were not used by your old kernel, you may want to start with a fresh set of default options for your kernel. Copying these defaults will give you a good starting point from which to proceed (assuming the directory ~/work/rasp/linux-rpi-3.10.y):

```
$ cp ./arch/arm/configs/bcmrpi_defconfig .config
```

At this point, you can modify the configuration, but for your first build, I suggest you leave it as is. Once you get a successful build and run of the kernel, you can go back with confidence and make changes. Otherwise, if the new kernel fails, you won't know whether it was the kernel, your build procedure, or the configuration that you chose.

If you downloaded your kernel from the Git repository, there is a likelihood that the first build of the kernel will fail if you copied the bcmrpi_defconfig configuration. The reason is that some of the configured modules may not be fully developed (or undergoing changes), but are enabled in the configuration for testing. For example, if an IPTables module fails to compile, you may need to disable it in the configuration. If the option is difficult to find in the menu (see make menuconfig next), it is an accepted practice to just edit the .config file. Things are often easier to find with the editor.

make menuconfig

The first time around, you should start make menuconfig and then just exit. When you decide later that you need to make configuration changes, you can either use the menu-driven approach here or edit the .config file directly. The menu-driven approach is usually best since it can guide you through the process:

```
$ make menuconfig
```

make

Now that the configuration has been established, start the build process. If you hadn't planned on making configuration changes, you might still be prompted with some configuration questions. To proceed without configuration changes, simply press Enter to accept the existing value for the parameter.

```
$ make
```

The build process takes a fair bit of time. On a MacBook Pro using an Intel i7 processor, hosting Ubuntu in VirtualBox, the process takes about 40 minutes to complete. You mileage will vary.

Next, build the modules for the kernel:

```
$ make modules
```

Now you are ready to install the new kernel and its modules.

■ **Tip** If your /tmp file system is not large enough for the build, you can direct the temporary files to another directory. For example, to use ./tmp in your work area:

```
$ mkdir ./tmp
```

```
$ export TMPDIR="$PWD/tmp"
```

Prepare Kernel Image

In the subdirectory arch/arm/boot/zImage is your built kernel image:

```
$ cd ~/work/rasp/linux-rpi-3.10.y/arch/arm/boot
$ ls -l zImage
-rwxr-xr-x  1  wwg  wwg     3696136  2014-06-22  13:58  zImage
```

Now let's prepare an image that can be booted by the Raspberry Pi.

The image tool seems to need to run from its own directory (otherwise, it is unable to locate the boot-uncompressed.txt file). So change to the image tool's directory and run it from there. It will create the file kernel.img in that directory, so make sure you have permissions there:

```
$ cd /opt/tools-master/mkimage
$ python /opt/tools-master/mkimage/imagetool-uncompressed.py \
    ~/work/rasp/linux-rpi-3.10.y/arch/arm/boot/zImage
```

```
$ ls -l
total 3160
-rw-rw-r--   1 root   root       157  May   8  08:14  args-uncompressed.txt
-rw-rw-r--   1 root   root       201  May   8  08:14  boot-uncompressed.txt
-rw-rw-r--   1 root   root     32768  Jun  24  08:28  first32k.bin
-rwxrwxr-x   1 root   root       822  May   8  08:14  imagetool-uncompressed.py
-rw-r--r--   1 root   root   3187280  Jun  24  08:28  kernel.img
```

From this, we see that it creates file kernel.img, which is 3, 187, 280 bytes in size.

Install Kernel Image

Here I assume that you have the SD card mounted on your desktop, rather than in VirtualBox. The SD card can be mounted in VirtualBox, but this takes some special care and additional effort. See the "VirtualBox Mount of SD Card" section at the end of the chapter (if this works for you, this will be more convenient).

With your SD card mounted, you can change out your kernel. It is recommended that you rename the original kernel.img file in case you want to reinstate it later. On the Mac, the session might look something like this:

```
$ cd /Volumes/Untitled/        # Where the SD card is mounted
$ ls
bootcode.bin     config.txt      issue.txt          kernel_emergency.img
cmdline.txt      fixup.dat       kernel.img         start.elf
config.bak       fixup_cd.dat    kernel_cutdown.img start_cd.elf
$ mv kernel.img kernel.orig
```

Once the original kernel is safely renamed on the SD card, you can copy the new kernel onto it:

```
$ scp wwg@osx-rpi:/opt/tools-master/mkimage/kernel.img /Volumes/Untitled/.
wwg@osx-rpi's password:
kernel.img                                      100%  2665KB   2.6MB/s   00:00
$ sync
```

Here I transferred the prepared image using scp, from VirtualBox machine osx-rpi, installing the new kernel as kernel.img. You may be able to boot the new kernel without updating the modules (obviously, the new modules will not be available). Once you boot up your Pi with the new kernel, then using scp you should be able to copy your new module's tarball to it (see the "Modules" section later). Try booting the new kernel and log in to check it (long lines edited):

```
$ ssh pi@rasp
...
$ dmesg | head
...
[    0.000000] Linux version 3.10.38 (wwg@osx-xpi) \
                (gcc version 4.8.2 20130603 (prerelease) \
                    (crosstool -NG 1.19.0)) \
                #3 PREEMPT Mon Jun 23 22:26:50 EST 2014
...
```

Here we have confirmation that the kernel was built by wwg@osx-xpi (on VirtualBox), using the crosstool-NG development tools and built on June 23. This is confirmation that the kernel is the new one that was installed. Next, of course, the modules need to be installed.

Boot Failure

If you see the initial colored flash screen remain on the console, this indicates that the kernel.img file failed to load/start.[43]

Modules

The modules need to be staged somewhere, so you can transfer them to the Pi's root file system (on the SD card). Here I'll stage them in ~/work/modules. Specify the full pathname to the staging directory by using the INSTALL_MOD_PATH variable:

```
$ mkdir -p ~/work/modules
$ make INSTALL_MOD_PATH=$HOME/work/modules modules_install
```

Note that $HOME is safer than the tilde (~) in the make command, since the shell may not substitute it properly. The bash shell, version 4.3.8, does seem to handle the tilde, however.

After this install step completes, you will have a subtree of kernel modules deposited there. These files now need to be installed in the Pi's root file system. Either mount the Pi's root file system under Linux, or use the existing kernel on the Pi itself. The following shows how the modules are put into a tar file for transport to the Pi:

```
$ cd ~/work/modules
$ tar czf modules.tar.gz.
$ tar tzf modules.tar.gz | head -4
. /
. /modules.tar.gz
. /lib/
. /lib/modules/
$ scp modules.tar.gz pi@rasp:.
```

On the Raspberry Pi, you can install it:

```
$ tar tzf modules.tar.gz | head -7
. /
. /modules.tar.gz
. /lib/
. /lib/modules/
. /lib/modules/3.2.27/
. /lib/modules/3.2.27/modules.symbols.bin
. /lib/modules/3.2.27/modules.usbmap
$ cd /
$ sudo tar xzf ~/modules.tar.gz
```

With the new modules installed, reboot your new kernel. Once the Pi boots up, log in and check whether any modules got loaded:

```
$ lsmod
Module                          Size    Used    by
snd_bcm2835                    16292    0
...
```

Firmware

From time to time, you should check to see whether new firmware is available. This code is available in binary form only. There are always two versions of the firmware available:[35]

> *Master*: The current firmware used in Raspbian

> *Next*: The firmware in development, which provides GPU updates

Depending on your needs, choose one of the following:

```
$ wget--no-check-certificate\
  https://github.com/raspberrypi/firmware/archive/master.tar.gz
```

```
$ wget--no-check-certificate\
  https://github.com/raspberrypi/firmware/archive/next.tar.gz
```

Of particular interest is the bootcode.bin firmware file. There are other files like the *.dat files. It is unclear when these dat files should be replaced. These may depend on the release of the Raspbian Linux kernel.

```
$ cd ./firmware-master/boot
$ ls -l
total 37248
-rw-r--r--  ..      18693  26 Jan 14:31  COPYING.linux
-rw-r--r--  ..       1447  26 Jan 14:31  LICENCE.broadcom
-rw-r--r--  ..      17764  26 Jan 14:31  bootcode.bin
-rw-r--r--  ..       5735  26 Jan 14:31  fixup.dat
-rw-r--r--  ..       2260  26 Jan 14:31  fixup_cd.dat
-rw-r--r--  ..       8502  26 Jan 14:31  fixup_x.dat
-rw-r--r--  ..    2800968  26 Jan 14:31  kernel.img
-rw-r--r--  ..    9609864  26 Jan 14:31  kernel_emergency.img
-rw-r--r--  ..    2539540  26 Jan 14:31  start.elf
-rw-r--r--  ..     569016  26 Jan 14:31  start_cd.elf
-rw-r--r--  ..    3472580  26 Jan 14:31  start_x.elf
```

If you think you need a firmware update, copy from this subdirectory to your Raspberry Pi's /boot directory.

VirtualBox Mount of SD Card

All this shuffling images around remotely using scp is a nuisance, but it gets the job done. If you are running VirtualBox, you may find that you can mount the SD card directly. This allows you to more easily update the SD card file systems, including the modules and firmware. I'll be showing the VirtualBox procedure for a Mac, but the process is similar for Windows.

The first step on the Mac is to determine which disk device the SD card is assigned to:

```
$ diskutil list
```

In my case, the SD card showed up as /dev/disk2 (this is obvious because it wasn't there prior to inserting the SD card).

Next you need to make sure that any mounted file systems from that SD card are unmounted (the Mac likes to automount everything it can). Using the diskutil command, unmount all file systems mounted from /dev/disk2:

```
$ diskutil unmountDisk /dev/disk2
```

Finally (for the Mac), you need to grant permissions to VirtualBox to use the raw device. Since VirtualBox likely runs under your own login, you need to grant permissions to it. I'll use the lazy approach here, to grant permissions to everyone on the device (the device will go away as soon as it is removed anyway):

```
$ sudo chmod 0666 /dev/disk2
```

Note that once you remove the SD card, and later insert it, you will need to repeat this step.

Next, you will need to locate the VBoxManage command. On the Mac you will find it here (Windows users may find it in C:\Program Files\Sun):

```
$ cd /Applications/VirtualBox.app/Contents/MacOS
```

You can either add that directory to your current PATH, or simply change to that directory. Then use the VBoxManage command to create a control file (*.vmdk). This control file informs VirtualBox how to access that raw device (place the *.vmdk wherever you find it convenient):

```
$ sudo VBoxManage internalcommands createrawvmdk \
    -filename /Volumes/VirtualBox/sddisk.vmdk \
    -rawdisk /dev/disk2
```

Now enter your VirtualBox console and open the storage settings. Click the Add Hard Disk icon and select the control file you created (in the example, it was created on /Volumes/VirtualBox/sddisk.vmdk). Make sure you add this device after your current boot device. Otherwise, VirtualBox will try to boot from your SD card instead.

After starting VirtualBox, you should see your new devices under Linux. In my case, the SD card devices showed up as /dev/sdb (entire SD card), /dev/sdb1 (partition 1), and /dev/sdb2 (partition 2). With this success, it is now possible to mount these partitions after creating mount points (I used ~/mnt1 and ~/mnt2):

```
$ sudo mount /dev/sdb1 ~/mnt1
$ sudo mount /dev/sdb2 ~/mnt2
```

Now you can list those mount points to see the Raspberry Pi file system content. This access makes it an easy matter to install your kernel:

```
$ cd /opt/tools-master/mkimage
$ sudo mv ~/mnt1/kernel.img ~/mnt1/kernel.orig        # Rename original kernel
$ sudo dd if=kernel.img ~/mnt1/kernel.img             # Install new kernel image
```

Likewise, you can now update the kernel modules:

```
$ cd ~/mnt2                                            # Raspberry Pi' Root file system
$ tar xzvf ~/work/modules/modules.tar.gz              # Unpack new modules into ~/mnt2/lib
```

With the modifications completed, change out of the file system (to unbusy them) and unmount them:

```
$ cd ~
$ sudo umount ~/mnt1
$ sudo umount ~/mnt2
```

If you are hosting VirtualBox on a Mac, the Mac will automount the first partition the moment that VirtualBox closes the SD card device. So be sure to undo that before pulling the SD card out (to prevent any file system corruption). You can use the Mac's diskutil to do this for you:

```
$ diskutil unmountDisk /dev/disk2
```

CHAPTER 22

■ ■ ■

DHT11 Sensor

The DHT11 humidity and temperature sensor is an economical peripheral manufactured by D-Robotics UK (www.droboticsonline.com). It is capable of measuring relative humidity between 20 and 90% RH within the operating temperature range of 0 to 50°C, with an accuracy of ±5% RH. Additionally, temperature is measured in the range of 0 to 50°C, with an accuracy of ±2°C. Both values are returned with 8-bit resolution.

Characteristics

The signaling used by the DHT sensor is similar to the 1-Wire protocol, but the response times differ. Additionally, there is no device serial number support. These factors make the device incompatible with the 1-Wire drivers within the Linux kernel. Figure 22-1 shows a DHT11 sensor.

Figure 22-1. DHT11 sensor

The DHT11 sensor also requires a power supply. In contrast, the signal line itself powers most 1-Wire peripherals. The datasheet states that the DHT11 can be powered by a range of voltages, from 3 V to 5.5 V. Powering it from the Raspberry Pi's 3.3 V source keeps the sensor signal levels within a safe range for GPIO. The device draws between 0.5 mA and 2.5 mA. Its standby current is stated as 100 μA to 150 μA, for those concerned about battery consumption.

Circuit

Figure 22-2 shows the general circuit connections between the Raspberry Pi and the DHT11 sensor. Pin 4 connects to the common ground, while pin 1 goes to the 3.3 V supply. Pin 2 is the signal pin, which communicates with a chosen GPIO pin. The program listing for dht11.c is configured to use GPIO 22. This is easily modified (look for gpio_dht11).

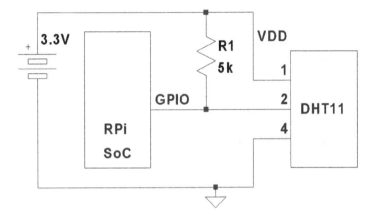

Figure 22-2. *DHT11 circuit*

When the Pi is listening on the GPIO pin and the DHT11 is not sending data, the line will float. For this reason, R_1 is required to pull the line up to a stable level of 3.3 V. The datasheet recommends a 5 kΩ resistor for the purpose (a more common 4.7 kΩ resistor can be substituted safely). This presents less than 1 mA of load on either the GPIO pin or the sensor when they are active. The datasheet also states that the 5 kΩ resistor should be suitable for cable runs of up to 20 meters.

Protocol

The sensor speaks only when spoken to by the master (Raspberry Pi). The master must first make a request on the bus and then wait for the sensor to respond. The DHT sensor responds with 40 bits of information, 8 of which are a checksum.

Overall Protocol

The overall signal protocol works like this:

1. The line idles high because of the pull-up resistor.

2. The master pulls the line low for at least 18 ms to signal a read request and then releases the bus, allowing the line to return to a high state.

3. After a pause of about 20 to 40 µs, the sensor responds by bringing the line low for 80 µs and then allows the line to return high for a further 80 µs. This signals its intention to return data.

4. Forty bits of information are then written out to the bus: each bit starting with a 50 μs low followed by:

    a.   26 to 28 μs of high to indicate a 0 bit

    b.   70 μs of high to indicate a 1 bit

5. The transmission ends with the sensor bringing the line low one more time for 50 μs.

6. The sensor releases the bus, allowing the line to return to a high idle state.

Figure 22-3 shows the overall protocol of the sensor. Master control is shown in thick lines, while sensor control is shown in thin lines. Initially, the bus sits idle until the master brings the line low and releases it (labeled Request). The sensor grabs the bus and signals that it is responding (80 μs low, followed by 80 μs high). The sensor continues with 40 bits of sensor data, ending with one more transition to low (labeled End) to mark the end of the last bit.

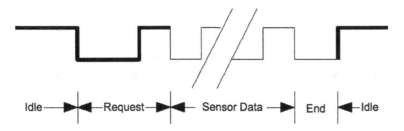

Idle ──►◄── Request ──►◄── Sensor Data ──► End ◄── Idle

Figure 22-3. *General DHT11 protocol*

Data Bits

Each sensor data bit begins with a transition to low, followed by the transition to high, as shown in Figure 22-4. The end of the bit occurs when the line is brought low again as the start of the next bit. The last bit is marked off by one final low-to-high transition.

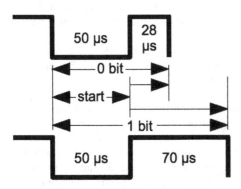

Figure 22-4. *DHT11 data bit*

Each data bit starts with a transition to low, lasting for 50 μs. The final transition to low after the last bit also lasts for 50 μs. After the bit's low-to-high transition, the bit becomes a 0 if the high lasts only 26 to 28 microseconds. A 1 bit stays high for 70 μs instead. Every data bit is completed when the transition from high to low occurs for the start of the next bit (or final transition).

Data Format

Figure 22-5 illustrates the 40-bit sensor response, transmitting the most significant bit first. The datasheet states 16 bits of relative humidity, 16 bits of temperature in Celsius, and an 8-bit checksum. However, the DHT11 always sends 0s for the humidity and temperature fractional bytes. Thus the device really has only 8 bits of precision for each measurement. Presumably, other models (or future ones) provide fractional values for greater precision.

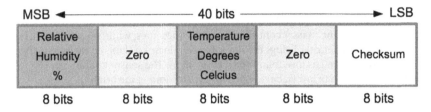

MSB ◄─────────────── 40 bits ───────────────► LSB

Relative Humidity %	Zero	Temperature Degrees Celcius	Zero	Checksum
8 bits	8 bits	8 bits	8 bits	8 bits

Figure 22-5. DHT11 data format

The checksum is a simple sum of the first 4 bytes. Any carry overflow is simply discarded. This checksum gives your application greater confidence that it has received correct values in the face of possible transmission errors.

Software

The user space software written to read the DHT11 sensor on the Raspberry Pi uses the direct register access of the GPIO pin. The challenges presented by this approach include the following:

- Short timings: 26 to 70 μs

- Preemptive scheduling delays within the Linux kernel

One approach is to count how many times the program could read the high-level signal before the end of the bit is reached (when the line goes low). Then decide on 0 bits for shorter times and 1s for longer times. After some experimentation, a dividing line could be drawn, where shorter signals mean 0 while the others are 1s.

The difficulty with this approach is that it doesn't adapt well if the Raspberry Pi is accelerated. When the CPU clock is increased through overclocking, the program will tend to fail. There is also the potential for future Raspberry Pis to include CPUs with higher clock rates.

The signal emitted by the sensor is almost a Manchester encoding. In Manchester encoding, one-half of the wave form is shorter than the other. This allows counting up for the first half and counting down for the second. Based on whether the counter underflows, a decision is made about the value of the bit seen.

The DHT11 signal uses a fixed first half of 50 μs The bit is decided based on how long the signal remains at a high level after that. So a "bit bang" application could get a relative idea by counting the number of times it could read the low-level signal. Based on that, it can get a relative idea of where the dividing line between a short and long high-level signal is.

This is the approach that was adopted by the program dht11.c. It counts the number of times in a spin loop that it can read the signal as low. On a 700 MHz nonturbo Raspberry Pi, I saw this count vary between 130 and 330 times, with an average of 292. This time period is supposed to be exactly 50 μs, which illustrates the real-time scheduling problem within a user space program. (The program did not use any real-time Linux priority scheduling.)

If the sensor waveform is true, a max count of 330 suggests that the Raspberry Pi can read the GPIO pin a maximum of

$$\frac{330}{50} = 6.6\,reads\,/\,\mu s$$

But the minimum of 130 GPIO reads shows a worst case performance of

$$\frac{130}{50} = 2.6\,reads\,/\,\mu s$$

This variability in preemptive scheduling makes it difficult to do reliable timings.

I have seen the high-level bit counts vary between 26 and 378. (The interested reader can modify the code to record the counts.) If the program is able to read 6.6 times per microsecond, a 1-bit time of 70 μs should yield a count of 462. Yet the maximum seen was 378. Preemptive scheduling prevents the code from performing that many reads without interruption.

The lower count of 26 represents the minimum count for 0 bits, where the line stays high for a shorter period of time. This suggests that each GPIO read is about 1 μs or longer during the 0-bit highs.

The preceding information is just a crude sampling of the problem to illustrate the variability that must be grappled with in a user space program, on a multitasking operating system.

Chosen Approach

The program shown in this chapter uses the following general approach:

1. Count the number of GPIO reads that report that the line is low (call it C_{low}).

2. Compute an adjustment bias B based on $B = \dfrac{C_{low}}{D}$, where D is some fixed divisor.

3. Compute a new count $K = B + C_{high}$, where C_{high} is the number of times the line was read as high.

4. If the count value $K > C_{low}$, the value is considered a 1-bit; otherwise, it's considered a 0-bit.

The method is intended to at least partially compensate for the level of preemption being seen by the application program. By measuring the low read counts, we get an idea of the number of times we can sample the line at the moment. The approach is intended to adapt itself to a faster-running Raspberry Pi.

Table 22-1 shows some experimental results on an idle Raspberry Pi running at the standard 700 MHz. Different divisors were tried and tested over 5-minute intervals. When the program runs, it attempts to read and report as many sensor readings as it can, tracking good reports, time-out, and error counts. The program was terminated by pressing ^C when an egg timer went off.

Table 22-1. *Bias Test Results*

Divisor	Results	Time-outs	Errors
2	1	17	103
3	48	17	63
4	30	25	56
5	49	14	63
6	45	20	52
7	60	16	47
8	41	20	56
9	42	17	62

(continued)

Table 22-1. (*continued*)

Divisor	Results	Time-outs	Errors
10	39	22	53
11	40	14	72
12	43	13	71
13	47	10	75
14	32	19	67
15	28	23	63
16	38	16	69
17	33	14	81
18	34	13	82
19	31	16	75
20	22	18	81

Using no bias at all, no successful reads result (which prompted the idea of applying a bias). Using a divisor of 2 applies too much adjustment, as can be seen by the low number of results (1). Increasing the divisor to the value 3 or more produced a much higher success rate, near 48, which is almost 10 reports per minute. Setting the divisor to 3 seems to yield the most repeatable results overall.

It is uncertain from the datasheets how rapidly the sensor can be requeried. The program takes the conservative approach of pausing 2 seconds between each sensor read attempt or waiting 5 seconds when a time-out has occurred.

The program reports an error when the checksum does not match. Time-outs occur if the code gets stuck waiting for the signal to go low, for too long. This can happen if the program misses a critical event because of preemptive scheduling. It sometimes happens that the high-to-low-to-high event can occur without the program ever seeing it. If the going-low event takes too long, the program performs a longjmp into the main loop, to allow a retry.

The errors are reported to stderr, allowing them to be suppressed by redirecting unit 2 to /dev/null from the command line.

The way that the Raspberry Pi relinquishes the sensor bus is by changing the GPIO pin from an output to an input. When configured as an input, the pull-up resistor brings the bus line high when the bus is idle (the pull-up applies when neither master or slave is driving the bus). When requested, the sensor grabs the bus and drives it high or low. Finally, when the master speaks, we configure the pin as an output, causing the GPIO pin to drive the bus.

Example Run

When the program dht11 is run, you should see output similar to the following:

```
$ sudo ./dht11
RH 37% Temp 18 C Reading 1
(Error # 1)
(Timeout # 1)
RH 37% Temp 18 C Reading 2
(Timeout # 2)
RH 37% Temp 18 C Reading 3
RH 37% Temp 18 C Reading 4
RH 37% Temp 18 C Reading 5
```

```
(Error # 2)
(Timeout # 3)
(Error # 3)
(Error # 4)
(Error # 5)
RH 37% Temp 18 C Reading 6
(Error # 6)
RH 37% Temp 18 C Reading 7
(Error # 7)
(Error # 8)
(Error # 9)
RH 36% Temp 19 C Reading 8
RH 37% Temp 18 C Reading 9
(Timeout # 4)
RH 36% Temp 19 C Reading 10
^C
Program exited due to SIGINT:

Last Read: RH 36% Temp 19 C, 9 errors, 4 timeouts, 10 readings
```

Source Code

The next few pages list the source code for the program. This was assembled into one compile unit by using the #include directive. This was done to save pages by eliminating additional header files and extern declarations.

■ **Note**   The source code for gpio_io.c is found in Chapter 12.

```
1   /*******************************************************************
2    * dht11.c: Direct GPIO access reading DHT11 humidity and temp sensor.
3    *******************************************************************/
4
5   #include <stdio.h>
6   #include <stdlib.h>
7   #include <fcntl.h>
8   #include <unistd.h>
9   #include <errno.h>
10  #include <setjmp.h>
11  #include <sys/mman.h>
12  #include <signal.h>
13
14  #include "gpio_io.c"                       /*GPIO routines */
15  #include "timed_wait.c"                    /*timed_wait() */
16
17  static const int gpio_dht11 = 22;          /*GPIO pin */
18  static jmp_buf timeout_exit;               /*longjmp on timeout */
19  static int is_signaled = 0;                /*Exit program if signaled */
20
```

```
21/*
22 * Signal handler to quit the program:
23 */
24 static void
25 sigint_handler(int signo) {
26         is_signaled = 1;                              /*Signal to exit program */
27 }
28
29 /*
30  * Read the GPIO line status:
31  */
32 static inline unsigned
33 gread(void) {
34          return gpio_read(gpio_dht11);
35 }
36
37 /*
38  * Wait until the GPIO line goes low:
39  */
40 static inline unsigned
41 wait_until_low(void) {
42         const unsigned maxcount = 12000;
43         unsigned count = 0;
44
45         while ( gread() )
46                 if ( ++count >=maxcount || is_signaled )
47                         longjmp(timeout_exit,1);
48         return count;
49 }
50
51 /*
52  * Wait until the GPIO line goes high:
53  */
54 static inline unsigned
55 wait_until_high(void) {
56         unsigned count = 0;
57
58         while ( !gread() )
59                 ++count;
60         return count;
61 }
62
63 /*
64  * Read 1 bit from the DHT11 sensor:
65  */
66 static unsigned
67 rbit(void) {
68         unsigned bias;
69         unsigned lo_count, hi_count;
70
```

```
71              wait_until_low();
72              lo_count = wait_until_high();
73              hi_count = wait_until_low();
74
75              bias = lo_count / 3;
76
77              return hi_count + bias > lo_count ? 1 : 0 ;
78  }
79
80  /*
81   * Read 1 byte from the DHT11 sensor :
82   */
83  static unsigned
84  rbyte(void) {
85              unsigned x, u = 0;
86
87              for ( x=0; x<8; ++x )
88                      u = (u << 1) | rbit();
89              return u;
90  }
91
92  /*
93   * Read 32 bits of data + 8 bit checksum from the
94   * DHT sensor. Returns relative humidity and
95   * temperature in Celsius when successful. The
96   * function returns zero if there was a checksum
97   * error.
98   */
99    static int
100 rsensor(int *relhumidity, int *celsius) {
101             unsigned char u[5], cs = 0, x;
102             for ( x=0; x<5; ++x ) {
103                     u[x] = rbyte();
104                     if ( x < 4 )                    /*Only checksum data..*/
105                             cs += u[x];             /*Checksum */
106             }
107
108             if ( (cs & 0xFF) == u[4] ) {
109                     *relhumidity = (int)u [0];
110                     *celsius = (int)u [2];
111                     return 1;
112     }
113         return 0;
114 }
115
116 /*
117  * Main program:
118  */
```

```
119 int
120 main(int argc, char **argv) {
121         int relhumidity = 0, celsius = 0;
122         int errors = 0, timeouts = 0, readings = 0;
123         unsigned wait;
124
125         signal(SIGINT,sigint_handler);              /*Trap on SIGINT */
126
127         gpio_init();                                /*Initialize GPIO access */
128         gpio_config(gpio_dht11,Input);              /*Set GPIO pin as Input */
129
130         for (;;) {
131                 if ( setjmp(timeout_exit) ) {            /*Timeouts go here */
132                         if ( is_signaled )              /*SIGINT? */
133                                 break;                  /*Yes, then exit loop */
134                         fprintf(stderr," (Timeout # %d)\n",++timeouts);
135                         wait = 5;
136                 } else  wait = 2;
137
138                 wait_until_high();              /*Wait GPIO line to go high */
139                 timed_wait(wait,0,0);           /*Pause for sensor ready */
140
141                 gpio_config(gpio_dht11,Output);  /*Output mode */
142                 gpio_write(gpio_dht11,0);        /*Bring line low */
143                 timed_wait(0,30000,0);           /*Hold low min of 18ms */
144                 gpio_write(gpio_dht11,1);        /*Bring line high */
145
146                 gpio_config(gpio_dht11,Input);   /*Input mode */
147                 wait_until_low();                /*Wait for low signal */
148                 wait_until_high();               /*Wait for return to high */
149
150                 if ( rsensor(&relhumidity,& celsius) )
151                         printf("RH %d%% Temp %d C Reading %d\n", relhumidity,
celsius,++readings);
152                 else fprintf(stderr," (Error # %d)\n",++errors);
153         }
154
155         gpio_config(gpio_dht11,Input);              /*Set pin to input mode */
156
157         puts("\ nProgram exited due to SIGINT: \n");
158         printf("Last Read: RH %d%% Temp %d C, %d errors, %d timeouts, %d readings \n",
159                 relhumidity, celsius, errors, timeouts, readings);
160         return 0;
161 }
162
```

```
163 /*End dht11.c */
```

```
1   /*****************************************************************
2    * Implement a precision "timed wait". The parameter early_usec
3    * allows an interrupted select(2) call to consider the wait as
4    * completed, when interrupted with only "early_usec" left remaining.
5    *****************************************************************/
6   static void
7   timed_wait(long sec,long usec,long early_usec) {
8       fd_set mt;
9       struct timeval timeout;
10      int rc;
11
12      FD_ZERO(&mt);
13      timeout.tv_sec = sec;
14      timeout.tv_usec = usec;
15      do {
16          rc = select (0,&mt,&mt,&mt,&timeout);
17          if ( ! timeout.tv_sec && timeout.tv_usec < early_usec )
18              return;    /*Wait is good enough, exit */
19      } while ( rc < 0 && timeout.tv_sec && timeout.tv_usec );
20  }
21
22  /*End timed_wait.c */
```

CHAPTER 23

MCP23017 GPIO Extender

Microchip's MCP23017 provides 16 additional GPIO pins that can be purchased for as little as $1.99. The chip communicates using the I2C bus. (The companion MCP23S17 is available for SPI bus.) The I2C bus allows the chip to be remote from the Raspberry Pi, requiring only a four-wire ribbon cable (power, ground, and a pair of I2C bus lines). This chapter explores the features and limits of this peripheral.

DC Characteristics

When shopping for chips or interface PCBs based on a particular chip, the first thing I look at is the operating supply voltage. 5 V parts are inconvenient for the Pi because of its 3.3 V GPIO interface. Many newer devices operate over a range of voltages, which include 3.3 V. The MCP23017 supply V_{DD} operates from an extended range of +1.8 V to +5.5 V. This clearly makes it compatible, if we power the chip from a +3.3 V source. Figure 23-1 shows the MCP23017chip pinout diagram.

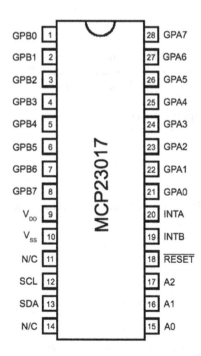

Figure 23-1. *MCP23017 pinout*

GPIO Output Current

Another factor in choosing a peripheral chip is its output drive capability. How well can the GPIO pin source or sink current? Chapter 12 notes that the Raspberry Pi's own GPIO pins can source/sink up to 16 mA, depending on configuration. The MCP23017 chip specifications indicate that it can source or sink up to 25 mA.

We still need to remember that if the MCP23017 is powered from the Raspberry Pi's 3.3 V regulator on header P1, the total current budget must not exceed 50 mA. This budget includes the Pi's own GPIO pin current usage. If, on the other hand, the MCP23017 is powered from a separate 3.3 V power supply, this limitation is eliminated.

There are still reasons to budget current, however. The chip must not consume more than 700 mW of power. This implies a total current limit as follows:

$$
\begin{aligned}
I_{V_{DD}} &= \frac{P}{V_{DD}} \\
&= \frac{0.7}{3.3} \\
&= 212 \ mA
\end{aligned}
$$

This power figure gives us an upper current limit. However, the datasheet of the MCP23017 also lists a maximum of 125 mA for supply pin V_{DD}. If every GPIO output is sourcing power, this leaves us with the following average pin limit:

$$
\frac{125 \ mA}{16} = 7.8 \ mA
$$

So while the output GPIO pins can *source* up to 25 mA, we cannot have all of them doing so simultaneously.

Likewise, the datasheet lists V_{ss} (ground) as limited to an absolute maximum of 150 mA. If every GPIO pin is an output and sinking current, the average for each output pin cannot exceed the following:

$$
\frac{150 \ mA}{16} = 9.4 \ mA
$$

Once again, while each output pin can *sink* up to 25 mA, we see that they cannot all do so at the same time without exceeding chip limits. This should not be discouraging, because in most applications, not all GPIO pins will be outputs, and not all will all be driving heavy loads. The occasional pin that needs driving help can use a transistor driver like the one discussed in Chapter 12.

Before we leave the topic of GPIO output driving, we can apply one more simple formula to help with interface design. With the foregoing information, we can calculate the number of 25 mA outputs available:

$$
\frac{125 \ mA}{25 \ mA} = 5
$$

From this, it is known that four to five GPIO pins can operate near their maximum limits, as long as the remaining GPIO pins are inputs or remain unconnected.

GPIO Inputs

In normal operation, the GPIO inputs should never see a voltage below the ground potential V_{ss}. Nor should they ever see a voltage above the supply voltage V_{DD}. Yet, variations can sometimes happen when interfacing with the external world, particularly with inductive components.

The datasheet indicates that clamping diodes provide some measure of protection against this. Should the voltage on an input drop below 0, it is clamped by a diode so it will not go further negative and cause harm. The voltage limit is listed at –0.6 V, which is the voltage drop of the clamping diode. Likewise, if the voltage goes over V_{DD} (+3.3 V in our case), the clamping diode will limit the excursion to $V_{DD} + 0.6\ V$ (+3.9 V).

This protection is limited by the current capability of the clamping diodes. The datasheet lists the maximum clamping current as 20 mA. If pins are forced beyond their limits and the clamping current is exceeded, damage will occur.

While we have focused on GPIO inputs in this section, the clamping diodes also apply to outputs. Outputs can be forced beyond their limits by external circuits like pull-up resistors. Pull-up resistors should not be attached to +5 V, for example, when the MCP23017 is operating from a +3.3 V supply.

Standby Current

If the MCP23017 device is not sourcing or sinking output currents, the standby current is stated as 3 μA (for 4.5 to 5.5 V operation). This operating parameter is important to designers of battery-operated equipment.

Input Logic Levels

Since the device operates over a range of supply voltages, the datasheet defines the logic levels in terms of the supply voltage. For example, the GPIO input low level is listed as $0.2 \times V_{DD}$. So if we operate with $V_{DD} = +\ 3.3V$, the input low voltage is calculated as follows:

$$V_{IL_{max}} = 0.2 \times V_{DD}$$
$$= 0.2 \times 3.3$$
$$= 0.66V$$

Therefore, a voltage in the range of 0 to 0.66 V is guaranteed to read as a 0 bit.

Likewise, let's calculate the input high voltage threshold, where the multiplier is given as 0.8:

$$V_{IH_{min}} = 0.8 \times V_{DD}$$
$$= 0.8 \times 3.3$$
$$= 2.64V$$

Thus any voltage greater than or equal to 2.64 V is read as a 1 bit, when powered from a +3.3 V supply. Any voltage between $V_{IL_{max}}$ and V_{IHmin} is undefined and reads as a 1 or a 0, and perhaps randomly so.

Output Logic Levels

The output logic levels are stated differently. The datasheet simply states that the output low voltage should not exceed a fixed limit. The high level is also stated as a minimum value relative to V_{DD}. This pair of parameters is listed here:

$$V_{OLmax} = 0.6\ V$$
$$V_{OHmin} = V_{DD} - 0.7\ V$$
$$= 3.3 - 0.7$$
$$= 2.7\ V$$

Reset Timing

The only parameter of interest for timing apart from the I2C bus is the device reset time. In order for the device to see a reset request, pin $\overline{RESET}$ must remain active (low) for a minimum of 1 μs. The device resets and places outputs into the high-impedance mode within a maximum of 1 μs.

Circuit

Figure 23-2 shows a circuit with two remote MCP23017 GPIO extenders connected to one I2C bus. In the figure, the power, ground, I2C data, and optional $\overline{RESET}$ and $\overline{INT}$ connections are shown connected through a six-conductor ribbon cable. This allows the Raspberry Pi to communicate remotely to peripherals in a robot, for example.

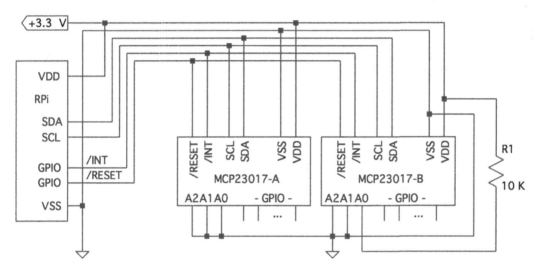

Figure 23-2. *MCP23017 circuit*

The data communication occurs over the pair of signals SDA and SCL. These are connected to the Raspberry Pi's pins P1-03 and P1-05, respectively (GPIO 2 and 3 for Rev 2.0+). The other end of the I2C data bus is common to all slave peripherals.

Each MCP23017 slave device is addressed by its individually configured A2, A1, and A0 pins. For device A, these pins are shown grounded to define it as device number 0x20 (low bits are zeroed). A1 is tied high for device B so that its peripheral address becomes 0x21. In this configuration, the Raspberry Pi will use addresses 0x20 and 0x21 to communicate with these slave devices.

Lines labeled $\overline{RESET}$ and $\overline{INT}$ are optional connections. The $\overline{RESET}$ line can be eliminated if you never plan to force a hardware reset of the slaves (tie to V_{DD} through a 10 K resistor). Usually the power-on reset is sufficient. The $\overline{INT}$ line is more desirable, since the MCP23017 can be programmed to indicate interrupts when a GPIO input has changed in value (or does not match a comparison value). The $\overline{INT}$ line is an open collector pin so that many can be tied together on the same line. However, the Pi will have to poll each peripheral to determine which device is causing the interrupt. Alternatively, each slave could provide a separate $\overline{INT}$ signal, with a corresponding increase in signal lines.

Each MCP23017 chip has two interrupt lines, named $\overline{INT\,A}$ and $\overline{INT\,B}$. There is the option of separate interrupt notifications for the A group or the B group of GPIO pins. For remote operation, it is desirable to take advantage of MCP23017's ability to configure these to work in tandem, so that only one $\overline{INT}$ line is required.

On the Raspberry Pi end, the GPIO pin used for the $\overline{RESET}$ line would be configured as an output and held high, until a reset is required. When activating a reset, the line must be held low for at least 1 microsecond, plus 1 more microsecond to allow for the chip reset operation itself (and possibly longer, if non-MCP23017 slaves are connected to the bus).

The $\overline{INT}$ line should be connected to a GPIO *input* on the Pi. This GPIO input either needs to be polled by the application, or to have the GPIO configured to trigger on changes. Then the select(2) or poll(2) system calls can be used to detect when an interrupt is raised by one or more peripherals.

The interrupt line, when used, should have a pull-up resistor configured (see Chapter 12 for information about internal pull-up resistors). It may be best to use an external pull-up resistor, especially for longer cable runs. To keep the sink current at 2 mA or less, the pull-up resistance used should be no lower than the following:

$$R_{pullup} = \frac{+3.3\,V}{2\,mA}$$
$$= 1650\Omega$$

A 2.2 $k\Omega$ 10% resistor will do nicely.

The +3.3 V line should be powered separately from the Raspberry Pi, unless the slaves expect to drive very low currents. The main concern here is to not overload the remaining 50 mA capacity of the Pi's +3.3 V regulated supply. See Chapter 12 about budgeting +3.3 V power.

I2C Bus

Throughout this chapter, we are assuming a Rev 2.0 or later Raspberry Pi. This matters for the I2C bus because the early versions wired I2C bus 0 to P1-03 and P1-05 (GPIO 0 and 1). Later this was changed to use bus 1. See Chapter 14 for more information about identifying your Pi and which I2C bus to use. If you are using an early Raspberry Pi revision, you'll need to substitute 0 for bus number 1, in commands and in the C source code that follows.

Wiring and Testing

The connections to the MCP23017 are simple enough that you can wire it up on a breadboard. The first step after wiring is to determine that you can detect the peripheral on the I2C bus.

But even before that, check your kernel module support. If lsmod doesn't show these modules loaded, you can manually load them now:

```
$ sudo modprobe i2c-dev
$ sudo modprobe i2c-bcm2708
```

If you haven't already done so, install i2c-tools:

```
$ sudo apt-get install i2c-tools
```

If your I2C support is there, you should be able to list the available I2C buses:

```
$ i2cdetect -l
i2c -0   unknown          bcm2708_i2c.0                    N/A
i2c -1   unknown          bcm2708_i2c.1                    N/A
```

The I2C device nodes should also appear in /dev. These nodes give us access to the I2C drivers:

```
$ ls -l /dev/i2c*
crw-rw---T  1  root root  89, 0  Feb 18 23:53  /dev/i2c-0
crw-rw---T  1  root root  89, 1  Feb 18 23:53  /dev/i2c-1
```

The ultimate test is to see whether the MCP23017 chip is detected (change the 1 to 0 for older Pi revisions):

```
$ sudo i2cdetect -y 1
     0  1  2  3  4  5  6  7  8  9  a  b  c  d  e  f
00:          -- -- -- -- -- -- -- -- -- -- -- -- --
10: -- -- -- -- -- -- -- -- -- -- -- -- -- -- -- --
20: 20 -- -- -- -- -- -- -- -- -- -- -- -- -- -- --
30: -- -- -- -- -- -- -- -- -- -- -- -- -- -- -- --
40: -- -- -- -- -- -- -- -- -- -- -- -- -- -- -- --
50: -- -- -- -- -- -- -- -- -- -- -- -- -- -- -- --
60: -- -- -- -- -- -- -- -- -- -- -- -- -- -- -- --
70: -- -- -- -- -- -- -- --
```

In this example, the A2, A1, and A0 pins of the MCP23017 were grounded. This gives the peripheral the I2C address of 0x20. In the session output, we see that address 0x20 was detected successfully.

The i2cdump utility can be used to check the MCP23017 register:

```
$  sudo  i2cdump  -y  -r   0x00-0x15 1 0x20 b
     0  1  2  3  4  5  6  7  8  9  a  b  c  d  e  f   0123456789abcdef
00: ff  ff  00  00  00  00  00  00  00  00  00  00  00  00  00  00   ................
10: 00  00  00  00  00  00                                          ......
```

Here we have dumped out registers 0x00 to 0x15 on I2C bus 1, at peripheral address 0x20, in byte mode. This was performed after a power-on reset, so we can check whether the register values match the datasheet values documented. As expected, IODIRA (register 0x00) and IODIRB (register 0x01) have the default of all 1s (0xFF). This also confirms that the registers are in BANK=0 mode (this is discussed in the following sections). All other MCP23017 registers default to 0 bits, which is also confirmed.

Software Configuration

The MCP23017 datasheet describes the full register complement and options available. In this chapter, we'll concern ourselves with a subset of its functionality, which is perhaps considered "normal use." The extended functionality is left as an exercise for you.

For this chapter's project, we're going to do the following:

- Configure some GPIOs as inputs

- Configure some GPIOs as outputs

- Configure the group A and B inputs to signal an interrupt on any change

General Configuration

The MCP23017 peripheral has 10 registers for the GPIO-A pins, 10 registers for the GPIO-B pins, and one shared register. In other words, there are 22 registers, with one pair of addresses referencing a common register. These registers may be accessed in banks or interleaved. We'll use interleaved mode in this chapter, to avoid having to reset the device.

Interleaved register addresses are shown in Table 23-1. These are valid addresses when the IOCON register value for BANK=0 (discussed later in this section).

Table 23-1. *MCP23017 Register Addresses*

Register	A	B	Description
IODIRx	0x00	0x01	I/O direction
IPOLx	0x02	0x03	Input polarity
GPINTENx	0x04	0x05	Interrupt on change control
DEFVALx	0x06	0x07	Default comparison value
INTCONx	0x08	0x09	Interrupt control
IOCONx	0x0A	0x0B	Configuration
GPPUx	0x0C	0x0D	Pull-up configuration
INTFx	0x0E	0x0F	Interrupt flags
INTCAPx	0x10	0x11	Interrupt captured value
GPIOx	0x12	0x13	General-purpose I/O
OLATx	0x14	0x15	Output latch

IOCON Register

This is the first register that must be configured, since it affects how registers are addressed. Additionally, other settings are established that affect the entire peripheral.

Table 23-2 illustrates the layout of the IOCON register. Setting the BANK bit determines whether we use banked or interleaved register addressing. The MCP23017 is in interleaved mode after a power-on reset. Once you set BANK=1, the register addresses change. However, once this change is made, it is impossible to tell, after a program restart, which register mode the peripheral is in. The only option is a hardware reset of the MCP23017 chip, to put it in a known state. For this reason, we'll keep the peripheral in its power-on reset state of BANK=0.

Table 23-2. *IOCON Register*

Bit	Meaning	R	W	Reset	Description
7	BANK	Y	Y	0	Set to 0 for interleaved access
6	MIRROR	Y	Y	0	Set to 1 to join INTA & INTB
5	SEQOP	Y	Y	0	Set to 0 for auto-address increment
4	DISSLW	Y	Y	0	Set to 1 to disable slew rate control
3	HAEN	Y	Y	0	Ignored: I2C always uses address
2	ODR	Y	Y	0	Set to 1 for open-drain INT pins
1	INTPOL	Y	Y	0	Set to 0 for INT active low
0	N/A	0	X	0	Ignored: reads as zero
		GPIO	**Address**	**Note**	
		A	0x0A	These access a shared register	
		B	0x0B		

In the tables that follow, a Y under the R (read) or W (write) column/row indicates that you can read or write the respective value. The Reset column indicates the state of the bit after a device reset. An X indicates a "don't care" or an undefined value when read. An N indicates no access or no effect when written.

The bit MIRROR=1 is used to make $\overline{INT\ A}$ equivalent to $\overline{INT\ B}$. In other words, GPIO A and B interrupts are reported to both pins. This allows a single pin to be used for A and B groups.

Setting bit SEQOP=0 allows the peripheral to automatically increment the register address as each byte is read or written. This eliminates the need to transmit a register address in many cases.

Bit DISSLW affects the physical handling of the SDA I2C bus line.

HAEN is applicable only to the MCP23S17 SPI device, since addresses are always enabled for I2C devices.

This project uses ODR=1 to configure the $\overline{INT\ A}$ pin as an open-drain pin. This allows multiple MCP23017 devices to share the same interrupt line. Use a pull-up resistor on the $\overline{INT}$ line when this is in effect. Otherwise, you may experience several sporadic interrupts.

Finally, INTPOL=0 is configured so that the interrupt is active low. This is required for an open-drain connected line along with a pull-up resistor.

OLATx Register

GPIO pins are all configured as inputs after a power-on reset (or use of $\overline{RESET}$). Prior to configuring pins as outputs, it is usually a good idea to set the required output values. This is accomplished by writing the OLAT register, for group A or B. For this project, we'll just write 0x00 to both OLATA and OLATB.

OLATx Register									GPIO	Address
Bit	7	6	5	4	3	2	1	0	A	0x14
R	Y	Y	Y	Y	Y	Y	Y	Y	B	0x15
W	Y	Y	Y	Y	Y	Y	Y	Y		
Reset	0	0	0	0	0	0	0	0		

OLATx Bit Value

0	Output set to 0
1	Output set to 1

GPPUx Register

A given project should also define a known value for its input pull-up resistors. Setting a given bit to 1 enables a weak $100\,K\Omega$ internal pull-up resistor. This setting affects only the inputs. The pull-up resistors are configured off after a reset. In our example code, we turn them on.

GPPUx Register									GPIO	Address
Bit	7	6	5	4	3	2	1	0	A	0x0C
R	Y	Y	Y	Y	Y	Y	Y	Y	B	0x0D
W	Y	Y	Y	Y	Y	Y	Y	Y		
Reset	0	0	0	0	0	0	0	0		

GPPUx Bit Value

0	Pull-up resistor disabled
1	100 KΩ pull-up resistor enabled

DEFVALx Register

This register is associated with interrupt processing. Interrupts are produced from conditions arising from input GPIO pins only. An interrupt can be generated if the input differs from the DEFVALx register or if the input value has *changed*. In the project presented, we simply zero this value because it is not used when detecting *changed* inputs.

DEFVALx Register									GPIO	Address
Bit	7	6	5	4	3	2	1	0	A	0x06
R	Y	Y	Y	Y	Y	Y	Y	Y	B	0x07
W	Y	Y	Y	Y	Y	Y	Y	Y		
Reset	0	0	0	0	0	0	0	0		

DEFVALx Bit Value

0	Interrupt when input not 0
1	Interrupt when input not 1

INTCONx Register

This register specifies how input comparisons will be made. In our project, we set all these bits to 0 so that inputs interrupt on *change*.

INTCONx Register									GPIO	Address
Bit	7	6	5	4	3	2	1	0	A	0x08
R	Y	Y	Y	Y	Y	Y	Y	Y	B	0x09
W	Y	Y	Y	Y	Y	Y	Y	Y		
Reset	0	0	0	0	0	0	0	0		

INTCONx Bit Value

0	Input compared against its previous value
1	Input compared against DEFCONx bit value

IPOLx Register

Bits set in this register will invert the logic sense of the corresponding GPIO inputs. In our project, we used no inversion and set the bits to 0.

IPOLx Register									GPIO	Address
Bit	7	6	5	4	3	2	1	0	A	0x02
R	Y	Y	Y	Y	Y	Y	Y	Y	B	0x03
W	Y	Y	Y	Y	Y	Y	Y	Y		
Reset	0	0	0	0	0	0	0	0		

IPOLx Bit Value

0	Read same logic as input pin
1	Read inverted logic of input pin

IODIRx Register

This register determines whether a given GPIO pin is an input or an output. Our project defines bits 4 through 7 as inputs, with the remaining bits 0 through 3 of each 8-bit port as outputs.

IPOLx Register									GPIO	Address
Bit	7	6	5	4	3	2	1	0	A	0x00
R	Y	Y	Y	Y	Y	Y	Y	Y	B	0x01
W	Y	Y	Y	Y	Y	Y	Y	Y		
Reset	1	1	1	1	1	1	1	1		

IPOLx Bit Value

0	Pin is configured as an output
1	Pin is configured as an input

GPINTENx Register

This register enables interrupts on input pin events. Only inputs generate interrupts, so any enable bits for output pins are ignored. How the interrupt is generated by the input is determined by registers DEFVALx and INTCONx.

GPINTENx Register									GPIO	Address
Bit	7	6	5	4	3	2	1	0	A	0x04
R	Y	Y	Y	Y	Y	Y	Y	Y	B	0x05
W	Y	Y	Y	Y	Y	Y	Y	Y		
Reset	0	0	0	0	0	0	0	0		

GPINTENx Bit Value

0	Disable interrupts on this input
1	Enable interrupts for this input

For this project, we enabled interrupts on all inputs for ports A and B.

INTFx Register

This interrupt flags register contains the indicators for each input pin causing an interrupt. This register is *unwritable.*
    Interrupt service routines start with this register to identify which inputs are the cause of the interrupt.
The DEFVALx and INTCONx registers configure how those interrupts are generated. The INTFx flags are cleared by reading the corresponding INTCAPx or GPIOx register.

INTFx Register									GPIO	Address
Bit	7	6	5	4	3	2	1	0	A	0x0E
R	Y	Y	Y	Y	Y	Y	Y	Y	B	0x0F
W	N	N	N	N	N	N	N	N		
Reset	0	0	0	0	0	0	0	0		

INTFx Bit Value

0	No interrupt for this input
1	Input has changed or does not compare

INTCAPx Register

The interrupt capture register reports the status of the inputs as the interrupt is being raised. This register is read-only. Reading this register clears the INTFx register, to allow new interrupts to be generated. When $\overline{INT\ A}$ is linked to $\overline{INT\ B}$, both INTCAPA and INTCAPB must be read to clear the interrupt (or read the GPIOx registers).

INTCAPx Register								GPIO	Address
Bit	7	6	5	4	3	2	1	0	A	0x10
R	Y	Y	Y	Y	Y	Y	Y	Y	B	0x11
W	N	N	N	N	N	N	N	N		
Reset	0	0	0	0	0	0	0	0		

INTCAPx Bit Value

0	Input state was 0 at time of interrupt
1	Input state was 1 at time of interrupt

GPIOx Register

Reading this register provides the current input pin values, for pins configured as inputs. Reading the GPIOx register also clears the interrupt flags in INTFx. When $\overline{INT\ A}$ is linked to $\overline{INT\ B}$, both GPIOA and GPIOB must be read to clear the interrupt (or read the INTCAPx registers).

Presumably, the OLATx register is read, for pins configured for output (the datasheet doesn't say). Writing to the GPIOx register alters the OLATx settings in addition to immediately affecting the outputs.

GPIOx Register								GPIO	Address
Bit	7	6	5	4	3	2	1	0	A	0x12
R	Y	Y	Y	Y	Y	Y	Y	Y	B	0x13
W	Y	Y	Y	Y	Y	Y	Y	Y		
Reset	X	X	X	X	X	X	X	X		

Value	R/W	GPIOx Bit Value
0	R	Current input pin state is low
	W	Write 0 to OLATx and output pin
1	R	Current input pin state is high
	W	Write 1 to OLATx and output pin

Main Program

Here are some change notes for the main program:

1. If you have a pre-revision 2.0 Raspberry Pi, change line 36 to use /dev/i2c-0.

2. Change line 55 if your MCP23017 chip is using a different I2C address than 0x20 (A2, A1, and A0 grounded).

3. Change line 56 if you use a different Raspberry Pi GPIO for your interrupt sense pin.

The main program is fairly straightforward. Here are the basic overall steps:

1. A signal handler is registered in line 180, so ^C will cause the program to exit cleanly.

2. Routine i2c_init() is called to open the I2C driver and initialize.

3. Routine mcp23017_init() is called to initialize and configure the MCP23017 device on the bus (only one is currently supported).

4. Routine gpio_open_edge() is called to open /sys/class/gpio17/value, so changes on the interrupt line can be sensed. This is discussed in more detail later.

5. Finally, the main program enters a loop in lines 190 to 200, looping until ^C is entered.

Once inside the main loop, the following events occur:

1. Execution stalls when gpio_poll() is called. This blocks until the interrupt on GPIO 17 transitions from a high to a low.

2. The interrupt flags are read using routine mcp23017_interrupts(). They're only reported and otherwise not used.

3. Routine mcp23017_captured() is used to read the INTCAPA and INTCAPB registers in order to clear the interrupt.

4. Finally, the routine post_outputs() reads the real-time input values and sends the bits to the outputs.

Program mcp23017.c is shown here:

```
1    /*******************************************************************
2     * mcp23017.c :  Interface with MCP23017 I/O Extender Chip
3     *
4     * This code assumes the following :
5     *
6     *       1.   MCP23017 is configured for address 0x20
7     *       2.   RPi's GPIO 17 (GEN0) will be used for sensing interrupts
8     *       3.   Assumed there is a pull up on GPIO 17.
9     *       4.   MCP23017 GPA4-7 and GPB4-7 will be inputs, with pull-ups.
10    *       5.   MCP23017 GPA0-3 and GPB0-3 will be ouputs.
11    *       6.   MCP23017 signals interrupt active low.
12    *       7.   MCP23017 operating in non-banked register mode.
13    *
14    *   Inputs sensed will be copied to outputs :
15    *       1. GPA4-7 copied to GPA0-3
16    *       2. GPB4-7 copied to GPB0-3
17    *
```

```
18      **********************************************************************/
19
20      #include <stdio.h>
21      #include <stdlib.h>
22      #include <fcntl.h>
23      #include <unistd.h>
24      #include <string.h>
25      #include <errno.h>
26      #include <signal.h>
27      #include <assert.h>
28      #include <sys/ioctl.h>
29      #include <sys/poll.h>
30      #include <linux/i2c.h>
31      #include <linux/i2c-dev.h>
32
33      #include "i2c_funcs.c"              /* I2C  routines  */
34
35      /* Change to i2c 0 if using early Raspberry Pi */
36      static const char * node = "/dev/i2c-1";
37
38      #define GPIOA               0
39      #define GPIOB               1
40
41      #define IODIR               0
42      #define IPOL                1
43      #define GPINTEN     2
44      #define DEFVAL      3
45      #define INTCON      4
46      #define IOCON               5
47      #define GPPU                6
48      #define INTF                7
49      #define INTCAP     ·8
50      #define GPIO                9
51      #define OLAT                10
52
53      #define MCP_REGISTER(r,g) (((r) <<1)|(g)) cc/* For I2C routines */
54
55      static unsigned gpio_addr = 0x20;     /* MCP23017 I2C Address */
56      static const int gpio_inta = 17 ;     /* GPIO pin for INTA connection */
57      static int is_signaled = 0;           /* Exit program if signaled * /
58
59      #include "sysgpio.c"
60
61      /*
62       * Signal handler to quit the program  :
63       */
64      static void
65      sigint_handler(int signo) {
66              is_signaled = 1;                    /* Signal to exit program */
67      }
68
```

```
69   /*
70    * Write to MCP23017 A or B register set:
71    */
72   static int
73   mcp23017_write(int reg,int AB,int value) {
74           unsigned reg_addr = MCP_REGISTER(reg,AB);
75           int rc;
76
77           rc = i2c_write8(gpio_addr,reg_addr,value);
78           return rc;
79   }
80
81   /*
82    * Write value to both MCP23017 register sets  :
83    */
84   static void
85   mcp23017_write_both(int reg,int value) {
86           mcp23017_write(reg,GPIOA,value);              /* Set A */
87           mcp23017_write(reg,GPIOB,value);              /* Set B */
88   }
89
90   /*
91    * Read the MCP23017 input pins (excluding outputs,
92    * 16-bits) :
93    */
94   static unsigned
95   mcp23017_inputs(void) {
96           unsigned reg_addr = MCP_REGISTER(GPIO,GPIOA);
97
98
99           return i2c_read16(gpio_addr,reg_addr) & 0xF0F0;
100  }
101
102  /*
103   * Write 16 bits to outputs  :
104   */
105  static void
106  mcp23017_outputs(int value) {
107          unsigned  reg_addr = MCP_REGISTER(GPIO,GPIOA);
108
109          i2c_write16 (gpio_addr,reg_addr,value & 0x0F0F);
110  }
111
112  /*
113   * Read MCP23017 captured values (16-bits):
114   */
115  static unsigned
116  mcp23017_captured(void) {
117          unsigned reg_addr = MCP_REGISTER(INTCAP,GPIOA);
118
```

```
119              return i2c_read16(gpio_addr,reg_addr) & 0xF0F0;
120 }
121
122 /*
123  * Read interrupting input flags (16-bits) :
124  */
125 static unsigned
126 mcp23017_interrupts(void) {
127          unsigned  reg_addr = MCP_REGISTER(INTF,GPIOA);
128
129          return i2c_read16(gpio_addr,reg_addr) & 0xF0F0;
130 }
131
132 /*
133  * Configure the MCP23017 GPIO Extender :
134  */
135 static void
136 mcp23017_init(void) {
137          int v, int_flags;
138
139          mcp23017_write_both(IOCON,0b01000100);        /* MIRROR=1,ODR=1 */
140          mcp23017_write_both(GPINTEN,0x00);            /* No interrupts enabled */
141          mcp23017_write_both(DEFVAL,0x00);             /* Clear default value */
142          mcp23017_write_both(OLAT,0x00);               /* OLATx=0 */
143          mcp23017_write_both(GPPU,0b11110000);         /* 4-7 are pull up */
144          mcp23017_write_both(IPOL,0b00000000);         /* No inverted polarity */
145          mcp23017_write_both(IODIR,0b11110000);        /* 4-7 are inputs, 0-3 outputs */
146          mcp23017_write_both(INTCON,0b00000000);       /* Cmp inputs to previous */
147          mcp23017_write_both(GPINTEN,0b11110000);      /* Interrupt on changes */
148
149          /*
150           * Loop until all interrupts are cleared:
151           */
152          do    {
153                  int_flags = mcp23017_interrupts();
154                  if ( int_flags != 0 ) {
155                      v = mcp23017_captured();
156                      printf("  Got change %04X values %04X\n",int_flags,v);
157                  }
158          } while ( int_flags  != 0x0000 && !is_signaled  );
159 }
160
161 /*
162  * Copy input bit settings to outputs :
163  */
164 static void
165 post_outputs(void) {
166          int inbits = mcp23017_inputs();     /* Read inputs */
167          int outbits = inbits >> 4;          /* Shift to output bits */
168          mcp23017_outputs(outbits);          /* Copy inputs to outputs */
```

```
169          printf ("   Outputs:      %04X\n",outbits);
170 }
171
172 /*
173  *Main program  :
174  */
175 int
176 main(int argc,char **argv) {
177          int int_flags, v;
178          int fd;
179
180          signal(SIGINT,sigint_handler);              /* Trap on SIGINT   */
181
182          i2c_init(node);                             /*  Initialize for I2C  */
183          mcp23017_init();                            /*  Configure MCP23017 @ 20  */
184
185          fd = gpio_open_edge(gpio_inta);             /*  Configure INTA pin  */
186
187          puts("Monitoring for MCP23017 input changes :\n");
188          post_outputs();                             /* Copy inputs to outputs */
189
190          do    {
191                  gpio_poll(fd) ;                     /* Pause until an interrupt */
192
193                  int_flags = mcp23017_interrupts();
194                  if ( int_flags )  {
195                          v = mcp23017_captured();
196                          printf("   Input change: flags %04X values %04X\n",
197                                       int_flags,v);
198                          post_outputs();
199                  }
200          } while ( !is_signaled  );                  /* Quit if ^C' d */
201
202          fputc('\n', stdout);
203
204          i2c_close();                                /* Close I2C driver */
205          close(fd);                                  /* Close gpio17/value */
206          gpio_close(gpio_inta) ;                     /* Unex port gpio17 */
207          return 0;
208 }
209
210 /* End mcp23017.c */
```

Module i2c_funcs.c

To compile code when making use of I2C, you will need to install the libi2c development library:

```
$ sudo apt-get install libi2c-dev
```

The i2c_funcs.c is a small module that wraps the ioctl(2) calls into neat little I/O functions:

> i2c_write8(): Writes 8-bit value to MCP23017 register

> i2c_write16(): Writes 16-bit value to MCP23017 register

> i2c_read8(): Reads 8-bit value from MCP23017 register

> i2c_read16(): Reads 16-bit value from MCP23017 register

Additionally, the open and close routines are provided:

> i2c_init(): Opens the bus driver for /dev/i2c-x

> i2c_close(): Closes the opened I2C driver

The C API for these I2C functions are described in Chapter 14.

```
1    /*************************************************************************
2     * i2c_funcs.c : I2C Access Functions
3     *************************************************************************/
4
5    static int i2c_fd = -1;                  /* Device node : /dev/i2c-1 */
6    static unsigned long i2c_funcs = 0;      /* Support flags */
7
8    /*
9     * Write 8 bits to I2C bus peripheral:
10    */
11   int
12   i2c_write8(int addr,int reg,int byte) {
13           struct i2c_rdwr_ioctl_data msgset;
14           struct i2c_msg iomsgs[1];
15           unsigned char buf[2];
16           int rc;
17
18           buf[0] = (unsigned char)reg;       /* MCP23017 register no. */
19           buf[1] = (unsigned char)byte;      /* Byte to write to register */
20
21           iomsgs[0].addr = (unsigned)addr;
22           iomsgs[0].flags = 0;               /* Write */
23           iomsgs[0].buf = buf;
24           iomsgs[0].len = 2;
25
26           msgset.msgs = iomsgs;
27           msgset.nmsgs = 1;
28
29           rc = ioctl(i2c_fd,I2C_RDWR,&msgset);
30           return rc < 0 ? -1 : 0;
31   }
32
33   /*
34    * Write 16 bits to Peripheral at address :
35    */
```

```
36  int
37  i2c_write16(int addr, int reg, int value) {
38          struct i2c_rdwr_ioctl_data msgset;
39          struct i2c_msg iomsgs[1];
40          unsigned char buf[3];
41          int rc;
42
43          buf[0] = (unsigned char)reg;
44          buf[1] = (unsigned char)(( value >> 8 ) & 0xFF);
45          buf[2] = (unsigned char)(value & 0xFF);
46
47          iomsgs[0].addr = (unsigned)addr;
48          iomsgs[0].flags = 0;                    /* Write */
49          iomsgs[0].buf = buf;
50          iomsgs[0].len = 3;
51
52          msgset.msgs = iomsgs;
53          msgset.nmsgs = 1;
54
55          rc = ioctl(i2c_fd,I2C_RDWR,&msgset);
56          return rc < 0 ? -1 : 0;
57  }
58
59  /*
60   * Read 8-bit value from peripheral at addr :
61   */
62  int
63  i2c_read8(int addr,int reg) {
64          struct i2c_rdwr_ioctl_data msgset;
65          struct i2c_msg iomsgs[2];
66          unsigned char buf[1], rbuf[1];
67          int rc;
68
69          buf[0] = (unsigned char)reg;
70
71          iomsgs[0].addr = iomsgs[1].addr = (unsigned)addr;
72          iomsgs[0].flags = 0;                    /* Write */
73          iomsgs[0].buf = buf;
74          iomsgs[0].len = 1;
75
76          iomsgs[1].flags = I2C_M_RD;             /* Read */
77          iomsgs[1].buf = rbuf;
78          iomsgs[1].len = 1;
79
80          msgset.msgs = iomsgs;
81          msgset.nmsgs = 2;
82
83          rc = ioctl(i2c_fd,I2C_RDWR,&msgset);
84          return rc < 0 ? -1 : ((int)(rbuf[0]) & 0x0FF);
85  }
86
```

```
87  /*
88   * Read 16- bits of data from peripheral :
89   */
90  int
91  i2c_read16(int addr,int reg)  {
92          struct i2c_rdwr_ioctl_data msgset;
93          struct i2c_msg iomsgs[2];
94          unsigned char buf[1], rbuf [2];
95          int rc;
96
97          buf[0] = (unsigned char)reg;
98
99          iomsgs[0].addr = iomsgs[1].addr = (unsigned)addr;
100         iomsgs[0].flags = 0;                        /* Write */
101         iomsgs[0].buf = buf;
102         iomsgs[0].len = 1;
103
104         iomsgs[1].flags = I2C_M_RD;
105         iomsgs[1].buf = rbuf ;                      /* Read */
106         iomsgs[1].len = 2;
107
108         msgset.msgs = iomsgs;
109         msgset.nmsgs = 2;
110
111         if ( (rc = ioctl(i2c_fd,I2C_RDWR,&msgset)) < 0 )
112                 return  -1;
113         return  (rbuf[0] << 8) | rbuf[1];
114 }
115
116 /*
117  * Open I2C bus and check capabilities :
118  */
119 static void
120 i2c_init(const char * node) {
121         int rc;
122
123         i2c_fd = open(node,O_RDWR);          /* Open driver /dev/i2s-1 */
124         if ( i2c_fd < 0 ) {
125                 perror("Opening /dev/i2s-1");
126                 puts("Check that the i2c dev & i2c-bcm2708  kernel modules "
127                      "are loaded.");
128                 abort();
129         }
130
131         /*
132          * Make sure the driver supports plain I2C I/O:
133          */
134         rc = ioctl(i2c_fd,I2C_FUNCS,&i2c_funcs);
135         assert(rc >= 0) ;
136         assert(i2c_funcs & I2C_FUNC_I2C);
137 }
138
```

```
139 /*
140  * Close the I2C driver  :
141  */
142 static void
143 i2c_close(void) {
144         close(i2c_fd);
145         i2c_fd = -1;
146 }
147
148 /* End i2c_funcs.c  */
```

Module sysgpio.c

The sysgpio.c module performs some grunt work in making the /sys/class/gpio17/value node available and configuring it. This node is opened for reading, so that poll(2) can be called upon it.

The interesting code in this module is found in lines 89 to 106, where gpio_poll() is defined. The file descriptor passed to it as fd is the /sys/class/gpio17/value file that is

- Configured as input

- Triggered on the falling edge (high-to-low transition)

The poll(2) system call in line 99 blocks the execution of the program until the input (GPIO 17) changes from a high state to a low state. This is connected to the MCP23017 $\overline{INT\ A}$ pin, so it can tell us when its GPIO extender input(s) have changed.

The poll(2) system call can return an error if the program has handled a signal. The error returned will be EINTR when this happens (as discussed in Chapter 11, section "Error EINTR"). If the program detects that ^C has been pressed (is_signaled is true), then it exits, returning -1, to allow the main program to exit.

A value of rc=1 is returned if /sys/class/gpio17/value has a changed value to be read. Before returning from gpio_poll(), a read(2) of any unread data is performed. This is necessary so that the next call to poll(2) will block until new data is available.

```
1    /*************************************************************
2     * sysgpio.c : Open/configure /sys GPIO pin
3     *
4     * Here we must open the /sys/class/gpio/gpio17/value and do a
5     * poll(2) on it, so that we can sense the MCP23017 interrupts.
6     *************************************************************/
7
8    typedef enum {
9            gp_export = 0,              /* /sys/class/gpio/export  */
10           gp_unexport,                /* /sys/class/gpio/unexport */
11           gp_direction,               /* /sys/class/gpo%d/direction  */
12           gp_edge,                    /* /sys/class/gpio%d/edge  */
13           gp_value                    /* /sys/class/gpio%d/value  */
14   } gpio_path_t;
15
16   /*
17    * Internal : Create a pathname for type in buf.
18    */
```

```
19  static const char *
20  gpio_setpath(int pin,gpio_path_t type,char *buf,unsigned bufsiz) {
21          static const char *paths[] = {
22                  "export",  "unexport",  "gpio%d/direction",
23                  "gpio%d/edge", "gpio%d/value" };
24          int slen;
25
26          strncpy(buf,"/sys/class/gpio/",bufsiz);
27          bufsiz -= (slen = strlen(buf));
28          snprintf(buf+slen,bufsiz,paths[type],pin);
29          return buf;
30  }
31
32  /*
33   * Open /sys/class/gpio%d/value for edge detection  :
34   */
35  static int
36  gpio_open_edge(int pin) {
37          char buf[128];
38          FILE *f;
39          int fd;
40
41          /* Export pin: /sys/class/gpio/export */
42          gpio_setpath(pin,gp_export,buf,sizeof buf);
43          f = fopen(buf, "w");
44          assert(f);
45          fprintf(f,"%d\n",pin);
46          fclose(f);
47
48          /* Direction: /sys/class/gpio%d/direction  */
49          gpio_setpath(pin,gp_direction,buf,sizeof buf);
50          f = fopen(buf,"w");
51          assert(f);
52          fprintf(f,"in\n");
53          fclose(f);
54
55          /* Edge: /sys/class/gpio%d/edge */
56          gpio_setpath(pin,gp_edge,buf,sizeof buf);
57          f = fopen(buf,"w");
58          assert(f);
59          fprintf(f,"falling\n");
60          fclose(f);
61
62          /* Value: /sys/class/gpio%d/value  */
63          gpio_setpath(pin,gp_value,buf,sizeof buf);
64          fd = open(buf,O_RDWR);
65          return fd;
66  }
67
68  /*
69   * Close (unexport) GPIO pin :
70   */
```

```
71  static void
72  gpio_close(int pin) {
73          char buf[128];
74          FILE *f ;
75
76          /* Unexport: /sys/class/gpio/unexport */
77          gpio_setpath(pin,gp_unexport,buf,size of buf);
78          f = fopen(buf,"w");
79          assert(f);
80          fprintf(f,"%d\n",pin);
81          fclose(f);
82  }
83
84  /*
85   * This routine will block until the open GPIO pin has changed
86   * value. This pin should be connected to the MCP23017 /INTA
87   * pin.
88   */
89  static int
90  gpio_poll(int fd) {
91          unsigned char buf[32];
92          struct pollfd polls;
93          int rc;
94
95          polls.fd = fd;                          /* /sys/class/gpio17/value */
96          polls.events = POLLPRI;                 /* Exceptions  */
97
98          do      {
99                  rc = poll(&polls,1,-1);         /* Block */
100                 if ( is_signaled )
101                         return -1;              /* Exit if ^Creceived */
102         } while ( rc < 0  && errno == EINTR );
103
104         (void)read(fd,buf,sizeof buf);       /* Clear interrupt */
105         return 0;
106 }
107
108 /* End sysgpio.c */
```

Example Run

The first time you run the program, you might encounter an error:

```
$ ./mcp23017
Opening /dev/i2s-1: No such file or directory
Check that the i2c-dev & i2c-bcm2708 kernel modules are loaded.
Aborted
$
```

As the program states in the error message, it is unable to open the I2C driver, because the I2C kernel modules have not been loaded. See Chapter 14 for modprobe information.

The following is a successful session. After the program is started, the program pauses after issuing the message "Monitoring for MCP23017 input changes." At this point, the program is in the poll(2) system call, waiting to be notified of an interrupt from the MCP23017 peripheral. If you open another session, you can confirm that little or no CPU resource is consumed by this.

```
$ sudo ./mcp23017
Monitoring for MCP23017 input changes :

  Outputs :        0F0F
  Input change :   flags 8000 values 70F0
  Outputs :        070F
  Input change :   flags 8000 values F0F0
  Outputs :        070F
  Input change :   flags 8000 values F0F0
  Outputs :        070F
  Input change :   flags 8000 values F0F0
  Outputs :        070F
  Input change :   flags 8000 values F0F0
  Outputs :        070F
  Input change :   flags 8000 values 70F0
  Outputs :        0F0F
^C
$
```

While this was running, I carefully grounded pin 28 of the MCP28017 chip, which is input GPA7. This is reflected immediately in the message:

```
Input change : flags 8000 values 70F0
```

The flags value reported as 8000 is decoded next, showing that GPA7 did indeed *change* in value:

INTFA								INTFB							
7	6	5	4	3	2	1	0	7	6	5	4	3	2	1	0
1	0	0	0	0	0	0	0	0	0	0	0	0	0	0	0

The value reported as 70F0 is from the INTCAPx register pair:

INTCAPA								INTCAPB							
7	6	5	4	3	2	1	0	7	6	5	4	3	2	1	0
0	1	1	1	0	0	0	0	1	1	1	1	0	0	0	0

This shows us that the GPA7 pin is found in the zero state at the time of the interrupt. All remaining inputs show high (0s indicate output pins).

While I grounded the GPA7 pin only once, you can see from the session output that several events occur. This is due to the *bounce* of the wire as it contacts. You'll also note that some events are lost during this bounce period. Look at the input events:

```
1    Input change:  flags 8000 values  70F0
2    Input change:  flags 8000 values  F0F0
3    Input change:  flags 8000 values  F0F0
4    Input change:  flags 8000 values  F0F0
5    Input change:  flags 8000 values  F0F0
6    Input change:  flags 8000 values  70F0
```

Each interrupt correctly shows that pin GPA7 changed. But look closely at the captured values for the inputs:

1. The captured level of the input is 0 (line 1).

2. The captured level change of the input is now 1 (line 2).

3. The next input change shows a captured level of 1 (line 3).

How does the state of an input change from a 1 to a 1? Clearly what happens is that the input GPA7 changes to low but returns to high by the time the interrupt is captured.

Push button, switch, and key bounces can occur often with a variety of pulse widths, in the range of microseconds to milliseconds, until the contact stabilizes (off or on). The very action of pushing a button can initiate a series of a thousand pulses. Some pulses will be too short for the software to notice, so it must be prepared to deal with this. Sometimes electronics circuits are applied to eliminate "key debouncing" so that the software will see a clean and singular event. This is what is accomplished in Chapter 29, where a flip-flop is used.

Response Times

You should be aware of the interrupt notification limitations provided by the poll(2) system call. The input lines could easily change faster than the Raspberry Pi can respond. Consider the process involved:

1. An input GPIO extender pin changes in value.

2. The MCP23017 device activates $\overline{INT\ A}$ by bringing it from a high to a low (a few cycles later).

3. The Raspberry Pi's GPIO 17 pin sees a falling input level change.

4. The device driver responds to the GPIO pin change by servicing an interrupt and then notifies the application waiting in poll(2).

5. The application sends some I2C traffic to query the INTFA and INTFB flag registers in the MCP23017.

6. Registers GPIOA and GPIOB must also be read to clear the interrupt, involving more I/O on the I2C bus.

Consequently, there is considerable delay in sensing a GPIO change and the clearing of the device interrupt.

An informal test using select(2) purely for delay purposes (no file descriptors) required a minimum of approximately 150 µs on a 700 MHz Pi. The poll(2) call is likely to be nearly identical. Attempting to set smaller timed delays bottomed out near 150 µs. This suggests that the quickest turnaround for reacting to an $\overline{INT}$ signal from the MCP23017 will be 150 µs (excluding the time needed to actually service the registers in the peripheral). This means that the absolute maximum number of interrupts per second that can be processed will be 6,600.

To estimate the effects of the IC2 bus, let's do some additional simplified calculations. The I2C bus operates at 100 kHz on the Raspberry Pi (Chapter 14). A single byte requires 8 data bits and an acknowledgment bit. This requires about 90 µs per byte. To read one MCP23017 register requires the following:

1. The peripheral's address byte to be sent (1 byte).

2. The MCP23017 register address to be sent (1 byte).

3. The MCP23017 responds back with 1 byte.

This requires $3 \times 90 = 270$ µs, just to read one register. Add to this the following:

1. Both interrupt flag registers INTFA and INTFB must be read.

2. Both GPIOA and GPIOB registers must be read, to clear the interrupt.

So, ignoring the start and stop bits, this requires $4 \times 270 = 1.80 \; ms$ to respond to one input level change. (This also ignores the effect of multiple peripherals on the bus.) This, added to the minimum of about 150 µs overhead for poll(2), leads to the minimum response time of about $1.08 + 0.150 = 1.23 \; ms$. This results in a practical limit of about 800 signal changes per second.

Because of the response-time limitations, it is recommended that the INTCAPx register values be ignored. By the time the application can respond to a signal change, it may have changed back again. This is why the program presented uses the values read in GPIOA and GPIOB, rather than the captured values in the INTCAPx. But if your application needs to know the state at the time of the event, the INTCAPx register values are available.

Some reduced I2C overhead can be attained by tuning the I/O operations. For example, with use of the auto-increment address feature of the MCP23017, it is possible to read both INTFx flags and GPIOx registers in one ioctl(2) call:

$$
\begin{aligned}
T &= t_{addr} + t_{register} + t_{INTFA} + t_{INTFB} + t_{register} + t_{GPIOA} + t_{GPIOB} \\
&= 7 \times 90 \\
&= 0.630 \; ms
\end{aligned}
$$

That approach reduces the I2C time to approximately 7-byte times. The total turnaround time can then be reduced to about $0.63 + 0.150 = 0.78 \; ms$.

CHAPTER 24

■ ■ ■

Nunchuk-Mouse

This chapter's project is about attaching the Nintendo Wii Nunchuk to the Raspberry Pi. The Nunchuk has two buttons; an X-Y joystick; and an X, Y, and Z accelerometer. The sensor data is communicated through the I2C bus. Let's have some fun using a Nunchuk as a pointing device for the X Window System desktop.

Project Overview

The challenge before us breaks down into two overall categories:

- The I2C data communication details of the Nunchuk device

- Inserting the sensed data into the X Window System desktop event queue

Since you've mastered I2C communications in other parts of this book, we'll focus more on the Nunchuk technical details. The remainder of the chapter looks at the Linux uinput API that will be used for the X-Windows interface. The final details cover a small but critical X-Windows configuration change, to bring about the Nunchuk-Mouse.

Nunchuk Features

The basic physical and data characteristics of the Nunchuk are listed in Table 24-1.

Table 24-1. *Nunchuk Controls and Data Characteristics*

User-Interface Features	Bits	Data	Hardware/Chip
C Button	1	Boolean	Membrane switch
Z button	1	Boolean	Membrane switch
X-Y joystick	8x2	Integers	30 $k\Omega$ potentiometers
X, Y, and Z accelerometer	10x3	Integers	ST LIS3L02 series

For application as a mouse, the C and Z buttons fill in for the left and right mouse buttons. The joystick is used to position the mouse cursor.

While the Nunchuk normally operates at a clock rate of 400 kHz, it works just fine at the Raspberry Pi's 100 kHz I2C rate.

■ **Note**   I encourage you to experiment with the accelerometer.

Connector Pinout

There are four wires, two of which are power and ground (some units may have two additional wires, one that connects to the shield and the other to the unused center pin). The remaining two wires are used for I2C communication (SDA and SCL). The connections looking into the cable-end connector are shown in Table 24-2.

Table 24-2. *Nuncheck Cable Connections*

SCL		Gnd
+3.3 V	N/C	SDA

The Nunchuk connector is annoyingly nonstandard. Some folks have rolled their own adapters using a double-sided PCB to mate with the inner connections. Others have purchased adapters for around $6. Cheap Nunchuk clones may be found on eBay for about half that price. With the growing number of clone adapters becoming available at more-competitive prices, there is less reason to cut off the connector.

■ **Tip**   Beware of Nunchuk forgeries and nonfunctional units.

If you do cut off the connector, you will quickly discover that there is no standard wire color scheme. The only thing you can count on is that the pins are laid out as in Table 24-2. If you have a genuine Wii Nunchuk, the listed wire colors in Table 24-3 might be valid. The column labeled Clone Wire lists the wire colors of my own clone's wires. *Yours will likely differ.*

Table 24-3. *Nunchuk Connector Wiring*

Pin	Wii Wire	CloneWire[†]	Description	P1
Gnd	White	White	Ground	P1-25
SDA	Green	Blue	Data	P1-03
+3.3 V	Red	Red	Power	P1-01
SCL	Yellow	Green	Clock	P1-05

[†]*Clone wire colors vary!*

Before you cut that connector off your clone, consider that you'll need to trace the connector to a wire color. Cut the cable, leaving about 3 inches of wire for the connector. Then you can cut the insulation off and trace the pins to a wire by using an ohmmeter (or by looking inside the cable-end connector).

Figure 24-1 shows the author's clone Nunchuk with the connector cut off. In place of the connector, solid wire ends were soldered on and a piece of heat shrink applied over the solder joint. The solid wire ends are perfect for plugging into a prototyping breadboard.

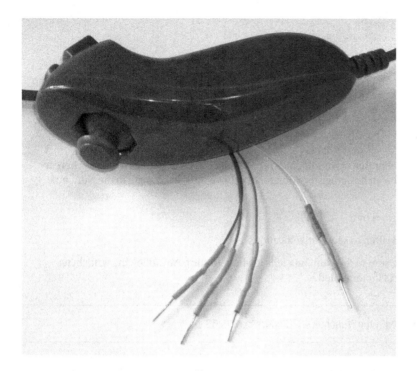

Figure 24-1. *Nunchuk with wire ends*

Testing the Connection

Once you've hooked up the Nunchuk to the Raspberry Pi, you'll want to perform some simple tests to make sure it is working. The first step is to make sure your I2C drivers are loaded:

```
$ lsmod | grep i2c
i2c_bcm2708          3759         0
i2c_dev              5620         0
```

If you see these modules loaded, you're good to go. Otherwise, manually load them now:

```
$ sudo modprobe i2c-bcm2708
$ sudo modprobe i2c-dev
```

Assuming the Raspberry Pi rev 2.0+, you'll use I2C bus 1 (see Chapter 14 if you're not sure). Scan to see whether your Nunchuk is detected:

```
$ sudo i2cdetect -y 1
     0  1  2  3  4  5  6  7  8  9  a  b  c  d  e  f
00:          -- -- -- -- -- -- -- -- -- -- -- -- --
10: -- -- -- -- -- -- -- -- -- -- -- -- -- -- -- --
20: -- -- -- -- -- -- -- -- -- -- -- -- -- -- -- --
30: -- -- -- -- -- -- -- -- -- -- -- -- -- -- -- --
40: -- -- -- -- -- -- -- -- -- -- -- -- -- -- -- --
```

```
50:  -- -- 52 -- -- -- -- -- -- -- -- -- -- -- -- --
60:  -- -- -- -- -- -- -- -- -- -- -- -- -- -- -- --
70:  -- -- -- -- -- -- -- --
```

If the Nunchuk is working, it will show up in this display at address 0x52. With the hardware verified, it is time to move on to the software.

Nunchuk I2C Protocol

The Nunchuk contains a quirky little controller that communicates through the I2C bus. In order to know where to store bytes written to it, the first byte must be an 8-bit register address. In other words, each write to the Nunchuk requires the following:

- One register address byte, followed by

- Zero or more data bytes to be written to sequential locations

Thus for write operations, the first byte sent to the Nunchuk tells it where to start. Any following write bytes received are written with the register address incremented.

■ **Tip**   Don't confuse the register address with the Nunchuk's I2C address of 0x52.

It is possible to write the register address and then read bytes instead. This procedure specifies the starting location of data bytes to be read.

A quirky aspect of the Nunchuk controller is that there must be a short delay between writing the register address and reading the data. Performing the write followed by an immediate read does not work. Writing data immediately after the register address does succeed, however.

■ **Note**   The Nunchuk uses I2C address 0x52.

Encryption

The Nunchuk is designed to provide an encrypted link. However, that can be disabled by initializing it a certain way. The defeat procedure is as follows:

1.   Write 0x55 to Nunchuk location 0xF0.

2.   Pause.

3.   Write 0x00 to Nunchuk location 0xFB.

The following illustrates the message sequence involved. Notice that this is performed as *two* separate I2C write operations:

Write		Pause	Write	
F0	55	-	FB	00

Once this is successfully performed, all future data is returned unencrypted.

Read Sensor Data

The whole point of the Nunchuk is to read its sensor data. When requested, it returns 6 bytes of data formatted as shown in Table 24-4.

Table 24-4. *Nunchuk Data*

Byte	Bits	Description
1		Analog stick x axis value
2		Analog stick y axis value
3		X acceleration bits 9:2
4		Y acceleration bits 9:2
5		Z acceleration bits 9:2
	0	Z button pressed (active low)
	1	C button pressed (active low)
6	3:2	X acceleration bits 1:0
	5:4	Y acceleration bits 1:0
	7:6	Z acceleration bits 1:0

Some of the data is split over multiple bytes. For example, the X acceleration bits 9:2 are obtained from byte 3. The lowest 2 bits are found in byte 6, in bits 3 and 2. These together form the 9-bit X acceleration value.

To retrieve this data, we are always required to tell the Nunchuk where to begin. So the sequence always begins with a write of offset 0x00 followed by a pause:

Write	Pause	Read 6 bytes					
00	-	01	02	03	04	05	06

The Nunchuk doesn't allow us to do this in one ioctl(2) call, using two I/O messages. A write of 0 must be followed by a pause. Then the 6 data bytes can be read as a separate I2C read operation. If the pause is too long, however, the Nunchuk controller seems to time out, resulting in incorrect data being returned. So we must do things the Nunchuk way.

Linux uinput Interface

While reading the Nunchuk is fun, we need to apply it to our desktop as a mouse. We need to insert mouse events based on what we read from it.

The Linux uinput driver allows programmers to develop nonstandard input drivers so that events can be injected into the input stream. This approach allows new input streams to be added without changing application code. Certainly the Nunchuk qualifies as a nonstandard input device!

A problem with this uinput API is its general lack of documentation. The best information available on the Internet seems to be from these three online sources:

- "Getting started with uinput: the user level input subsystem"
  http://thiemonge.org/getting-started-with-uinput

- "Using uinput driver in Linux- 2.6.x to send user input"
  http://www.einfochips.com/download/dash_jan_tip.pdf

- "Types"
  http://www.kernel.org/doc/Documentation/input/event-codes.txt

The only other source of information seems to be the device driver source code itself:

drivers/input/misc/uinput.c

The example program provided in this chapter can help pull all the necessary details together for you.

Working with Header Files

The header files required for the uinput API include the following:

```
#include <sys/ioctl.h>
#include <linux/input.h>
#include <linux/uinput.h>
```

To compile code, making use of I2C, you also need to install the libi2c development library, if you have not done that already:

```
$ sudo apt-get install libi2c-dev
```

Opening the Device Node

The connection to the uinput device driver is made by opening the device node:

/dev/uinput

The following is an example of the required open(2) call:

```
int fd;

fd = open("/dev/uinput",O_WRONLY|O_NONBLOCK);
if ( fd < 0 ) {
    perror("Opening /dev/uinput");
    ...
```

Configuring Events

In order to inject events, the driver must be configured to accept them. Each call to ioctl(2) in the following code enables one class of events based on the argument *event*. The following is a generalized example:

```
int rc;
unsigned long event = EV_KEY;

rc = ioctl(fd,UI_SET_EVBIT,event);
assert(!rc);
```

The list of UI_SET_EVBIT event types is provided in Table 24-5. The most commonly needed event types are EV_SYN, EV_KEY, and EV_REL (or EV_ABS).

Table 24-5. *List of uinput Event Types*

From Header File input.h	
Macro	**Description**
EV_SYN	Event synchronization/separation
EV_KEY	Key/button state changes
EV_REL	Relative axis mouse-like changes
EV_ABS	Absolute axis mouse-like changes
EV_MSC	Miscellaneous events
EV_SW	Binary (switch) state changes
EV_LED	LED on/off changes
EV_SND	Output to sound devices
EV_REP	For use with autorepeating devices
EV_FF	Force feedback commands to input device
EV_PWR	Power button/switch event
EV_FF_STATUS	Receive force feedback device status

■ **Caution** Do not or the event types together. The device driver expects each event type to be registered *separately*.

Configure EV_KEY

Once you have registered your intention to provide EV_KEY events, you need to register all key codes that might be used. While this seems a nuisance, it does guard against garbage being injected by an errant program. The following code registers its intention to inject an Escape key code:

```
int rc;

rc = ioctl(fd,UI_SET_KEYBIT,KEY_ESC);
assert(!rc);
```

To configure all possible keys, a loop can be used. But do not register key code 0 (KEY_RESERVED) nor 255; the include file indicates that code 255 is reserved for the special needs of the AT keyboard driver.

```
int rc;
unsigned long key;

for ( key=1; key<255; ++key ) {
    rc = ioctl(fd,UI_SET_KEYBIT,key);
    assert(!rc);
}
```

Mouse Buttons

In addition to key codes, the same ioctl(2,UI_SET_KEYBIT) call is used to register mouse, joystick, and other kinds of button events. This includes touch events from trackpads, tablets, and touchscreens. The long list of button codes is defined in header file linux/input.h. The usual suspects are shown in Table 24-6.

Table 24-6. *Key Event Macros*

Macro	Synonym	Description
BTN_LEFT	BTN_MOUSE	Left mouse button
BTN_RIGHT		Right mouse button
BTN_MIDDLE		Middle mouse button
BTN_SIDE		Side mouse button

The following example shows the application's intention to inject left and right mouse button events:

```
int rc;

rc=ioctl(fd,UI_SET_KEYBIT,BTN_LEFT);
assert(!rc);
rc = ioctl(fd,UI_SET_KEYBIT,BTN_RIGHT);
assert(!rc);
```

Configure EV_REL

In order to inject EV_REL events, the types of relative movements must be registered in advance. The complete list of valid argument codes is shown in Table 24-7. The following example indicates an intention to inject x and y relative axis movements:

```
rc = ioctl(fd,UI_SET_RELBIT,REL_X);
assert(!rc);
rc = ioctl(fd,UI_SET_RELBIT,REL_Y);
assert(!rc);
```

Table 24-7. *UI_SET_RELBIT Options*

Macro	Intention
REL_X	Send relative X changes
REL_Y	Send relative Y changes
REL_Z	Send relative Z changes
REL_RX	x-axis tilt
REL_RY	y- axis tilt
REL_RZ	z- axis tilt
REL_HWHEEL	Horizontal wheel change
REL_DIAL	Dial-turn change
REL_WHEEL	Wheel change
REL_MISC	Miscellaneous

Configure EV_ABS

While we don't use the EV_ABS option in this project, it may be useful to introduce this feature at this point. This event represents absolute cursor movements, and it too requires registration of intentions. The complete list of EV_ABS codes is defined in linux/input.h. The usual suspects are defined in Table 24-8.

Table 24-8. *Absolute Cursor Movement Event Macros*

Macro	Description
ABS_X	Move X to this absolute X coordinate
ABS_Y	Move Y to this absolute Y coordinate

The following is an example of registering intent for absolute x- and y-axis events:

```
int rc;

rc = ioctl(fd,UI_SET_ABSBIT,ABS_X);
assert(!rc);
rc = ioctl(fd,UI_SET_ABSBIT,ABS_X);
assert(!rc);
```

In addition to registering your intentions to inject these events, you need to define some coordinate parameters. The following is an example:

```
struct uinput_user_dev uinp;

uinp.absmin[ABS_X] = 0;
uinp.absmax[ABS_X] = 1023;
```

```
uinp.absfuzz[ABS_X] = 0;
uinp.absflat[ABS_X] = 0;

uinp.absmin[ABS_Y] = 0;
uinp.absmax[ABS_Y] = 767;

uinp.absfuzz[ABS_Y] = 0;
uinp.absflat[ABS_Y] = 0;
```

These values must be established as part of your ioctl(2,UI_DEV_CREATE) operation, which is described next.

Creating the Node

After all registrations with the uinput device driver have been completed, the final step is to create the uinput node. This will be used by the receiving application, in order to read injected events. This involves two programming steps:

1. Write the struct uinput_user_dev information to the file descriptor with write(2).

2. Perform an ioctl(2,UI_DEV_CREATE) to cause the uinput node to be created.

The first step involves populating the following structures:

```
struct input_id {
    __u16       bustype;
    __u16       vendor;
    __u16       product;
    __u16       version;
};

struct uinput_user_dev {
    char        name[UINPUT_MAX_NAME_SIZE];
    struct input_id id;
    int         ff_effects_max;
    int         absmax[ABS_CNT];
    int         absmin[ABS_CNT];
    int         absfuzz[ABS_CNT];
    int         absflat[ABS_CNT];
};
```

An example populating these structures is provided next. If you plan to inject EV_ABS events, you must also populate the abs members, mentioned in the "Configure EV_ABS" section.

```
    struct uinput_user_dev uinp;
    int rc;

    memset(&uinp,0,sizeof uinp);

    strncpy(uinp.name,"nunchuk",UINPUT_MAX_NAME_SIZE);

    uinp.id.bustype = BUS_USB;
    uinp.id.vendor = 0x1;
    uinp.id.product = 0x1;
    uinp.id.version = 1;
```

```
//      uinp.absmax[ABS_X] = 1023; /*EV_ABS only */
//        ...

        rc = write(fd,&uinp,sizeof(uinp));
        assert(rc == sizeof(uinp));
```

The call to write(2) passes all of this important information to the uinput driver. Now all that remains is to request a device node to be created for application use:

```
int rc;

rc = ioctl(fd,UI_DEV_CREATE);
assert(!rc);
```

This step causes the uinput driver to make a device node appear in the pseudo directory /dev/input. An example is shown here:

```
$ ls -l /dev/input
total 0
drwxr-xr-x 2 root root      120 Dec 31  1969 by-id
drwxr-xr-x 2 root root      120 Dec 31  1969 by-path
crw-rw---T 1 root input 13, 64 Dec 31  1969 event0
crw-rw---T 1 root input 13, 65 Dec 31  1969 event1
crw-rw---T 1 root input 13, 66 Dec 31  1969 event2
crw-rw---T 1 root input 13, 67 Feb 23 13:40 event3
crw-rw---T 1 root input 13, 63 Dec 31  1969 mice
crw-rw---T 1 root input 13, 32 Dec 31  1969 mouse0
crw-rw---T 1 root input 13, 33 Feb 23 13:40 mouse1
```

The device /dev/input/event3 was the Nunchuck's created uinput node, when the program was run.

Posting EV_KEY Events

The following code snippet shows how to post a key down event, followed by a key up event:

```
 1 static void
 2 uinput_postkey(int fd,unsigned key) {
 3     struct input_event ev;
 4     int rc;
 5
 6     memset(&ev,0,sizeof(ev));
 7     ev.type = EV_KEY;
 8     ev.code = key;
 9     ev.value = 1;
10
11     rc = write(fd,&ev,sizeof(ev));
12     assert(rc == sizeof(ev));
13
14     ev.value = 0;
15     rc = write(fd,&ev,sizeof(ev));
16     assert(rc == sizeof(ev));
17 }
```

From this example, you see that each event is posted by writing a suitably initialized input_event structure. The example illustrates that the member named type was set to EV_KEY, code was set to the key code, and a keypress was indicated by setting the member value to 1 (line 9).

To inject a key up event, value is reset to 0 (line 14) and the structure is written again.

Mouse button events work the same way, except that you supply mouse button codes for the code member. For example:

```
memset(&ev,0,sizeof(ev));
ev.type = EV_KEY;
ev.code = BTN_RIGHT;        /*Right click */
ev.value = 1;
```

Posting EV_REL Events

To post a relative mouse movement, we populate the input_event as a type EV_REL. The member code is set to the type of event (REL_X or REL_Y in this example), with the value for the relative movement established in the member value:

```
static void
uinput_movement(int fd,int x,inty) {
    struct input_event ev;
    int rc;

    memset(&ev,0,sizeof(ev));
    ev.type = EV_REL;
    ev.code = REL_X;
    ev.value = x;

    rc = write(fd,&ev,sizeof(ev));
    assert(rc == sizeof(ev));

    ev.code = REL_Y;
    ev.value = y;
    rc = write(fd,&ev,sizeof(ev));
    assert (rc == sizeof(ev));
}
```

Notice that the REL_X and REL_Y events are created separately. What if you want the receiving application to avoid acting on these separately? The EV_SYN event helps out in this regard (next).

Posting EV_SYN Events

The uinput driver postpones delivery of events until the EV_SYN event has been injected. The SYN_REPORT type of EV_SYN event causes the queued events to be flushed out and reported to the interested application. The following is an example:

```
static void
uinput_syn(int fd) {
    struct input_event ev;
    int rc;
```

```
    memset(&ev,0,sizeof(ev));
    ev.type = EV_SYN;
    ev.code = SYN_REPORT;
    ev.value = 0;
    rc = write(fd,&ev,sizeof(ev));
    assert(rc == sizeof(ev));
}
```

For a mouse relative movement event, for example, you can inject a REL_X and REL_Y, followed by a SYN_REPORT event to have them seen by the application as a group.

Closing uinput

There are two steps involved:

1.   Destruction of the /dev/input/event%d node

2.   Closing of the file descriptor

The following example shows both:

```
int rc;

rc = ioctl(fd,UI_DEV_DESTROY);
assert(!rc);
close(fd);
```

Closing the file descriptor implies the ioctl(2,UI_DEV_DESTROY) operation. The application has the option of destroying the device node while keeping the file descriptor open.

X-Window

The creation of our new uinput device node is useful only if our desktop system is listening to it. Raspbian Linux's X-Windows system needs a little configuration help to notice our Frankenstein creation. The following definition can be added to the /usr/share/X11/xorg.config.d directory. Name the file 20-nunchuk.conf:

```
# Nunchuck event queue

Section "InputClass"
        Identifier "Raspberry Pi Nunchuk"
        Option "Mode" "Relative"
        MatchDevicePath "/dev/input/event3"
        Driver "evdev"
EndSection

# End 20-nunchuk.conf
```

This configuration change works only if your Nunchuk uinput device shows up as /dev/input/event3. If you have other specialized input device creations on your Raspberry Pi, it could well be event4 or some other number. See the upcoming section "Testing the Nunchuk" for troubleshooting information.

Restart your X-Windows server to have the configuration file noticed.

■ **Tip** Normally, your Nunchuk program should be running already. But the X-Windows server will notice it when the Nunchuk does start.

Input Utilities

When writing uinput event-based code, you will find the package input-utils to be extremely helpful. They can be installed from the command line as follows:

```
$ sudo apt-get install input-utils
```

The following commands are installed:

> lsinput(8): List uinput devices
>
> input-events(8): Dump selected uinput events
>
> input-kbd(8): Keyboard map display

This chapter uses the first two utilities: lsinput(8) and input-events(8).

Testing the Nunchuk

Now that the hardware, drivers, and software are ready, it is time to exercise the Nunchuk. Unfortunately, there is no direct way for applications to identify your created uinput node. When the Nunchuk program runs, the node may show up as /dev/input/event3 or some other numbered node if event3 already exists. If you wanted to start a Nunchuk driver as part of the Linux boot process, you need to create a script to edit the file with the actual device name. The affected X-Windows config file is as follows:

```
/usr/share/X11/xord.conf.d/20-nunchuk.conf
```

The script (shown next) determines which node the Nunchuk program created. The following is an example run, while the Nunchuk program was running:

```
$ ./findchuk
/dev/input/event3
```

When the node is not found, the findchuk script exits with a nonzero code and prints a message to stderr:

```
$ ./findchuk
Nunchuk uinput device not found.
$ echo $?
1
```

The findchuk script is shown here:

```
#!/bin/bash
##########################################################################
# Find the Nunchuck
##########################################################################
#
# This script locates the Nunchuk uinput device by searching the
# /sys/devices/virtual/input pseudo directory for names of the form:
# input[0_9]*. For all subdirectories found, check the ./name pseudo
# file, which will contain "nunchuk". Then we derive the /dev path
# from a sibling entry named event[0_9]*. That will tell use the
# /dev/input/event%d pathname, for the Nunchuk.

DIR=/sys/devices/virtual/input  # Top level directory
set_eu

cd "$DIR"
find . -type d -name 'input[0-9]*' | (
    set -eu
    while read dirname ; do
            cd "$DIR/$dirname"
            if [-f "name"] ; then
                    set +e
                    name=$(cat name)
                    set -e
                    if [ $(cat name) = nunchuk ] ; then
                            event="/dev/input/$ (ls-devent[0-9]*)"
                            echo $event
                            exit 0              # Found it
                    fi
            fi
    done

    echo "Nunchuk uinput device not found." >&2
    exit 1
)

# End findchuk
```

Testing ./nunchuk

When you want to see what Nunchuk data is being received, you can add the -d command-line option:

```
$ ./nunchuk -d
Raw nunchuk data: [83] [83] [5C] [89] [A2] [63]
.stick_x = 0083 (131)
.stick_y = 0083 (131)
.accel_x = 0170 (368)
.accel_y = 0226 (550)
.accel_z = 0289 (649)
.z_button= 0
.c_button= 0
```

The first line reports the raw bytes of data that were received. The remainder of the lines report the data in its decoded form. While the raw data reports the button presses as active low, the Z and C buttons are reported as 1 in the decoded data. The value in the left column is in hexadecimal format, while the value in parenthesis is shown in decimal.

Utility lsinputs

When the Nunchuk program is running, you should be able to see the Nunchuk uinput device in the list:

```
$ lsinput
...
/dev/input/event2
   bustype    : BUS_USB
   vendor     : 0x45e
   product    : 0x40
   version    : 272
   name       : "Microsoft Micro soft 3-Button Mou"
   phys       : "usb-bcm2708_usb-1.3.4/input0"
   uniq       : ""
   bitsev     : EV_SYN EV_KEY EV_REL EV_MSC

/dev/input/event3
   bustype     : BUS_USB
   vendor      : 0x1
   product     : 0x1
   version     : 1
   name        : "nunchuk"
   bits ev     : EV_SYN EV_KEY EV_REL
```

In this example, the Nunchuk shows up as event3.

Utility input-events

When developing uinput-related code, the input-events utility is a great help. Here we run it for event3 (the argument 3 on the command line), where the Nunchuk mouse device is:

```
$ input-events 3
/dev/input/event3
   bustype    : BUS_USB
   vendor     : 0x1
   product    : 0x1
   version    : 1
   name       : "nunchuk"
   bits ev    : EV_SYN EV_KEY EV_REL

waiting for events
23:35:15.345105: EV_KEY BTN_LEFT (0x110) pressed
23:35:15.345190: EV_SYN code=0 value=0
23:35:15.517611: EV_KEY BTN_LEFT (0x110) released
23:35:15.517713: EV_SYN code=0 value=0
```

```
23:35:15.833640: EV_KEY BTN_RIGHT (0x111) pressed
23:35:15.833727: EV_SYN code=0 value=0
23:35:16.019363: EV_KEY BTN_RIGHT (0x111) released
23:35:16.019383: EV_SYN code=0 value=0
23:35:16.564129: EV_REL REL_X -1
23:35:16.564213: EV_REL REL_Y 1
23:35:16.564261: EV_SYN code=0 value=0
...
```

The Program

The code for nunchuk.c is presented on the following pages. The source code for timed_wait.c is shown in Chapter 22. We've covered the I2C I/O in other chapters. The only thing left to note is the difficulty of providing a smooth interface for events produced by the Nunchuk. Here are a few hints for the person who wants to experiment:

1. If the mouse moves too quickly, one major factor is the timed delay used. The timed_wait() call in line 107 spaces out read events for the Nunchuk (currently 15 ms). This also lightens the load on the CPU. Reducing this time-out increases the number of Nunchuk reads and causes more uinput events to be injected. This speeds up the mouse pointer.

2. The function curve() in line 349 attempts to provide a somewhat exponential movement response. Small joystick excursions should be slow and incremental. More-extreme movements will result in faster mouse movements.

3. The Z button is interpreted as the left-click button, while the C button is the right-click button.

4. No keystrokes are injected by this program, but it can be modified to do so. The function uinput_postkey() on line 244 can be used for that purpose.

```
1    /******************************************************************
2     * nunchuk.c: Read events from nunchuck and stuff as mouse events
3     ******************************************************************/
4
5    #include <stdio.h>
6    #include <math.h>
7    #include <stdlib.h>
8    #include <fcntl.h>
9    #include <unistd.h>
10   #include <string.h>
11   #include <errno.h>
12   #include <signal.h>
13   #include <assert.h>
14   #include <sys/ioctl.h>
15   #include <linux/i2c-dev.h>
16   #include <linux/input.h>
17   #include <linux/uinput.h>
18
19   #include "timed_wait.c"
20
21   static int is_signaled = 0;          /*Exit program if signaled */
22   static int i2c_fd = -1;              /*Open/dev/i2c-1 device */
23   static int f_debug = 0;              /*True to print debug messages */
```

```
24
25   typedef struct {
26           unsigned char stick_x;                /*Joystick X */
27           unsigned char stick_y;                /*Joystick Y */
28           unsigned accel_x;                     /*Accel X */
29           unsigned accel_y;                     /*Accel Y */
30           unsigned accel_z;                     /*Accel Z */
31           unsigned z_button: 1;                 /*Z button */
32           unsigned c_button: 1;                 /*C button */
33           unsigned char raw[6];                 /*Raw received data */
34   } nunchuk_t;
35
36   / *
37    * Open I2C bus and check capabilities:
38    * /
39   static void
40   i2c_init(const char *node) {
41           unsigned long i2c_funcs = 0;          /*Support flags */
42           int rc;
43
44           i2c_fd = open(node,O_RDWR);            /*Open driver/dev/i2s-1 */
45           if ( i2c_fd < 0 ) {
46                   perror("Opening/dev/i2s-1");
47                   puts("Check that the i2c-dev & i2c-bcm2708 kernel modules"
48                           "are loaded.");
49                   abort();
50           }
51
52           /*
53            * Make sure the driver supports plain I2C I/O:
54            */
55           rc = ioctl(i2c_fd,I2C_FUNCS,&i2c_funcs);
56           assert(rc >=0);
57           assert(i2c_funcs & I2C_FUNC_I2C);
58   }
59
60   /*
61    * Configure the nunchuk for no encryption:
62    */
63   static void
64   nunchuk_init(void) {
65           static char init_msg1[] = {0xF0, 0x55};
66           static char init_msg2[] = {0xFB, 0x00};
67           struct i2c_rdwr_ioctl_data msgset;
68           struct i2c_msg iomsgs[1];
69           int rc;
70
71           iomsgs[0].addr = 0x52;                 /*Address of Nunchuk */
72           iomsgs[0].flags = 0;                   /*Write */
73           iomsgs[0].buf = init_msg1;             /*Nunchuk 2 byte sequence */
74           iomsgs[0].len = 2;                     /*2 bytes */
75
```

```
76          msgset.msgs = iomsgs;
77          msgset.nmsgs = 1;
78
79          rc = ioctl(i2c_fd,I2C_RDWR,&msgset);
80          assert(rc == 1);
81
82          timed_wait(0,200,0);                    /*Nunchuk needs time */
83
84          iomsgs[0].addr = 0x52;                  /*Address of Nunchuk */
85          iomsgs[0].flags = 0;                    /*Write */
86          iomsgs[0].buf = init_msg2;              /*Nunchuk 2 byte sequence */
87          iomsgs[0].len = 2;                      /*2 bytes */
88
89          msgset.msgs = iomsgs;
90          msgset.nmsgs = 1;
91
92          rc = ioctl(i2c_fd,I2C_RDWR,&msgset);
93          assert(rc == 1);
94 }
95
96 /*
97  * Read nunchuk data :
98  */
99 static int
100 nunchuk_read(nunchuk_t *data) {
101         struct i2c_rdwr_ioctl_data msgset;
102         struct i2c_msg iomsgs[1];
103         char zero[1] = {0x00};                  /*Written byte */
104         unsigned t;
105         int rc;
106
107         timed_wait(0,15000,0);
108
109         /*
110          * Write the nunchuk register address of 0x00:
111          */
112         iomsgs[0].addr = 0x52;                  /*Nunchuk address */
113         iomsgs[0].flags = 0;                    /*Write */
114         iomsgs[0].buf = zero;                   /*Sending buf */
115         iomsgs[0].len = 1;                      /*6 bytes */
116
117         msgset.msgs = iomsgs;
118         msgset.nmsgs = 1;
119
120         rc = ioctl(i2c_fd,I2C_RDWR,&msgset);
121         if ( rc < 0 )
122                 return -1;                      /*I /O error */
123
124         timed_wait(0,200,0);                    /*Zzzz, nunchuk needs time */
125
```

```
126             /*
127              * Read 6 bytes starting at 0x00:
128              */
129             iomsgs[0].addr = 0x52;               /*Nunchuk address */
130             iomsgs[0].flags = I2C_M_RD;          /*Read */
131             iomsgs[0].buf = (char *)data->raw;   /*Receive raw bytes here */
132             iomsgs[0].len = 6;                   /*6 bytes */
133
134             msgset.msgs = iomsgs;
135             msgset.nmsgs = 1;
136
137             rc = ioctl(i2c_fd,I2C_RDWR,&msgset);
138             if ( rc < 0 )
139                     return -1;                   /*Failed */
140
141             data->stick_x = data->raw[0];
142             data->stick_y = data->raw[1];
143             data->accel_x = data->raw[2] << 2;
144             data->accel_y = data->raw[3] << 2;
145             data->accel_z = data->raw[4] << 2;
146
147             t = data->raw[5];
148             data->z_button = t & 1 ? 0 : 1;
149             data->c_button = t & 2 ? 0 : 1;
150             t >>=2;
151             data->accel_x |= t & 3;
152             t >>=2;
153             data->accel_y |= t & 3;
154             t >>=2;
155             data->accel_z |= t & 3;
156             return 0;
157 }
158
159 /*
160  * Dump the nunchuk data:
161  */
162 static void
163 dump_data(nunchuk_t *data) {
164             int x;
165
166             printf("Raw nunchuk data : ");
167             for ( x=0; x<6; ++x )
168                     printf("[%02X]",data->raw[x]);
169             putchar('\n');
170
171             printf(".stick_x = %04X (%4u)\n",data->stick_x,data->stick_x);
172             printf(".stick_y = %04X (%4u)\n",data->stick_y,data->stick_y);
173             printf(".accel_x = %04X (%4u)\n",data->accel_x,data->accel_x);
174             printf(".accel_y = %04X (%4u)\n",data->accel_y,data->accel_y);
175             printf(".accel_z = %04X (%4u)\n",data->accel_z,data->accel_z);
```

```
176            printf(".z_button= %d\n",data->z_button);
177            printf(".c_button= %d\n\n",data->c_button);
178 }
179
180 /*
181  * Close the I2C driver :
182  */
183 static void
184 i2c_close(void) {
185            close(i2c_fd);
186            i2c_fd = -1;
187 }
188
189 /*
190  * Open a uinput node :
191  */
192 static int
193 uinput_open(void) {
194        int fd;
195        struct uinput_user_dev uinp;
196        int rc;
197
198        fd = open("/dev/uinput",O_WRONLY|O_NONBLOCK);
199        if ( fd < 0 ) {
200                perror("Opening/dev/uinput");
201                exit(1);
202         }
203
204        rc = ioctl(fd,UI_SET_EVBIT,EV_KEY);
205        assert(!rc);
206        rc = ioctl(fd,UI_SET_EVBIT,EV_REL);
207        assert(!rc);
208
209        rc = ioctl(fd,UI_SET_RELBIT,REL_X);
210        assert(!rc);
211        rc = ioctl(fd,UI_SET_RELBIT,REL_Y);
212        assert(!rc);
213
214        rc = ioctl(fd,UI_SET_KEYBIT,KEY_ESC);
215        assert(!rc);
216
217        ioctl(fd,UI_SET_KEYBIT,BTN_MOUSE);
218        ioctl(fd,UI_SET_KEYBIT,BTN_TOUCH);
219        ioctl(fd,UI_SET_KEYBIT,BTN_MOUSE);
220        ioctl(fd,UI_SET_KEYBIT,BTN_LEFT);
221        ioctl(fd,UI_SET_KEYBIT,BTN_MIDDLE);
222        ioctl(fd,UI_SET_KEYBIT,BTN_RIGHT);
223
224        memset(&uinp,0,sizeof uinp);
225        strncpy(uinp.name,"nunchuk",UINPUT_MAX_NAME_SIZE);
226        uinp.id.bustype = BUS_USB;
227        uinp.id.vendor = 0x1;
```

```
228             uinp.id.product = 0x1;
229             uinp.id.version = 1;
230
231             rc = write(fd,&uinp,sizeof(uinp));
232             assert(rc == sizeof(uinp));
233
234             rc = ioctl(fd,UI_DEV_CREATE);
235             assert(!rc);
236             return fd;
237 }
238
239 /*
240  * Post keystroke down and keystroke up events:
241  * (unused here but available for your own experiments)
242  */
243 static void
244 uinput_postkey(int fd,unsigned key) {
245             struct input_event ev;
246             int rc;
247
248             memset(&ev,0,sizeof(ev));
249             ev.type = EV_KEY;
250             ev.code = key;
251             ev.value = 1;                   /*Key down */
252
253             rc = write(fd,&ev,sizeof(ev));
254             assert(rc == sizeof(ev));
255
256             ev.value = 0;                   /*Key up */
257             rc = write(fd,&ev,sizeof(ev));
258             assert(rc == sizeof(ev));
259 }
260
261 /*
262  * Post a synchronization point :
263  */
264 static void
265 uinput_syn(int fd) {
266             struct input_event ev;
267             int rc;
268
269             memset(&ev,0,sizeof(ev));
270             ev.type = EV_SYN;
271             ev.code = SYN_REPORT;
272             ev.value = 0;
273             rc = write(fd,&ev,sizeof(ev));
274             assert(rc == sizeof(ev));
275 }
276
277 /*
```

```
278    * Synthesize a button click :
279    *        up_down          1=up,     0=down
280    *        buttons          1=Left, 2=Middle, 4=Right
281    */
282  static void
283  uinput_click(int fd,int up_down,int buttons) {
284          static unsigned codes[] = {BTN_LEFT, BTN_MIDDLE, BTN_RIGHT};
285          struct input_event ev;
286          int x;
287
288          memset(&ev,0,sizeof(ev));
289
290          /*
291           * Button down or up events:
292           */
293          for ( x=0; x < 3; ++x )  {
294                  ev.type = EV_KEY;
295                  ev.value = up_down;              /*Button Up or down */
296                  if ( buttons & (1 << x) ) {    /*Button 0, 1 or 2 */
297                          ev.code = codes[x];
298                          write(fd,&ev,sizeof(ev));
299                  }
300          }
301  }
302
303  /*
304   * Synthesize relative mouse movement:
305   */
306  static void
307  uinput_movement(int fd,int x,int y) {
308          struct input_event ev;
309          int rc;
310
311          memset(&ev,0,sizeof(ev));
312          ev.type = EV_REL;
313          ev.code = REL_X;
314          ev.value = x;
315
316          rc = write(fd,&ev,sizeof(ev));
317          assert(rc == sizeof(ev));
318
319          ev.code = REL_Y;
320          ev.value = y;
321          rc = write(fd,&ev,sizeof(ev));
322          assert(rc == sizeof(ev));
323  }
324
325  /*
326   * Close uinput device :
```

```
327  */
328  static void
329  uinput_close(int fd) {
330          int rc;
331
332          rc = ioctl(fd,UI_DEV_DESTROY);
333          assert(!rc);
334          close(fd);
335  }
336
337  /*
338   * Signal handler to quit the program:
339   */
340  static void
341  sigint_handler(int signo) {
342          is_signaled = 1;                    /*Signal to exit program */
343  }
344
345  /*
346   * Curve the adjustment :
347   */
348  static int
349  curve(int relxy) {
350          int ax = abs(relxy);                /*abs (re lxy) */
351          int sgn = relxy < 0 ? -1 : 1;       /*sign (relxy) */
352          int mv = 1;                          /*Smallest step */
353
354          if ( ax > 100 )
355                  mv = 10;                     /*Take large steps */
356          else if ( ax > 65 )
357                  mv = 7;
358          else if ( ax > 35 )
359                  mv = 5;
360          else if ( ax > 15 )
361                  mv = 2;                      /*2nd smallest step */
362          return mv * sgn;
363  }
364
365  /*
366   * Main program:
367   */
368  int
369  main(int argc,char **argv) {
370          int fd, need_sync, init = 3;
371          int rel_x=0, rel_y = 0;
372          nunchuk_t data0, data, last;
373
```

```
374         if ( argc > 1 && !strcmp(argv [1]," -d") )
375                 f_debug = 1;                    /*Enable debug messages */
376
377         (void)uinput_postkey;                   /*Suppress compiler warning about unused */
378
379         i2c_init("/dev/i2c-1");                 /*Open I2C controller */
380         nunchuk_init();                         /*Turn off encrypt ion */
381
382         signal(SIGINT,sigint_handler);          /*Trap on SIGINT */
383         fd = uinput_open();                     /*Open/dev/uinput */
384
385         while ( !is_signaled ) {
386                 if ( nunchuk_read(&data) < 0 )
387                         continue;
388
389                 if ( f_debug )
390                         dump_data(&data);       /*Dump nunchuk data */
391
392                 if ( init > 0 && !data0.stick_x && !data0.stick_y ) {
393                         data0 = data;                   /*Save initial values */
394                         last = data;
395                         --init;
396                         continue;
397                 }
398
399                 need_sync = 0;
400                 if ( abs(data.stick_x - data0.stick_x) > 2
401                   || abs(data.stick_y - data0.stick_y) > 2) {
402                         rel_x = curve (data.stick_x - data0.stick_x);
403                         rel_y = curve (data.stick_y - data0.stick_y);
404                         if ( rel_x || rel_y ) {
405                             uinput_movement(fd,rel_x,-rel_y);
406                             need_sync = 1;
407                         }
408                 }
409
410                 if ( last.z_button != data.z_button ) {
411                         uinput_click(fd, data.z_button,1);
412                         need_sync = 1;
413                 }
414
415                 if ( last.c_button != data.c_button ) {
416                         uinput_click(fd,data.c_button,4);
417                         need_sync = 1;
418                 }
419
420                 if ( need_sync )
421                         uinput_syn(fd);
422                 last = data;
423         }
```

```
424
425          putchar('\n');
426          uinput_close(fd);
427          i2c_close();
428          return 0;
429 }
430
431 /*End nunchuk.c */
```

CHAPTER 25

Real-Time Clock

The Dallas Semiconductor DS1307 Real-Time Clock is the perfect project for the Raspberry Pi, Model A. Lacking a network port, the Model A cannot determine the current date and time when it boots up. A 3 V battery attached to the DS1307 will keep its internal clock running for up to 10 years, even when the Pi is powered off. If you have a Model B, don't feel left out. There is no reason that you can't try this project too; a Model B not connected to a network could use the DS1307.

DS1307 Overview

The pinout of the DS1307 chip is provided in Figure 25-1. The chip is available in PDIP-8 form or in SO format (150 mils). Hobbyists who like to build their own will prefer the PDIP-8 form.

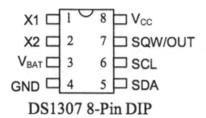

Figure 25-1. DS1307 pinout

A crystal is wired between pins 1 and 2 (X1 and X2). The battery powers the chip through pin 3 and flows to ground (pin 4). This keeps the clock alive while the main power is absent. When there is power, it is supplied through pin 8 (V_{CC}). The I2C communication occurs via pins 5 and 6. Pin 7 provides an optional output clock signal or can operate as an open collector output.

While you could build this circuit yourself, you can find fully assembled PCB modules using the DS1307 on eBay for as little as $2.36 (with free shipping). These are available as Buy It Now offers, so you don't have to waste your time trying to win auctions. Just keep in mind that some are not shipped with a 3 V battery. (Check the product. The Tiny RTC I used came with a 3.6 V battery.) It is claimed that there are mailing restrictions on batteries to certain countries. So you may want to shop for suitable batteries while you wait for the mail.

Tip Buying a fresh battery ahead of time is recommended, as batteries often arrive exhausted.

Figure 25-2 shows a PCB unit that I purchased through eBay. This unit came paired with the AT24C32 EEPROM chip. The auction was labeled "Tiny RTC I2C Modules." You don't have to use this specific PCB, of course. The wiring for each chip is fairly basic and can be prototyped on a breadboard if you can't find one. But if you do choose this PCB, a modification is *required* before you attach it to the Raspberry Pi.

Figure 25-2. *An assembled DS1307 PCB purchased through eBay*

■ **Caution**   *I2C pull-up resistors R_2 and R_3 must be removed before wiring the PCB to the Raspberry Pi.* Also, if you plan to attach the SQW/OUT output of this PCB to a GPIO input, be sure to track down and remove its pull-up resistor as well.

Pins X1 and X2

These pins are for connection to a 32.768 kHz crystal. The datasheet states that the "internal oscillator circuitry is designed for operation with a crystal having a specified load capacitance (C_L) of 12.5 pF."

Pin SQW/OUT

This is an open-drain output from the DS1307 chip that you can choose to ignore if you like. It can be used as follows:

- A GPIO-like output. If you plan on wiring this to a Pi GPIO pin, be sure to remove the pull-up resistor (on PCB) first. The +5 V from the pull-up will damage the Pi.

- A square wave clock output, at one of the following programmable frequencies:

  - 1 Hz

  - 4.096 kHz

  - 8.192 kHz

  - 32.768 kHz

The datasheet lists a current rating for output when low:

Parameter	Symbol	Min	Typ	Max	Units
Logic 0 Output ($IOL = 5\ mA$)	V_{OL}			0.4	Volts

Without more-specific information, we arrive at the conclusion that a given logic pin is capable of sinking a maximum of 5 mA (SDA). While doing so, the maximum voltage appearing at the pin is 0.4 V. This is well under the 0.8 V maximum, for the V_{IL} voltage level of the Raspberry Pi.

The datasheet indicates that the SQW/OUT pin is an open-drain output. As such, you can use a pull-up to +3.3 V or +5 V as your interface requires. It could be used to drive a small LED at 1 Hz, if the current is limited to less than 5 mA (although the datasheet doesn't indicate the current capability of this open-drain transistor). Alternatively, it can be used to drive other external logic with a pull-up resistor.

The datasheet indicates that the SQW/OUT pin can pulled as high as 5.5 V, even when V_{CC} is lower in voltage (such as +3.3 V.) This is safe, provided that these higher voltages never connect to the Pi's GPIO pins.

Power

If you've looked at the datasheet for the DS1307 before, you might be wondering about the power supply voltage. The datasheet lists it as a +5 V part, and by now you are well aware that the Pi's GPIO pins operate at +3 V levels. The DC operating conditions are summarized here:

Parameter	Symbol	Min	Typ	Max	Units
Supply voltage	V_{CC}	4.5	5.0	5.5	Volts
Battery voltage	V_{BAT}	2.0		3.5	Volts

It is tempting to consider that the PCB might operate at +3.3 V, given that the battery in the unit is 3 V. However, that will not work because the DS1307 chip considers a V_{CC} lower than $1.25 \times V_{BAT} = 3.75$ V to be a *power-fail* condition (for a typical operation). When it senses a power fail, it relies on battery operation and will cease to communicate by I2C, among other things. Power-fail conditions are summarized here:

Parameter	Symbol	Min	Typ	Max	Units
Power-fail voltage	V_{PF}	$1.26 \times V_{BAT}$	$1.25 \times V_{BAT}$	$1.284 \times V_{BAT}$	Volts

The note in the datasheet indicates that the preceding figures were measured when $V_{BAT} = 3$ V. So these figures will likely deviate when the battery nears expiry. Given the power-fail conditions, we know that the device must be powered from a +5 V power supply. But the only connections made to the Raspberry Pi are the SDA and SCL I2C lines. So let's take a little closer look at those and see if we can use them.

3-Volt Compatibility

The SCL line is always driven by the master, as far as the DS1307 is concerned. This means that SCL is always seen as an input signal by the RTC clock chip. All we have to check here is whether the Raspberry Pi will meet the input-level requirements. Likewise, the AT24C32 EEPROM's SCL pin is also an input only.

The SDA line is driven by both the master (Pi) and the DS1307 chip (slave). The SDA is driven from the Pi as a 3 V signal, so again we need to make certain that the DS1307 will accept those levels. But what about the DS1307 driving the SDA line? The Pi must not see +5 V signals.

The DS1307 datasheet clearly states that "the SDA pin is open drain, which requires an external pull-up resistor." The Raspberry Pi already supplies the pull-up resistor to +3.3 V. This means that the DS1307's open drain will allow the line to be pulled up to +3.3 V for the high logic level, when the output transistor is in the off state. When the transistor is on, it simply pulls the SDA line down to ground potential. Thus with open-drain operation, we can interoperate with the Raspberry Pi. A check of the AT24C32 EEPROM datasheets leads to the same conclusion.

Logic Levels

How do the I2C logic levels compare between the Raspberry Pi and the DS1307?

Signal	Raspberry Pi	DS1307
V_{IL}	≤ 0.8 volts	≤ 0.8 volts
V_{IH}	≥ 1.3 volts	≥ 2.2 volts

The V_{IL} figure matches perfectly for both sides. As long as the Raspberry Pi provides a high level exceeding 2.2 V, the DS1307 chip should read high levels just fine. Given that the Pi's pull-up resistor is connected to +3.3 V, there is very little reason to doubt problems meeting the DS1307 V_{IH} requirement.

To summarize, we can safely power the DS1307 from +5 V, while communicating between it and the Raspberry Pi at +3 V levels. The Pi already supplies pull-up resistors for the SCL and SDA lines, and these are attached to +3.3 V. If, however, you choose to use other GPIO pins to bit-bang I2C (say), you'll need to provide these pull-up resistors (they must go to only +3.3 V).

Tiny RTC Modifications

In the preceding section, you saw that even though the DS1307 is a +5 V part, the SDA pin is driven by an open-drain transistor. With the Raspberry Pi tying the SDA line to +3.3 V, the highest voltage seen will be exactly that. The open-drain transistor can only pull it down to ground (this also applies to the AT24C32 EEPROM). Both chips have the SCL pins as inputs (only), which are not pulled high by the chips themselves.

If you purchased a PCB like the one I used, however, be suspicious of pull-up resistors! I knew that the parts would support +3.3 V I2C bus operation before the PCB arrived in the mail. However, I was suspicious of added pull-up resistors. So when the PCB arrived, I quickly determined that the PCB did indeed include pull-up resistors connected to the +5 V supply. *The extra +5 V pull-up resistors must be tracked down and removed for use with the Raspberry Pi.*

Checking for Pull-up Resistors

There are two methods to test for pull-up resistors: a DMM resistance check and a voltage reading. I recommend that you apply them both.

Since this modification is important to get correct, the following sections will walk you through the two different procedures in detail.

Performing a DMM Resistance Check

Use these steps for the DMM resistance check:

1. Attach one probe of your DMM (reading kΩ) to the +5 V line of the PCB.

2. Attach the other probe to the SDA line and take the resistance reading.

3. Reverse the leads if you suspect diode action.

On my PCB, I read 3.3 $k\Omega$. Reversing the DMM leads should read the same (proving only resistance). Performing the same test with the SCL input, I also read 3.3 $k\Omega$.

Performing a Voltage Reading

Do not skip this particular test. The result of this test will tell you whether your Raspberry Pi will be at risk.

1. Hook up your PCB to the +5 V supply it requires, but do not attach the SDA/SCL lines to the Pi yet. Just leave them loose for measuring with your DMM.

2. With the DMM negative probe grounded, measure the voltage seen at the PCB's SDA and SCL inputs. If there is no pull-up resistor involved, you should see a low reading of approximately 0.07 V. The reading will be very near ground potential.

On my unmodified PCB, these readings were +5 V because of the 3.3 kΩ pull-up resistors. If this also applies to your PCB unit, a modification is *required*.

Performing a Tiny RTC Modification

If you have the exact same PCB that I used, you can simply remove resistors R_2 and R_3 (but I would double-check with the preceding tests). These resistors are shown in Figure 25-3. Carefully apply a soldering iron to sweep them off the PCB. Make sure no solder is left, shorting the remaining contacts. I highly recommend that you repeat the tests to make sure you have corrected the pull-up problem and test for short circuits.

Figure 25-3. R_2 and R_3 of the Tiny RTC I2C PCB

Working with Other PCB Products

If you have a different PCB product, you may have optional resistors that you can *leave uninstalled*. Even though they may be optional, someone might have done you the favor of soldering them in. So make sure you check for that (use the earlier tests).

The Adafruit RTC module (http://www.adafruit.com/products/264) is reportedly *sometimes* shipped with the 2.2 kΩ resistors installed. For the Raspberry Pi, they must be removed.

Locating the Pull-up Resistors

Even if you don't have a schematic for your PCB product, you will need to locate the pull-up resistors. Since there aren't many components on the PCB to begin with, they tend to be easy to locate:

1. Observe static electricity precautions.

2. Attach one DMM (kΩ) probe to the +5 V input to the PCB.

3. Look for potential resistors on the component side.

4. Locate all resistors that have one lead wired directly to the +5 V supply (resistance will read 0 Ω). These will be the prime suspects.

5. Now attach your DMM (range kΩ) to the SDA input. With the other DMM probe, check the opposite ends of the resistors, looking for readings of 0 Ω. You should find one resistor end (the other end of the resistor will have been previously identified as connected to the +5 V supply).

6. Likewise, test the SCL line in the same manner as step 5.

7. Double-check: take a resistance reading between the SDA input and the +5 V supply. You should measure a resistance of 2 to 10 kΩ, depending on the PCB manufacturer. You should get the same reading directly across the resistor identified.

8. Repeat step 7 for the SCL line.

If you've done this correctly, you will have identified the two resistors that need to be removed. If you plan to interface the SQW/OUT pin to a Pi GPIO, you'll want to remove the pull-up used on that as well.

DS1307 Bus Speed

The DS1307 datasheet lists the maximum SCL clock speed at 100 kHz:

Parameter	Symbol	Min	Typ	Max	Units
SCL clock frequency	f_{SCL}	0		100	kHz

The Raspberry Pi uses 100 kHz for its I2C clock frequency (see Chapter 14 for more information). The specification also states that there is no minimum frequency. If you wanted to reserve the provided I2C bus for use with other peripherals (perhaps at a higher frequency), you could bit-bang interactions with the DS1307 by using another pair of GPIO pins. (Pull-up resistors to +3.3 V will be required; the internal pull-up resistors are not adequate.) That is an exercise left for you.

Now that we have met power, signaling, and clock-rate requirements, "Let's light this candle!"

RTC and RAM Address Map

The DS1307 has 56 bytes of RAM in addition to the real-time clock registers. I/O with this chip includes an implied address register, which ranges in value from 0x00 to 0x3F. The address register will wrap around to zero after reaching the end (don't confuse the register address with the I2C peripheral address).

■ **Note**   The DS1307 RTC uses I2C address 0x68.

The address map of the device is illustrated in Table 25-1. The date and time components are BCD encoded. In the table, *10s* represents the tens digit, while *1s* represents the ones digit.

Table 25-1. *DS1307 Register Map*

Address	Register	Format							
		7	6	5	4	3	2	1	0
0x00	Seconds	CH	10s			1s			
0x01	Minutes	0	10s			1s			
0x02	Hours	0	24hr	10s		1s			
			12hr	PM	10s	1s			
0x03	Weekday	0	0	0	0	0	1s		
0x04	Day	0	0	10s		1s			
0x05	Month	0	0	0	10s	1s			
0x06	Year	10s				1s			
0x07	Control	OUT	0	0	SQWE	0	0	RS1	RS2
0x08	RAM 00	byte							
...	...								
0x3F	RAM 55	byte							

The components of the register map are further described in Table 25-2. Bit CH allows the host to disable the oscillator and thus stop the clock. This also disables the SQW/OUT waveform output (when SQWE=1). Bit 6 of the Hours register determines whether 12- or 24-hour format is used. When in 12-hour format, bit 5 becomes an AM/PM indicator.

Table 25-2. *RTC Register Map Components*

Bit		Meaning			
CH	0	Clock running			
	1	Clock (osc) halt			
24hr	0	24-hour format			
12hr	1	12-hour format	**RS1**	**RS0**	**Meaning**
OUT	0	SQW/OUT = Low	0	0	1 Hz
	1	SQW/OUT = High	0	1	4.096 kHz
SQWE	0	SQW/OUT is OUT	1	0	8.192 kHz
	1	SQW/OUT is SQW	1	1	32.768 kHz

The Control register at address 0x07 determines how the SQW/OUT pin behaves. When SQWE=1, a square wave signal is produced at the SQW/OUT pin. The frequency is selected by bits RS1 and RS0. In this mode, the OUT setting is ignored.

When SQWE=0, the SQW/OUT pin is set according to the bit placed in OUT (bit 7 of the control register). In this mode, the pin behaves as an open-drain GPIO output pin.

Reading Date and Time

When the DS1307 device is being read, a snapshot of the current date and time is made when the I2C start bit is seen. This copy operation allows the clock to continue to run while returning a stable date/time value back to the master. If this were not done, time components could change between reading bytes. The application should therefore always read the full date/time set of registers as one I/O operation. The running clock does not affect reading the control register or the RAM locations.

I2C Communication

The DS1307 registers and RAM can be written randomly, by specifying an initial starting register address, followed by 1 or more bytes to be written. The register address is automatically incremented with each byte written and wraps around to 0. The DS1307 slave device will ACK each byte as it is received, continuing until the master writes a stop bit (P). The first byte sent is always the peripheral's I2C address, which should not be confused with the selected peripheral's register address (that immediately follows). The DS1307 I2C address is always 0x68. The general form of the write message is shown here:

DS1307 <u>Write</u> Register Message:

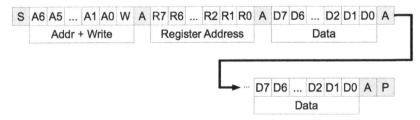

The DS1307 supports multibyte reads. You can read multiple bytes from the DS1307 simply by starting with an I2C start bit (S), and peripheral address sent as a read request. The slave will then serve up bytes one after another for the master. Receiving terminates when the master sends a NAK.

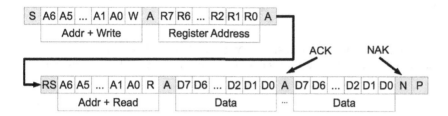

If you want to be certain that the register address is established with a known value, you should always issue a write request first. In the preceding diagram, the write request immediately follows the start bit (S). Only the peripheral's register address byte is written out prior to the repeating start bit (RS), which follows.

After the RS bit, the peripheral address is transmitted once more to re-engage the DS1307, but this time as a read request. From that point on, the master reads bytes sequentially from the DS13017 until a NAK is sent. The final stop bit (P) sent by the master ends the exchange. This peripheral provides us with a good example of a multimessage I/O.

This is demonstrated in lines 27 to 45 of the program ds1307get.c, in the upcoming pages. The entire I/O is driven by the structures iomsgs[0] and iomsgs[1]. Structure iomsgs[0] directs the driver to write to peripheral address 0x68 and writes 1 0x00 data byte out to it. This establishes the RTC's internal register with a value of 0x00. The read request is described in iomsgs[1], which is a read from the same peripheral 0x68, for 8 bytes. (Only 7 bytes are strictly required for the date and time, but we read the additional control byte anyway.)

The data structure is laid out in C terms in the file ds1307.h. An optional exercise for you is to add a command-line option to ds1307set to stop the clock and turn it on again using the ch bit (line 8 of ds1307.h).

Source module i2c_common.c has the usual I2C open/initialization and close routines in it.

Wiring

Like any I2C project for the Pi, you'll wire the SDA and SCL lines as follows:

Pre Rev 2.0		Rev 2.0+		
GPIO	Line	GPIO	Line	P1
0	SDA0	2	SDA1	P1-03
1	SCL0	3	SCL1	P1-05

The DS1307 PCB (or chip) is powered from the +5 V supply. Prior to attaching it to the Raspberry Pi, it is a good idea to power the DS1307 and measure the voltage appearing on its SDA and SCL lines. Both should measure near ground potential. If you see +5 V instead, stop and find out why.

Running the Examples

Since these programs use the I2C Linux drivers, make sure these kernel modules are either already loaded, or load them manually now:

```
$ sudo modprobe i2c-bcm2708
$ sudo modprobe i2c-dev
```

Program `ds1307set.c` (executable `ds1307set`) is used to reset the RTC to a new date/time value of your choice. For example:

```
$ ./ds1307set 20130328215900
2013-03-28 21:59:00 (Thursday)
$
```

This sets the date according to the command-line value, which is in YYYYMMDDHHMMSS format.

Once the RTC date has been established, you can use the executable `ds1307get` to read back the date and time:

```
$ ./ds1307get
2013-03-28 22:00:37 (Thursday)
$
```

In this case, a little time had passed between setting the date and reading it. But we can see that the clock is ticking away.

If you don't like the date/time format used, you can either change the source code or set the environment variable `DS1307_FORMAT`. For example:

```
$ export DS1307_FORMAT="%a %Y-%m-%d %H:%M:%S"
$ ./ds1307get
Thu 2013-03-28 22:03:38
$
```

For a description of the date/time format options available, use this:

```
$ man date
```

The setting of `DS1307_FORMAT` also affects the display format used by `ds1307set`.

The Ultimate Test

The ultimate test is to shut down the Raspberry Pi and turn off its power. Wait a minute or so to make sure that all of the power has been drained out of every available capacitor. Then bring up the Pi again and check the date/time with the program `ds1307get`. Did it lose any time?

The Startup Script

To put the RTC to good practical use, you'll want to apply `ds1307get` at a suitable point in the Linux startup sequence. You'll need to wait until the appropriate I2C driver support is available (or can be arranged). You'll need to develop a short shell script, using the `DS1307_FORMAT` environment variable in order to produce a format suitable for the console date command. To set the system date (as root), you would use this command:

```
# date [-u|--utc|--universal] [MMDDhhmm[[CC]YY][.ss]]
```

The startup script for doing all of this has not been provided here. I don't want to spoil your fun when you can develop this yourself. You learn best by doing. Review Chapter 17 if you need some help.

As a further hint, you'll want to develop a script for the `/etc/rc2.d` directory, with a name starting with *S* and two digits. The digits determine where the script runs in the startup sequence (you'll want to make sure your script runs after the system has come up far enough that I2C drivers are loaded).

Once your startup script is developed, your Raspberry Pi can happily reboot after days, even years, of being powered off, and still be able to come up with the correct date and time.

■ **Note** If you're running the older Model B, where the I2C bus 0 is used instead of 1, change line 21 in ds1307set.c and line 21 in ds1307get.c. See Chapter 14 for more information.

```
 1 /*******************************************************************
 2  * ds1307.h: Common DS1307 types and macro definitions
 3  *******************************************************************/
 4
 5 typedef struct {
 6         /* Register Address 0x00 : Seconds */
 7         unsigned char       secs_1s : 4;    /*Ones digit : seconds */
 8         unsigned char       secs_10s : 3;   /*Tens digit : seconds */
 9         unsigned char       ch : 1;         /*CH bit */
10         /* Register Address 0x01 : Minutes */
11         unsigned char       mins_1s : 4;    /*Ones digit : minutes */
12         unsigned char       mins_10s : 3;   /*Tens digit : minutes */
13         unsigned char       mbz_1 : 1;      /*Zero bit */
14         /* Register Address 0x02 : Hours */
15         unsigned char       hour_1s : 4;    /*Ones digit : hours */
16         unsigned char       hour_10s : 2;   /*Tens digit : hours (24 hr mode) */
17         unsigned char       mode_1224 : 1;  /*Mode bit : 12/24 hour format */
18         /* Register Address 0x03 : Weekday */
19         unsigned char       wkday : 3;      /*Day of week (1-7) */
20         unsigned char       mbz_2 : 5;      /*Zero bits */
21         /* Register Address 0x04 : Day of Month */
22         unsigned char       day_1s : 4;     /*Ones digit : day of month (1-31) */
23         unsigned char       day_10s : 2;    /*Tens digit : day of month */
24         unsigned char       mbz_3 : 2;      /*Zero bits */
25         /* Register Address 0x05 : Month */
26         unsigned char       month_1s : 4;   /*Ones digit : month (1-12) */
27         unsigned char       month_10s : 1;  /*Tens digit : month */
28         unsigned char       mbz_4 : 3;      /*Zero */
29         /* Register Address 0x06 : Year */
30         unsigned char       year_1s : 4;    /*Ones digit : year (00-99) */
31         unsigned char       year_10s : 4;   /*Tens digit : year */
32         /* Register Address 0x07 : Control */
33         unsigned char       rs0 : 1;        /*RS0 */
34         unsigned char       rs1 : 1;        /*RS1 */
35         unsigned char       mbz_5 : 2;      /*Zeros */
36         unsigned char       sqwe : 1;       /*SQWE */
37         unsigned char       mbz_6 : 2;
38         unsigned char       outbit : 1;     /*OUT */
39 } ds1307_rtc_regs;
40
41 /* End ds1307 . h */
```

```
 1  /*******************************************************************
 2   * i2c_common.c : Common I2C Access Functions
 3   *******************************************************************/
 4
 5  static int i2c_fd = -1;                     /*Device node : /dev/ i2c-1 */
 6  static unsigned long i2c_funcs = 0;         /*Support flags */
 7
 8  /*
 9   * Open I2C bus and check cap abilities:
10   */
11  static void
12  i2c_init(const char *node) {
13        int rc;
14
15        i2c_fd = open(node,O_RDWR);     /*Open driver /dev/i2s-1 */
16        if ( i2c_fd < 0 ) {
17            perror("Opening /dev/ i 2 s -1");
18                puts("Check that the i2c-dev & i2c-bcm2708 kernelmodules "
19                    " are loaded . " ) ;
20            abort();
21        }
22
23        /*
24         * Make sure the driver suppor tsplain I2C I /O:
25         */
26        rc = ioctl(i2c_fd,I2C_FUNCS,&i2c_funcs);
27        assert(rc >=0);
28        assert(i2c_funcs & I2C_FUNC_I2C);
29  }
30
31    /*
32     * Close the I2C driver :
33     */
34    static void
35    i2c_close(void) {
36        close(i2c_fd);
37        i2c_fd = -1;
38    }
39
40    /*End i2c_common.c */

 1  /*******************************************************************
 2   * ds1307set.c : Set real-time DS1307 clock on I2C bus
 3   *******************************************************************/
 4
 5  #include <stdio.h>
 6  #include <stdlib.h>
 7  #include <ctype.h>
 8  #include <time.h>
 9  #include <fcntl.h>
10  #include <unistd . h>
11  #include <string . h>
```

```
12 #include <errno . h>
13 #include <assert . h>
14 #include <sys / i octl . h>
15 #include <l inux / i2c-dev . h>
16
17 #include "i2c_common.c"        /*I2C routines */
18 #include "ds1307.h"            /*DS1307 types */
19
20  /*Change to i2c-0 if using early Raspberry Pi */
21  static const char *node = "/dev/i2c-1";
22
23 /*
24  * Write [ S ] 0xB0 <regaddr> <rtcbuf[0]> . . . <rtcbuf[n-1]> [P]
25  */
26  static int
27  i2c_wr_rtc(ds1307_rtc_regs *rtc) {
28          struct i2c_rdwr_ioctl_data msgset;
29          struct i2c_msg iomsgs[1];
30          char buf[sizeof *rtc+1] ;                 /*Work buffer */
31
32          buf[0] = 0x00 ;                           /*Register 0x00 */
33          memcpy(buf+1,rtc,sizeof *rtc);            /*Copy RTC info */
34
35          iomsgs[0].addr = 0x68;                    /*DS1307 Address */
36          iomsgs[0].flags = 0;                      /*Write */
37          iomsgs[0].buf = buf;                      /*Register + data */
38          iomsgs[0].len = sizeof *rtc + 1;          /*Total msg len */
39
40          msgset.msgs = &iomsgs[0];
41          msgset.nmsgs = 1;
42
43          return ioctl(i2c_fd,I2C_RDWR,&msgset);
44 }
45
46 /*****************************************************************
47  * Set the DS1307 real-time clock on the I2C bus :
48  *
49  * ./ds1307set YYYYMMDDHHMM[ss]
50  *****************************************************************/
51 int
52 main(int argc,char **argv) {
53          ds1307_rtc_regs rtc ;          /*8 DS1307 Register Values */
54          char buf[32];                  /*Extraction buffe r */
55          struct tm t0, t1;              /*Unix date / time values */
56          int v, cx, slen;
57          char *date_format = getenv("DS1307_FORMAT");
58          char dtbuf[256];               /*Formatted date/time */
59          int rc;                        /*Return code */
60
```

```
61        /*
62         * If no environment variable named DS1307_FORMAT, then
63         * set a default date/time format.
64         */
65        if ( !date_format )
66              date_format = "%Y-%m-%d %H:%M:%S (%A) " ;
67
68        /*
69         * Check command line usage :
70         */
71        if ( argc != 2 || (slen = strlen(argv[1])) < 12 || slen > 14 ) {
72   usage: fprintf(stderr,
73                    "Usage : %s YYYYMMDDhhmm[ss]\n",
74                  argv[0]);
75              exit(1);
76        }
77
78        /*
79         * Make sure every character is a digit in argument 1 .
80         */
81        for ( cx=0; cx<slen; ++cx )
82              if ( !isdigit(argv[1][cx]) )
83              goto usage;            /*Not a numeric digit */
84
85        /*
86         * Initialize I2C and clear rtc and t1 structures :
87         */
88        i2c_init(node) ;                /*Initialize for I2C */
89        memset(&rtc,0,sizeof rtc);
90        memset(&t1,0,sizeof t1);
91
92        /*
93         * Extract YYYYMMDDhhmm[ss] from argument 1:
94         */
95        strncpy(buf,argv[1],4)[4] = 0;        /*buf[] = "YYYY" */
96        if ( sscanf(buf,"%d",&v)  != 1 || v < 2000 || v > 2099 )
97            goto usage;
98        t1.tm_year = v - 1900;
99
100       strncpy(buf,argv[1]+4,2)[2] = 0;      /*buf[] = "MM" */
101       if ( sscanf(buf,"%d",&v) != 1 || v <= 0 || v > 12 )
102       goto usage;
103       t1.tm_mon = v-1;                      /*0 - 11 */
104
105       strncpy(buf,argv[1]+6,2)[2] = 0;      /*buf[] = "DD" */
106       if ( sscanf(buf,"%d",&v) != 1 || v <= 0 || v > 31 )
107       goto usage ;
108       t1.tm_mday = v;                       /*1 - 31 */
109
```

```
110            strncpy(buf,argv[1]+8,2)[2] = 0;      /*buf[] = "hh" */
111            if ( sscanf(buf,"%d",&v) != 1 || v < 0 || v > 23 )
112            goto usage;
113            t1.tm_hour = v;
114
115            strncpy(buf,argv[1]+10,2)[2] = 0;     /*buf[] = "mm" */
116            if ( sscanf(buf,"%d",&v) != 1 || v < 0 || v > 59 )
117            goto usage;
118            t1.tm_min = v;
119
120            if ( slen > 12 ) {
121                /* Optional ss was provided : */
122                strncpy(buf,argv[1]+12,2)[2] = 0;       /*buf[] = "ss" */
123                if ( sscanf(buf,"%d",&v) != 1 || v < 0 || v > 59 )
124                    goto usage;
125            t1.tm_sec = v;
126        }
127
128        /*
129         * Check the validity of the date :
130         */
131        t1.tm_isdst = -1;                   /*Determine if daylight savings */
132        t0 = t1;                            /*Save initial values */
133        if ( mktime(&t1) == 1L ) {          /*t1 is modified */
134 bad_date : printf("Argument '%s ' is not avalid calendar date.\n",argv[1]) ;
135                exit(2);
136        }
137
138        /*
139         * If struct t1 was adjusted , then the original date/time
140         * values were invalid :
141         */
142        if ( t0.tm_year != t1.tm_year || t0.tm_mon != t1.tm_mon
143         || t0.tm_mday != t1.tm_mday || t0.tm_hour != t1.tm_hour
144         || t0.tm_min != t1.tm_min || t0.tm_sec != t1.tm_sec )
145            goto bad_date;
146
147        /*
148         * Populate DS1307 registers :
149         */
150        rtc.secs_10s = t1.tm_sec / 10;
151        rtc.secs_1s = t1.tm_sec % 10;
152        rtc.mins_10s = t1.tm_min / 10;
153        rtc.mins_1s = t1.tm_min % 10;
154        rtc.hour_10s = t1.tm_hour / 10;
155        rtc.hour_1s = t1.tm_hour % 10;
156        rtc.month_10s = (t1.tm_mon + 1) / 10;
157        rtc.month_1s = (t1.tm_mon + 1) % 10;
158        rtc.day_10s = t1.tm_mday / 10;
159        rtc.day_1s = t1.tm_mday % 10;
```

```
160              rtc.year_10s = (t1.tm_year + 1900 - 2000) / 10;
161              rtc.year_1s = (t1.tm_year + 1900 - 2000) % 10;
162
163              rtc.wkday = t1.tm_wday + 1;          /*Weekday 1-7 */
164              rtc.mode_1224 = 0;                   /*Use 24 hour format */
165
166 #if 0        /*Change to a 1 for debugging */
167     printf("%d%d-%d%d-%d%d %d%d:%d%d:%d%d (wkday %d )\n",
168              rtc.year_10s,rtc.year_1s,
169              rtc.month_10s,rtc.month_1s,
170              rtc.day_10s,rtc.day_1s,
171              rtc.hour_10s,rtc.hour_1s,
172              rtc.mins_10s,rtc.mins_1s,
173              rtc.secs_10s,rtc.secs_1s,
174              rtc.wkday);
175 #end if
176     rc = i2c_wr_rtc(&rtc );
177
178     /*
179      * Display RTC values submitted :
180      */
181         strftime(dtbuf,sizeof dtbuf,date_format,&t1);
182         puts(dtbuf);
183
184         if ( rc < 0 )
185             perror("Writing to DS1307 RTC");
186         else if ( rc != 1 )
187             printf(" Incomplete write : %d msgs of 2written \n",rc);
188
189         i2c_close();
190         return rc ==1? 0 : 4;
191 }
192
193 /* End ds1307set.c */

  1 /*****************************************************************
  2  * ds1307get.c : Read real-time DS1307 clock on I2C bus
  3  *****************************************************************/
  4
  5 #include <stdio.h>
  6 #include <stdlib.h>
  7 #include <ctype.h>
  8 #include <time h>
  9 #include <fcntl.h>
 10 #include <unistd.h>
 11 #include <string.h>
 12 #include <errno.h>
 13 #include <assert.h>
 14 #include <sys/ioctl.h>
 15 #include <linux/i2c-dev.h>
 16
```

```
17 #include "i2c_common.c"              /*I2C routines */
18 #include "ds1307.h"                  /*DS1307 types */
19
20 /* Change to i2c-0 if using early Raspberry Pi */
21 static const char *node = "/dev/i2c-1";
22
23 /*
24  * Read : [ S ] 0xB1 <regaddr> <rtcbuf[0]> . . . <rtcbuf[n-1]> [P]
25  */
26 static int
27 i2c_rd_rtc(ds1307_rtc_regs *rtc) {
28         struct i2c_rdwr_ioctl_data msgset;
29         struct i2c_msg iomsgs[2];
30         char zero = 0x00;                    /*Register 0x00 */
31
32         iomsgs[0].addr = 0x68;               /*DS1307 */
33         iomsgs[0].flags = 0;                 /*Write */
34         iomsgs[0].buf = &zero;               /*Register 0x00 */
35         iomsgs[0].len = 1;
36
37         iomsgs[1].addr = 0x68;               /*DS1307 */
38         iomsgs[1].flags = I2C_M_RD;          /*Read */
39         iomsgs[1].buf = (char *)rtc;
40         iomsgs[1].len = size of *rtc;
41
42         msgset.msgs=iomsgs;
43         msgset.nmsgs=2;
44
45         return ioctl(i2c_fd,I2C_RDWR,&msgset);
46 }
47
48 /*
49  * Main program :
50  */
51 int
52 main(int argc,char **argv) {
53         ds1307_rtc_regs rtc;         /* 8 DS1307 Register Values */
54         struct tm t0, t1;            /*Unix date / time values */
55         char *date_format = getenv("DS1307_FORMAT");
56         char dtbuf[256];             /*Formatted date/time */
57         int rc;                      /*Return code */
58
59         /*
60          * If no environment variable named DS1307_FORMAT, then
61          * set a default date/time format.
62          */
63         if ( !date_format )
64             date_format = "%Y-%m-%d%H:%M:%S(%A)";
65
66         /*
67          * Initialize I2C and clear rtc and t1 structures:
68          */
```

```
69          i2c_init(node);                 /*Initialize for I2C */
70          memset(&rtc,0,sizeof rtc);
71          memset(&t1,0,sizeof t1);
72
73          rc = i2c_rd_rtc(&rtc);
74          if ( rc < 0 ) {
75                  perror("Reading DS1307 RTC clock.");
76                  exit(1);
77          } else if ( rc != 2 ) {
78                  fprintf(stderr,"Read error: got %d of 2 msgs.\n",rc);
79                  exit(1);
80          } else
81                  rc = 0;
82
83          /*
84           * Check the date returned by the RTC:
85           */
86          memset(&t1,0,sizeof t1);
87          t1.tm_year = (rtc.year_10s * 10 + rtc.year_1s) + 2000 - 1900;
88          t1.tm_mon = rtc.month_10s * 10 + rtc.month_1s - 1;
89          t1.tm_mday = rtc.day_10s * 10 + rtc.day_1s;
90          t1.tm_hour = rtc.hour_10s * 10 + rtc.hour_1s;
91          t1.tm_min = rtc.mins_10s * 10 + rtc.mins_1s;
92          t1.tm_sec = rtc.secs_10s * 10 + rtc.secs_1s;
93          t1.tm_isdst = -1;               /*Determine if daylight savings */
94
95          t0 = t1;
96          if ( mktime(&t1) == 1L         /*t1 i s modi f ied */
97            || t1.tm_year != t0.tm_year || t1.tm_mon != t0.tm_mon
98            || t1.tm_mday != t0.tm_mday || t1.tm_hour != t0.tm_hour
99            || t1.tm_min != t0.tm_min || t1.tm_sec != t0.tm_sec ) {
100         strftime(dtbuf,sizeof dtbuf,date_format,&t0);
101         fprintf(stderr,"Read RTC date is not valid: %s\n",dtbuf);
102         exit(2);
103       }
104
105     if ( t1.tm_wday != rtc.wkday-1 ) {
106         fprintf(stderr,
107            "Warning:RTC weekday is incorrect %d but should be %d\n",
108            rtc.wkday,t1.tm_wday);
109     }
110
111 #if 0              /*Change to a 1 for debugging */
112     printf("%d%d-%d%d-%d%d%d%d:%d%d:%d%d(wkday %d)\n",
113         rtc.year_10s,rtc.year_1s ,
114         rtc.month_10s,rtc.month_1s ,
115         rtc.day_10s, rtc.day_1s ,
116         rtc.hour_10s,rtc.hour_1s ,
117         rtc.mins_10s,rtc.mins_1s ,
```

```
118            rtc.secs_10s,rtc.secs_1s ,
119            rtc.wkday);
120 #end if
121    strftime (dtbuf,size of dtbuf,date_format,&t1);
122    puts(dtbuf);
123
124    i2c_close();
125    return rc == 8 ? 0 : 4;
126 }
127
128 /* End ds1397get.c */
```

CHAPTER 26

VS1838B IR Receiver

The VS1838B is a PIN photodiode high-gain amplifier IC in an epoxy package with an outer shield. It consists of three pins and is about the size of a signal transistor. This inexpensive part can be purchased for about $2 on eBay to give your Raspberry Pi the ability to read many IR remote-control signals.

Operating Parameters

Figure 26-1 is a close-up photo of the VS1838B.

Figure 26-1. *The VS1838B PIN photodiode*

The datasheet provided for this part is mostly in Chinese. The most important parameter to decipher is the supply voltage range, which is listed in English here:

Parameter	Symbol	Min	Typ	Max	Units
Supply voltage	V_{CC}	2.7		5.5	Volts

Given that 3.3 V is within the operating range for the device, we can use it for the Raspberry Pi. We simply power it from the +3.3 V supply pin P1. The device requires only 1 mA of current, as seen in the other datasheet parameters here:

Parameter	Symbol	Test Conditions	Min	Typ	Max	Units
Supply current	I_{CC}	$V_{CC} = 5.0$ volts	0.6	0.8	1.0	mA
Receiving distance	L		11	13		m
Acceptance angle	$\theta\frac{1}{2}$			±35		Deg
Carrier frequency	f_0			37.9		kHz
Bandwidth	f_{BW}			8		kHz
Voltage out low	V_{OL}	$R_{pullup} = 2.4\ k\Omega$			0.25	Volts
Voltage out high	V_{OH}		$V_{CC}-0.3$		V_{CC}	Volts
Operating temp.	T_{opr}		−30		+85	°C

Pinout

With the lens of the part facing toward you, the pins are as follows, from left to right:

VS1838B		
	Front View	
Out	*Gnd*	V_{CC}

VS1838B Circuit

Figure 26-2 illustrates the VS1838B wired to the Raspberry Pi. Any GPIO pin can be used, but this text uses GPIO 17 for ease of reference. If you choose to use a different GPIO, changes to the source code will be necessary.

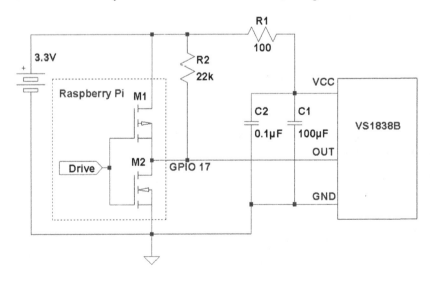

Figure 26-2. *VS1838B wired to the Raspberry Pi using GPIO 17*

The circuit may appear somewhat daunting to students, compared to some of the other projects in this book. The datasheet lists several components as being required: 100 Ω resistor R_1, and capacitors C_1 and C_2. Finally, there is the pull-up resistor R_2, shown here as 22 $k\Omega$.

■ **Note** The datasheet simply shows the pull-up as being > 20 kΩ.

If you're breadboarding this in a hurry, you can probably leave out R_1, C_1, and C_2. I wired mine with R_1 but forgot about the capacitors. If you leave out the capacitors, R_1 is not required either. R_1 is not a current-limiting resistor here; R_1 and the capacitors are simply a low-pass filter designed to provide a quieter power supply to the part (which should normally be used). But if you're soldering this up, do include all of the recommended components for best results. Don't leave out the pull-up resistor. R_2 is required.

The IR Receiver

Most IR remote controls today use the 38 kHz carrier frequency on an infrared beam of light. Even if you know that your brand of remote uses a slightly different carrier frequency, the VS1838B may still work. The important point to realize about this part is that it tries to detect the remote control while ignoring other light sources in the room. To discriminate between fluorescent lighting and the remote control, it looks for this 38 kHz carrier signal. When it sees a steady stream of pulses, it can ignore the interference.

The 22 $k\Omega$ pull-up resistor in the schematic diagram is necessary to pull the Out line up to V_{CC} level, when no 38 kHz beam is seen. (The datasheet block diagram shows the output as a CMOS totem-pole output, but the pull-up suggests open-drain configuration instead.) When the device sees a carrier for a minimum burst of 300 μs, it pulls the Out line low. This line remains driven low as long as the carrier signal is detected. As soon as the carrier is removed for 300 μs or more, the line is pulled high again by the resistor.

Out	Description
High	No 38 kHz carrier seen
Low	38 kHz carrier is detected

Wired as shown, the Raspberry Pi will be able to see the effect of the carrier being turned on and off, many times per second, as it receives remote-control bursts of IR light.

Software

This is where I apologize in advance. No matter which brand of TV or remote control is supported by the software in this chapter, most people will own something *different*. However, if you own a relatively recently produced Samsung TV, the software *might* just work for you out of the box. The software presented in this chapter was developed for the remote control of a Samsung plasma HDTV (Model series 50A400).

If the software doesn't work for you as is, then consider yourself blessed. When you dig into the program and make it work for your remote, you'll come away from the experience knowing much more than when you started.

Signal Components

Here's where it gets fun. While most manufacturers have agreed on the 38 kHz carrier frequency, they haven't agreed on how the signaling works. Most protocols work on the principle of turning bursts of IR on and off, but how that encodes a "key" differs widely.

An informative website (www.techdesign.be/projects/011/011_waves.htm) documents a few of the common IR waveforms.[54] The one we're interested in is the Samsung entry, listed as protocol number 8.

Table 26-1 summarizes the technical aspects of the waveforms shown at the website. All times shown are in milliseconds.

Table 26-1. *IR Remote Waveform Times*

Protocol	Brand	Component	High	Low	High
				ms	
2	NEC	Start bit	9	4.5	-
		0 bit	0.56	0.56	-
		1 bit	0.56	1.69	-
		Stop bit	0.56	0.56	-
4	SIRCS	Start bit	2.4	0.6	-
		0 bit	0.6	0.6	-
		1 bit	1.2	0.6	-
5	RC5	Start bit	-	0.889	0.889
		0 bit	-	0.889	0.889
		1 bit	0.889	0.889	-
7	Japan	Start bit	3.38	1.69	-
		0 bit	0.42	0.42	-
		1 bit	0.42	1.69	-
8	Samsung	Start bit	4.5	4.5	-
		0 bit	0.56	0.56	-
		1 bit	0.56	1.69	-
		Stop bit	0.56	0.56	-

The High/Low values shown in the table agree with the website. For our circuit, the signals are *inverted* because of the way that the VS1838B brings the line *low* when a carrier is detected. The logic sense of these signals are documented in Table 26-2 for clarity.

Table 26-2. *Carrier Signals as Seen by the Raspberry Pi GPIO*

Level	GPIO	Meaning
High (1)	Low	Carrier present
Low (0)	High	Carrier absent

The waveform diagrams at the website are pleasant to look at, but the essential ingredients boil down to the timings of three or four waveform components, which are listed in Table 26-3.

Table 26-3. *Waveform Components*

Component	Description
Start bit	Marks the start of a key-code
0 bit	0 bit for the code
1 bit	1 bit for the code
Stop bit	Stop bit (end of code)

Table 26-1 shows that only the NEC and the Samsung signals use a stop bit. In both cases, each stop bit is simply an extra 0 bit added onto the end of the stream.

All protocols use a *special* "start bit" to identify where the code transmission begins. RC5 just uses a 0-bit waveform (in other words, the start and the 0 bits are identical).

A signal component always begins with a burst (seen as a GPIO low) followed by a time of no carrier (GPIO high). The only thing that varies among manufacturers is the timings of these two signal components.

The RC5 protocol is unusual by allowing a start- or 0-bit transmission to begin with no carrier (GPIO high). Only the 1 bit begins with an IR burst followed by no carrier. So if the remote is going from idle to transmission, the first half of the bit cell for the start bit is *unseen*. But after the first transition, to mark the start, the receiver need only expect a transition every 0.889 ms for 0 bits, and double that if the bits are changing state.

Looking at Table 26-1 again, notice that the shortest signal time occurs for type 7 (Japan) with a time of 0.42 ms. The smallest detectable unit of time for the GPIO signal changes approaches 150 μs (0.15 ms) for the Raspberry Pi. But if the Linux kernel is busy with other events, 420 μs events may not be reliably detected. Expect some trouble with that particular protocol. Otherwise, the smallest unit of time shown is 560 μs for the other protocols.

Code Organization

If you experiment, you may find occurrences of other pulses within the IR data stream. For example, the Samsung remote occasionally included a 46.5 ms pulse. Others may do something similar. I believe that these are key repeat signals, which happen when you hold down a remote key.

In the Samsung bit stream, the bits gather into a 32-bit code. Your remote *might* use a different code length, but 32 bits is a convenient storage unit for a key code. For that reason, I expect that you'll find that in other brands as well.

Command-Line Options

The irdecode utility program has been designed to take some options. These are listed when –h is used:

```
$ ./irdecode -h
Usage : ./irdecode [-d] [-g] [-n] [-p gpio]
where :
 -d         dumps event s
 -g         gnuplot waveforms
 -n         don't invert GPIO input
 -p gpio    GPIO pin to use (17)
$
```

Without any options provided, the utility tries to decode Samsung remote-control codes (some of the output is suppressed in this mode). The -p option can be provided to cause the command to use a different GPIO port. In Samsung decode mode, stderr receives reports of the key codes. Redirect unit 2 to /dev/null if you don't want them.

In this example, we capture the stderr output to file codes.out. The GPIO port is specified as 17 here, but this is the command's default:

```
$ ./irdecode -p17 2>codes.out
Monitoring GPIO 17 f or changes :

<POWER>
123
<RETURN>
73
<EXIT>

Exit .
$
```

While the program runs, it reports recognized key presses to stdout. Special keys are shown in angle brackets, while the numeric digits just print as digits. In this mode, the program exits if it sees an <EXIT> key press on the remote. You can also enter ^C in the terminal session to exit the program.

When the program exits, the codes.out file is displayed with the cat command:

```
$ cat codes.out
CODE E0E040BF
CODE E0E020DF
CODE E0E0A05F
CODE E0E0609F
CODE E0E0609F
CODE E0E01AE5
CODE E0E030CF
CODE E0E0609F
CODE E0E0B44B
$
```

Dump Mode

When the -d option is used, the program runs in *dump mode*. In this mode, the program will report level changes on your selected GPIO pin:

```
$ ./irdecode -d
Monitoring GPIO 17 f or changes :
    30524.573    1
     4.628       0
     4.322       1
     0.696       0
     1.555       1
```

■ **Tip** By default, irdecode dumps out a 1 level when the carrier is present. To invert this to match the GPIO level, use the -n option.

The left column of numbers is the time in milliseconds, prior to the level change. The number in the right column shows you the level of the GPIO input after the change. In this example, the first event took a long time before it changed (I was picking up the remote). The next change to low (0) occurs only 4.628 ms later, and so on.

This is a good format for getting a handle on the average pulse widths. From this output, you should see pulse widths centered about certain ranges of numbers.

Each line reported is a signal change event. Either the GPIO pin changes to high, or it changes to a low level. When reporting changes, therefore, you should never see two or more lines in a row change to a 0, for example. The reported level should always alternate between 0 and 1.

If, however, you do see repeated highs or lows, *this indicates that the program has missed events.* Events spaced closer together than about 150 µs are not likely to be seen on the Raspberry Pi. Noise and spikes can also cause these kinds of problems.

Gnuplot Mode

Dump mode is great for analyzing pulse widths but it isn't very helpful if you want to visualize the waveform. To produce an output suitable for gnuplot, add the -g option:

```
$ ./irdecode -dg
Monitoring GPIO 17 f or changes :
   31337.931      1
   31342.528      1
   31342.528      0              4.597
   31342.528      0
   31346.860      0
   31346.860      1              4.332
   31346.860      1
   31347.594      1
   31347.594      0              0.734
   31347.594      0
   31349.110      0
```

When the -g option is used, three lines are produced for each event:

- Time of prior event, with previous state

- Time of current event, with previous state

- Time of current event, with current state, with time lapse in column 3

If gnuplot is absent, you can install it on your Raspberry Pi as follows:

```
$ sudo apt-get install gnuplot-x11
```

These data plots can then be read into gnuplot to display a waveform. Create a file named gnuplot.cmd with these commands in it:

```
set title "IR Remote Waveform"
set xlabel "Time (ms)"
set ylabel "Level"
set autoscale
set yrange [-.1:1.2]
plot "gnuplot.dat" using 1:2 with lines
```

Collect your output into a file named gnuplot.dat (or change the file gnuplot.cmd to use a different file name). Then run gnuplot on the data:

```
$ gnuplot -p gnuplot.cmd
```

Figure 26-3 shows an example plot display. Note that you'll normally have to edit out all but the most interesting lines of data. Otherwise, your plot will be a rather crowded display of vertical lines.

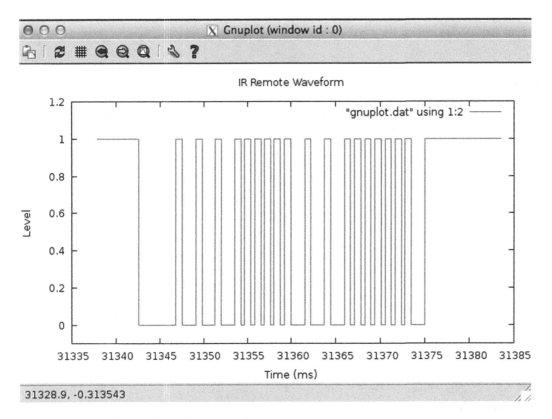

Figure 26-3. *gnuplot waveform of an IR signal*

If running gnuplot doesn't pop up a window, you may need to set the DISPLAY variable, or run xhost on the X-Window server machine. If you are using the Raspberry Pi desktop, this should not be necessary.

The following xhost command enables anyone to create a window on your X-Window server:

```
# xhost +
```

The source code for the irdecode program is listed here:

```
1    /*****************************************************************
2     * irdecode.c : Read IR remote control on GPIO 17 (GEN0)
3     *****************************************************************/
4    #include <stdio.h>
5    #include <stdlib.h>
6    #include <fcntl.h>
7    #include <unistd.h>
8    #include <string.h>
```

```
9    #include <errno.h>
10   #include <signal.h>
11   #include <setjmp.h>
12   #include <assert.h>
13   #include <sys/time.h>
14   #include <sys/poll.h>
15   #include <getopt.h>
16
17   static int gpio_inpin = 17;          /* GPIO input pin */
18   static int is_signaled = 0;          /* Exit program if signaled */
19   static int gpio_fd = -1;             /* Open file descriptor */
20
21   static jmp_buf jmp_exit;
22
23   typedef enum {
24           gp_export=0,         /* /sys/class/gpio/export */
25           gp_unexport,         /* /sys/class/gpio/unexport */
26           gp_direction,        /* /sys/class/gpio%d/direction */
27           gp_edge,             /* /sys/class/gpio%d/edge */
28           gp_value             /* /sys/class/gpio%d/value */
29   } gpio_path_t ;
30
31   /*
32    *Samsung Remote Codes :
33    */
34   #define IR_POWER     0xE0E040BF
35   #define IR_0         0xE0E08877
36   #define IR_1         0xE0E020DF
37   #define IR_2         0xE0E0A05F
38   #define IR_3         0xE0E0609F
39   #define IR_4         0xE0E010EF
40   #define IR_5         0xE0E0906F
41   #define IR_6         0xE0E050AF
42   #define IR_7         0xE0E030CF
43   #define IR_8         0xE0E0B04F
44   #define IR_9         0xE0E0708F
45   #define IR_EXIT      0xE0E0B44B
46   #define IR_RETURN    0xE0E01AE5
47   #define IR_MUTE      0xE0E0F00F
48
49   static struct {
50           unsigned long        ir_code;        /* IR Code */
51           const char           *text;          /* Display text */
52   } ir_codes[] = {
53           { IR_POWER,   "\n<POWER>\n" } ,
54           { IR_0,            "0"},
55           { IR_1,            "1" } ,
56           { IR_2,            "2" } ,
57           { IR_3,            "3" } ,
58           { IR_4,            "4" } ,
59           { IR_5,            "5" } ,
```

```
60          { IR_6,              "6" } ,
61          { IR_7,              "7" } ,
62          { IR_8,              "8" } ,
63          { IR_9,              "9" } ,
64          { IR_EXIT,    "\n<EXIT>\n" } ,
65          { IR_RETURN, "\n<RETURN>\n" } ,
66          { IR_MUTE,    "\n<MUTE>\n" } ,
67          { 0,                  0 }      /* End marker */
68  } ;
69
70  /*
71   * Compute the time difference in milliseconds :
72   */
73  static double
74  msdiff(struct timeval *t1,struct timeval *t0) {
75          unsigned long ut;
76          double ms;
77
78          ms = ( t1->tv_sec - t0->tv_sec ) * 1000.0;
79          if ( t1->tv_usec > t0->tv_usec )
80                  ms += ( t1->tv_usec - t0->tv_usec ) / 1000.0;
81          else {
82                  ut = t1->tv_usec + 1000000UL;
83                  ut -= t0->tv_usec;
84                  ms += ut / 1000.0;
85          }
86          return ms;
87  }
88
89  /*
90   * Create a pathname fo r type in buf.
91   */
92  static const char *
93  gpio_setpath(int pin,gpio_path_t type,char *buf,unsigned bufsiz) {
94          static const char *paths[] = {
95                  "export", "unexport", "gpio%d/direction",
96                  "gpio%d/edge", "gpio%d/value"};
97          int slen;
98
99          strncpy(buf,"/sys/class/gpio/",bufsiz);
100         bufsiz -= (slen = strlen(buf));
101         snprintf(buf+slen,bufsiz,paths[type],pin);
102         return buf;
103 }
104
105 /*
106  * Open /sys/class/gpio%d/value for edge detection :
107  */
```

```
108 static int
109 gpio_open_edge(int pin,const char *edge) {
110         char buf[128];
111         FILE *f;
112         int fd;
113
114         /* Export pin: /sys/class/gpio/export */
115         gpio_setpath(pin gp_export,buf,sizeof buf);
116         f = fopen(buf,"w");
117         assert(f);
118         fprintf(f,"%d\n",pin);
119         fclose(f);
120
121         /* Direction: /sys/class/gpio%d/direction */
122         gpio_setpath(pin,gp_direction,buf,sizeof buf);
123         f = fopen(buf,"w");
124         assert(f);
125         fprintf(f,"in\n");
126         fclose(f);
127
128         /* Edge: /sys/class/gpio%d/edge */
129         gpio_setpath(pin,gp_edge,buf,sizeof buf);
130         f = fopen(buf,"w");
131         assert(f);
132         fprintf(f,"%s\n",edge);
133         fclose(f);
134
135         /* Value: /sys/class/gpio%d/value */
136         gpio_setpath(pin,gp_value,buf,sizeof buf);
137         fd = open(buf,O_RDWR);
138         return fd;
139 }
140
141 /*
142  * Close ( unexport ) GPIO pin :
143  */
144 static void
145 gpio_close(int pin) {
146         char buf[128];
147         FILE *f;
148
149         /* Unexport: /sys/class/gpio/unexport */
150         gpio_setpath(pin,gp_unexport,buf,sizeof buf);
151         f = fopen(buf,"w");
152         assert(f);
153         fprintf(f,"%d\n",pin);
154         fclose(f);
155 }
156
```

```
157  /*
158   * This routine will block until the open GPIO pin has changed
159   * value .
160   */
161  static int
162  gpio_poll(int fd,double *ms) {
163          static char needs_init = 1;
164          static struct timeval t0;
165          static struct timeval t1;
166          struct pollfd polls;
167          char buf[32];
168          int rc, n;
169
170          if ( needs_init ) {
171                  rc = gettimeofday(&t0,0);
172                  assert(!rc);
173                  needs_init = 0;
174          }
175
176          polls.fd = fd;                   /* /sys/class/gpio17/value */
177          polls.events = POLLPRI;          /* Exceptions */
178
179          do    {
180                  rc = poll(&polls,1,-1);      /* Block */
181                  if ( is_signaled )
182                          longjmp(jmp_exit,1);
183          } while ( rc < 0 && errno == EINTR );
184
185          assert(rc > 0);
186
187          rc = gettimeofday(&t1,0);
188          assert(!rc);
189
190          *ms = msdiff(&t1,&t0);
191
192          lseek(fd,0,SEEK_SET);
193          n = read(fd,buf,sizeof buf);     /* Read value */
194          assert(n>0);
195          buf[n] = 0;
196
197          rc = sscanf(buf,"%d",&n) ;
198          assert(rc==1);
199
200          t0 = t1;                         /* Save for next call */
201          return n;                        /* Return value */
202  }
203
204  /*
205   * Signal handler to quit the program :
206   */
```

```
207 static void
208 sigint_handler(int signo) {
209         is_signaled = 1;                    /* Signal to exit program */
210 }
211
212 /*
213  * Wait until the line changes :
214  */
215 static inline int
216 wait_change(double *ms) {
217         /* Invert the logic of the input pin */
218         return gpio_poll(gpio_fd,ms) ? 0 : 1;
219 }
220
221 /*
222  * Wait until line changes to "level" :
223  */
224 static int
225 wait_level(int level) {
226         int v;
227         double ms;
228
229         while ( (v = wait_change(&ms)) != level )
230                 ;
231         return v;
232 }
233
234 /*
235  * Get a 32 bit code from remote control :
236  */
237 static unsigned long
238 getword(void) {
239         static struct timeval t0 = { 0, 0 };
240         static unsigned long last = 0;
241         struct timeval t1;
242         double ms;
243         int v, b, count;
244         unsigned long word = 0;
245
246 Start: word = 0;
247         count = 0;
248
249         /*
250          * Wait for a space of 46 ms :
251          */
252         do      {
253                 v = wait_change(&ms);
254         } while ( ms < 46.5 );
255
256         /*
257          * Wait for start : 4.5ms high, then 4.5ms low :
258          */
```

```
259            for ( v=1;; ) {
260                 if ( v )
261                      v = wait_level(0);
262                 v = wait_level(1);
263                 v = wait_change(&ms);        /* High to Low */
264                 if ( !v && ms >=4.0 && ms <= 5.0 ) {
265                      v = wait_change(&ms);
266                      if ( v && ms >=4.0 && ms <= 5.0 )
267                              break ;
268                 }
269            }
270
271            /*
272             * Get 32 bi t code :
273             */
274            do    {
275                 /* Wait for line to go low */
276                 v = wait_change(&ms);
277                 if ( v || ms < 0.350 || ms > 0.8500 )
278                      goto Start;
279
280                 /* Wait for line to go high */
281                 v = wait_change(&ms);
282                 if ( !v || ms < 0.350 || ms > 2.0 )
283                         goto Start;
284
285                 b = ms < 1.000 ? 0 : 1;
286                 word = (word << 1) | b;
287            } while ( ++count < 32 );
288
289            /*
290             * Eliminate key stutter :
291             */
292            gettimeofday(&t1,0);
293            if ( word == last && t0.tv_sec && msdiff (&t1,&t0) < 1100.0 )
294                 goto Start;           /* Too soon */
295
296            t0 = t1;
297            fprintf(stderr,"CODE %08lX\n",word);
298            return word;
299 }
300
301 /*
302  * Get text form of remote key :
303  */
304 static const char *
305 getircode(void) {
306         unsigned long code;
307         int kx;
308
```

```
309            for (;;) {
310                    code = getword();
311                    for ( kx=0; ir_codes[kx].text; ++kx )
312                            if ( ir_codes[kx].ir_code == code )
313                                    return ir_codes[kx].text;
314            }
315 }
316
317 /*
318  * Main program :
319  */
320 int
321 main(int argc,char **argv) {
322         const char *key;
323         int optch;
324         int f_dump = 0, f_gnuplot = 0, f_noinvert = 0;
325
326         while ( (optch = getopt(argc,argv,"dgnsp:h")) != EOF )
327                 switch ( optch ) {
328                 case 'd' :
329                         f_dump = 1;
330                         break;
331                 case 'g' :
332                         f_gnuplot = 1;
333                         break;
334                 case 'n':
335                         f_noinvert = 1;
336                         break;
337                 case 'p' :
338                         gpio_inpin = atoi(optarg);
339                         break;
340                 case 'h' :
341                         /* Fall thru */
342                 default :
343 usage :         fprintf (stderr,
344                                 "Usage: %s [-d ] [-g ] [-n ] [-p gpio]\n",argv[0]);
345                         fputs("where: \n"
346                            "  -d\t\t\tdumps events\n"
347                            "  -g\t\t\tgnuplot waveforms\n"
348                            "  -n\ t \tdon't invert GPIO input \n"
349                            "  -p gpio\tGPIO pin to use (17)\n",
350                                 stderr);
351                         exit(1);
352                 }
353
354         if ( gpio_inpin < 0 || gpio_inpin >=32 )
355                 goto usage;
356
357         if ( setjmp(jmp_exit) )
358                 goto xit;
359
```

```
360          signal(SIGINT,sigint_handler);                        /* Trap on SIGINT */
361          gpio_fd = gpio_open_edge(gpio_inpin,"both");          /* GPIO input */
362
363          printf("Monitoring GPIO %d for changes:\n",gpio_inpin);
364
365          if ( !f_dump ) {
366                  /*
367                   * Remote control read loop :
368                   */
369                  for (;;) {
370                          key = getircode();
371                          fputs(key,stdout);
372                          if ( !strcmp(key,"\n<EXIT>\n") )
373                                  break;
374                          fflush(stdout);
375                  }
376          } else {
377                  /*
378                   * Dump out IR level changes
379                   */
380                  int v;
381                  double ms, t =0.0;
382
383                  wait_change(&ms);          /* Wait for first change */
384
385                  for (;;) {
386                          v = wait_change(&ms) ^ f_noinvert;
387                          if ( !f_gnuplot )
388                                  printf("%12.3 f\t%d\n",ms,v);
389                          else  {
390                                  printf("%12.3 f\t%d\n",t,v^1);
391                                  t += ms;
392                                  printf("%12.3 f\t%d\n",t,v^1);
393                                  printf("%12.3 f\t%d\t%12.3 f\n",t,v,ms);
394                          }
395                  }
396          }
397
398 xit :    fputs("\nExit.\n",stdout);
399          close(gpio_fd);              /* Close gpio%d/value */
400          gpio_close(gpio_inpin);      /* Unexport gpio */
401          return 0;
402 }
403 /* End irdecode.c */
```

CHAPTER 27

■ ■ ■

Stepper Motor

A *stepper motor* is a brushless device with multiple windings, where one rotation is divided into several small *steps*. Stepper motors are used when precise positioning is required. Unipolar stepper motors have multiple windings connected to a common connection.

In this chapter, we'll recycle an old floppy-disk stepper motor. Modern stepper motors are smaller and operate at lower voltages. This particular stepper motor presents a good example of the challenges that exist when driving a motor from a 12 V power supply.

Floppy-Disk Stepper Motor

Figure 27-1 shows an old 5.25-inch floppy-disk stepper motor that was sitting on a shelf in my furnace room. Perhaps you have a gem like this in your own junk box.

Figure 27-1. *A salvaged 5.25-inch floppy-disk motor*

This particular stepper motor has these markings on it:

12 V	0.16	A/Ø
75 Ω	100	S/R
	Date 42-83	

This motor was clearly marked as a 12 V device. The 0.16 A/Ø marking tells us that each winding (phase Ø) is rated for 160 mA. The following calculation confirms that the winding resistance is 75 Ω, which is consistent with the printed current rating:

$$I = \frac{V}{R}$$
$$= \frac{12}{75}$$
$$= 160 \; mA$$

The 100 S/R marking tells us that this motor has 100 steps per revolution. It's really nice when you get all the information you need up front.

Your Junk-Box Motor?

Old 5.25-inch floppy-disk drives are getting scarcer these days. So what about other stepper motors that you might have in your junk box? How can you determine whether you can use one?

The first thing you must check is the type of motor. This chapter focuses on unipolar motors that have three or more step windings with a common connection. The floppy-disk stepper motor that I'm using in this chapter is shown in Figure 27-2. Notice that this motor has four separate windings, labeled L_1 through L_4. These have a common connection to a black wire coming out of the motor. To make this motor step, each winding must be activated in sequence.

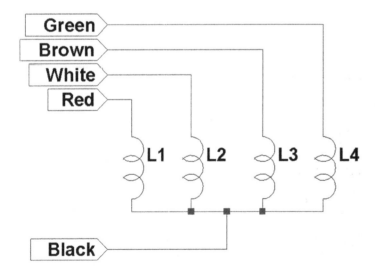

Figure 27-2. *Floppy-disk stepper motor windings*

If you have a stepper motor on hand but don't know much about it, you can test it with a DMM. Measure the DC resistance of the windings between each pair of wires. You won't need to measure every combination, but start a chart something like the following I'll use my motor as an example:

Wire 1	Wire 2	Reading
Black	Red	84 Ω
Red	White	168 Ω
White	Brown	168 Ω
Brown	Black	84 Ω
	etc.	

What does this tell you? The lowest readings show 84 Ω (the reading should be 75 Ω for this motor, but my DMM doesn't read low resistances accurately). The other readings are double that. This indicates that each winding should read 84 Ω, and when it doesn't, it means that we are measuring the resistance of two windings in series.

Looking again at the chart, we see that whenever we find an 84 Ω reading, the black wire is common to each. Knowing that the black wire is common to the windings means that all of the other wires should read 84 Ω relative to it. Now you know which wire is the common one.

Some motors you might encounter use two separate split windings. These won't have a wire common to *all* windings. You'll find that some paired wires have infinite resistance (no connection). If this applies, you have a motor that is applicable to the project in Chapter 28.

Another ingredient that you need to check is the DC resistance of each winding. Assuming you already measured this while determining the common wire, perform this calculation:

$$I_{winding} = \frac{V}{R_{winding}}$$

Let's assume that you think your stepper motor is a 6 V part, or simply that you plan to operate it at 6 V. Assume also that the measured DC resistance of the winding is 40 Ω. What will be the maximum current necessary to drive this motor?

$$I_{winding} = \frac{6}{40}$$
$$= 150\ mA$$

This figure is important to the driving electronics. In this chapter, I am using an economical PCB purchased from eBay that uses the ULN2003A driver chip. I'll describe the chip and the PCB in more detail later. The ULN2003A chip has a maximum drive rating of 500 mA. But this figure must be derated by the duty cycle used and the number of simultaneous drivers. If you computed a figure of 300 mA or more, you may need to seek out a more powerful driver.

■ **Note** In addition to stepper motors, the ULN2003A can drive lightbulbs and other loads.

Driver Circuit

Clearly, the GPIO outputs of the Raspberry Pi cannot drive a stepper motor directly. You could build your own driver circuit (or breadboard one) using the ULN2003A chip. I chose instead to buy a PCB from eBay for $2 (with free shipping), which provided the advantage of four LEDs. These light when a winding is activated, which is useful for testing. Figure 27-3 shows the schematic of the PCB that I used.

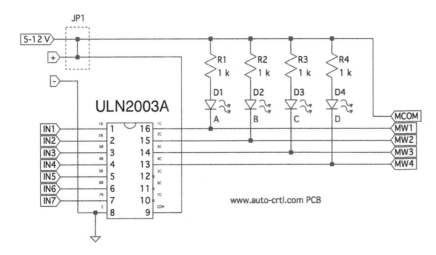

Figure 27-3. *ULN2003A PCB schematic*

The PCB includes two holes that power connections can be soldered into. There are also two pins marked (+) and (-) for a push-on connector.

Beside the power connections is a small jumper with the text *5 – 12 V* under it. This jumper is shown as JP1 in the schematic. You'll normally want to leave the jumper *in.*

The input connections are clearly labeled IN1 through IN7. However, only outputs 1C through 4C are used (outputs for IN1 through IN4). The other ULN2003A outputs 5C through 7C are unconnected. Wires could be carefully soldered to these pins, if you needed additional drivers for lamps, relays, or a second stepper motor.

The LEDs are connected from the (+) side, in series with a 1 $k\Omega$ current–limiting resistor. The voltage drop $V_{CE(sat)}$ in the ULN2003A ranges from about 0.9 to 1.6 V (use the worst case of 0.9 V). Assuming that the voltage drop is 1.6 V for red LEDs[55] and the maximum of 12 V is applied, each LED conducts about this:

$$I_{LED} = \frac{V_{CC} - V_{CE(sat)} - V_{LED}}{R_{LED}}$$

$$= \frac{12 - 0.9 - 1.6}{1000}$$

$$= 9.5 \; mA$$

The LEDs are the main reason the PCB lists a maximum voltage of 12 V. The ULN2003A chip has an absolute maximum V_{CC} voltage of 50 V. If, for example, you need to drive a 24 V stepper motor from an old *8-inch* floppy drive, you can remove jump JP1 to take the LEDs out of the circuit. Then you would supply the +24 V directly to the common wire of the stepper motor itself. If you do this, you'll also want to connect the PCB (+) to the motor's supply. This connects the motor to the COM pin of the ULN2003A, which provides reverse-biased diodes to drain away induced voltages.

When purchased, the PCB included a white socket for connection to the stepper motor. I removed that and replaced it with a soldered-in ribbon cable. These wires connect the driver outputs 1C through 4C to the stepper-motor windings.

The Raspberry Pi will drive pins IN1 through IN4 from the GPIO ports. When a given INx pin is driven high, the Darlington pair of transistors will sink up to 500 mA of current from a positive (motor supply) source to ground.

Darlington Pair

It is tempting to look at the ULN2003A chip as a black box: a signal goes into it, and a bigger one comes out. But when interfacing to voltages higher than the Raspberry Pi's own +3.3 V system, extra caution is warranted. If any of this higher voltage leaks back into the Pi, the GPIO pins will get "cooked" (if not the whole system).

Figure 27-4 shows input 1B being driven high by a GPIO line. This forward-biases Q_2, which in turn biases Q_1. A small amount of current flows in dashed lines from 1B, into the base of Q_2, and then from Q_1 to ground. This small amount of current flow allows a much greater current to flow from the collector of Q_1 to ground. The dashed lines on the right show the motor-winding current flowing from the motor power supply (12 V, for example), through Q_1 to ground through the E terminal.

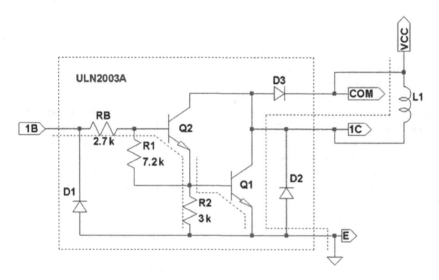

Figure 27-4. *ULN2003A driving a winding*

When the GPIO ceases to drive input 1B as shown in Figure 27-5, the transistors Q_2 and Q_1 turn off. With no more current flowing through L_1, the magnetic field collapses, generating a reverse current. As the field collapses, current flows into terminal 1C, through the diode D_3 and back to the upper side of L_1. In effect, diode D_3 shorts out this generated-back EMF. Diode D_3 is necessary to prevent the rest of the electronics from seeing a high voltage, which can cause damage and disruption.

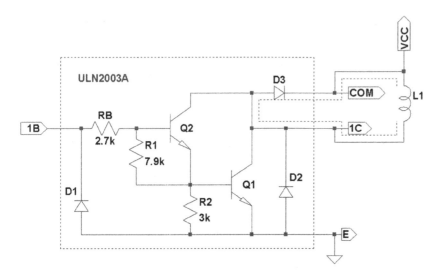

Figure 27-5. *ULN2003A driver turning off*

One side effect of the reverse-biased diode is that it slows down the decay of the magnetic field. As current flows in the reverse direction, the magnetic collapse is resisted. This results in magnetic forces inside the motor, which affect its speed. (This same effect also slows the release of relay contacts.) When greater speed is required, a resistor is sometimes used in series with the diode to limit its effect.

So what about voltage safety of our Raspberry Pi GPIO pins? Reexamine the Darlington pair Q_2 and Q_1. Pins COM and 1C can be as high as 50 V. But current cannot leak through D_3 (from COM) because the diode junction is reverse-biased. Current cannot leak from the collectors of Q_2 and Q_1 (from 1C) into the base circuits because those base-collector junctions are behaving as reverse-biased diodes. The main point of caution is that Q_2 and Q_1 *must remain intact.*

If Q_1 were allowed to overheat, for example, it might break down. If Q_1 or Q_2 breaks down, current will be allowed to flow from its collector into the base circuit, which is connected to the GPIO. Therefore, the breakdown of the driver transistors must be strictly prevented!

Driving the Driver

In this section, we look at the Raspberry Pi (GPIO) interface to the ULN2003A. There are two things we are most interested in here:

- The usual input logic-level interface

- Power-on reset and boot conditions

Input Levels

The output current of the ULN2003A Darlington pair rises as the input voltage rises above the *turn-on* level. We know from the Darlington configuration that there are two base-emitter junctions in the path from input to ground. Therefore, the ULN2003A driver requires a $2 \times V_{BE}$ voltage to forward-bias the pair. If we assume $V_{BE} = 0.6$ V, we can compute a V_{IL} for the driver as follows:

$$V_{IL} = 2 \times V_{BE}$$
$$= 2 \times 0.6$$
$$= 1.2\,V$$

Clearly, the Pi GPIO low (0.8 V) easily turns off the ULN2003A input with margin to spare. The datasheets state that a maximum output drive of 300 mA can be achieved with a 3 V input drive signal. The ULN2003A drive characteristics are shown here:

Signal	Raspberry Pi	ULN2003A	
		V_I	I_c
V_{OL}	≤ 0.8 V	1.2 V	500 μA
V_{OH}	≥ 1.3 V	2.4 V	100 mA
		2.7 V	250 mA
		3.0 V	300 mA

If we had a TTL signal driving the ULN2003A, we could get closer to the 500 mA maximum drive (interpolating from the characteristics shown). However, for our purposes, we need only 160 mA, so a 3 V drive signal meets the requirements well enough.

■ **Note** TTL levels approach +5V.

Power-on Reset/Boot

The one serious matter that remains is what our circuit will be doing as the Raspberry Pi is reset and is spending time booting up. The maximum ratings of the ULN2003A have to be derated when more than one Darlington pair is operating simultaneously. This is because each driver that is *on* heats up the chip substrate. For this reason, it is highly desirable for the ULN2003A to be "quiet" at reset time and subsequent boot-up. If a boot problem occurs, requiring a lot of time to correct, the drivers could overheat.

This potentially requires that we use GPIO pins that

- Are automatically configured as *inputs* at reset

- Are not configured with high pull-up resistors

Input pins with high pull-up resistors are *potentially* bad news. A high level appearing on ULN2003A inputs might activate drivers. In the worst-case scenario, all inputs become *active.*

Table 27-1 lists the acceptable GPIO pins as well as the reasons that others should be avoided.

Table 27-1. *GPIOs for Motor Control at Reset/Boot Time*

GPIO					
OK		Bad	Reason	Bad	Reason
09	23	00	Pull-up high	08	Pull-up high
10	24	01	Pull-up high	14	TXD0
11	25	02	Pull-up high	15	RXD0
12	28†	03	Pull-up high	16	Output
17	29†	04	Pull-up high	27	Output
18	30	05	Pull-up high		
21	31	06	Output		
22		07	Pull-up high		

(†) No pull-up resistor

The pull-up resistance provided by the Broadcom SoC is weak (50 $k\Omega$). Because of this, the worst-case input drive, due to the pull-up resistance, is calculated as follows:

$$I_I = \frac{V_{CC}}{R_{pullup}}$$
$$= \frac{3.3V}{50\,k\Omega}$$
$$= 66\,\mu A$$

The ULN2003A datasheet states that it takes an input drive of 250 μA to produce an output current flow of 100 mA. *Some* GPIO pins are pulled up by external resistors (GPIO 2 and 3 for SDA and SCL). These GPIO pins should *not* be used as motor drivers, for this reason.

The Darlington pair includes resistances that naturally pull down the input signal (review Figure 27-5). Resistances R_B, R_1, and R_2 are connected in series between the input and ground. This effectively provides a pull-down resistance of approximately 13.6 $k\Omega$. If the ULN2003A is attached to a floating input like GPIO 28 or 29, the input voltage will automatically be pulled down as a result (this is desirable here).

Modes of Operation

A unipolar stepper motor may be operated in four modes. The first three of these modes use digital on/off signals to drive each winding. The fourth *micro-stepping* mode requires driving each winding with varying analog signals. Since we are driving with digital GPIO pins, we'll examine only the first three modes.

Wave Drive (Mode 0)

Wave drive mode is the simplest of the modes, in which only one winding of the motor is activated at one time (see Figure 27-6). Each winding is energized in sequence to cause the rotation to occur in full steps. The motor will have significantly less torque than in full-step drive mode and is therefore rarely used.[57]

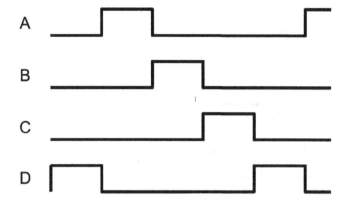

Figure 27-6. *Wave drive (mode 0)*

Full-Step Drive (Mode 1)

Figure 27-7 shows how full-step drive mode operates. Each field is energized in turn like a wave drive, but the next field is activated prior to turning off the prior field. In this way, an overlapping drive is affected in the direction of travel. This is the usual drive method delivering full-rated torque.[58]

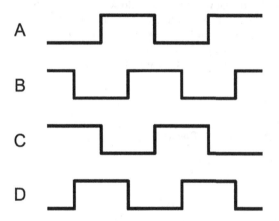

Figure 27-7. *Full-step drive (mode 1)*

Half-Step Drive (Mode 2)

Figure 27-8 illustrates the drive waveforms for half-step drive mode. As in full-step mode, an overlapped drive is applied to the field coils. Unlike full-step mode, the overlap occurs on the first third and the last third of a given coil's drive. For two-thirds of the waveform, there is overlapped drive. In the middle third, only one winding is active.

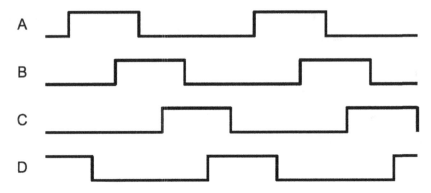

Figure 27-8. *Half-step drive*

This mode provides increased angular resolution but suffers from having less torque (about 70% of full-rated torque).[59]

Software

To demonstrate stepper-motor driving without getting into a complex assignment, the program unipolar.c simply positions the shaft of the motor to various hour positions of the clock, based on single-key commands.

With a pointer attached to the shaft of your motor, press 6, and the motor will point at 6 o'clock. Press 3, and the motor figures out that it is quickest to step counterclockwise back to the 3 o'clock position. Press 7, and the motor steps forward to 7 o'clock. All of this, of course, requires that you point the shaft at 12 o'clock before you begin (the motor provides no information to the program about where it is currently pointing).

The program presented uses the GPIO pin assignments in Table 27-2 for driving the stepper motor (your wire colors may differ):

Table 27-2. *GPIO Assignments Used by the Program unipolar.c*

GPIO	GENX	P1	Mode	Stepper Wire	ULN2003A	Description
17	GEN0	P1-11	Output	Red	1B	Field A
24	GEN5	P1-18		White	2B	Field B
22	GEN3	P1-15		Brown	3B	Field C
23	GEN4	P1-16		Green	4B	Field D

Figure 27-9 shows how a pointer knob can be used for a pointer. Otherwise, this is your opportunity to get creative.

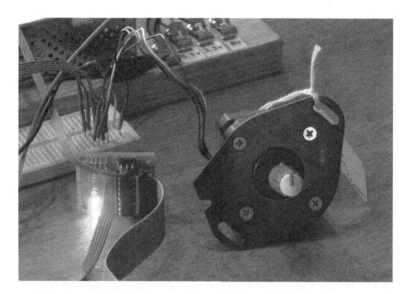

Figure 27-9. *Stepper motor with knob used as a pointer*

At power-on reset and boot time, the selected GPIO lines are all input pins with pull-down resistors. After boot-up, when the program starts and configures its GPIO pins, it will do the following:

1. Configure an output low value for each GPIO (while still an input)

2. Configure the GPIO pin as an output

Step 1 eliminates the possibility of a stepper winding being driven before the software is ready to drive it. If this were not done, a driver could be activated when the GPIO is first configured as an output. Step 2, of course, is necessary to drive the ULN2003A chip. But no glitch occurs in the output when step 1 is performed first.

After the main program has begun, it saves the current terminal settings in sv_ios and then sets up a raw mode, permitting single-character I/O interaction (lines 167–173). See Chapter 11 for a review of the serial API.

Lines 175–178 initialize the GPIO lines to drive the stepper-motor field windings. The default stepper-motor mode is configured on line 182, which may be overruled by a command-line argument. The program can also change modes by using keystroke commands.

The remainder of the program is a while loop that extends from lines 185–241. It reads a single-character command at line 187 and then dispatches to sections of code in the switch statement. The single-character commands are summarized in Table 27-3.

Table 27-3. Single-Character Commands

Char	Command	Char	Command
Q	Quit	0	12 o'clock (noon)
<	Slower steps	1	1 o'clock
>	Faster steps	2	
?	Help		...
H		9	9 o'clock
J	Stepper mode 0	A	10 o'clock
K	Stepper mode 1	B	11 o'clock
L	Stepper mode 2	+/=	Step clockwise
P	Show current position	-	Step counterclockwise
O	Toggle drive on/off		

The < and > commands double or halve the step time interval. This slows and increases the rotational speed, respectively. Stepper modes can be changed using the J, K, or L commands. These reposition the stepper to 12 o'clock prior to changing modes. The digits 0 through 9 and letters A and B reposition the shaft to point to the hour of the clock.

You can test whether your rotation is properly working by using the + and - keystrokes to step one step clockwise or counterclockwise. Pressing O (the letter O, not zero) toggles the drive power on or off for the motor. This is useful for turning off the motor drive when you want to manually reposition the shaft.

The source code used in this program for gpio_io.c is provided in Chapter 12, and timed_wait.c in Chapter 22. The main source module of interest is unipolar.c, which is presented at the end of this chapter.

Testing

Be careful setting up this project because of the voltages involved. One careless wiring error could bring higher voltage into your GPIO pins and fry the Pi. In the following procedures, I refer to the driver PCB (as I used), but this procedure applies equally to breadboarded circuits.

Here is the first part of the setup and checkout procedure:

1. Set up the power to the driver PCB without connecting it to the Raspberry Pi. Leave the motor unconnected also.

2. Make sure that the driver inputs are not connected.

3. Apply the power to the PCB. No LEDs will light if everything is OK. No smoke? Good!

4. Apply +3.3 V one at a time to the driver inputs 1B through 4B (IN1 through IN4 on the PCB) with a wire, which should cause the corresponding LED to light. (These driver inputs will also accept +5 V for testing, if that is what you have available.) If you breadboarded the circuit, consider adding LEDs to each driver output.

5. Measure the voltage at each unconnected driver *input* 1B through 4B (IN1 through IN4). Each should measure 0 V (or very nearly). If you measure anything higher, you have either a wiring error or a bad driver chip. Don't use a defective driver.

If this procedure tests out OK, the next step is to wire up the motor (with PCB still unconnected from the Pi):

1. Put some kind of pointer on the motor shaft (like a pointer knob) and wire up the motor to the PCB driver outputs.

2. Make sure that the COM pin of the driver chip is connected to the + power connection used for the motor (+12 V in my case). This is important for bleeding off the inductive kick that occurs when the motor winding is turned off.

3. Apply power to the PCB and check for smoke. No smoke or crackling sounds means you can proceed to the next step.

4. With the PCB power applied, you should be able to drive each motor winding with +3.3 V applied to individual inputs, as before. If the motor is wired up correctly, it should twitch. If the twitch is not visible, put your hand on the shaft. You should feel it when the winding activates.

The next step is to make sure you wired the windings for the correct sequence. When applying step 4 of the preceding procedure to each winding's driver input, the motor should take one step clockwise. Watch for double steps, or twitches in the reverse direction. As you strobe inputs 1B, 2B, 3B, and 4B (IN1 through IN4) in sequence, the motor should step in an orderly clockwise direction. Reversing that activation sequence should cause the motor to step counterclockwise. Keep your nose alert for smoke or funny smells. Then follow these steps:

1. Measure the inputs of the drivers 1B through 4B one last time, while the motor is connected and all motor voltages are present. Each input should measure near 0 V (due to its internal pull-down resistances).

2. Now power everything off.

3. Make sure there is a ground-wire connection between your Raspberry Pi's ground and the stepper-motor power supply's ground. *Don't try operating without this critical link.*

4. With everything still off, and observing care for static electricity, connect the GPIO pins to each of the ULN2003A driver inputs 1B through 4B (IN1 through IN4).

Now turn everything on and keep alert, just in case. The Raspberry Pi should begin booting with no visible activity on the stepper motor (or LEDs). If there is, you might have a GPIO wiring error. Turn off the stepper-motor power supply if you can and bring the Pi down and recheck.

Assuming all went well, point your motor at 12 o'clock and start the program:

```
$ ./unipolar
```

If the motor struggles or moves erratically when you give it movement commands, you may need to correct the motor wiring. Use the + and - commands to check whether the motor steps properly in one direction.

```
1    /*********************************************************
2     * unipolar.c : Drive unipolar stepper motor
3     *********************************************************/
4
5    #include <stdio.h>
6    #include <stdlib.h>
7    #include <fcntl.h>
8    #include <unistd.h>
9    #include <errno.h>
```

```
10   #include <math.h>
11   #include <ctype.h>
12   #include <termio.h>
13   #include <sys/mman.h>
14   #include <signal.h>
15   #include <assert.h>
16
17   #include "gpio_io.c"                          /* GPIO routines */
18   #include "timed_wait.c"                       /* timed_wait () */
19
20   static const int steps_per_360 = 100;         /* Full steps per rotation */
21
22   /*                 GPIO Pins :  A    B    C    D */
23   static const int gpios[] = { 17, 24, 22, 23 };
24
25   static float step_time = 0.1;                 /* Seconds */
26   static int drive_mode = 0;                    /* Drive mode 0, 1, or 2 */
27   static int step_no = 0;                       /* Step number */
28   static int steps_per_r = 100;                 /* Steps per rotation */
29   static int position = 0;                      /* Stepper position */
30   static int on_off = 0;                        /* Motor drive on/off */
31
32   static int quit = 0;                          /* Exit program if set */
33
34   /***********************************************************
35    * Await so many fractional seconds
36    ***********************************************************/
37   static void
38   await(float seconds) {
39           long sec, usec;
40
41           sec = floor(seconds);                 /* Seconds to wait */
42           usec = floor((seconds_sec)*1000000);  /* Microseconds */
43           timed_wait(sec,usec,0);               /* Wait */
44   }
45
46   /***********************************************************
47    * Set motor drive mode
48    ***********************************************************/
49   static void
50   set_mode(int mode) {
51           int micro_steps = mode < 2 ? 1 : 2;
52
53           step_no = 0;
54           drive_mode = mode;
55           steps_per_r = steps_per_360 * micro_steps;
56           printf("Drive mode %d\n",drive_mode);
57   }
58
```

```
59   /***********************************************************
60    * Drive all fields according to bit pattern in pins
61    ***********************************************************/
62   static void
63   drive(int pins) {
64           short x;
65           for ( x=0; x<4; ++x )
66                   gpio_write(gpios [x],pins & (8>>x) ? 1 : 0);
67   }
68
69   /***********************************************************
70    * Advance motor:
71    *       dir =                   -1 Step counter_clockwise
72    *       dir =                    0 Turn on exist ing fields
73    *       dir =                   +1 Step clockwise
74    ***********************************************************/
75   static void
76   advance(int dir) {
77           static int m0drv[] = {8, 4, 2, 1};
78           static int m1drv[] = {9, 12, 6, 3};
79           static int m2drv[] = {9, 8, 12, 4, 6, 2, 3, 1};
80
81           switch ( drive_mode ) {
82           case 0:                                 /* Simple mode 0 */
83               step_no = (step_no + dir) & 3;
84               drive(m0drv[step_no]);
85               await(step_time/4.0);
86               break;
87           case 1:                                 /* Mode 1 drive */
88               step_no = (step_no + dir) & 3;
89               drive(m1drv[step_no]);
90               await(step_time/6.0);
91               break;
92           case 2 :                                /* Mode 2 drive */
93               step_no = (step_no + dir) & 7;
94               drive(m2drv[step_no]);
95               await(step_time/1 2.0);
96               ;
97           }
98
99           on_off = 1;                             /* Mark as drive enabled */
100  }
101
102  /***********************************************************
103   * Move +/- n steps, keeping track of position
104   ***********************************************************/
105  static void
106  move(int steps) {
107          int movement = steps;
108          int dir = steps >=0 ? 1 : -1;
109          int inc = steps >=0 ? -1 : 1;
110
```

```
111              for ( ; steps != 0; steps += inc )
112                      advance(dir);
113          position = (position + movement + steps_per_r) % steps_per_r;
114 }
115
116 /************************************************************
117  * Move to an hour position
118  ************************************************************/
119 static void
120 move_oclock(int hour) {
121          int new_pos = floor((float)hour * steps_per_r/12.0);
122          int diff;
123
124          printf("Moving to %d o'clock.\n",hour);
125
126          if ( new_pos >=position ) {
127                  diff = new_pos - position;
128                  if ( diff <= steps_per_r/2 )
129                          move(diff);
130                  else move(-(position + steps_per_r - new_pos));
131          } else {
132                  diff = position - new_pos;
133                  if ( diff <= steps_per_r/2 )
134                          move(-diff);
135                  else move (new_pos + steps_per_r - position);
136          }
137 }
138
139 /************************************************************
140  * Provide usage info :
141  ************************************************************/
142 static void
143 help(void) {
144     puts("Enter 0-9,A,B for 0_9,10,11 o'clock.\n"
145          " '<' to slow motor speed, \n"
146          " '>' to increase motor speed, \n"
147          " 'J ', 'K' or 'L' for modes 0-2,\n"
148          " '+'/ '-' to step 1 step,\n"
149          " 'O' to toggle drive on/off, \n"
150          " 'P' to show position, \n"
151          " 'Q' to quit.\n");
152 }
153
154 /************************************************************
155  * Main program
156  ************************************************************/
157 int
158 main(int argc,char **argv) {
159          int tty = 0;                                    /* Use stdin */
160          struct termios sv_ios, ios;
```

```
161          int x, rc;
162          char ch;
163
164          if ( argc >=2 )
165                  drive_mode = atoi(argv[1]);           /* Drive mode 0_2 */
166
167          rc = tcgetattr(tty,&sv_ios);                 /* Save current settings */
168          assert(!rc);
169          ios = sv_ios;
170          cfmakeraw(&ios);                             /* Make into a raw config */
171          ios.c_oflag = OPOST | ONLCR;                 /* Keep output editing */
172          rc = tcsetattr(tty,TCSAFLUSH,& ios);         /* Put terminal into raw mode */
173          assert(!rc);
174
175          gpio_init();                                 /* Initialize GPIO access */
176          drive(0);                                    /* Turn off output */
177          for ( x=0; x<4; ++x )
178          gpio_config(gpios[x],Output);                /* Set GPIO pin as Output */
179                             .
180          help();
181
182          set_mode(drive_mode);
183          printf("Step time: %6.3f seconds\n",step_time);
184
185          while ( !quit ) {
186                  write(1," : ",2);
187                  rc = read(tty,&ch,1);                /* Read char */
188                  if ( rc != 1 )
189                          break;
190                  if ( islower(ch) )
191                          ch = toupper(ch);
192
193                  write(1,&ch,1);
194                  write(1,"\n",1);
195
196                  switch ( ch ) {
197                  case 'Q':                            /* Quit */
198                      quit = 1;
199                      break;
200                  case '<' :                           /* Go slower */
201                      step_time *= 2.0;
202                      printf ("Step time : %6.3 f seconds \n", step_time);
203                      break;
204                  case '>':                            /* Go faster */
205                      step_time /=2.0;
206                      printf ("Step time: %6.3 f seconds \n", step_time);
207                      break;
208                  case '?':                            /* Provide help */
209                  case 'H':
210             help ();
211             break;
```

```
212                     case 'J':                        /* Mode 0 */
213                     case 'K':                        /* Mode 1 */
214                     case 'L':                        /* Mode 2 */
215                         move_oclock(0);
216                         set_mode((int) ch - (int) 'J');
217                         break;
218                     case 'A':                        /* 10 o'clock */
219                     case 'B':                        /* 11 o'clock */
220                         move_oclock ((int) ch - (int) 'A'+10);
221                         break;
222                     case 'O':                        /* Toggle on/ off drive */
223                         on_off ^= 1;
224                         if ( !on_off )
225                                 drive(0);            /* Turn off motor drive */
226                         else advance(0);             /* Re_assert motor drive */
227                         break;
228                     case '+':                        /* Advance +1 */
229                     case '=':                        /* Tread '=' as '+' for convenience */
230                     case '-':                        /* Counter clock_wise 1 */
231                         move(ch == '-' ? -1 : 1);
232                         /* Fall thru */
233                     case 'P':                        /* Display Position */
234                         printf("Position: %d of %d\n",position,steps_per_r);
235                         break;
236                     default:                         /* 0 to 9'oclock */
237                         if ( ch >= '0' && ch <= '9' )
238                                 move_oclock((int) ch - (int) '0');
239                         else write (1,"???\n",4);
240                 }
241         }
242
243         puts("\nExit.");
244
245         drive(0);
246         for ( x=0; x<4; ++x )
247                 gpio_config(gpios[x],Input);         /* Set GPIO pin as Input */
248
249         tcsetattr(tty,TCSAFLUSH,&sv_ios);            /* Restore terminal mode */
250         return 0;
251 }
252
253 /* End unipolar.c */
```

■ ■ ■

## CHAPTER 28

The H-Bridge Driver

One of the challenges of driving DC electric motors is that they sometimes need the capability to operate in reverse. To do this, the current flow must be reversed. Arranging for this requires additional hardware.

The H-Bridge driver can be used to drive a reversible DC motor *or* a bipolar stepper motor (also LEDs as in chapter 12). Unlike the unipolar motor, the field windings of a bipolar stepper motor require reversible current flow to operate. This chapter demonstrates the utility of the H-Bridge driver, using a bipolar stepper motor.

The L298 Driver

The L298 integrated circuit implements a convenient H-Bridge driver circuit. An H-Bridge can be built from discrete components, but integrated circuits are more convenient for lower-current applications. Figure 28-1 shows the block diagram for the L298 driver IC. You can see the *H* composed from the driver transistors Q_1 through Q_4, and the driven motor in the center (in this case, a DC motor).

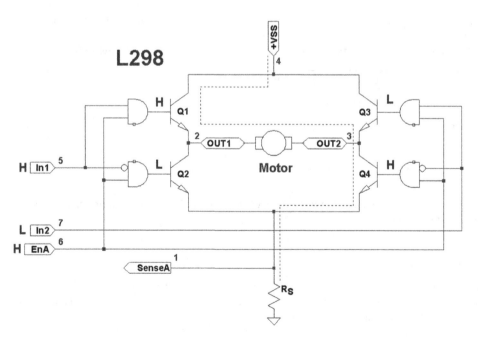

Figure 28-1. *L298 full-bridge driver*

The motor in the figure is driven when Q_1 and Q_4 are turned on. Q_2 and Q_3 are kept off when the other transistors are on. If Q_1 and Q_2 were allowed to be on at the same time, a short circuit would exist from V_{SS} to ground. The *and* logic gates driving these transistors prevent this.

Returning to Figure 28-1, with Q_1 and Q_4 on, the current flows through the motor from left to right. Turning all transistors off results in no current flow. Turning Q_3 and Q_2 on causes the current to flow from V_{SS} to ground, passing this time through the motor from right to left. By controlling pairs of transistors, current can be made to flow in one direction or the other.

Sensing Resistor

When used, the sensing resistor R_S is a low-resistance resistor for sensing how much current flows through the motor (the datasheet suggests a *non-wire-wound* resistance of $R_S = 0.5\,\Omega$). As current flow increases, the voltage V_{RS} across the resistor increases. When the motor stalls, for example, V_{RS} will exceed a certain threshold voltage, allowing protective circuitry to turn the drivers (and thus the motor) off. In this chapter, we will simply wire the sense pins to ground and omit the protective circuitry for simplicity.

Enable A and B

The L298 is a dual-bridge driver, with units A and B. Figure 28-1 shows only unit A. The enable inputs EnA and EnB enable or disable the drive to units A and B, respectively. Without a high signal on the enable input, no current will flow through the bridge, no matter what the other input signals are. The enable input can be used by the protective circuitry to disable the motor outputs, should the V_{RS} voltage rise too high. Otherwise, the enable inputs can be tied to the logic high or controlled by the microprocessor.

Inputs In1 and In2

Each half of the dual-bridge driver has a pair of logic inputs. They are In1 and In2 for bridge A, and In3 and In4 for bridge B. We'll focus on bridge A.

When the enable EnA pin is enabled, the In1 and In2 inputs have the following results for the motor drive:

In1	In2	Q1	Q2	Q3	Q4	Motor Current
0	0		On		On	No current flow
0	1		On	On		Right to left
1	0	On			On	Left to right
1	1	On		On		No current flow

A simple way to think about this is that one input must be high, while the other is low for the motor drive. The direction is selected by the input that is high.

Protection Diodes

No inductive driver circuit is complete without protective diodes. When the applied voltage is suddenly removed from the motor coil, the magnetic field collapses, producing an electric current. Recall in Chapter 27 that the reverse-biased diode was used to bleed off the inductive kick in the unipolar motor drive.

Figure 28-2 shows the L298 with the external protective diodes wired in (these are not included in the IC). If the current flow was as shown in the earlier block diagram, the sudden off would cause the current to flow through diodes D_3 and D_2. The SGS-Thomson Microelectronics datasheet specifies that these should be 1A fast-recovery diodes ($t_{rr} \leq 200\ ns$). A slow-reacting diode can allow the voltage to spike into the surrounding circuit.

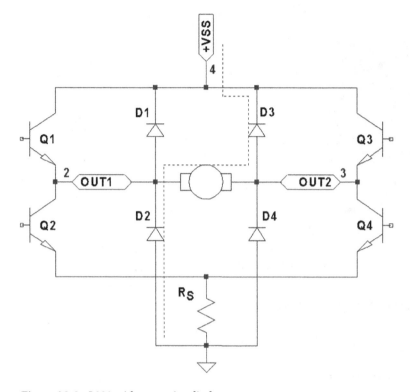

Figure 28-2. *L298 with protective diodes*

L298 PCB

You could build your own L298 driver circuit, but with the availability of PCBs around $4 on eBay, you'd have to have a good reason to bother. Figure 28-3 shows the unit that I purchased and used for this project.

Figure 28-3. *L298 driver PCB*

■ **Note**   I purchased this PCB as an eBay Buy It Now offer with free shipping.

The PCB has three power connections:

- V_s, which is labeled as +12 V (yellow wire in the photo)
- Gnd (black wire)
- V_{ss}, which is labeled as +5 V (red wire)

This particular PCB has a jumper (removed in Figure 28-3), with its two pins visible just above the power-connection block and below the round capacitor. With the jumper installed, an onboard regulator supplies V_{ss} with +5 V from the V_s (+12 V) input. The regulated +5 V is also available for external circuitry at the block connector (where the red wire is shown).

When the motor (V_s) voltage is higher than 12 V, it is best to remove the jumper and supply the +5 V into the block instead. The reason for this is that the linear regulator must dissipate additional heat from the higher input voltage. I am using a salvaged power supply with both a +5 V supply and a +16 V supply, so the jumper was removed.

To the right of the power-input block are header connection pins as follows:

+5V					+5V
EnA	In1	In2	In3	In4	EnB

The EnA and EnB connections have jumpers installed to enable both driver units (tying the enable A and B inputs up to the +5 V supply). If you don't need to control the enable inputs, leave the jumpers in. Otherwise, remove them and then use the edge pins for inputs to enables A and B.

The pins In1 through In4 are the inputs to the bridge drivers (see In1 and In2 in Figure 28-1). The remaining connections are two blocks with paired connections:

- OUT1 and OUT2, bridge connections for unit A

- OUT3 and OUT4, bridge connections for unit B

You don't have to install any protective diodes, since they are already included on the PCB. Price and convenience were the reasons I chose to buy the PCB. If you breadboard the driver instead, be sure to wire in the fast-acting protection diodes, since these are not included in the IC.

Driving from GPIO

Of course, before we attach the inputs of these drivers to the GPIO pins of the Raspberry Pi, we need to be certain that the voltage levels are safe and that the interface logic levels work.

The L298 IC has the following power requirements:

Symbol	Parameter	Min	Typ	Max	Unit
V_S	Supply voltage (pin 4)	$V_{IH} + 2.5$		46	Volts
V_{SS}	Logic supply voltage (pin 9)	4.5	5	7	Volts

From this, we see that the motor side (V_s) can operate up to 46 V. The logic side, however, must have a minimum of 4.5 V. In other words, the L298 driver operates at 5V TTL levels.

■ **Note**   Be sure to remove the regulator jumper when using high voltages.

But we've seen this kind of problem before, in Chapter 27. There we were still able to drive the ULN2003A safely from the GPIO outputs at 3 V levels. So let's check the signal requirements of GPIO outputs vs. L298 inputs:

GPIO		L298	
Signal	Volts	Volts	Signal
V_{OL}	$\leq 0.8\ V$	$\leq 1.5\ V$	V_{IL}
V_{OH}	$\geq 1.3\ V$	$\geq 2.3\ V$	V_{IH}

If you look carefully at the chart, there is a dodgy area where the GPIO output can be as low as $V_{OH} \geq 1.3\ V$ and still be in spec *as far as the Raspberry Pi is concerned*. We see that the L298 considers signals $V_{IL} \leq 1.5V$ as a *low*. Worse, only voltages $\geq 2.3\ V$ are considered high by the L298. The good news is that the L298 input current is very low:

		L298			
Symbol	Parameter	Test Conditions	Typ	Max	Unit
I_{IH}	High-voltage input current	$V_I = H \leq V_{SS} - 0.6\ V$	30	100	μA

The input current necessary to drive the L298 input high is a maximum of 100 μA. The lowest configured output drive capability of a GPIO pin is 2 mA. The L298 input current requirement is thus only 5% of the minimum current drive available. If the GPIO pin had to drive a 2 mA signal, its output voltage might be as low as 1.3 V. But having to supply only 100 μA of signal current means that the GPIO voltage should be almost as high as it can go.

For this reason, it is not that unreasonable to expect the GPIO output voltage to be near 3 V (allowing for a drop from the +3.3 V supply). However, we must allow for variation in the +3.3 V power supply as well. If the supply is within the standard range of +3.125 to +3.465 V, and we allow a GPIO output drop of, say, 0.3 V due to the output transistor R_{on}, then the unloaded GPIO output voltage could be as low as 3.135 – 0.3 = 2.835 V. This is only 0.535 V above the minimum V_{IH} = 2.3 V that we need for the L298. This is cutting things rather close, but sufficient for hobby and educational use (for products that are sold, you would want a greater margin for error). If this remains a concern for a project build, external pull resistors to +3.3 V can be added.

The DMM Check

The final word is the voltage measurement of the L298 chip's inputs. You must make certain there is no pull-up resistor to +5 V on the PCB. The datasheet doesn't indicate that any L298 chip internal pull-up resistors exist. But seeing is believing, so don't skip this check. A purchased PCB is more likely to contain pull-up resistors than not.

Without attaching it to the Pi, supply the circuit with +5 V for its logic (the motor supply need not be applied). When using the onboard regulator, supply the +12 V to the +VS input instead. Then check the voltage appearing at the EnA, EnB, In1, In2, In3, and In4 inputs. When measured, there should be nearly no voltage present (with respect to ground). If you read +5 V instead, the PCB likely has provided a pull-up resistor somewhere. For the enable inputs, jumpers may need to be removed. Do not wire these inputs to the Raspberry Pi until these inputs have passed this check. Anything measured less than 0.6 V is probably OK. Measurements higher than this probably mean a defective driver IC or a wiring error.

If you are supplying the L298 logic from a separate +5 V supply, it is a good idea to perform one more test with the +12 V (or higher) motor supply applied. The measured voltage at each input pin should remain as before, near zero. Anything else suggests a bad PCB or defective L298 chip leaking current into the inputs.

Bipolar Stepper Modes

Before we look at the schematic and software, let's review how the bipolar stepper motor works. There are three basic modes of operation for a *bipolar* stepper motor:

- Wave drive, one-phase-on drive
- Wave drive, two-phase-on drive
- Half-step drive

One-Phase-On Mode

Figure 28-4 shows the first two of four possible drive states for wave drive, one phase on. Each winding is energized in turn for the first two steps. The final two steps energize the same two windings in sequence except that the current polarity is reversed. In other words, the south pole of the rotor follows the positive input polarity (as wired in the figure). In this mode, there are a total of four steps.

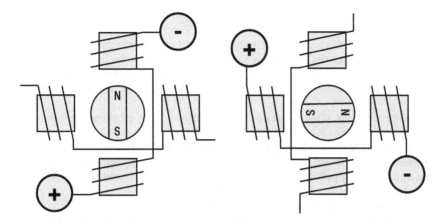

Figure 28-4. *Wave drive, one phase on*

This simple mode of operation suffers from the loss of precision that the half-step drive has and lacks the torque of two-phase-on mode.

Two-Phase-On Mode

Wave drive, two-phase-on mode energizes both windings for each step. This is where the extra torque comes from. Figure 28-5 shows two of the four possible steps for this mode. Notice how the south pole centers itself between two poles, as it follows the two positive polarities. Like the one-phase mode, there are only four possible steps.

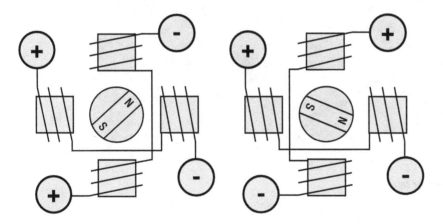

Figure 28-5. *Wave drive, two phase on*

While this mode lacks the precision of half-step mode (next), it does enjoy the extra torque advantage over all three modes.

Half-Step Mode

In half-step mode, a combination of the two prior modes is used. First, only one winding is energized to point the rotor at the winding's pole (like one-phase mode). Then the next pole is energized while keeping the prior winding energized. In this way, the rotor moves a half step between the two poles, as with two-phase mode. Finally, the previous winding is turned off, producing another half step. The precision is increased to a total of eight steps in this manner.

This is clearly the most precise of the three modes. While it lacks some of the torque of two-phase mode, it has on average more torque than one-phase mode.

In all of these modes, it is necessary to first pass current through the windings in one direction, and then later in the reverse direction. This allows the bipolar stepper motor to be built with less wire than the unipolar motor. In the unipolar design, only one or two of the four center-tapped windings are used at one time. Consequently, the bipolar motor is cheaper to manufacture and lighter in weight.

Figure 28-6 illustrates my test setup. At the left is a power supply that I rescued from a discarded piece of equipment. To the right of the Raspberry Pi station, I have the L298 PCB wired up to the power and the Pi's GPIO pins. The remaining four wires go from the drive PCB to the bipolar stepper motor (I left some sort of shaft attachment to the motor, to make the rotation more visible).

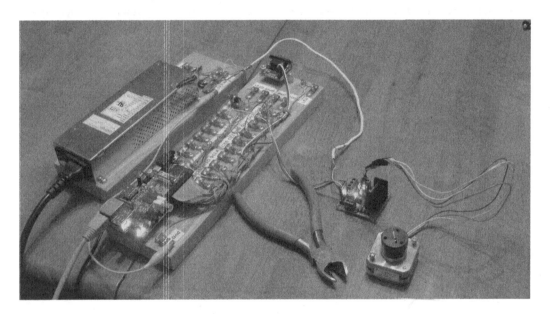

Figure 28-6. *My bipolar stepper motor setup*

Choosing Driving GPIOs

Recall from Chapter 27's Table 27-1 that some GPIO pins are more suitable than others for motor controls. While the Raspberry Pi is booting up, we don't want driver circuits and motors running amok. It is best that the motor remains disabled until the Pi boots up and the motor-controlling software takes proper control.

When using the L298, we can take one of two design approaches:

- Tie enable inputs high, but choose *motor-safe* GPIO pins for the driver inputs.

- Drive the enable inputs from a *motor-safe* GPIO and configure the other GPIO pins after boot-up.

The first option does not use the enable inputs at all. For that, you must make sure that all In GPIO pins are safe for motor control at boot time. The disadvantage is that all *four* input controls need to be taken from the *safe* GPIO pool. If you need to drive more than one motor, your options start to become limited.

The second approach uses motor-safe GPIO pin(s) on the *two* enable inputs of the L298 driver. This way, the enable inputs are pulled down during the boot-up process, disabling the motor controls, regardless of the state of the In pins. This gives you flexibility to choose any other GPIO pins for use for the In signals. This is the approach adopted for this chapter's project. (Note that you can tie the enable pins together so that only one safe GPIO pin is required to drive the enable input.) Because a bipolar stepper motor needs a bridge driver for each of its two windings, we'll use both bridge driver units provided by the L298 IC.

The enable inputs for the two windings can be ganged together and driven by one GPIO pin. This, of course, increases the load on the GPIO output, but at a worst case of 200 μA, the driving voltage requirements will be easily met.

Project Schematic

Figure 28-7 shows the schematic for the bipolar motor driver. If you are using a purchased PCB, the only important details are the connections to it. The schematic, however, helps us visualize all the separate components involved.

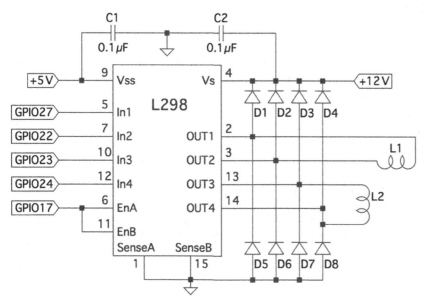

Figure 28-7. *L298 schematic*

In this circuit, the enable inputs A and B have been tied together so that only GPIO 17 needs to be allocated to drive it.

Junk-Box Motors

If you've been an electronics hobbyist for a while, you likely have a bipolar motor in your junk box. If not, salvage one from an old 3.5-inch floppy disk. Its seek motor will likely be a bipolar stepper. Another source of stepper motors is an old flat-top scanner.

Bipolar motors are easier to figure out than unipolar motors. There are only four wires, and they operate in pairs. To identify the pairs, simply take resistance readings. A low reading will identify one pair of wires. Once that pair is identified, the remaining two wires should be the second pair and read similarly. Make sure there is no connection between the windings. They should be electrically isolated from each other.

Program Operation

The program used in this chapter is named `bipolar.c` and is listed at the end of the chapter. The program is designed similarly to the unipolar program in Chapter 27. The bipolar program, however, does not do clock positioning, but instead operates in free-running mode when instructed to do so.

The program starts in one-phase mode, but the stepper-motor mode can be changed with any of the following single-character commands:

Character	Command
1	Wave mode, one phase
2	Wave mode, two phase
3	Half-step mode

Entering a mode command will automatically stop the motor if it is in free-running mode.

To test your motor connections, these single-step commands are available:

Character	Command
+	Single step clockwise
-	Single step counterclockwise

The + command steps the motor one step clockwise, while the – (minus) key steps the motor counterclockwise. If your motor turns the wrong way, you can fix your wiring after testing it.

Similarly, use these single-step commands to make sure your motor is wired up correctly. In one-phase mode (the default), the motor should step equally with each + or - step command. If not, one of the two pairs needs its connections reversed.

The free-running commands (and Quit) are listed here:

Character	Command
F	Forward (free running)
R	Reverse (free running)
S	Stop
>	Go faster (halve the step time)
<	Go slower (double the step time)
Q	Quit

Entering F starts the motor running, in the forward (clockwise) direction. To speed it up, press > while it is running, or prior to starting it. Pressing the same direction command F toggles the motor off again. Alternatively, S is available to stop the motor if that seems more intuitive. The R command starts the motor in the reverse direction. Pressing R again stops it. Direction can be changed while the motor is running. This tests how well it recovers when operated at higher speeds.

Program Internals

This program requires the use of a thread to run the motor in free-running mode. This design allows the main program to continue to read user commands from the keyboard while supplying the motor with stepping commands. The user can change the stepping speed, reverse the motor, or stop the motor.

The main user input dispatch loop is in the main program (lines 230 to 305). The threaded code resides in lines 125 to 140. Unless the free-running F or R commands are in effect, the thread blocks in line 131, waiting for a command. Once a command is received, the loop in lines 133 to 136 keeps the motor stepping, until the main loop sets the stop flag.

The mutex and cond variables (lines 36 and 37) provide a simple arrangement to implement a queue from the main thread to the free-running thread. The queue get function is implemented in lines 105 to 119. The code must first successfully lock the mutex in line 109. Once that is accomplished, the while loop in lines 111 and 112 is executed. If the cmd variable is still zero, this indicates that no command has been queued. When that happens, pthread_cond_wait() in line 112 is executed. This unlocks the mutex and blocks the execution of the program. Control blocks until the cond variable is signaled in line 158. When control returns from pthread_cond_wait(3), the kernel has relocked the mutex.

Queuing the command occurs in the routine queue_cmd() (lines 146 to 159). After locking the mutex (line 149), the while loop checks whether the cmd variable is nonzero. If it is, this indicates that the motor thread has not received the last command yet, and control blocks in the pthread_cond_wait() call (line 152). Again, when control blocks, the kernel releases the mutex. The cond variable is signaled from line 117, when the command is taken off the one-element queue.

The stepping functions are performed by the routine step() in lines 73 to 91. The motor drive is disabled in line 86 so the GPIO signals can be changed (line 87). Once the new GPIO output settings are established, the drive to the motor is enabled in line 88.

If you choose to use different GPIO pins for this project, change the constant declarations in lines 23 to 27.

```
1    /*********************************************
2     * bipolar.c : Drive a bipolar stepper motor
3     *********************************************/
4
5    #include <stdio.h>
6    #include <stdlib.h>
7    #include <fcntl.h>
8    #include <unistd.h>
9    #include <errno.h>
10   #include <math.h>
11   #include <ctype.h>
12   #include <termio.h>
13   #include <sys/mman.h>
14   #include <pthread.h>
15   #include <assert.h>
16
17   #include "gpio_io.c"            /* GPIO routines */
18   #include "timed_wait.c"         /* timed_wait() */
19
```

```
20   /*
21    * GPIO definitions :
22    */
23   static const int g_enable      = 17;              /* L298 EnA and EnB */
24   static const int g_in1            = 27;           /* L298 In1 */
25   static const int g_in2            = 22;           /* L298 In2 */
26   static const int g_in3            = 23;           /* L298 In3 */
27   static const int g_in4            = 24;           /* L298 In4 */
28
29   static volatile int stepper_mode = 0;             /* Stepper mode - 1 */
30   static volatile float step_time = 0.1;            /* Step time in seconds */
31
32   static volatile char cmd = 0;                     /* Thread command when nonzero */
33   static volatile char stop = 0;                    /* Stop thead when nonzero */
34   static volatile char stopped = 0;                 /* True when thread has stopped */
35
36   static pthread_mutex_t mutex;                     /* For inter-thread locks */
37   static pthread_cond_t cond;                       /* For inter-thread signaling */
38
39   /*
40    * Await so many fractional seconds
41    */
42   static void
43   await(float seconds) {
44           long sec, usec;
45
46           sec = floor(seconds);                     /* Seconds to wait */
47           usec = floor((seconds-sec)*1000000);      /* Microseconds */
48           timed_wait(sec, usec, 0);                 /* Wait */
49   }
50
51   /*
52    * Enable/Disable drive to the motor
53    */
54   static inline void
55   enable(int enable) {
56           gpio_write(g_enable, enable);
57   }
58
59   /*
60    * Drive the appropriate GPIO outputs :
61    */
62   static void
63   drive(int L1L2) {
64           gpio_write(g_in1, L1L2&0x08);
65           gpio_write(g_in2, L1L2&0x04);
66           gpio_write(g_in3, L1L2&0x02);
67           gpio_write(g_in4, L1L2&0x01);
68   }
69
```

```
70   /*
71    * Take one step in a direction :
72    */
73   static void
74   step(int direction) {
75           static const int modes[3][8] = {
76                   { 0b1000, 0b0010, 0b0100, 0b0001 },         /* Mode 1 */
77                   { 0b1010, 0b0110, 0b0101, 0b1001 },         /* Mode 2 */
78                   { 0b1000, 0b1010, 0b0010, 0b0110, 0b0100, 0b0101, 0b0001, 0b1001 }
79           } ;
80           static int stepno = 0;                              /* Last step no. */
81           int m = stepper_mode < 2 ? 4 : 8;                   /* Max steps for mode */
82
83           if ( direction < 0 )
84                   direction = m - 1;
85
86           enable(0);                                          /* Disable motor */
87           drive(modes[stepper_mode][stepno]);                 /* Change fields */
88           enable(1);                                          /* Drive motor */
89
90           stepno = (stepno+direction) % m;                    /* Next step */
91   }
92
93   /*
94    * Set the stepper mode of operation :
95    */
96   static inline void
97   set_mode(int mode) {
98           enable(0);
99           stepper_mode = mode;
100  }
101
102  /*
103   * Take a command off the input queue
104   */
105  static char
106  get_cmd(void) {
107          char c;
108
109          pthread_mutex_lock(&mutex);
110
111          while ( !cmd )
112                  pthread_cond_wait(&cond,&mutex);
113
114          c = cmd;
115          cmd = stop = 0;
116          pthread_mutex_unlock(&mutex);
117          pthread_cond_signal (&cond);                        /* Signal that cmd is taken */
118
119          return c;
120  }
121
```

```
122 /*
123  * Stepper controller thread :
124  */
125 static void *
126 controller(void * ignored) {
127         int command;
128         int direction;
129
130         for ( stopped = 1; ; ) {
131                 command = get_cmd();
132                 direction = command == 'F' ? 1 : -1;
133
134                 for ( stopped = 0; !stop; ) {
135                         step(direction);
136                         await(step_time);
137                 }
138                 stopped = 1;
139         }
140         return 0;
141 }
142
143 /*
144  * Queue up a command for the controller thread :
145  */
146 static void
147 queue_cmd( char new_cmd) {
148
149         pthread_mutex_lock(&mutex);          /* Gain exclusive access */
150
151         /* Wait until controller grabs and zeros cmd */
152         while ( cmd )
153                 pthread_cond_wait(&cond ,&mutex);
154
155         cmd = new_cmd ;                      /* Deposit new command */
156
157         pthread_mutex_unlock(&mutex );       /* Unlock */
158         pthread_cond_signal(&cond);          /* Signal that cmd is there */
159 }
160
161 /*
162  * Stop the current operation :
163  */
164 static void
165 stop_cmd(void) {
166         for ( stop = 1; !stopped; stop = 1 )
167                 await(0.100);
168 }
169
170 /*
171  * Provide usage info :
172  */
```

```
173 static void
174 help(void) {
175         puts("Enter :\n"
176            "  1 - One phase mode\n"
177            "  2 - Two phase mode\n"
178            "  3 - Half step mode\n"
179            "  R - Toggle Reverse (counter-clockwise)\n"
180            "  F - Toggle Forward (clockwise)\n"
181            "  S - Stop motor\n"
182            "  + - Step forward\n"
183            "  - - Step backwards\n"
184            "  > - Faster step times \n"
185            "  < - Slower step times \n"
186            "  ? - Help\n"
187            "  Q - Quit\n " ) ;
188 }
189
190 /*
191  * Main program
192  */
193 int
194 main(int argc,char **argv) {
195         pthread_t tid;                              /* Thread id */
196         int tty = 0;                                /* Use stdin */
197         struct termios sv_ios, ios;
198         int rc, quit;
199         char ch, lcmd = 0;
200
201         rc = tcgetattr (tty,&sv_ios);               /* Save current settings */
202         assert(!rc);
203         ios = sv_ios;
204         cfmakeraw(&ios);                            /* Make into a raw config */
205         ios.c_oflag = OPOST | ONLCR;                /* Keep output editing */
206         rc = tcsetattr(tty,TCSAFLUSH,&ios);         /* Put terminal into raw mode */
207         assert(!rc);
208
209         /*
210          * Initialize and configure GPIO pins :
211          */
212         gpio_init();
213         gpio_config(g_enable,Output);
214         gpio_config(g_in1,Output);
215         gpio_config(g_in2,Output);
216         gpio_config(g_in3,Output);
217         gpio_config(g_in4, Output);
218
219         enable(0);                                  /* Turn off output */
220         set_mode(0);                                /* Default is one phase mode */
221
222         help();
223
```

```
224          pthread_mutex_init(&mutex,0);              /* Mutex for inter-thread locking */
225          pthread_cond_init(&cond,0);                /* For inter-thread signaling */
226          pthread_create(&tid,0,controller,0);       /* The thread itself */
227
228          /*
229           * Process single-character commands :
230           */
231          for ( quit=0; !quit; ) {
232                  /*
233                   * Prompt and read input char :
234                   */
235                  write(1,": ",2);
236                  rc = read(tty,&ch,1);
237                  if ( rc != 1 )
238                          break;
239                  if ( islower (ch) )
240                          ch = toupper(ch);
241
242                  write(1,&ch,1);
243                  write(1,"\n",1);
244
245                  /*
246                   * Process command char :
247                   */
248                  switch ( ch ) {
249                  case '1' :                          /* One phase mode */
250                          stop_cmd();
251                          set_mode(0);
252                          break;
253                  case '2' :                          /* Two phase mode */
254                          stop_cmd();
255                          set_mode(1);
256                          break;
257                  case '3' :                          /* Half step mode */
258                          stop_cmd();
259                          set_mode(2);
260                          break;
261                  case '<' :                          /* Make steps slower */
262                          step_time *= 2.0;
263                          printf("Step time is now %.3f ms\n",step_time *1000.0);
264                          break;
265                  case '>' :                          /* Make steps faster */
266                          step_time /=2.0;
267                          printf("Step time is now %.3f ms\n",step_time *1000.0);
268                          break;
269                  case 'F' :                          /* Forward : run motor */
270                          if ( !stopped && lcmd != 'R' ) {
271                                  stop_cmd();         /* Stop due to toggle */
272                                  lcmd = 0;
```

```
273                            } else  {
274                                    stop_cmd();        /* Stop prior to change direction */
275                                    queue_cmd(lcmd='F');
276                            }
277                    break;
278            case 'R' :                        /* Reverse : run motor */
279                    if ( !stopped && lcmd != 'F' ) {
280                            stop_cmd();
281                            lcmd = 0;
282                    } else  {
283                            stop_cmd();
284                            queue_cmd(lcmd='R');
285                    }
286                    break ;
287            case 'S' :                        /* Just stop */
288                    stop_cmd();
289                    break;
290            case '+' :                        /* Step clockwise */
291            case '=' :                        /* So we don't have to shift for + */
292                    stop_cmd();
293                    step(1);
294                    break;
295            case '-' :                        /* Step counterclockwise */
296                    stop_cmd();
297                    step(-1);
298                    break;
299            case 'Q' :                        /* Quit */
300                    quit = 1;
301                    break;
302            default :                        /* Unsupported */
303                    stop_cmd();
304                    help();
305            }
306        }
307
308        stop_cmd();
309        enable(0);
310
311        puts("\nExit.");
312
313        tcsetattr(tty,TCSAFLUSH,&sv_ios);        /* Restore terminal mode */
314        return 0;
315 }
316
317 /* End bipolar.c */
```

CHAPTER 29

■ ■ ■

Remote-Control Panel

Because of the Raspberry Pi's small size and low cost, it is an attractive platform for remote-sensing applications. A remote station might need to sense control panel switches or push button events. This electronic problem sounds simple until you discover that switches and buttons suffer from *contact bounce*.

The remaining challenge resides on the software side. When your sensing stations are *remote,* some kind of local software console needs to exist. In fact, your console may monitor several remote Raspberry Pis. Then add redundant consoles, or consoles in multiple locations. Each of these has the ability to monitor *and* control the same remote devices. It doesn't take long before the problem becomes complex.

This chapter's project aims to solve two problems:

- Debouncing a switch or push button (hardware)

- Controlling remote consoles (software)

Let's first examine the contact bounce problem.

Switched Inputs

One of the aggravations of dealing with push buttons and switches in an electronic computing environment is that contacts *bounce*. When you close a switch or push a button, the contacts can bounce a thousand times before they settle and produce a stable contact. A modern computer might see thousands of on/off transitions before the contacts stabilize.

This is not only a nuisance for software design, but also wasteful of the CPU. Each time the signal from the switch changes state, the CPU must be interrupted to make note of this event and pass the information on to the interested software (for example, GPIO change events). The software must then apply algorithms to smooth out these pulses and arrive at a conclusion when the switch is fully on, or fully off. This is all very ugly and messy!

The same problem happens in reverse when contacts release. Thousands of pulses are delivered to the CPU as the contacts slowly release and alternate between being in contact and being disconnected.

There are several ways to reduce or eliminate the problem. One approach is to apply a flip-flop ahead of the GPIO pins, as shown in Figure 29-1. One end of a SPDT switch is wired to the flip-flop reset input, while the other is wired to the set input. In this manner, a single pulse on either end changes the flip-flop state and keeps it stable.

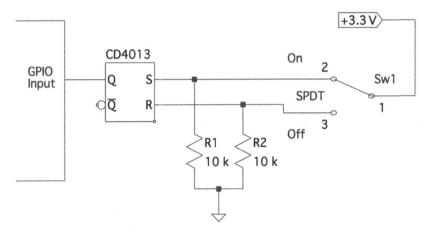

Figure 29-1. *Using a flip-flop for debouncing*

When the switch is releasing one contact, there is no change in the flip-flop output. After the arm has flown through its switching arc, the opposite contact eventually starts to bounce at the end of its swing. At this point, it takes only a single pulse to change the output of the flip-flop to its new state. After that, it remains constant.

The pull-down resistors R_1 and R_2 are necessary because the CMOS inputs would otherwise float when the switch arm disconnects from the switch's contacts. While disconnected, the resistors pull the input voltage down to ground potential.

The CD4013

The CD4013 is a CMOS part that is able to operate from +3 V and up. The pinout for the CD4013 is provided in Figure 29-2. The supply voltage V_{DD} is applied to pin 14, with pin 7 (V_{SS}) performing as the ground return. From the pinout diagram, you can see that this is a dual flip-flop IC, with pins labeled for units 1 and 2.

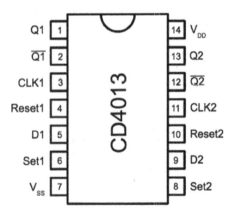

Figure 29-2. *The CD4013 pinout*

The datasheet for this part from various manufacturers shows the V_{IL} and V_{IH} levels when V_{DD} = +5 V (and higher). The values shown for V_{OH} for each V_{DD} are all listed at a value of V_{DD} – 0.5 V. Extrapolating from that, I have assumed V_{OH} = 3.3 – 0.5 = 2.8 V in the following table. The V_{OL} is listed as 0.05 V for all V_{DD} values listed, so we'll assume the same for 3.3 V.

The following table compares the Raspberry Pi GPIO logic levels with those of the CD4013 chip operating at +3.3 V.

Raspberry Pi, GPIO		CD4013, V_{DD} = +3.3 V	
Parameter	Volts	Volts	Parameter
V_{IL}	$\leq 0.8\ V$	$\leq 0.05\ V$	V_{OL}
V_{IH}	$\geq 1.3\ V$	$\geq 2.8\ V$†	V_{OH}

†Derived from a National Semiconductor datasheet

From Figure 29-1, recall that we are using the flip-flop output Q to drive a GPIO input. The flip-flop's V_{OL} is much lower than the maximum value for V_{IL}, so that works well. Additionally, from the table, notice that the V_{OH} level of the CD4013 output is well above the minimum required for V_{IH} for the GPIO input as well. From this signal comparison, we can conclude that the CD4013 part should play very nice with the Pi when powered from 3.3 V.

▨ **Caution**   Unused CMOS *inputs* should not be left unconnected. If an unused input has no contribution to your design, ground it. If you must have the input in a high state, wire it directly to the +3.3 V supply. No limiting resistor is required, since a CMOS input draws no current. Likewise, do not omit R_1 and R_2, shown in Figure 29-1. Unused CMOS *outputs*, however, can be left unconnected.

Unused CMOS inputs should not be left to float. In the presented flip-flop circuit, the following unused pins will be grounded:

Pin	Function	Wired to	Notes
3	Clock 1	Ground	Not used
5	Data 1	Ground	Not used
8	Set 2	Ground	If FF2 not used
9	Data 2	Ground	Not used
10	Reset 2	Ground	If FF2 not used
11	Clock 2	Ground	Not used

If the second flip-flop is used, simply ground unused pins 9 and 11. Otherwise, unused pins 8 and 10 should also be grounded. With two flip-flops in the CD4013, you could debounce two switches/buttons.

Testing the Flip-Flop

After wiring up the CD4013 circuit, you can do a preliminary test before hooking it up to your Pi. Simply apply +3.3 V to the circuit and measure the voltage on pin 1 (Q_1). When you throw the switch from one position to the next, the output of Q_1 should follow.

Hooked up to the Pi, you can test the circuit with the evinput program developed in Chapter 12. You can choose any suitable GPIO input, or one that you configured for input. Consult Chapter 12 for a list of GPIOs that boot up in input mode. I chose to use GPIO 22 (GEN3):

```
$ ./evinput 22
Monitoring for GPIO input changes :

GPIO 22 changed :   0
GPIO 22 changed :   1
GPIO 22 changed :   0
GPIO 22 changed :   1
GPIO 22 changed :   0
^C
$
```

Here the switch was initially off (Q_1 reads low). Then I threw the switch on, and then off, on, and then off again. Notice that there are no intervening glitches or other contact bounce events.

If you have a microswitch available with SPDT contacts, you can wire it as a push button. Push it on, release it, push it on again, and release again. The Raspberry Pi will read nice clean events without any contact bounce. That's how we like it on the software side!

The LED

Figure 29-3 shows the wiring for the LED. The resistor R_1 was chosen to provide a red LED, about 8 mA. If you're using a lower-powered LED, you can increase the resistance of R_1. Students may want to review Chapter 12 for the procedure on how to calculate the resistance for R_1.

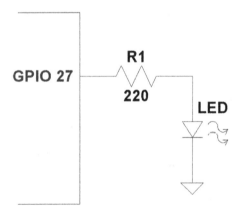

Figure 29-3. *Sensor LED hookup*

ØMQ

Some open source projects are just too good not to use. ØMQ is one of them. It exists to solve a difficult problem close to our hearts. Using this library, we can have each Raspberry Pi act as a *publisher* of information for the multiple software consoles acting as *subscribers*.

To allow multiple consoles to control each Pi sensing station, each sensing station also becomes a *subscriber* to the console *publishers*. In effect, we have many-to-many communication in a tidy software API, thanks to ØMQ.

■ **Note**   For interesting reading, a nice overview of ØMQ is available here: `http://zguide.zeromq.org/page:all`.

Performing Installation

The download and installation of ØMQ is almost painless for the Raspberry Pi. Simply allow some time for the compile, which might take a while (step 3):

1.   wget `http://download.zeromq.org/zeromq-3.2.2.tar.gz`

2.   `./configure -prefix=/usr/local`

3.   `make`

4.   `make check` (optional)

5.   `make install`

If you also want C++ support for ØMQ, you can perform the following additional steps (we'll use only the C API in this chapter):

1.   git clone `https://github.com/zeromq/cppzmq.git`

2.   `cd cppzmq`

3.   `sudo cp zmq.hpp /usr/local/include/`

Compiling and Linking

When compiling source code using ØMQ, you need to specify only the directory where the include files were installed:

- `-I /usr/local/include`

For linking, you need the following linker options:

- `-L/usr/local/lib -lzmq`

- `-Wl,-R/usr/local/lib`

The last option tells the executable where to find the ØMQ shared libraries at runtime. Exclude that option when linking on the Mac (or use the provided makefile `target mac_console`).

```
$ make
gcc -c -Wall -O0 -g -I/usr/local/include -Wall -O0 -g sensor.c -o sensor.o
gcc sensor.o -o sensor -L/usr/local/lib -lzmq -lncurses -Wl, -R/usr/local/lib
sudo chown root ./sensor
sudo chmod u+s ./sensor
gcc -c -Wall -O0 -g -I/usr/local/include -Wall -O0 -g console.c -o console.o
gcc -console.o -o console -L/usr/local/lib -lzmq -lncurses -Wl, -R/usr/local/lib
```

Sensing Station Design

Our Raspberry Pi sensing station will use the CD4013 flip-flop circuit to debounce one switch or SPDT push button. The Pi station will also consist of one LED that will be controlled by the multiple software consoles.

If you need to imagine some kind of use case, imagine that the Raspberry Pi is controlling a jail cell door. The guard who wants to open a door pushes a microswitch button to show SW1=On on the remote consoles (as a request indication). After the monitoring agents check their video monitor, one of them agrees to honor the request by entering 1 on the console (which lights the LED) to open the jail cell door. Pressing 0 closes the latch again (turns off the LED).

The great thing about using ØMQ for networking is that you can do the following:

- Run ./sensor with no consoles running

- Run any number of ./console (or ./mac_console) programs without the sensor running yet

- Run as many consoles as you like

- Bring down consoles anytime you like

With a little homework and extra effort, you could monitor multiple sensors as well. That was avoided here, to keep the example as simple as possible.

Sensing Station Program

The sensing station (Raspberry Pi) is started as follows:

```
$ ./sensor
```

The station runs quietly until terminated (it can be shut down from a console).

While it runs, it periodically broadcasts (publishes) updates to the consoles with the current status of SW_1 and LED. This is necessary because a console may be offline when the last switch or LED change occurs.

Whenever SW_1 changes, a broadcast is immediately sent with its new status sw1:%d, where %d is a 1 when the switch is on, and otherwise, a 0.

The LED is changed only at the command of the console program. When the sensor program receives a console message of the form led:%d (over the network), the LED is turned on or off, according to the value of %d (1 or 0). Once the LED is changed, however, it is rebroadcasted to all consoles, so that the other consoles can see that this has changed.

Finally, if the console sends stop: to the sensor, the sensor program shuts down and exits. Pressing ^C in its terminal session will also terminate it.

Console Program

The console program should be compilable for any Linux or Mac OS X platform. If you use the downloaded makefile, use the target mac_console when building it on Mac OS X:

```
$ make mac_console
```

For the Raspberry Pi or any other Linux distribution, you can build the program simply as follows:

```
$ make
```

You'll need the ncurses development library installed, in addition to ØMQ:

```
# apt-get install libncurses5-dev
```

To run the console program, simply launch it with the optional hostname as the first command-line argument (the default is localhost):

```
$ ./console 192.145.200.14      # Raspberry Pi by IP no.
```

Mac users will use the following:

```
$ ./mac_console myrasp      # Raspberry Pi by hostname
```

Figure 29-4 shows the appearance of the console when it first starts up. The ??? show that the console does not yet know the status of the switch or LED. Beside the command-line input, it also shows Online?, indicating that it does not yet know whether the sensor is online. As soon as one message is received, that changes to ONLINE.

```
Receiving sensor at: tcp://localhost:9999

   SW1: ???

   LED: ???

Commands: ▊   Online?

0 - Turn remote LED off.
1 - Turn remote LED on.
X - Shutdown sensor node.
Q - Quit the console.
```

Figure 29-4. *Console at startup*

Console Commands

The console commands are all single-character commands and are displayed on the screen. Typing 0 turns off the LED on the sensor, and typing 1 turns it on. Typing q or Q quits the console.

Typing x or X terminates the sensor program. (It would not be good to have this option on a real jail cell control.)

Sensor Source Code

Every attempt was made to keep these listings short. But despite these attempts, the code is a bit "winded" for this simple-minded task. The important thing here is the basic concept and how to leverage it in your own more sophisticated designs.

Except for the use of pthreads and ØMQ, not much is new in the source code. Consequently, I'll just provide some highlights.

The sensor.c main program gets everything started, by opening the GPIO files (input and output), opening the ØMQ sockets, and creating two threads. The main thread is contained within the main program, within the for loop starting at line 298. The loop simply pulls console commands from the ØMQ socket console at line 299 and then acts upon them.

There are only two supported console commands:

led:%d: Change LED status

stop:: Shut down the ./sensor program

Line 286 of the main program creates the SW1_monitor_thread. This thread is located in lines 211 to 223. It uses the poll(2) system call in the routine gpio_poll(), to determine when the switch setting changes. This GPIO input is coming from Q_1 of the flip-flop, which is connected to either a switch or a microswitch push-button.

Program execution blocks at line 216, until the switch changes state. Then the status of the switch is captured in rc and relayed to all interested consoles by calling the routine publish_SW1().

The remaining thread is launched in the main program from line 289. It runs in lines 228 through 237. It is a very small loop, which simply updates the consoles every 3 seconds, with the current status of the LED and SW_1. This is necessary so that consoles that are restarted can eventually know the current state of these items.

The mutex_lock() and mutex_unlock() routines are designed to guard against two threads using the same ØMQ resources at the same time. Doing so would cause program aborts.

The ØMQ library supports a routine named zmq_poll(), which would have simplified things if it could have been used. Unfortunately, it supports only ZMQ_POLLIN for input. Our switch change driver requires the use of poll(2)'s POLLPRI event, so zmq_poll() will not support us there.

```
1      /*********************************************************************
2       * sensor.c - Sense SW1, send to console (and take LED cmd from console)
3       *********************************************************************/
4
5      #include <stdio.h>
6      #include <stdlib.h>
7      #include <unistd.h>
8      #include <string.h>
9      #include <fcntl.h>
10     #include <assert.h>
11     #include <poll.h>
12     #include <pthread.h>
13
14     #include <zmq.h>
15
16     static const char *service_sensor_pub =  "tcp ://*:9999";
17     static const char *service_sensor_pull = "tcp ://*:9998";
18
19     static void *context = 0;                    /* ZMQ context */
20     static void *publisher = 0;                  /* Publishing socket */
21     static void *console = 0;                    /* Pull socket */
22
23     static int SW1 = 0;                          /* Switchstatus */
24     static int LED = 0;                          /* LED status */
25     static int stop = 0;                         /* Nonzero when shutting down */
26
27     static int gp_SW1 = 22;                      /* GPIO 22 (input) */
28     static int gp_LED = 27;                      /* GPIO 22 (output) */
29     static int fd_SW1 = -1;                      /* Open fd for SW1 */
30
31     #include "mutex.c"
32
```

```
33    /*
34     * Publish the LED setting to the console(s)
35     */
36    static void
37    publish_LED(void) {
38              char buf [256];
39              size_tn;
40              int rc;
41
42        n = sprintf(buf,"led:%d",LED);
43        mutex_lock();
44        rc = zmq_send(publisher,buf,n,0);
45        assert(rc!=-1);
46        mutex_unlock();
47    }
48
49    /*
50     * Publish the switch setting to the console(s)
51     */
52    static void
53    publish_SW1(void) {
54        char buf[256];
55        size_t n;
56        int rc;
57
58        n = sprintf(buf,"sw1:%d",SW1);
59
60        mutex_lock();
61        rc = zmq_send(publisher,buf,n,0);
62        assert(rc!=-1);
63        mutex_unlock();
64    }
65
66    typedef enum {
67              gp_export = 0,        /* /sys/class/gpio/export */
68              gp_unexport,          /* /sys/class/gpio/unexport */
69              gp_direction,         /* /sys/class/gpio%d/direction */
70              gp_edge,              /* /sys/class/gpio%d/edge */
71              gp_value              /* /sys/class/gpio%d/value */
72    } gpio_path_t;
73
74    /*
75     * Internal : Create a pathname for type in buf.
76     */
77    static const char *
78    gpio_setpath(int pin,gpio_path_t type,char *buf,unsigned bufsiz) {
79        static const char *paths [] = {
80              "export", "unexport", "gpio%d/ direction",
81              "gpio%d/edge", "gpio%d/value" };
82        intslen;
83
```

```
84      strncpy(buf,"/sys/class/gpio/",bufsiz);
85      bufsiz -= (slen == strlen(buf));
86      snprintf(buf+slen,bufsiz,paths[type],pin);
87      return buf;
88  }
89
90  /*
91   * Open/sys/class/gpio%d/value for edge detection :
92   */
93  static int
94  gpio_open_edge(int pin,const char *edge) {
95      char buf[128];
96      FILE *f;
97      int fd;
98
99      /* Export pin : /sys/class/gpio/export */
100     gpio_setpath(pin,gp_export,buf,sizeof buf);
101     f = fopen(buf,"w");
102     assert(f);
103     fprintf(f,"%d\n",pin);
104     fclose(f);
105
106     /* Direction : /sys/class/gpio%d/direction */
107     gpio_setpath(pin,gp_direction,buf,sizeof buf);
108     f = fopen(buf,"w");
109     assert(f);
110     fprintf(f,"in\n");
111     fclose(f);
112
113     /* Edge : /sys/class/gpio%d/edge */
114     gpio_setpath(pin, gp_edge,buf,sizeof buf);
115     f = fopen(buf,"w");
116     assert(f);
117     fprintf(f,"%s\n",edge);
118     fclose(f);
119
120     /* Value : /sys/class/gpio%d/value */
121     gpio_setpath(pin,gp_value,buf,sizeof buf);
122     fd = open(buf,O_RDWR);
123     return fd;
124 }
125
126 /*
127  * Open/sys/class/gpio%d/value for output :
128  */
129 static int
130 gpio_open_output(int pin) {
131     char buf[128];
132     FILE *f;
133     int fd;
134
```

```
135        /* Export pin : /sys/class/gpio/export */
136        gpio_setpath(pin,gp_export,buf,sizeof buf);
137        f = fopen(buf,"w");
138        assert(f);
139        fprintf(f,"%d\n",pin);
140        fclose(f);
141
142        /* Direction : /sys/class/gpio%d/direction */
143        gpio_setpath(pin,gp_direction,buf,sizeof buf);
144        f = fopen(buf,"w");
145        assert(f);
146        fprintf(f,"out\n");
147        fclose(f);
148
149        /* Value : /sys/class/gpio%d/value */
150        gpio_setpath(pin,gp_value,buf,sizeof buf);
151        fd = open(buf,O_WRONLY);
152        return fd;
153    }
154
155    /*
156     * Close (unexport) GPIO pin :
157     */
158    static void
159    gpio_close(int pin) {
160        char buf [128];
161        FILE *f ;
162
163        /* Unexport : /sys/class/gpio/unexport */
164        gpio_setpath(pin,gp_unexport,buf,sizeof buf);
165        f = fopen(buf,"w");
166        assert(f);
167        fprintf(f,"%d\n",pin);
168        fclose(f);
169    }
170
171    /*
172     * This routine will block until the open GPIO pin has changed
173     * value.
174     */
175    static int
176    gpio_poll(int fd) {
177        struct poll fd_polls;
178        char buf[32];
179        int rc, n;
180
181        polls.fd = fd;              /* /sys/class/gpio17/value */
182        polls.events = POLLPRI;     /* Exceptions */
183
```

```
184      do  {
185            rc = poll (&polls,1, -1);          /* Block */
186      } while ( rc < 0 && errno == EINTR );
187
188      assert(rc > 0);
189
190      lseek(fd,0,SEEK_SET);
191      n = read(fd,buf,sizeof buf);             /* Read value */
192      assert(n>0);
193      buf[n] = 0;
194
195      rc = sscanf(buf,"%d",&n);
196      assert(rc==1);
197      return;                                  /* Return value */
198  }
199
200  /*
201   * Write to the GPIO pin
202   */
203  static void
204  gpio_write(int fd,int dbit) {
205      write(fd,dbit ? "1\n" : "0\n",2);
206  }
207
208  /*
209   * Monitor switch changes on GPIO
210   */
211  static void *
212  SW1_monitor_thread(void *arg) {
213      int rc;
214
215      while ( !stop ) {
216          rc = gpio_poll(fd_SW1);              /* Watch for SW1 changes */
217          if ( rc < 0 )
218              break;
219          SW1 = rc;
220          publish_SW1();
221      }
222      return 0;
223  }
224
225  /*
226   * Periodic broadcast to consoles thread
227   */
228  static void *
229  console_thread(void *arg) {
230
231      while ( !stop ) {
232          sleep(3);
233          publish_SW1();
```

```
234            publish_LED();
235        }
236        return 0;
237    }
238
239    /*****************************************************************
240     * Main thread : read switch changes and publish to console (s)
241     *****************************************************************/
242    int
243    main(int argc,char **argv) {
244        pthread_t tid;
245        int rc = 0;
246        char buf[256];
247        int fd_LED = -1;                    /* GPIO 27 */
248
249        mutex_init();
250
251        /* Open GPIO for LED */
252        fd_LED = gpio_open_output(gp_LED);
253        if ( fd_LED < 0 ) {
254            printf("%s : Opening GPIO %d for output.\n",
255                strerror (errno),gp_LED);
256            return 1;
257        }
258
259        /* Open GPIO for SW1 */
260        fd_SW1 = gpio_open_edge(22,"both");    /* GPIO input */
261        if ( fd_SW1 < 0 ) {
262            printf("%s: Opening GPIO %d for input.\n",
263                strerror(errno),gp_SW1);
264            return 1;
265        }
266
267        context = zmq_ctx_new();
268        assert(context);
269
270        /* Create a ZMQ publishing socket */
271        publisher = zmq_socket(context,ZMQ_PUB);
272        assert(publisher);
273        rc = zmq_bind(publisher,service_sensor_pub);
274        assert(!rc);
275
276        /* Create a console PULL socket */
277        console = zmq_socket(context, ZMQ_PULL);
278        assert(console);
279        rc = zmq_bind(console,service_sensor_pull);
280        assert(rc != -1);
281
282        SW1 = 0;
283        publish_SW1();
284        publish_LED();
285
```

```
286        rc = pthread_create(&tid,0,SW1_monitor_thread,0);
287        assert(!rc);
288
289        rc = pthread_create(&tid,0,console_thread,0);
290        assert(!rc);
291
292        /*
293         * In this thread, we "pull" console commands :
294         *
295         * led:n change state of LED
296         * stop: shutdown the sensor
297         */
298        for (;;) {
299            rc = zmq_recv(console,buf,sizeof buf -1,0);
300            if ( rc > 0 ) {
301                buf[rc] = 0;
302                if ( !strncmp(buf,"led:",4) ) {
303                    /* LED command from console */
304                    buf[rc] = 0;
305                    sscanf(buf,"led:%d",&LED);
306                    gpio_write(fd_LED,LED);
307                    publish_LED();
308                }
309                if ( !strncmp(buf,"stop:",5) ) {
310                    stop = 1;
311                    break;
312                }
313            }
314        }
315
316        mutex_lock();
317        zmq_close(console);
318        console = 0;
319
320        rc = zmq_send(publisher,"off: " 4,0);
321        assert(rc !=-1);
322        sleep(3);
323        zmq_close(publisher);
324        publisher = 0;
325
326        gpio_close(gp_SW1);
327        gpio_close(gp_LED);
328        mutex_unlock();
329
330        return 0;
331    }
332
333    /* End sensor.c */
```

Console Source Code

The console program is an ncurses-based program. It provides the user with a full-screen display without the complexity of programming a GUI program (an exercise left to the interested reader).

The main program initiates curses mode in lines 204 through 207. Prior to that, the ØMQ library is used to subscribe to the sensor's published data in lines 184 through 196. Notice that when subscribing, you *must* indicate what subscriptions you want. Not setting any ZMQ_SUBSCRIBE options will result in no messages being received.

Lines 198 to 202 initiate a push connection to the sensor, so commands may be delivered from the console to the sensor. Note that all running consoles will also establish this connection. Any console can control the sensor.

The main console loop from lines 226 through 243 receives the subscribed messages and displays them on the console. That's all it does.

The command_center thread is shown in lines 112 to 161. It simply reads a keystroke in line 125 and then dispatches the command in line 132.

The ncurses library is not thread safe, so mutex locking is used to prevent more than one thread from attempting to use that library simultaneously.

```
1    /************************************************
2     * console.c - Raspberry Pi Sensor Console
3     ************************************************/
4
5    #include <stdio.h>
6    #include <stdlib.h>
7    #include <unistd.h>
8    #include <string.h>
9    #include <assert.h>
10   #include <pthread.h>
11   #include <curses.h>
12
13   #include <zmq.h>
14
15   #include "mutex.c"
16
17   static char*host_name = "local host";      /* Default host name */
18   static char service_sensor_pub[128];       /* Service name for sensor */
19   static char service_sensor_pull[128];      /* Service name for sensor's cmds */
20
21   static void *context = 0;                   /* ZMQ context object */
22   static void *subscriber = 0;                /* Subscriber socket */
23   static void *console = 0;                   /* Push socket */
24
25   static int SW1 = -1;                        /* Known status of SW1 */
26   static int LED = -1;                        /* Known status of LED */
27
28   /*
29    * Post the status of SW1 to the console screen
30    */
```

```
31  static void
32  post_SW1(void) {
33
34      mutex_lock();                           /* Lock for shared curses access */
35      attrset(A_REVERSE);
36      mvprintw(3,4,"SW1:");
37      attrset(A_NORMAL);
38      move (3,9);
39      if ( SW1 < 0 ) {
40          addstr("???");
41      } else {
42          if ( SW1 ) {
43              attrset(A_BOLD);                /* Blink when switch on */
44              addstr("On ");
45          } else {
46              attrset(A_NORMAL);
47              addstr("Off");                  /* SW1 is off */
48          }
49      }
50      attrset(A_NORMAL);
51      if ( SW1 >=0 || LED >=0 )
52          mvprintw(7,15,"ONLINE ");
53      move(7,12);
54      refresh();
55      mutex_unlock();                         /* Done with curses */
56  }
57
58   /*
59    * Post LED status to console screen
60    */
61  static void
62  post_LED(void) {
63
64      mutex_lock();                           /* Lock shared curses access */
65      attrset(A_REVERSE);
66      mvprintw(5,4,"LED:");
67      attrset(A_NORMAL);
68      move(5,9);
69
70      if ( LED < 0 ) {
71          addstr("???");
72      } else {
73          if ( LED ) {
74              attrset(A_BOLD);
75              addstr("On ");                  /* LED is now on */
76          } else {
77              attrset(A_NORMAL);
78              addstr("Off");/* LED is now off */
79          }
80      }
81
```

416

```
82      attrset(A_NORMAL);
83      if ( SW1 >=0 || LED >=0 )
84          mvprintw(7,15,"ONLINE ");
85      move(7, 12);
86      refresh();
87      mutex_unlock();                     /* Release hold on cur ses */
88  }
89
90  /*
91   * Post online status to screen
92   */
93  static void
94  post_offline(void) {
95
96      SW1 = -1;
97      LED = -1;
98
99      mutex_lock();                       /* Lock for shared curses access */
100     attrset(A_REVERSE|A_BLINK);
101     mvprintw(7,15,"OFFLINE");
102     refresh();
103     mutex_unlock();                     /* Done with curses */
104
105     post_LED();
106     post_SW1();
107 }
108
109 /*
110  * Main console thread for command center
111  */
112 static void *
113 command_center(void *ignored) {
114     int rc;
115
116     post_LED();                         /* Post unknown LED status */
117     post_SW1();                         /* Post unknown SW1 status */
118
119     for (;;) {
120         mutex_lock();                   /* Lock curses */
121         move (7,12);                    /* Move cursor to command point */
122         refresh();
123         mutex_unlock();                 /* Release curses*/
124
125         rc = getch();                   /* Wait for keystroke */
126
127         mutex_lock();                   /* Lock curses */
128         mvaddch(7,12,rc);               /* Echo character that was typed */
129         refresh();
130         mutex_unlock();                 /* Release curses */
131
```

```
132            switch ( rc ) {
133            case '0' :
134                /* Tell sensor to turn off LED */
135                rc = zmq_send(console,"led : 0",5,0);
136                assert(rc !=-1);
137                break;
138            case '1' :
139                /* Tell sensor to turn on LED */
140                rc = zmq_send(console,"led: 1",5,0);
141                assert(rc!=-1);
142                break ;
143            case'x' :
144            case'X' :
145                rc = zmq_send(console,"stop :",5,0);
146                assert(rc!=-1);
147                break;
148            case 'q' :
149            case 'Q' :
150                /* Quit the command console */
151                sleep(1);
152                clear();
153                refresh();
154                endwin();
155                exit(0);
156                break;
157            default :
158                ;
159            }
160        }
161 }
162
163 /*
164  * Main thread : init/receive published SW1/LED status updates
165  *
166  * Specify the IP number or hostname of the sensor on the command
167  * line as argument one : $ ./console myrasp
168  */
169 int
170 main(int argc,char **argv) {
171     char buf[1024];
172     int rc;
173     pthread_t tid;
174
175     if ( argc > 1 )
176         host_name = argv[1];
177     sprintf(service_sensor_pub,"tcp://%s:9999",host_name);
178     sprintf(service_sensor_pull,"tcp://%s:9998",host_name);
179
180     mutex_init();
181     context = zmq_ctx_new();
182     assert(context);
183
```

```
184        subscriber = zmq_socket(context,ZMQ_SUB);
185        assert(subscriber);
186
187        rc = zmq_connect(subscriber,service_sensor_pub);
188        if (rc == -1) perror("zmq_connect\n");
189        assert(rc!=-1);
190
191        rc = zmq_setsockopt(subscriber,ZMQ_SUBSCRIBE,"sw1:", 4);
192        assert(rc!=-1);
193        rc = zmq_setsockopt(subscriber,ZMQ_SUBSCRIBE,"led:", 4);
194        assert(rc!=-1);
195        rc = zmq_setsockopt(subscriber,ZMQ_SUBSCRIBE, "off:",4);
196        assert(rc!=-1);
197
198        console = zmq_socket(context,ZMQ_PUSH);
199        assert(console);
200
201        rc = zmq_connect(console, service_sensor_pull);
202        assert(!rc);
203
204        initscr();
205        cbreak();
206        noecho();
207        nonl();
208
209        clear();
210        box(stdscr,0,0);
211        move(1,2);
212        printw("Receiving sensor at: %s",service_sensor_pub);
213
214        attrset(A_UNDERLINE);
215        mvaddstr(7,2,"Commands:");
216        attrset(A_NORMAL);
217        mvaddstr(9,2,"0 - Turn remote LED off.");
218        mvaddstr(10,2,"1 - Turn remote LED on.");
219        mvaddstr(11,2,"X - Shutdown sensor node.");
220        mvaddstr(12,2,"Q - Quit the console.");
221        mvprintw(7,15,"Online ?");
222
223        rc = pthread_create(&tid,0,command_center,0);
224        assert(!rc);
225
226        for(;;) {
227            rc = zmq_recv(subscriber,buf,sizeof buf - 1,0);
228            assert(rc >=0 && rc < sizeof buf -1);
229            buf[rc] = 0;
230
231            if ( !strncmp(buf,"off:",4) )
232                post_offline();
233
```

```
234          if ( !strncmp(buf,"sw1:",4) ) {
235              sscanf(buf,"sw1:%d",&SW1);
236              post_SW1();
237          }
238
239          if ( !strncmp(buf,"led:",4) ) {
240              sscanf(buf,"led:%d",&LED);
241              post_LED();
242          }
243      }
244
245      return 0;
246  }
247
248  /* console.c */
```

```
1   /*****************************************
2    * Mutex . c
3    *****************************************/
4
5   static pthread_mutex_t mutex;
6
7   static void
8   mutex_init(void) {
9       int rc = pthread_mutex_init(&mutex, 0);
10      assert(!rc);
11  }
12
13  static void
14  mutex_lock(void) {
15      intrc = pthread_mutex_lock(&mutex);
16      assert(!rc);
17  }
18
19  static void
20  mutex_unlock(void) {
21      int rc = pthread_mutex_unlock(&mutex);
22      assert(!rc);
23  }
24
25  /* End mutex.c */
```

■ ■ ■

## CHAPTER 30

Pulse-Width Modulation

This chapter explores pulse-width modulation (PWM) using the Raspberry Pi. PWM is applied in motor control, light dimming, and servo controls, to name a few examples. To keep the hardware simple and the software small enough to read, we're going to apply PWM to driving an analog meter in this chapter.

While the CPU percent-busy calculation used here is a bit cheesy, it is simple and effective for our demonstration. The meter deflection will indicate how busy your Raspberry Pi's CPU is. We'll demonstrate this using a hardware and software PWM solution.

Introduction to PWM

The GPIO output signal is a digital signal that may be only on or off. You can program it to deliver only 3 V or 0 V. Consequently, there is no means for the software to ask the GPIO to deliver 1 or 2 V. Despite this limitation, an analog meter can be driven from a digital output using PWM.

PWM is a technique that works on the principle of averaging the signal. If the signal is on for 10% of the total cycle, then when the signal is averaged out, the result is an analog 10% of the two digital extremes. If the highest voltage produced by the GPIO output is 3.3 V, a repeating digital signal that is only on for 75% of that cycle produces an average voltage that's determined as follows:

$$V_{avg} = 3.3 \times 0.75$$
$$= 2.475\,V$$

If the GPIO output signal was high only 10% of the time, the averaged result is $V_{avg} = 0.33$ V. The on time as a percentage of the total cycle time is known as the *duty cycle*.

Obviously, there is an averaging aspect to all of this. If you applied the 10% signal to the probes of an oscilloscope, you'd see a choppy digital-looking signal. The duty cycle may be there, but the averaging effect is not.

The averaging effect is accomplished in several ways. In a lightbulb, the element is heated up by the on pulses but does not cool immediately, so its brightness reflects the averaged current flow. A DC motor does not immediately stop when the current is withdrawn, because the rotational inertia keeps the rotor spinning. A meter's pointer does not immediately move back to zero when the current is removed. All of these physical effects have an averaging effect that can be exploited.

PWM Parameters

PWM involves modulating the width of the pulse. But the pulse's width is one aspect relative to a whole cycle. Defining a PWM signal requires three parameters:

- Frequency (or period) of the cycle
- The time period that the signal is on
- The time period that the signal is off

It is tempting to think that the cycle time is unimportant. But consider a cycle lasting 10 seconds, where the signal is on for 1 second and off for the remaining 9 (10%). Apply that signal to a meter, and the needle will show 100% for 1 second and zero for the remaining time. Clearly the cycle is too long for the meter's movement to average out.

If you produce a software-derived PWM signal, a high-frequency rate will average well on the meter movement. But the amount of CPU effort expended is also needlessly high, wasting computing power. Planning the operating frequency is an important aspect of PWM. Hardware PWM peripherals also have design frequency limits that must be considered.

The remaining two parameters form the *duty* in *duty cycle*, and are often expressed as a fraction:

$$\frac{N}{M}$$

The denominator M = 100 when we talk of percentages. However, M may be any integer that divides the complete cycle into equal units of time. The value N defines the number of units that the PWM device is to be *on*. The remaining M − N step represents the *off* time.

PWM Hardware Peripheral

The Raspberry Pi makes one hardware PWM peripheral available to the user. It is available on GPIO 18 (GEN1), but you must give up one of the audio channels to use it (or both, if you consider that the clock is also reconfigured for PWM clock rates). If your application does not use audio, the peripheral makes a great resource for effortlessly delivering fast and relatively clean pulse waveforms. And all this without having your software even "think" about it. If you don't need to change the duty cycle, you can set up the peripheral and let it run free on its own.

PWM Software

The servo folks would be wringing their hands at the thought of only one PWM signal. Fortunately, the Pi is quite capable of generating more PWM signals if you can accept a little jitter in the signal output and a little CPU overhead (about 6% of the CPU for each thread-driven PWM signal, in nonturbo mode). While separate processes could be used to generate multiple PWM signals, this is best accomplished in one process using threads. The softpwm program at the end of this chapter demonstrates this.

Meter Circuit

Figure 30-1 shows the circuit used for this chapter's CPU percent meter. The resistor R1 = 3.3 kΩ when you use a 1 mA meter movement.

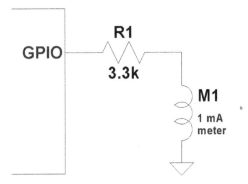

Figure 30-1. *PWM-driven meter*

If you know the current-handling capability for the meter you would like to use, you can calculate the resistance needed as follows:

$$R_1 = \frac{V}{I_m}$$

where:

- V is the voltage (3.3 V) at the GPIO pin.

- I_m is the current for your meter movement.

If your meter is known to use a 100 µA movement, for example, the series-dropping resistor would work out to be the following:

$$R_1 = \frac{3.3}{0.0001}$$
$$= 33 \ k\Omega$$

For all projects in this book, I encourage you to substitute and try parts that you have on hand. You may have a junk-box meter somewhere that you can use. Don't use automotive ammeters, since they will usually have a shunt installed. Almost any voltmeter or meter with a sufficiently sensitive movement can be used. The limit is imposed by the GPIO output pin, which supports up to 8 mA (unless reconfigured).

If you don't know its movement sensitivity, start with high resistances and work down (try lowest currents first). With care, you can sort this out without wrapping the needle around the pin.

pwm Program

The program software pwm is listed at the end of this chapter. To facilitate discussion, I'll show excerpts of it here. The hardware example driven by pwm.c is the nastier of the two programs presented. This is due to the difficulty of programming the PWM hardware registers and the clock-rate registers.

The main program invokes pwm_init(), which gains access to the Pi's peripherals in much the same way that the other examples did in gpio_init(). The same mmap() techniques are used for access to the PWM and CLK control registers.

Whether operating pwm to just set the PWM peripheral or to use the CPU percent-busy function, the PWM frequency must be set by the function pwm_frequency():

```
static int
pwm_frequency(float freq) {
...
```

This function stops the clock that is running and computes a new integer divisor. After disabling the clock, a little sleep time is used to allow the clock peripheral to stop. The maximum clock rate appears to be 19.2 MHz. To compute the divisor, the following calculation is used:

$$I_{div} = \frac{19200000}{f}$$

where:

- I_{div} is the computed integer divisor.

- f is the desired PWM frequency.

The range of the resulting I_{div} is checked against the peripheral's limits. The value of I_{div} is then forced to remain in range, but the return value is -1 or +1 depending on whether the frequency is under or over the limits.

```
idiv = (long)( clock_rate / (double) freq );
if ( idiv < 1 ) {
    idiv = 1;                    /* Lowest divisor */
    rc = -1;
} else if ( idiv >=0x1000 ) {
    idiv = 0xFFF;                /* Highest divisor */
    rc = +1;
}
```

Once that is calculated, the value of I_{div} is loaded:

```
ugclk[PWMCLK_DIV] = 0x5A000000 | ( idiv << 12 );
```

Finally, the clock source is set to use the oscillator, and the clock is enabled:

```
ugclk[PWMCLK_CNTL] = 0x5A000011;
```

After this, GPIO 18 is configured for ALT function 5, to gain access to the PWM peripheral:

```
INP_GPIO(18);                    /* Set ALT = 0 */
SET_GPIO_ALT(18,5);              /* Or in '5' */
```

The way the SET_GPIO_ALT() macro is defined requires that the INP_GPIO() macro be used first. The INP_GPIO() macro clears the ALT function bits so that SET_GPIO_ALT() can *or* in the new bits (the value 5, in this case).

The remaining steps ready the PWM peripheral:

```
pwm_ctl->MODE1 = 0;              /* PWM mode */
pwm_ctl->RPTL1 = 0;
pwm_ctl->SBIT1 = 0;
pwm_ctl->POLA1 = 0;
pwm_ctl->USEF1 = 0;
pwm_ctl->MSEN1 = 0;              /* PWM mode */
pwm_ctl->CLRF1 = 1;
```

Now, at this point, the PWM peripheral is almost ready to go. It needs the ratio $\frac{N}{M}$ and then to be enabled. This is done in the routine pwm_ratio():

```
static void
pwm_ratio(unsigned n,unsigned m) {
...
```

This function allows the $\frac{N}{M}$ ratio be changed without having to fully reinitialize the other aspects, including the clock. With our CPU percent-busy function, this ratio will be changing often.

```
pwm_ctl->PWEN1 = 0;              /* Disable */

*pwm_rng1 = m;
*pwm_dat1 = n;
```

After initialization, the PWM peripheral is already disabled. But the first step here disables it, because it may be running when the ratio is being changed. The following pair of statements put the value of M into the PWM register RNG1, while N goes into the DAT1 register.

A few more statements check for errors and reset if necessary (these may not be strictly necessary). Then the following two statements provide a short pause and re-enable the PWM peripheral:

```
usleep(10);             /* Pause  */
pwm_ctl->PWEN1 = 1;     /* Enable */
```

That covers the interesting aspects of the hardware PWM control.

Hardware PWM Set Command

When program pwm is provided with command-line arguments, it simply sets up and starts the PWM peripheral. The command takes up to three arguments:

```
$ ./pwm N [M] [ F ]
```

where:

- N is the N in the PWM ratio.

- M is the M in the PWM ratio.

- F is the frequency required.

Once the command is started with these parameters, the PWM peripheral is started and the program exits:

```
$ . /pwm 40 100 1000
PWM set for 40/100, frequency 1000.0
$
```

If you have an oscilloscope available, you can attach probes to GPIO 18 and the ground to see a 40% PWM signal. If you attach the meter circuit of Figure 30-1, it should read near 40% of the full deflection. Figure 30-2 shows my milliampere meter showing nearly 40% (the deflection reading is nearly 0.4). The DMM in the background is measuring the +3.3 V supply voltage, which is showing good voltage regulation.

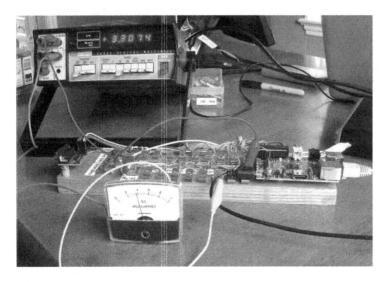

Figure 30-2. *A milliampere meter showing 40% deflection*

To get a more accurate reading, you could put a potentiometer or Trimpot in series with a lower-valued resistor and adjust for full deflection (with GPIO set to high).

Alternatively, you could take a voltage reading of the GPIO output when set to high and calculate the 1% resistor value needed. At the time I took the photo for Figure 30-2, I measured 3.275 V when the GPIO was set high while supplying current to the milliampere meter (through a 3.3 kΩ 10% resistor). Using that for the basis for calculations, you could use a 3.24 kΩ 1% resistor.

Hardware Based CPU Percent-Busy Display

The same pwm command can be used as a CPU percent-busy command when started with no command-line arguments:

```
$ ./pwm
CPU Meter Mode:
1.4%
```

The percent of CPU that is busy will be repeatedly shown on the same console line. Simultaneously, the hardware PWM ratio is being changed. This will cause the meter deflection to indicate the current CPU percent-busy reading. The pwm command itself requires about 0.6% CPU, so you will never see the meter reach zero.

The CPU percent is determined in a cheesy manner, but it is simple and good enough for this demonstration.

```
for (;;) {
    pipe = popen("ps -eo pcpu|sed 1d","r");
    for ( total=0.0; fgets(buf,sizeof buf,pipe); ) {
        sscanf(buf,"%f",&pct);
        total += pct;
    }
    pclose(pipe);
    printf("\r%.1f%%    ",total);
    fflush(stdout);
    pwm_ratio(total,100);
    usleep(300000);
}
```

In this section of code, we open a piped command to ps, with options to report the percent of CPU used by each process. The sed command deletes the header line from the ps command output.

The for loop reads each line, totaling the percent of CPU used. Occasionally, the total exceeds 100% because of timing and other roughness in the calculations.

Once the CPU percent total is known, the function pwm_ratio() is called to alter the ratio, thus changing the position of the meter's indicator.

```
1    /*********************************************************
2     * pwm. c - PWM example program
3     *********************************************************/
4
5    #include <stdio.h>
6    #include <stdlib.h>
7    #include <unistd.h>
8    #include <fcntl.h>
9    #include <sys/mman.h>
10   #include <errno . h>
11   #include <string . h>
12
13   #define BCM2835_PWM_CONTROL 0
14   #define BCM2835_PWM_STATUS  1
15   #define BCM2835_PWM0_RANGE  4
16   #define BCM2835_PWM0_DATA   5
17
18   #define BCM2708_PERI_BASE      0x20000000
19   #define BLOCK_SIZE             (4*1024)
20
21   #define GPIO_BASE              (BCM2708_PERI_BASE + 0x200000)
22   #define PWM_BASE               (BCM2708_PERI_BASE + 0x20C000)
23   #define CLK_BASE               (BCM2708_PERI_BASE + 0x101000)
24
25   #define PWMCLK_CNTL 40
26   #define PWMCLK_DIV  41
27
28   static volatile unsigned *ugpio = 0;
29   static volatile unsigned *ugpwm = 0;
30   static volatile unsigned *ugclk = 0;
31
32   statics struct S_PWM_CTL {
33           unsigned      PWEN1 : 1;
34           unsigned      MODE1 : 1;
35           unsigned      RPTL1 : 1;
36           unsigned      SBIT1 : 1;
37           unsigned      POLA1 : 1;
38           unsigned      USEF1 : 1;
39           unsigned      CLRF1 : 1;
40           unsigned      MSEN1 : 1;
41   } volatile *pwm_ctl = 0;
42
```

```
43 static struct S_PWM_STA {
44          unsigned      FULL1 : 1;
45          unsigned      EMPT1 : 1;
46          unsigned      WERR1 : 1;
47          unsigned      RERR1 : 1;
48          unsigned      GAP01 : 1;
49          unsigned      GAP02 : 1;
50          unsigned      GAP03 : 1;
51          unsigned      GAP04 : 1;
52          unsigned      BERR : 1;
53          unsigned      STA1 : 1;
54 } volatile *pwm_sta = 0;
55
56 static volatile unsigned *pwm_rng1 = 0;
57 static volatile unsigned *pwm_dat1 = 0;
58
59 #define INP_GPIO(g) *( ugpio+((g )/10)) &= ~(7<<(((g)%10)*3))
60 #define SET_GPIO_ALT(g,a) \
61     *(ugpio+(((g)/10))) |= (((a)<=3?(a)+4:((a)==4?3:2))<<(((g)%10)*3))
62
63 /*
64  * Establish the PWM frequency :
65  */
66 static int
67 pwm_frequency(float freq) {
68     const double clock_rate = 19200000.0;
69     long idiv;
70     int rc = 0;
71
72     /*
73      * Kill the clock :
74      */
75     ugclk[PWMCLK_CNTL] = 0x5A000020;               /* Kill clock */
76     pwm_ctl->PWEN1 = 0;                            /* Disable PWM */
77     usleep(10);
78
79     /*
80      * Compute and set the divisor:
81      */
82     idiv = (long)( clock_rate / (double)freq );
83     if ( idiv < 1 ) {
84         idiv = 1;                                 /* Lowest divisor */
85         rc = -1;
86     } else if ( idiv >=0x1000 ) {
87         idiv = 0xFFF;                             /* Highest divisor */
88         rc = +1;
89     }
90
91     ugclk[PWMCLK_DIV] = 0x5A000000 | ( idiv << 12 );
92
```

```
93      /*
94       * Set source to oscillator and enable clock :
95       */
96      ugclk[PWMCLK_CNTL] = 0x5A000011;
97
98      /*
99       * GPIO 18 is PWM, when set to Alt Func 5 :
100      */
101     INP_GPIO(18);                       /* Set ALT = 0 */
102     SET_GPIO_ALT(18,5);                 /* Or in '5 ' */
103
104     pwm_ctl->MODE1 = 0;                 /* PWM mode */
105     pwm_ctl->RPTL1 = 0;
106     pwm_ctl->SBIT1 = 0;
107     pwm_ctl->POLA1 = 0;
108     pwm_ctl->USEF1 = 0;
109     pwm_ctl->MSEN1 = 0;                 /* PWM mode */
110     pwm_ctl->CLRF1 = 1;
111     return rc ;
112 }
113
114 /*
115  * Initialize GPIO/PWM/CLK Access
116  */
117 static void
118 pwm_init() {
119     int fd;
120     char *map;
121
122     fd = open("/dev/mem",O_RDWR|O_SYNC);   /* Needs root access */
123     if ( fd < 0 ) {
124         perror("Opening /dev/mem");
125         exit(1);
126     }
127
128     map = (char *)mmap(
129         NULL,                           /* Any address */
130         BLOCK_SIZE,                     /* # of bytes */
131         PROT_READ|PROT_WRITE,
132         MAP_SHARED,                     /* Shared */
133         fd,                             /* /dev/mem */
134         PWM_BASE                        /* Offset to GPIO */
135     );
136
137     if ( (long)map == -1L ) {
138         perror("mmap(/dev/mem)");
139         exit(1);
140     }
141
142     /* Access to PWM */
143     ugpwm = (volatile unsigned *)map;
144     pwm_ctl = (struct S_PWM_CTL *) &ugpwm[BCM2835_PWM_CONTROL];
```

```
145      pwm_sta = (struct S_PWM_STA *) &ugpwm[BCM2835_PWM_STATUS];
146      pwm_rng1 = &ugpwm[BCM2835_PWM0_RANGE];
147      pwm_dat1 = &ugpwm[BCM2835_PWM0_DATA];
148
149      map = (char *)mmap(
150          NULL,                           /* Any address */
151          BLOCK_SIZE,                     /* # of bytes */
152          PROT_READ|PROT_WRITE,
153          MAP_SHARED,                     /* Shared */
154          fd,                             /* /dev/mem */
155          CLK_BASE                        /* Offset to GPIO */
156      );
157
158      if ( (long )map == -1L ) {
159          perror("mmap(/dev/mem)");
160          exit(1);
161      }
162
163      /* Access to CLK */
164      ugclk = (volatile unsigned *)map;
165
166      map = (char *)mmap(
167          NULL,                           /* Any address */
168          BLOCK_SIZE,                     /* # of bytes */
169          PROT_READ|PROT_WRITE,
170          MAP_SHARED,                     /* Shared */
171          fd,                             /* /dev/mem */
172          GPIO_BASE                       /* Offset to GPIO */
173      );
174
175      if ( (long)map == -1L ) {
176          perror("mmap(/dev/mem)");
177          exit(1);
178          }
179
180      /* Access to GPIO */
181      ugpio = (volatile unsigned *)map;
182
183      close(fd);
184  }
185
186  /*
187   * Set PWM to ratio N/M, and enable it :
188   */
189  static void
190  pwm_ratio(unsigned n,unsigned m) {
191
192      pwm_ctl->PWEN1 = 0;                  /* Disable */
193
194      *pwm_rng1 = m;
195      *pwm_dat1 = n;
196
```

```
197     if ( !pwm_sta->STA1 ) {
198         if ( pwm_sta->RERR1 )
199             pwm_sta->RERR1 = 1;
200             if ( pwm_sta->WERR1 )
201                 pwm_sta->WERR1 = 1;
202                 if ( pwm_sta->BERR )
203                     pwm_sta->BERR = 1;
204     }
205
206     usleep(10);              /* Pause */
207     pwm_ctl->PWEN1 = 1;      /* Enable */
208 }
209
210 /*
211  * Main program :
212  */
213 int
214 main(int argc,char **argv) {
215     FILE *pipe;
216     char buf[64];
217     float pct, total;
218     int n, m = 100;
219     float f = 1000.0;
220
221     if ( argc > 1 )
222         n = atoi(argv[1]);
223     if ( argc > 2 )
224         m = atoi(argv[2]);
225     if ( argc > 3 )
226         f = atof(argv[3]);
227     if ( argc > 1 ) {
228         if ( n > m || n < 1 || m < 1 || f < 586.0 || f > 19200000.0 ) {
229             fprintf(stderr,"Value error: N=%d , M=%d , F=%.1f \n",n,m,f);
230             return 1;
231         }
232     }
233
234     pwm_init();
235
236     if ( argc > 1 ) {
237         /* Start PWM */
238         pwm_frequency(f);
239         pwm_ratio(n,m);
240         printf("PWM set for %d/%d, frequency %.1f \n",n,m,f);
241     } else {
242         /* Run CPU Meter */
243         puts("CPU Meter Mode : ");
244         for (;;) {
245             pipe = popen("ps -eo pcpu | sed 1d","r");
```

```
246                 for ( total =0.0; fgets(buf,sizeof buf,pipe); ) {
247                     sscanf(buf,"%f",&pct);
248                     total += pct;
249                 }
250             pclose(pipe);
251             printf("\r%.1f%%",total);
252             fflush(stdout);
253             pwm_ratio(total,100);
254             usleep(300000);
255         }
256     }
257
258     return 0 ;
259 }
260
261 /* End pwm.c */
```

Software PWM Program

The program softpwm works from the command line very similarly to the hardware PWM program pwm. One difference, however, is that the software PWM requires that the program continue to run to maintain the signal. The hardware program can exit and leave the PWM peripheral running.

The design of the program differs in that a thread is used for each PWM signal being maintained. With a little bit of work, the softpwm.c module could be formed into a PWM software library. The data type PWM is created with the same idea as the stdio FILE type:

```
typedef struct {
        int             gpio;       /* GPIO output pin */
        double          freq;       /* Operating frequency */
        unsigned        n;          /* The N in N/M */
        unsigned        m;          /* The M in N/M */
        pthread _t       thread;     /* Controlling thread */
        volatile char   chgf;       /* True when N/M changed */
        volatile char   stopf;      /* True when thread to stop */
} PWM;
```

The comments identify the purpose of the structure object members. The last two members are flags that are used to control the thread.

The function pwm_open(), establishes the GPIO line and the PWM frequency, and returns the PWM control block. Note that no thread is started just yet:

```
PWM *
pwm_open(int gpio,double freq) {
    PWM *pwm = malloc(sizeof *pwm);

    pwm->gpio = gpio;
    pwm->freq = freq;
    pwm->thread = 0;
    pwm->n = pwm->m = 0;
    pwm->chgf  = 0;
    pwm->stopf = 0;
```

```
        INP_GPIO(pwm->gpio);
        OUT_GPIO(pwm->gpio);
        return pwm;
}
```

The reverse of open is the pwm_close() call. Here the thread is instructed to stop (stopf=1), and if there is a thread running, a join with the thread is performed. The join causes the caller to block until the thread itself has ended. Then the PWM structure is freed, completing the close operation.

```
void
pwm_close(PWM *pwm) {
        pwm->stopf = 1;
        if ( pwm->thread )
                pthread_join(pwm->thread,0);
        pwm->thread = 0;
        free(pwm);
}
```

The software PWM signal starts when the ratio is established by a call to pwm_ratio():

```
void
pwm_ratio(PWM *pwm,unsigned n,unsigned m) {
        pwm->n = n <= m ? n : m;
        pwm->m = m;
        if ( !pwm->thread )
                pthread_create(&pwm->thread,0,soft_pwm,pwm);
else
        pwm->chgf = 1;
}
```

This call establishes the values for N and M. Then if no thread is currently running, one is created with the thread's ID saved in the PWM structure. If the thread is already running, we simply point out to the thread that the $\frac{N}{M}$ values have changed so that it can adapt to it at the cycle's end.

The function soft_pwm() is the software PWM engine itself. The pthread_create() call passes the PWM structure into the call as a void *arg, which is used by the function to access the PWM structure. The entire procedure is an outer and inner loop. The outer loop runs as long as the stopf flag is zero. Then the floating-point period variables fperiod, percent, and ontime are calculated.

From there, the inner loop continues until either the chgf or stopf flag variables become nonzero. If the stopf becomes nonzero, both loops are exited. Once the thread function exits, the thread ends. The thread resources are reclaimed in the pwm_close() call when it joins.

```
static void *
soft_pw(void *arg) {
        PWM *pwm = (PWM *)arg;
        double fperiod, percent, ontime;

        while ( !pwm->stopf ) {
                fperiod = 1.0 / pwm->freq;
                percent = (double) pwm->n / (double)pwm->m;
                ontime = fperiod * percent;
```

```
            for ( pwm->chgf=0; !pwm->chgf && !pwm->stopf; ) {
                gpio_write(pwm->gpio,1);
                float_wait(ontime);

                gpio_write(pwm->gpio,0);
                float_wait(fperiod-ontime);
        }
    }

    return 0;
}
```

One final note about the PWM structure members concerns the use of the C keyword volatile. Both chgf and stopf structure members are declared volatile so that the compiler will generate code that will access these values every time they are required. Otherwise, compiler optimization may cause the generated code to reuse values held in registers. This would cause the thread to not notice a change in these values, which are critical.

```
volatile char       chgf;       /* True when N/M changed */
volatile char       stopf;      /* True when thread to stop */
```

How Many PWMs?

The design of the preceding PWM software routines is such that you can open as many PWM instances as you require. The limiting factors are as follows:

- Number of free GPIO output lines
- CPU resource utilization

On a nonturbo mode Raspberry Pi, the code shown seems to require approximately 6% CPU for each soft PWM created. (The CPU utilization rises with frequency, however.) This leaves you with a certain latitude in the number of PWM signals you generate.

Running the Software PWM Command

To generate a fixed software PWM signal on GPIO 22 (GEN3), run the command like this:

```
$ ./ softpwm 60 100 2000
PWM set for 60 / 100 , frequency 2000.0 (for 60 seconds )
```

Obviously, the PWM signal is present for only as long as the softpwm program continues to run.

Software Based CPU Percent-Busy Display

Without command-line arguments, the softpwm command defaults to being a CPU percent-busy driver. It drives pin GPIO 22 (GEN3), which when attached to a meter as shown in Figure 30-1, will display CPU utilization.

```
$  ./softpwm
CPU  Meter  Mode :
6.5%
```

Press ^C after the fascination of the CPU meter wears off.

```
1  /*********************************************************
2   * softpwm.c Software PWM example program
3   *********************************************************/
4
5  #include <stdio.h>
6  #include <stdlib.h>
7  #include <unistd.h>
8  #include <fcntl.h>
9  #include <sys/mman.h>
10 #include <errno.h>
11 #include <string.h>
12 #include <math.h>
13 #include <pthread.h>
14
15 #include "gpio_io.c"
16
17 typedef struct {
18         int        gpio;        /* GPIO out put pin */
19         double     freq;        /* Operating frequency */
20         unsigned   n;           /* The N in N/M */
21         unsigned   m;           /* The M in N/M */
22         pthread_t  thread;      /* Controlling thread */
23         volatile char   chgf;   /* True when N/M changed */
24         volatile char   stopf;  /* True when thread to stop */
25 } PWM;
26
27 /*
28  * Timed wait from a float
29  */
30 static void
31 float_wait(double seconds) {
32     fd_set mt ;
33     struct timeval time out;
34     int rc;
35
36     FD_ZERO(&mt);
37     timeout.tv_sec = floor(seconds);
38     timeout.tv_usec = floor((seconds - floor(seconds)) * 1000000);
39
40     do {
41         rc = select(0,&mt,&mt,&mt,&timeout);
42     } while ( rc < 0 && time out.tv_sec && timeout.tv_usec );
43 }
44
45 /*
46  * Thread performing the PWM function :
47  */
```

```
48 static void *
49 soft_pwm(void *arg) {
50     PWM *pwm = (PWM *)arg;
51     double fperiod, percent, ontime;
52
53     while ( !pwm >stopf ) {
54         fperiod = 1.0 / pwm->freq;
55         percent = (double ) pwm->n / (double) pwm->m;
56         ontime = fperiod * percent ;
57         for ( pwm->chgf =0; !pwm->chgf && !pwm->stopf; ) {
58             gpio_write (pwm->gpio,1);
59             float_wait(ontime);
60
61             gpio_write(pwm->gpio,0);
62             float_wait(fperiod ontime);
63         }
64     }
65
66     return 0;
67 }
68
69 /*
70  * Open a soft PWM object:
71  */
72 PWM *
73 pwm_open(int gpio,double freq) {
74     PWM *pwm = malloc(sizeof **pwm);
75
76     pwm->gpio = gpio;
77     pwm->freq = freq;
78     pwm->thread = 0;
79     pwm->n = pwm->m = 0;
80     pwm->chgf = 0;
81     pwm->stopf = 0;
82
83     INP_GPIO(pwm->gpio);
84     OUT_GPIO(pwm->gpio);
85     return pwm;
86 }
87
88 /*
89  * Close the soft PWM object:
90  */
91 void
92 pwm_close(PWM *pwm) {
93     pwm->stopf = 1;
94     if ( pwm->thread )
95         pthread_join(pwm->thread,0);
96         pwm->thread = 0;
97         free(pwm);
98 }
99
```

```
100  /*
101   * Set PWM Ratio:
102   */
103  void
104  pwm_ratio(PWM *pwm,unsigned n,unsigned m) {
105      pwm->n = n <= m ? n : m;
106      pwm->m = m;
107      if ( !pwm->thread )
108          pthread_create(&pwm->thread,0,soft_pwm,pwm);
109      else pwm->chgf = 1;
110  }
111
112  /*
113   * Main program:
114   */
115  int
116  main(int argc,char **argv) {
117      int n, m = 100;
118      float f = 1000.0;
119      PWM *pwm;
120      FILE *pipe;
121      char buf[64];
122      float pct, total;
123
124      if ( argc > 1 )
125          n = atoi(argv[1]);
126      if ( argc > 2 )
127          m = atoi(argv[2]);
128      if ( argc > 3 )
129          f = atof(argv[3]);
130      if ( argc > 1 ) {
131          if ( n > m || n < 1 || m < 1 || f < 586.0 || f > 19200000.0 ) {
132              fprintf(stderr,"Value error: N=%d, M=%d, F=%.1f \n",n,m,f);
133              return 1;
134          }
135      }
136
137      gpio_init();
138
139      if ( argc > 1 ) {
140          /* Run PWM mode */
141          pwm = pwm_open(22,1000.0);          /* GPIO 22 (GEN3) */
142          pwm_ratio(pwm,n,m) ;                /* n% , Start it */
143
144          printf ("PWM set for %d/%d, frequency %.1f (for 60 seconds)\n",n,m,f);
145
146          sleep(60);
147
148          printf("Closing PWM..\n");
149          pwm_close(pwm);
```

```
150        } else {
151            /* Run CPU Meter */
152            puts("CPU Meter Mode: ");
153
154            pwm = pwm_open(22,500.0);        /* GPIO 22 (GEN3) */
155            pwm_ratio(pwm,1,100);           /* Start at 1% */
156
157            for (;;) {
158                pipe = popen("ps -eo pcpu | sed 1d","r");
159                for ( total = 0.0 ; fgets(buf,sizeof buf,pipe); ) {
160                    sscanf(buf,"%f ",&pct);
161                    total += pct;
162                }
163                pclose(pipe);
164
165                pwm_ratio(pwm,total,100);
166
167                printf("\r%.1f%%        ",total);
168                fflush (stdout) ;
169
170                usleep(300000);
171            }
172        }
173
174        return 0;
175  }
176
177  /* End softpwm.c */
```

APPENDIX A

Glossary

AC

   Alternating current

Amps

   Amperes

ATAG

   ARM tags, though now used by boot loaders for other architectures

AVC

   Advanced Video Coding (MPEG-4)

AVR

   Wikipedia states that "it is commonly accepted that AVR stands for Alf (Egil Bogen) and Vegard (Wollan)'s RISC processor."

BCD

   Binary-coded decimal

Brick

   To accidently render a device unusable by making changes to it

CEA

   Consumer Electronics Association

cond

   Condition variable

CPU

   Central processing unit

CRC

   Cyclic redundancy check, a type of hash for error detection

CVT

   Coordinated Video Timings standard (replaces GTF)

daemon

   A Unix process that services requests in the background

DC

   Direct current

DCD

RS-232 data carrier detect

DCE

RS-232 data communications equipment

Distro

A specific distribution of Linux software

DLNA

Digital Living Network Alliance, whose purpose is to enable sharing of digital media between multimedia devices

DMM

Digital multimeter

DMT

Display Monitor Timing standard

DPI

Display Pixel Interface (a parallel display interface)

DPVL

Digital Packet Video Link

DSI

Display Serial Interface

DSR

RS-232 data set ready

DTE

RS-232 data terminal equipment

DTR

RS-232 data terminal ready

ECC

Error-correcting code

EDID

Extended display identification data

EEPROM

Electrically erasable programmable read-only memory

EMMC

External mass media controller

Flash

Similar to EEPROM, except that large blocks must be entirely rewritten in an update operation

FFS

Flash file system

FIFO

First in, first out

FSP

Flash storage processor

FTL

Flash translation layer

FUSE

Filesystem in Userspace (File system in USerspace)

GNU

GNU is not Unix

GPIO

General-purpose input/output

GPU

Graphics processing unit

GTF

Generalized Timing Formula

H.264

MPEG-4 Advanced Video Coding (AVC)

H-Bridge

An electronic circuit configuration that allows voltage to be reversed across the load

HDMI

High-Definition Multimedia Interface

HID

Human interface device

I2C

Two-wire interface invented by Philips

IC

Integrated circuit

IDE

Integrated development environment

IR

Infrared

ISP

Image Sensor Pipeline

JFFS2

Journalling Flash File System 2

LCD

Liquid-crystal display

LED

Light-emitting diode

mA
    Milliamperes, a measure of current flow

MCU
    Microcontroller unit

MMC
    MultiMedia Card

MISO
    Master in, slave out

MOSI
    Master out, slave in

MTD
    Memory technology device

mutex
    Mutually exclusive

NTSC
    National Television System Committee (analog TV signal standard)

PAL
    Phase Alternating Line (analog TV signal standard)

PC
    Personal computer

PCB
    Printed circuit board

PLL
    Phase-locked loop

PoE
    Power over Ethernet (supplying power over an Ethernet cable)

POSIX
    Portable Operating System Interface (for Unix)

pthreads
    POSIX threads

PWM
    Pulse-width modulation

Pxe
    Preboot execution environment, usually referencing booting by network

RAM
    Random-access memory

RI
    RS-232 ring indicator

RISC

Reduced instruction set computer

RH

Relative humidity

ROM

Read-only memory

RPi

Raspberry Pi

RS-232

Recommended standard 232 (serial communications)

RTC

Real-time clock

SBC

Single-board computer

SD

Secure Digital Association memory card

SDIO

SD card input/output interface

SDRAM

Synchronous dynamic random-access memory

SoC

System on a chip

SMPS

Switched-mode power supply

SPI

Serial Peripheral Interface (bus)

Stick parity

Mark or space parity, where the bit is constant

TWI

Two-wire interface

UART

Universal asynchronous receiver/transmitter

USB

Universal Serial Bus

V3D

Video for 3D

VAC

Volts AC

VESA
Video Electronics Standards Association

VFS
Virtual file system

VNC
Virtual Network Computing

V_{SB}
ATX standby voltage

YAFFS
Yet Another Flash File System

APPENDIX B

Power Standards

The following table references the standard ATX power supply voltages, regulation (tolerance), and voltage ranges.[15]

The values listed here for the +5 V and +3.3 V supplies were referenced in Chapter 4 as a basis for acceptable power supply ranges. When the BroadCom power specifications become known, they should be used instead.

Supply (Volts)	Tolerance		Minimum	Maximum	Ripple (Peak to Peak)
+5 V	±5%	± 0.25 V	+4.75 V	+5.25 V	50 mV
-5 V	±10%	±0.50 V	−4.50 V	−5.50 V	50 mV
+12 V	±5%	±0.60 V	+11.40 V	+12.60 V	120 mV
-12 V	±10%	±1.2 V	−10.8 V	−13.2 V	120 mV
+3.3 V	±5%	±0.165 V	+3.135 V	+3.465 V	50 mV
+5 V_{SB}	±5%	±0.25 V	+4.75 V	+5.25 V	50 mV

APPENDIX C

Electronics Reference

The experienced electronic hobbyist or engineer will already know these formulas and units well. This reference material is provided as a convenience for the student or beginning hobbiest.

Ohm's Law

Using the following triangle, cover the unknown property to determine the formula needed. For example, if current (I) is unknown, cover the I, and the formula $\frac{V}{R}$ remains.

Power

Power can be computed from these formulas:

$$P = I \times V$$
$$P = I^2 \times R$$
$$P = \frac{V^2}{R}$$

Units

The following chart summarizes the main metric prefixes used in electronics.

	Name	Prefix	Factor
Multiples	mega	M	10^6
	kilo	k	10^3
Fraction	milli	m	10^{-3}
	micro	μ	10^{-6}
	nano	n	10^{-9}
	pico	p	10^{-12}

■ ■ ■

Raspbian apt Commands

This appendix highlights the usage of commonly used package management commands under Raspbian Linux.

List Available Packages

```
$ apt-cache pkgnames
tesseract-ocr-epo
pipenightdreams
openoffice.org-l10n-mn
mumudvb
tbb-examples
libsvm-java
libsalck3-dev
libboost-timer1.50-dev
snort-rules-default
freediams-doc-fr
...
```

List Installed Packages

```
$ dpkg -l
Desired=Unknown/Install/Remove/Purge/Hold
| Status=Not/Inst/Conf-files/Unpacked/halF-conf/Half-inst/trig-aWait/Trig-pend
|/ Err?=(none)/Reinst-required (Status,Err: uppercase=bad)
||/ Name           Version         Architecture  Description
+++ -============= -============== -============ -================================
ii  adduser        3.113+nmu3      all           add and remove users and groups
ii  alsa-base      1.0.25+2+nmu2   all           ALSA driver configuration files
ii  alsa-utils     1.0.25-3        armhf         Utilities for configuring and \
                                                 using ALSA
ii  apt            0.9.7.6+rpi1    armhf         commandline package manager
ii  apt-utils      0.9.7.6+rpi1    armhf         package managment related \
                                                 utility programs
```

List Files for Package

```
$dpkg -L apt
/.
/etc
/etc/cron.daily
/etc/cron.daily/apt
/etc/logrotate.d
/etc/logrotate.d/apt
/etc/apt
/etc/apt/apt.conf.d
/etc/apt/apt.conf.d/01autoremove
/etc/apt/preferences.d
...
```

Perform Package Search

```
$ apt-cache search gnuplot
...
devscripts - scripts to make the life of a Debian Package maintainer easier
gnuplot - Command -line driven interactive plotting program
gnuplot-doc - Command -line driven interactive plotting program. Doc-package
gnuplot-mode - Yet another Gnuplot mode for Emacs
gnuplot-nox - Command-line driven interactive plotting program. No-X package
gnuplot-qt - Command-line driven interactive plotting program. QT-package
gnuplot-x11 - Command-line driven interactive plotting program. X-package
libchart-gnuplot -perl - module for generating two - and three-dimensional plots
libgnuplot-ocaml -dev - OCaml interface to the gnuplot utility
libgnuplot-ruby - Transitional package for ruby-gnuplot
libgnuplot-ruby1 .8 - Transitional package for ruby-gnuplot
libgraphics-gnuplotif-perl - dynamic Perl interface to gnuplot
libploticus0 - script driven business graphics library
libploticus0-dev - Development files for the ploticus library
...
```

Install a Package

```
$ sudo apt-get install gnuplot-x11
Reading package lists...
Building dependency tree...
Reading state information...
The following extra packages will be installed:
libglu1-mesa liblua5.1-0 libwxbase2.8-0 libwxgtk2.8-0
Suggested packages:
gnuplot-doc libgnomeprintui2.2-0
The following NEW packages will be installed:
gnuplot-x11 libglu1-mesa liblua5.1-0 libwxbase2.8-0 libwxgtk2.8-0
```

```
0 upgraded, 5 newly installed, 0 to remove and 107 not upgraded.
Need to get 4,967 kB of archives.
After this operation, 12.4 MB of additional disk space will be used.
Do you want to continue [Y/n]? y
Get:1 http :// mirrordirector.raspbian.org/raspbian/ wheezy/main libglu1-mesa armhf 8.0.5-3 [152 kB]
Get:2 http :// mirrordirector.raspbian.org/raspbian/ wheezy/main liblua5.1-0 armhf 5.1.5-4 [145 kB]
Get:3 http :// mirrordirector.raspbian.org/raspbian/ wheezy/main libwxbase2.8-0 armhf 2.8.12.1-12
[599 kB]
Get:4 http :// mirrordirector.raspbian.org/raspbian/ wheezy/main libwxgtk2.8-0 armhf 2.8.12.1-12
[3 ,011 kB]
Get:5 http :// mirrordirector.raspbian.org/raspbian/ wheezy/main gnuplot-x11 armhf 4.6.0-8 [1 ,059 kB]
Fetched 4,967 kB in 12s (408 kB/s)
Selecting previously unselected package libglu1-mesa:armhf.
(Reading database ... 60788 files and directories currently installed .)

Unpacking libglu1 -mesa:armhf (from .../libglu1-mesa_8.0.5-3 _armhf.deb) ...
Selecting previously unselected package liblua5.1-0: armhf.
Unpacking liblua5.1-0: armhf (from .../liblua5.1-0_5.1.5-4 _armhf.deb) ...
Selecting previously unselected package libwxbase2.8-0: armhf.
Unpacking libwxbase2.8-0: armhf (from .../libwxbase2.8-0_2.8.12.1-12_armhf.deb) ...
Selecting previously unselected package libwxgtk2.8-0: armhf.
Unpacking libwxgtk2.8-0: armhf (from .../libwxgtk2.8-0_2.8.12.1-12_armhf.deb) ...
Selecting previously unselected package gnuplot-x11.
Unpacking gnuplot-x11 (from .../gnuplot-x11_4.6.0-8_armhf.deb) ...
Processing triggers for menu ...
Processing triggers for man-db ...
Setting up libglu1-mesa:armhf (8.0.5-3) ...
Setting up liblua5.1-0:armhf (5.1.5-4) ...
Setting up libwxbase2.8-0:armhf (2.8.12.1-12) ...
Setting up libwxgtk2.8-0:armhf (2.8.12.1-12) ...
Setting up gnuplot-x11 (4.6.0-8) ...
Processing triggers for menu ...
$
```

Remove a Package

```
# apt-get remove pkg_name
# apt-get purge pkg_name
```

Install Updates

```
# apt-get update
```

Upgrade

```
# apt-get upgrade
```

Obtain Kernel Sources

```
$ wget --no-check-certificate \
  -O raspberrypi-linux-3.6.11.tar.gz \
  http://github.com/raspberrypi/linux/tarball/rpi-3.6.y
```

APPENDIX E

ARM Compile Options

For ARM platform compiles, the following site makes compiler option recommendations: http://elinux.org/RPi_Software.

The site states the following:

- The gcc compiler flags that produce the most optimal code for the Raspberry Pi are as follows:

  - -Ofast -mfpu=vfp -mfloat -abi=hard -march=armv6zk -mtune=arm1176jzf-s

- For some programs, -Ofast may produce compile errors. In these cases, -O3 or -O2 should be used instead.

- -mcpu=arm1176jzf-s can be used in place of -march=armv6zk -mtune=arm1176jzf-s.

APPENDIX F

■ ■ ■

Mac OS X Tips

This appendix offers a couple of tips pertaining to Raspberry Pi SD card operations under Mac OS X. Figure F-1 shows an SD card reader and a built-in card slot being used.

Figure F-1. *USB card reader and MacBook Pro SD slot*

The one problem that gets in the way of working with Raspberry Pi images on SD cards is the automounting of partitions when the card is inserted. This, of course, can be disabled, but the desktop user will find this inconvenient. So you need a way to turn it off, when needed.

Another problem that occurs is determining the OS X device name for the card. When copying disk images, you need to be certain of the device name! Both of these problems are solved using the Mac diskutil command (found in /usr/sbin/diskutil).

■ **Caution**   Copying to the wrong device on your Mac can destroy all of your files. Be afraid!

Before inserting your SD cards, do the following:

```
$ diskutil list
/dev/disk0
#:        TYPE NAME                 SIZE           IDENTIFIER
0:        GUID_partition_scheme     750.2 GB       disk0
1:        EFI                       209.7 MB       disk0s1
2:        Apple_HFS Macintosh HD    749.3 GB       disk0s2
3:        Apple_Boot Recovery HD    650.0 MB       disk0s3
```

Check the mounts:

```
$ mount
/dev/disk0s2 on / (hfs, NFS exported, local, journaled)
...
```

Insert the SD card:

```
$ diskutil list
/dev/disk0
#:                    TYPE NAME        SIZE           IDENTIFIER
0:        GUID_partition_scheme        750.2 GB       disk0
1:                          EFI        209.7 MB       disk0s1
2:    Apple_HFS    Macintosh HD        749.3 GB       disk0s2
3:    Apple_Boot    Recovery HD        650.0 MB       disk0s3
          /dev/disk1
#:                    TYPE NAME        SIZE           IDENTIFIER
0:    FDisk_partition_scheme            3.9 GB        disk1
1:            Windows_FAT_32           58.7 MB        disk1s1
2:                    Linux            3.8 GB         disk1s2
```

Unmount any automounted partitions for disk1:

```
$ diskutil unmountDisk /dev/disk1
Unmount of all volumes on disk1 was successful
$
```

Likewise, insert the destination SD card and use diskutil to get its device name (mine was /dev/disk2). Unmount all file systems that may have been automounted for it (diskutil unmountDisk).

At this point, you can perform a file system image copy:

```
$ dd if=/dev/disk1 of=/dev/disk2 bs=1024k
3724+0 records in 3724+0 records out
3904897024 bytes transferred in 2571.524357 secs (1518515 bytes/sec)
$
```

Bibliography

1. "Byte (magazine)", From Wikipedia, the free encyclopedia.
   `< http://en.wikipedia.org/wiki/Byte_Magazine>`

2. "Moore's law", From Wikipedia, the free encyclopedia.
   `<http://en.wikipedia.org/wiki/Moore%27s_law>`

3. "EEPROM", From Wikipedia, the free encyclopedia.
   `<http://en.wikipedia.org/wiki/EEPROM>`

4. "Microcontroller", From Wikipedia, the free encyclopedia.
   `<http://en.wikipedia.org/wiki/Micro-controller>`

5. "Wiring", From Wikipedia, the free encyclopedia.
   `<en.wikipedia.org/wiki/Wiring_(development_platform)>`

6. "AVR Freaks Articles", AVR Freaks.
   `<http://www.avrfreaks.net/index.php?module=FreaksArticles&func=viewArticles>`

7. "Atmel AVR", From Wikipedia, the free encyclopedia.
   `<http://en.wikipedia.org/wiki/Atmel_AVR>`

8. "USB Boarduino (Arduino compatible) Kit w/ATmega328 - v2.0", Adafruit Industries,
   `<www.adafruit.com/products/91>`

9. "Raspberry Pi", From Wikipedia, the free encyclopedia.
   `<http://en.wikipedia.org/wiki/Raspberry_Pi>`

10. "Power supply confirmed as 5V micro-USB", Raspberry Pi.
    `<http://www.raspberrypi.org/archives/260>`

11. "Upcoming board revision", Upcoming board revision.
    `<http://www.raspberrypi.org/archives/1929>`

12. "Nine-Volt battery", Wikipedia, the free encyclopedia.
    `<http://en.wikipedia.org/wiki/Nine-volt_battery>`

13. "Introduction To The USB Power Form", USB As A Power Source.

     <http://www.girr.org/mac_stuff/usb_stuff.html>

14. "Model B revision 2.0 schematics", Model B revision 2.0 schematics.

     <http://www.raspberrypi.org/wp-content/uploads/2012/10/Raspberry-Pi-R2.0-
     Schematics-Issue2.2_027.pdf>

15. "Power Supply", ATX.

     <http://encyclopedia.thefreedictionary.com/ATX>

16. "Raspberry Pi", Raspberry Pi - Revision 2.0,

     <http://www.raspberrypi.org/wp-content/uploads/2012/10/Raspberry-Pi-R2.0-
     Schematics-Issue2.2_027.pdf>

17. "Broadcom: BCM2835 ARM Peripherals", www.farnell.com.

     <http://www.farnell.com/datasheets/1521578.pdf>

18. "Secure Digital" From Wikipedia, the free encyclopedia.

     <http://en.wikipedia.org/wiki/Secure_Digital>

19. "Chapter 3, SD Bus Topology", SD Card Interface Description, SD Card Product Manual.

     <http://media.digikey.com/pdf/Data%20Sheets/M-Systems%20Inc%20PDFs/SD%20
     Card%20Prod%20Family%20OEM%20Manual.pdf>

20. "System Features", SD Specifications Part 1 Physical Layer Simplified Specification Version
     3.01 May 18, 2010.

     <https://www.sdcard.org/downloads/pls/simplified_specs/archive/part1_301.pdf>

21. "Wear Leveling Methodology", White Paper, SanDisk Flash Memory Cards Wear Leveling

     <http://ugweb.cs.ualberta.ca/~c274/resources/hardware/SDcards/
     WPaperWearLevelv1.0.pdf>

22. "Defect and Error Management", SanDisk SD Card, Product Manual Version 2.2,
     Document No. 80-13-00169, November 2004

     <http://dlnmh9ip6v2uc.cloudfront.net/datasheets/Components/General/SDSpec.pdf>

23. "Overview", RPi Software

     <http://elinux.org/RPi_Software>

24. "See Also", YAFFS, From Wikipedia, the free encyclopedia

     <http://en.wikipedia.org/wiki/YAFFS>

25. Booting ARM Linux, Vincent Sanders

     <http://www.simtec.co.uk/products/SWLINUX/files/booting_article.html>

26. "Apple iPhone charger teardown: quality in a tiny expensive package", Ken Shirriff's blog

     <http://www.arcfn.com/2012/05/apple-iphone-charger-teardown-quality.html>

27. "meminfo:", "The /proc Filesystem"

    <http://www.kernel.org/doc/Documentation/filesystems/proc.txt>

28. "Programming GPIO output current", Programming GPIO output current

    <http://www.raspberrypi.org/phpBB3/viewtopic.php?f=44&t=9867>

29. "Errata", GPIO Pads Control

    <http://www.scribd.com/doc/101830961>

30. "Colors and Materials", Light-emitting Diode

    <http://en.wikipedia.org/wiki/Light-emitting_diode>

31. "Microchip 3V Tips 'n Tricks"

    <http://www.newark.com/pdfs/techarticles/microchip/3_3vto5vAnalogTipsnTricks
    Brchr.pdf>

32. "Interfacing 3V and 5V applications AN240", Application Note, Phillips Semiconductors

    <http://www.nxp.com/documents/application_note/AN240.pdf>

33. "GPIO Driving Example (C)", RPi Low Level Peripherals

    <http://elinux.org/RPi_Low-level_peripherals>

34. "Prepare the image file", RPi Kernel Compilation

    <http://elinux.org/RPi_Kernel_Compilation>

35. "Transfer the Firmware", RPi Kernel Compilation

    <http://elinux.org/RPi_Kernel_Compilation>

36. "1-Wire FAQ", Design Guide v1.0

    <http://www.1wire.org/Files/Articles/1-Wire-Design%20Guide%20v1.0.pdf>

37. "1-Wire", From Wikipedia, the free encyclopedia

    <http://en.wikipedia.org/wiki/1-Wire>

38. "1-Wire® (Protocol)", Company: Dallas Semiconductor/Maxim, Linus Wong

    <coecsl.ece.illinois.edu/ge423/sensorprojects/1-wire_full.doc>

39. "Serial Peripheral Interface Bus", From Wikipedia, the free encyclopedia

    <http://en.wikipedia.org/wiki/Serial_Peripheral_Interface_Bus>

40. "Raspberry Pi Revision identification", Raspberry Pi

    <http://www.raspberrypi.org/phpBB3/viewtopic.php?t=32733&p=281035>

41. "Automatic Raspberry Pi board revision detection: model A, B1 and B2", RASPBERRY
    ALPHA OMEGA, Raspberry Pi from start to finish

    <http://raspberryalphaomega.org.uk/2013/02/06/automatic-raspberry-pi-board-
    revision-detection-model-a-b1-and-b2/>

42. "Ping only works in console not from Desktop", Raspberry PI Community Projects

    <http://www.raspians.com/knowledgebase/errors/ping-only-works-in-console-not-from-desktop>

43. "Coloured splash screen", R-Pi Troubleshooting

    <http://elinux.org/R-Pi_Troubleshooting#Coloured_splash_screen>

44. "Ethernet connection is lost when a USB device is plugged in", R-Pi Troubleshooting

    <http://elinux.org/R-Pi_Troubleshooting#Ethernet_connection_is_lost_when_a_USB_device_is_plugged_in>

45. "GPIO", R-Pi Troubleshooting

    <http://elinux.org/R-Pi_Troubleshooting#GPIO>

46. "RS-232", RS-232, From Wikipedia, the free encyclopedia

    <http://en.wikipedia.org/wiki/RS-232>

47. "Baudot Code", Baudo Code, From Wikipedia, the free encyclopedia

    <http://en.wikipedia.org/wiki/Baudot_code>

48. "BCM2835 GPIO functions", RPi BCM2835 GPIOs

    <http://elinux.org/RPi_BCM2835_GPIOs>

49. "I² C", I² C, From Wikipedia, the free encyclopedia

    <http://en.wikipedia.org/wiki/I%C2%B2C>

50. "Hardware", Wiimote/Extension Controllers/Nunchuck

    <http://wiibrew.org/wiki/Wiimote/Extension_Controllers/Nunchuck>

51. "Getting started with uinput: the user level input subsystem"

    <http://thiemonge.org/getting-started-with-uinput>

52. "Using uinput driver in Linux- 2.6.x to send user input"

    <http://blog.csdn.net/outblue/article/details/5288760>

53. "Types"

    <http://www.kernel.org/doc/Documentation/input/event-codes.txt>

54. "Waveforms"

    <http://www.techdesign.be/projects/011/011_waves.htm>

55. "LED voltage drops", LED Characteristics & Colours

    <http://www.radio-electronics.com/info/data/semicond/leds-light-emitting-diodes/characteristics.php>

56. "BCM3825 Pull-Up Resistor Value?"

    <http://www.raspberrypi.org/phpBB3/viewtopic.php?f=44&t=35771&p=301563#p301563>

57. "Wave drive", Stepper motor

    <http://en.wikipedia.org/wiki/Stepper_motor>

58. "Full step drive (two phases on)", Stepper motor

    <http://en.wikipedia.org/wiki/Stepper_motor>

59. "Half Stepping", Stepper motor

    <http://en.wikipedia.org/wiki/Stepper_motor>

60. "The Old Way", Wiimote/Extension Controllers

    <http://wiibrew.org/wiki/Wiimote/Extension_Controllers>

61. "What does the current value mean?", GPIO pads control,

    <http://www.scribd.com/doc/101830961/GPIO-Pads-Control2>

62. "Brief history", Atmel AVR

    <http://en.wikipedia.org/wiki/Atmel_AVR>

63. "Meminfo", Raspberry PI UART Debugger

    <http://diy.powet.eu/2012/07/14/raspberry-pi-jtag-debugger>

Index

Get the eBook for only $10!

Now you can take the weightless companion with you anywhere, anytime. Your purchase of this book entitles you to 3 electronic versions for only $10.

This Apress title will prove so indispensible that you'll want to carry it with you everywhere, which is why we are offering the eBook in 3 formats for only $10 if you have already purchased the print book.

Convenient and fully searchable, the PDF version enables you to easily find and copy code—or perform examples by quickly toggling between instructions and applications. The MOBI format is ideal for your Kindle, while the ePUB can be utilized on a variety of mobile devices.

Go to www.apress.com/promo/tendollars to purchase your companion eBook.

Apress®
THE EXPERT'S VOICE™

All Apress eBooks are subject to copyright. All rights are reserved by the Publisher, whether the whole or part of the material is concerned, specifically the rights of translation, reprinting, reuse of illustrations, recitation, broadcasting, reproduction on microfilms or in any other physical way, and transmission or information storage and retrieval, electronic adaptation, computer software, or by similar or dissimilar methodology now known or hereafter developed. Exempted from this legal reservation are brief excerpts in connection with reviews or scholarly analysis or material supplied specifically for the purpose of being entered and executed on a computer system, for exclusive use by the purchaser of the work. Duplication of this publication or parts thereof is permitted only under the provisions of the Copyright Law of the Publisher's location, in its current version, and permission for use must always be obtained from Springer. Permissions for use may be obtained through RightsLink at the Copyright Clearance Center. Violations are liable to prosecution under the respective Copyright Law.